THE REIGN OF
KING GEORGE THE FIFTH
AN ENGLISH CHRONICLE

THE REIGN OF
KING
GEORGE THE FIFTH
AN ENGLISH CHRONICLE

BY

D. C. SOMERVELL

LONDON
FABER & FABER LIMITED
24 RUSSELL SQUARE

FIRST PUBLISHED IN FEBRUARY MCMXXXV
BY FABER AND FABER LIMITED
24 RUSSELL SQUARE LONDON W.C.I
PRINTED IN GREAT BRITAIN BY
LATIMER TREND AND CO PLYMOUTH
ALL RIGHTS RESERVED

PREFACE

I have called this book 'An English Chronicle' in order to indicate two of its many limitations: 'A Chronicle', because the time has not yet come when the latter and longer part of the period surveyed is susceptible of treatment deserving the name of History: 'English' because, though the world is now more than ever one, and though the British sovereign is king or emperor in many lands all over the world, I have taken my stand in England, and not looked farther afield than an English standpoint seemed to require. Such a limitation of a subject in any case immense seems hardly to call for apology.

There is another limitation which I should avow at once in order that the reader may not waste his time looking for things that he will not find. I have excluded from my survey not all but very much the greater part of all that might have been included under the heading of manners and customs, modes of fashion and modes of thought. I have tried to put into plain and con-tinuous narrative a sequence of events, bewilderingly varied as they often seemed to me when engaged on the task of marshal-ling them in order, but much less varied than they might have been if I had been more ambitious. My sequence of events is mainly political in the wider sense of that term; it excludes much that is more superficial and much that is, perhaps, more pro-found. I have not chronicled the rise of the cinema, the wireless, the motor, nor attempted to estimate the influence exercised by these and a score of other conspicuous novelties upon the form and habit of society. The reason for all these omissions is not that I am unaware of their significance. I am prepared to admit that much of what I have omitted is as important and as inter-esting as the subjects of which I have chosen to treat. But I felt that there was in what I had included quite enough to make a book.

Preface

I wish to add a word on a feature of the book which will not escape the reader's notice and might incur his criticism.

The Greek tragedians held no play to be complete until they had provided the actors with a Chorus, a dozen citizens, it might be, of the city in which the tragic events were about to be enacted. One of the functions of the Chorus was to make intelligent remarks, or to chant emotional meditations, on the events enacted under their eyes; they were, as every classically educated schoolboy has been told, ideal spectators, enriching by their performance the insight of the actual spectators, who inevitably suffered the drawbacks, as well as enjoying the advantages, of knowing how the story was going to end. They express the feelings which the actual audience would have experienced if they had themselves been living in close contact with the events they merely witness from the safe distance of the auditorium.

At various points in the course of my narrative I have used quotations from the quarterly review called *The Round Table* to serve the same purpose as the interventions of the Chorus in a Greek play. *The Round Table* began to appear in the first year of King George's reign. Its contributions, like those of the Chorus, are invariably anonymous; they are carefully considered, and free from, at any rate, the more obvious kinds of party prejudice. The fact that they were written for a quarterly review appearing usually some months after the events discussed is an advantage rather than otherwise; they may be accepted as being fairly representative of a strand of sober contemporary opinion. It would have been easy to introduce diversity by drawing upon a wide variety of journalistic comment. But the space available for such comment was limited, and it seemed better to select a single eye-witness, and to allow him to accompany the reader throughout the book. His intrusions will not, I think, be resented as either uninteresting or excessively frequent.

CONTENTS

PART I

THE UNFINISHED MELODRAMA: 1910-1914

PART II

THE EPIC: 1914-1918

PART III

THE AFTERMATH: 1918-1922

Contents

PART I
THE UNFINISHED MELODRAMA
1910-1914

CHAPTER I

PRELIMINARIES

When King Edward VII died on May 6th, 1910, someone asked 'Who killed the King?' and, answering his own question according to his own folly, indicated Mr. Asquith, the Liberal Prime Minister. King Edward had passed his sixty-eighth birthday and his health had for some time been declining; it was, said this commentator, Mr. Asquith who had hustled him onwards to his grave by raising the issue of the powers of the House of Lords, which inevitably brought the crown down into the arena of party politics; for the King would have to consent, or refuse to consent, to create peers—five hundred peers perhaps—and, by his consent or his refusal, to identify himself with one or other of the embattled factions into which his subjects were divided.

In fact the curtain had rung down on the first act of the melodrama some few months before, when Mr. Lloyd George's budget, called for purposes of controversy 'The People's Budget', had been rejected in the House of Lords by a majority of three hundred and fifty to seventy-five votes.

To understand the embittered state of party politics at the beginning of the reign of George V it is necessary to look back for a moment to the general election of January 1906. That election had produced the most sensational turnover of votes since the passage of the first Reform Bill. At the end of eleven consecutive years of power the Conservatives had still retained a majority of sixty-eight over the Liberals and Irish Nationalists combined. In the new Parliament their party was reduced to a

3

miserable rump of one hundred and fifty-seven, less than a quarter of the House. Over against them were three hundred and ninety-seven Liberals, a larger host than Gladstone had ever led to battle; fifty-one Labour members, an entirely new party which might be safely reckoned an advanced guard of the new Liberalism; and eighty-three Nationalists—the number of these was always fairly constant. It was an overwhelming defeat and an overwhelming victory.

But in politics as in war defeat is certainly defeat, while the fruits of victory are always problematical. What was to be done with it? It was, of course, a victory for Free Trade, but there was nothing to be done about that, for free trade was there already, having been enacted long ago. It was a victory over the Tory policy of supplying Chinese labour for the Transvaal gold mines, 'Chinese Slavery' it was called, and that could be stopped; indeed the Transvaal could be given self-government; but the Transvaal was very far away and would be forgotten almost before the last tatters of that poster with the hideous yellow face had been torn off the hoardings. It was also a victory for the Nonconformist conscience.

Victorian Nonconformity had always been the backbone of the Liberal party, a fact rather ominous in an age no longer Victorian, and the Nonconformists considered that they had been made the victims of a gross injustice by Mr. Balfour's Education Act of 1902, which compelled them to contribute as ratepayers to the support of Church schools in which the children received, unless specially exempted, a religious instruction in accordance with the tenets of the Church of England. There had been very strong feeling about this, and the stalwarts of Nonconformity had refused to pay the rate; nearly a hundred of them had proudly gone to prison as 'passive resisters'—or, as Mr. Gandhi would say, 'non-violent non-co-operators'. Liberalism had solemnly dedicated itself to the righting of this wrong, and one hundred and eighty Liberal Nonconformists secured election in 1906. Accordingly in the same year Mr. Birrell, the elegant humourist and man of letters to whom, as Minister of Education in the Liberal Government, this most unamusing task had fallen, introduced his Education Bill. It would be unfair to say that the grievance of the Nonconformists was an unreal one. But it was immersed in complicated and uninteresting technicalities and it seemed almost impossible to remove it without creating another grievance on the other side. In short, though the grievance had been an excitement, the task of its removal gradually became a bore. Mr. Birrell's Bill, a laborious attempt to do justice to all sections of opinion, pleased none very much and displeased some a great deal. It had a troubled passage through the Commons and was drastically amended in the Lords. The Government thereupon took the unprecedented step of inviting the House of Commons by resolution to reject the Lords' amendments 'as a whole'. The resolution was carried by a majority of three hundred and ten. The Lords insisted on their amendments and the Bill was abandoned. In the following year another Education Bill was introduced by Mr. McKenna; intended for the satisfaction of all parties, it failed to satisfy the Archbishop of Canterbury, and was therefore dropped. There was also a third abortive Education Bill. Not many dogs barked, and most of the barkers, it may be suspected, were no longer young. The crusade of the Passive Resisters had petered out without reaching Jerusalem, and indeed the grievance created by the Act of 1902 is still today unrectified. It was a Victorian grievance born out of due time.

The Temperance movement had long been closely associated with Nonconformity, and consequently with the Liberal party, and in 1908 Mr. Asquith introduced a drastic Licensing Bill, the upshot of which would be the suppression of thirty thousand licensed premises in the course of the next fourteen years. It was intensely unpopular with the powerful class which supplies, and the large class which consumes, alcoholic drinks in licensed premises, and its unpopularity was dramatically focussed on an uproarious by-election in Peckham where the Conservative candidate won a smashing victory. The Conservative peers did not wait for the Bill to reach them in the 'other place'; they decided on its rejections at a private gathering in Lansdowne House. This looked like a studied insult, but here again the Liberal government had no good ground for a popular appeal. The Bill was out of date. Drunkenness was an old-fashioned vice; it was markedly declining, and with the decline of drunkenness there declined whatever force there might have been in arguments for aggressive temperance legislation.

There had also been a curious attempt to settle the Irish question by offering the Irish something very much less than Home Rule. The Irish Councils Bill of 1907 seemed innocuous enough, but the Irish Nationalists derided it, and it was abandoned. Once more the Government—the Government with the greatest voting strength of modern times—had to pocket a rebuff, and English Liberals were reminded that the dreadful incubus of the Home Rule demand was waiting to descend upon their shoulders as soon as another general election should have reduced their numbers in the House of Commons to normal proportions.

Needless to say, not all the legislative babies of the Liberal Government were still-born. Much useful work was done. Mr. Haldane reorganized the Army, succeeding where Conservative predecessors had conspicuously failed. Mr. Asquith and Mr. Lloyd George shared the credit for the introduction of Old Age Pensions, a boon to which Conservatives could raise no objection for they had themselves promised to confer it. The establishment of Labour Exchanges, and the establishment of Trade Boards for the regulation of wages in sweated industries, were excellent measures. None the less, after three years of office the Liberal Government had become a disappointment to its most earnest supporters.

Moreover foreign affairs had taken a turn distinctly unfavourable to the Liberal interest. The German fleet was a growing menace. In 1904 the Kaiser had publicly described himself as 'Admiral of the Atlantic'. It was, no doubt, difficult to take

6

quite seriously a potentate who used phrases of this order, but it was even more difficult to dismiss as innocuous the threat behind the phrase, when its author was the ruler of the most powerful State in the world. By 1906 the general public were beginning to be acutely aware of the naval menace from Germany, but the Liberal Prime Minister can hardly have shared their alarm when he entrusted the Admiralty to Lord Tweedmouth, an old Gladstonian and one of the least notable members of the Liberal Cabinet. In March 1908 the *Times* disclosed the fact that Lord Tweedmouth had been in private correspondence with the German Emperor on naval policy. There was an outburst of patriotic indignation and Lord Tweedmouth resigned;[1] he was succeeded by Mr. McKenna, not a name to conjure with, perhaps, but a first-class administrator in the prime of life. People were beginning to realize that the battle fleet must be entirely rebuilt in *Dreadnoughts*, the name of the new battleship launched a few years before, which had reduced all earlier types to the category of second-class ships. Mr. McKenna demanded six *Dreadnoughts* for his 1909 programme and the Cabinet forced him down to four. At once the popular cry was raised 'We want eight, and we won't wait.' The Government eventually decided not to keep them waiting; it gave the full eight.

No doubt Mr. Asquith, Mr. Haldane, and Sir Edward Grey

[1] The Kaiser's letter to Lord Tweedmouth was not published until October 1914. It is a long dissertation, the drift of which seemed to be that Navies do not exist to fight against each other but to guard commerce. For example: 'It is absolutely *nonsensical* and *untrue* that the German Naval Bill is to provide a navy meant as a challenge to British naval supremacy. The German fleet is built *against* nobody at all. It is solely built *for* Germany's needs in relation with that country's rapidly growing trade.' England may, on her side, build a navy as large as she pleases, 'and nobody anywhere would lose a word about it and whether it be 60 or 90 or 100 battleships that would make no difference, and certainly no change in the German Naval Bill. May the numbers be as you think fit. Everybody here would understand it, but people would be very grateful over here if at last Germany was left out of the discussion.' (*Sic*: the Kaiser's English was not absolutely correct.)

Preliminaries

were themselves accepted as 'sound' on foreign policy and national defence, but would they be able to hold their ground against their colleagues and their party? The Liberal and Labour parties contained within their ranks the whole body of pacifist opinion; the Conservative party was untrammelled by such doubts and scruples. Any further development of Anglo-German rivalry would automatically swing the pendulum of public opinion still further in the Conservative direction.

What was to swing it back again? What in fact was the message of twentieth-century Liberalism? Had it a message at all? Back in 1892 John Morley had said: 'There is an old Indian idea that, when a great chief dies, his friends and horses and dogs should be buried with him. So it must be with us.' The great chief, of course, was Gladstone. Was Liberalism to loiter for ever round Gladstone's grave, enacting, or failing to enact, the dull remainders of Gladstonian programmes?

There was at any rate one member of the Cabinet who knew better than that. Mr. Lloyd George considered that the mission of the new Liberalism was the redistribution of the national income. If one emphasized the fact that twenty-five incomes of £200 a year could be carved out of one income of £5000 a year one would gain twenty-five votes and lose one. Mr. Lloyd George was not a classical economist, and the hypothetical remoter consequences of such a proceeding did not engage his attention. Indeed he was not a 'classical' person at all. Most of his colleagues were either scholars or aristocrats, and neither scholarship nor aristocracy inspired his respect. It is not necessary to say that he was a disloyal colleague but he certainly did not suffer in the least from that team-spirit which is the English gentleman's especial heritage and incubus. He had made his reputation unaided by his present colleagues, by his extremely brave championship of the Boers during the South African War. He had proved his capacities for business by two years' very successful administration of the Board of Trade. When, on the retirement of Sir Henry Campbell-Bannerman, Mr. Asquith

8

became Prime Minister, he had secured promotion to Mr. Asquith's former position as Chancellor of the Exchequer. He was more of a salient figure in the public eye than his chief, and he knew it. He would fashion a new Liberalism which would 'dish the Socialists', and secure a voting strength such as would free the party for good and all from the incubus of the Irish Nationalists. He had visited Germany and had been impressed by its 'superb system' of national industrial insurance. He would attack the landlords, a class he had disliked since early boyhood, for it is reported that, like Shakespeare, he had begun with poaching. Indeed, when one came to think of it, was not the redistribution of the national income bound to be the one fundamental demand of a democratic electorate slowly awakening to the realization of its powers?

This question of inequalities in the distribution of the national income had at this very time been brought conspicuously before the public eye by certain official statistics of Estate Duty, popularized by Mr. Chiozza Money and compared by him with similar statistics published by the French Government, from which it appeared that in France there were twice as many small estates, ranging from £500 to £10,000, as in the United Kingdom, but in the United Kingdom three times as many estates over £50,000 and four times as many over £250,000, the populations of the two countries being approximately the same.

But the immediate task was the Budget of 1909. It was an excellent opportunity, for sixteen additional millions of revenue were required, a large sum in those days. One-third of the sum was for Mr. McKenna's *Dreadnoughts*, the other two-thirds for the newly established Old Age Pensions. Lord Lansdowne, regretfully admitting the Pensions to the Statute Book, had declared that they would cost as much as a war without a war's advantages, since 'a war has at any rate the effect of raising the moral fibre of the nation whereas this measure, I am much afraid, will weaken the moral fibre and diminish the self-respect of the people'. Indeed Old Age Pensions were going to cost consider-

Preliminaries

ably more than had been at first estimated, the demand from Ireland in particular surpassing all expectations. In Ireland it appeared there was one septuagenarian among every twenty-five persons compared with one in eighty-eight on this side of St. George's Channel. Was it that wholesale emigration had endowed Ireland with a radically different age-distribution of its population? or that in that primitive island false statements regarding both age and income were less easily checked? or that sinister influences dissuaded officials from checking them? Perhaps all these causes operated, but in any case the result was financially the same. All through the early months of 1909 Conservative statisticians were proving to the satisfaction of Conservative newspaper readers that the cost of the Pensions must infallibly bring the Liberal Government to disaster on its next Budget. They did not see the card up Mr. Lloyd George's sleeve, and even if they had seen it they would not have known it for a trump.

The reader is prepared for a sensational disclosure, and it only remains to disappoint him. The 'People's Budget' strikes one today as a very modest and commonplace affair. The grading of the income tax was steepened, reaching on the biggest incomes the dizzy height of one shilling and eightpence in the pound. There was a heavy tax on licensed premises—revenge for the rejected Licensing Bill—and additional duties on spirits and tobacco; the ordinary bottle of whisky would henceforth cost four shillings instead of three-and-sixpence. There were the first taxes on motor cars and petrol, and there were some exceedingly complicated taxes on land values. These last were certainly as vindictive in intention as they were obscure in substance, but they would bring in very little money.

What sort of Budget Mr. Lloyd George would have produced if he had enjoyed the authority of a Mussolini cannot be known. He was, after all, a member of a Cabinet of very moderate men, scholars and aristocrats, and sixteen millions, though it may have sounded a large sum at the time, does not offer scope for

any very heroic redistributions. If the Budget had been subjected to no more than the undramatic opposition that is the
fate of most Budgets, no wizardry on its author's part could have
made of it the opening act of a melodrama. But the Conservatives had possessed themselves of the idea that in opposition to
this Budget lay the salvation of their party. They fastened upon
the land-tax clauses with a most injudicious industry, and presented themselves to the electorate as the impassioned champions of aristocratic privilege. In fact they served Mr. Lloyd
George's cause as neither he nor any of his friends could have
served it. For his own part he did his best to encourage them in
the good work. His Budget might not be the whole of his heart's
desire, but he was free to put the whole of himself into his platform speeches; free to suggest that this Budget, which so evidently
struck monied worldlings with dismay, was but a small beginning of good things to come. The name of Limehouse, as the
scene of the most famous of these orations, is still remembered.
Intolerable in cold print a quarter of a century old are these
tawdry harangues, with their cheap Dives-and-Lazarus senti-
mentality, their vulgar abuse of 'Dukes' and their astonishing
mixed metaphors. But the man who spoke them was dynamic;
there had been no such intoxicating verbosity since the palmy
days of the Midlothian campaign.

Throughout the previous sessions of the Liberal Government
the House of Lords had played their hand with great astuteness.
They had accepted a Trades Disputes Bill dangerously enlarging the privileges of Trade Unions; a Workmen's Compensation
Bill extending to the point of universality the employer's responsibility for the industrial accidents of his employees, and a
Miners' Eight Hours Bill, restricting for the first time the day's
work of adult male workers. All these were popular 'Labour'
measures, stages in that organization of industrial democracy to
which, since Disraeli's time, Conservative governments had
contributed at least as much as the Liberals. They had rejected
only what was specifically 'Liberal' and partisan—the Educa-

tion Bills, the Licensing Bill and a few other trifles. They had snubbed the party politicians but they had manifestly refrained from defying the democracy.

But now they were provoked out of all caution. Before the Budget had been so much as introduced in the House of Commons, Mr. Lloyd George had dared the Lords to reject it. They decided to do so and, in Lord Milner's phrase, to 'damn the consequences'—consequences which included everything of a purely political character from that date onwards to August 1914. The rejection of the Budget was a bold measure. It was also a very unwise one, for it was an established convention that the Lords could neither amend nor reject the annual Budget; Mr. Balfour himself had acknowledged the validity of this convention only two years before. Useless for the Conservative party to say that this was not an 'ordinary' Budget. A new issue had been raised, on which the merits of the Budget did not arise; a constitutional issue of Lords versus Commons; an issue on which conservative traditions were against the Conservative party. Parliament was at once dissolved, and Mr. Asquith appealed to the country in January 1910.

There followed the usual confused tournament of oratory. The Conservatives officially staked their prospects on Tariff Reform, i.e. Protection, which at that date included taxes on imported food. They exhibited dumped goods 'made in Germany', to which the Liberals retorted with exhibitions of an unappetizing substance alleged to be the bread consumed by 'protected' German working-class families. All this was 1906 over again. Mr. Balfour declared that the alternative to Tariff Reform was simply socialism, but Mr. Balfour always looked too far ahead for electoral purposes. More effective as a Conservative weapon was the German menace. No doubt it lost the Liberals many seats, and would have lost them many more but that the quiet efficiency of Mr. McKenna's administration at the Admiralty had secured the public approval of Lord Fisher, who was generally recognized as the greatest living sailor. The

Preliminaries

Liberals held firmly to the constitutional issue, which Mr. Lloyd George embroidered with fancy pictures of impossibly luxurious Dukes.

In the result the Conservatives gained and the Liberals lost about a hundred seats. If we include the wear and tear of the previous four years' by-elections the Liberal majority over their historic rivals had fallen from two hundred and forty to two. But at any rate there was no Conservative majority, and on the Liberal side were to be reckoned a somewhat reduced Labour party of forty-one, and eighty-two Irish Nationalists, though eleven of these last were pledged to oppose the whisky clause of the rejected Budget. In fact the whole of the Irish party was restive on this subject, and was inclined to think it would be master of the situation; for if the Irish chose to vote with the Opposition, the Liberal-Labour combination would be defeated at the outset. There were many who foresaw a very short life for Mr. Asquith's government. The thing looked like a stalemate. Some active-minded editors toyed with the notion of a National Government—under Lord Rosebery! The *Times* desired a Round Table Conference.

It turned out that, for good or for evil, Mr. Asquith maintained his government in office for another five years of unprecedented political excitement, finally leading a united nation into the Great War. It was an astonishing triumph of nerve and political dexterity, beyond the reach of any other British statesman of that generation. Yet through it all Mr. Asquith remained a curiously impersonal figure. The man in the street never got a clear idea of him until well on in the Great War, and then he got an idea—from the Northcliffe and Beaverbrook newspapers —which, though clear enough, was libellously wrong. Mr. Asquith was a difficult man to label; he owed his position neither to birth nor to influence, yet there was in him not a trace of the demagogue; nor had he caught the fancy of the popular press by any oddity of taste or temperament. Everyone knew that Mr. Balfour was a philosopher, that Sir Edward Grey was a fisherman who knew all about British birds and nothing about foreign languages; Mr. Chamberlain had been 'Joe', Mr. Churchill was 'Winston', and as for Mr. Lloyd George he went without saying. Mr. Asquith was a barrister—like so many rather dim politicians: he was indeed the first barrister to be Prime Minister since the younger Pitt, whom in many respects he resembled. His initials were H.H. but even those who knew that these stood for Henry and Herbert were for the most part uncertain which name had the preference. Yet there he was, and there he stayed. In 1913 Max Beerbohm put him into one of his cartoons—a sturdy figure, unexciting and unexcited. A peer with a hunting crop, a trade unionist with a crowbar, a suffragette with a hatchet, a German soldier with a bayonet, Sir Edward Carson with his blackthorn stick, threatening him from five different points of the compass. He crosses his legs, folds his hands, and puffs at his cigar:

> 'Come one, come all, this rock shall fly
> From its firm base as soon as I.'

The King's Speech on opening Parliament in February 1910 contained the eagerly awaited announcement. 'Proposals will be laid before you to define the relations between the Houses of Parliament, so as to secure the undivided authority of the House of Commons over finance, and its predominance in legislation. These measures, in the opinion of my advisers, should provide that this House (i.e. the House of Lords, in which the King's Speech is delivered) should be so constituted and empowered as to exercise impartially, in regard to proposed legislation, the functions of initiation, revision and, subject to proper safeguards, of delay.' So there was to be a reform of the constitution of the House of Lords as well as a curtailment of its powers. A few weeks later, however, it was apparent that the 'Veto' problem was to be tackled at once and the reform of the membership of the Second Chamber postponed until a more convenient season. The Veto was a simple matter, and a Veto Bill acceptable to all three parties in what was now derisively described as the Coalition could be written out on half a sheet of notepaper. Reform of the House of Lords, establishment of an ideal Second Chamber, was, on the other hand, a problem complicated to the verge of insolubility. Most members of the Coalition were uninterested in, or even hostile to, any such measure: they believed that the 'will of the people' as expressed by a House of Commons majority ought in all circumstances to prevail, and, so long as there was a Second Chamber at all, they preferred that it should wallow in the discredit of undiluted aristocracy. So when Mr. Asquith introduced Resolutions in the House of Commons, it was found that they confined themselves to the three points subsequently enshrined in the Parliament Act. The Lords' veto on bills certified by the Speaker as Money Bills was to be abolished; other Bills were to become law, in spite of the House of Lords, if they had been passed by the House of Commons in three successive sessions; and the duration of Parliament was to be reduced from seven to five years. These Resolutions were passed by the House of Commons in April, as also was the Budget which should have belonged to 1909, for the Irish Nationalists had come to heel as soon as they saw that they could not frighten Mr. Asquith. They swallowed the whisky tax.

The safe passage of the Budget through the House of Lords had been assured, but there was every likelihood of a fight to the finish over the Parliament Bill. In view of this contingency the Prime Minister made one of those carefully guarded statements, at once elaborate and lucid, with which he was so often in the next few years to exasperate his adversaries.

'If the Lords fail to accept our policy . . . we shall feel it our duty immediately to tender advice to the Crown as to the steps which will have to be taken if that policy is to have statutory effect in this parliament. . . . If we do not find ourselves in a position to ensure that statutory effect, we shall then either resign our offices or recommend a dissolution of parliament. Let me add this that in no case should we recommend a dissolution except under such conditions as will secure that in the new parliament the judgment of the people, as expressed at the election, will be carried into law.'

This was all Mr. Asquith had to say, and he chose his time for saying it. Those who wanted to know it earlier, or to know more, had been answered with an ironical refusal: 'The Honourable Member had better wait and see.' The last three words, recurring again and again, caused intense irritation, and they were, years afterwards, to be retorted upon their author with deadly effect. 'Wait and see', became the popular description of Mr. Asquith's alleged deficiencies as a wartime Prime Minister; what was then wanted was a minister who saw without waiting and, if necessary, acted without seeing. So 'old Wait and See' had to go at last, and Mr. Lloyd George secured the long-coveted promotion. But those events were nearly seven years ahead in the unimaginable future. It was in April 1910 that Honourable Members were told that they had better wait and see. Before the first week of May was over the reign of King George V had begun.

CHAPTER II

THE PARLIAMENT BILL

We have learnt from Sir Sidney Lee, King Edward's official yet most candid biographer, that he disliked both Mr. Lloyd George and his Budget. None the less he had been most anxious that the House of Lords should accept it, and to secure this end he had, on his own initiative but with Mr. Asquith's cordial approval, sent for Lord Lansdowne and Mr. Balfour, the Conservative leaders in the two Houses, and pressed upon them the advisability of moderation. In so doing he was following precedents set by Queen Victoria on similar occasions of conflict between the two Houses; but where she had succeeded, he failed. When the worst happened, he viewed the prospect, as it affected both the nation and himself, with intense disrelish. His health was failing and he knew it. He was rightly proud of the success with which he had maintained intact a reputation never approached by any previous British sovereign, for Olympian impartiality and detachment from domestic controversy. He was proud to be known as Edward the Peacemaker. It was intolerable that, old and enfeebled, he should be dragged down into the arena of party politics, and compelled to play, or to refuse to play, the thankless part that had fallen to William IV in the days of the first Reform Bill. He was vexed by suggestions thrown out in the course of electioneering speeches that he had in fact given 'guarantees' which would secure, by the creation of Liberal peers, the passage of either the rejected Budget, or the unborn Parliament Bill, or both. As a matter of fact the Prime Minister had asked for no such guarantees. Mr. Asquith may sometimes have been too late, but he was never too early with any of the fateful steps of his political career.

The King left England for Biarritz early in March, to return at the end of April. Mr. Balfour is said to have remarked that the King's absence was a 'good thing'; he hoped that he would be away a long time, as there was much to be gained by his 'not having any personal intercourse with his ministers just at present'. However that may be, nothing of importance occurred in the nine days between the King's return and his death on May 6th. He died uncommitted by the granting or the refusal of any political pledges; uncommitted his son succeeded him.

'Edward the Peacemaker'. The phrase provided the text of ten thousand eulogies from the pulpit and the press. The title had been well won in Paris, by that marvellously successful visit in 1903, which had opened amid cries of 'Vivent les Boers' and ended with 'Vive notre roi'. It was King Edward who had made of the French Entente what the Russian Entente could never be, a real union of hearts. 'He had', wrote Sir Edward Grey long afterwards, 'a rare if not unique power of combining dignity with bonhomie. . . . Warm human kindness was of the very substance of the man . . . genius for projecting his personality over a crowd.' And yet there surely lurked a tragic irony in the phrase, and still more in its too easy acceptance. Outside France the Peacemaker had failed. In Germany he was regarded as the most insidious of enemies, the secret designer of a policy of 'encirclement', a man who smiled, and smiled, and was a villain. He could no more persuade the Kaiser to reduce the German naval programme than he could persuade the Lords to accept the Budget. He had tried very hard, but he had failed. His death was to be followed by an orgy of strife—malice domestic, foreign levy. Simple souls believed that, if King Edward the Peacemaker had lived, all the next few years would have been different, but almost certainly they would not.

The Parliament Bill

Lord Rosebery, though long withdrawn from party politics for which he never had any great aptitude, was still the most impressive spokesman of the nation on solemn and ceremonial occasions. He struck on this occasion the note which, in different circumstances, Lincoln had struck at Gettysburg. Dedication was not for the dead but for the living. The meeting, he said, of the German Emperor and King George in the presence of Death had struck the imagination of the world. Was it too much to hope that King Edward, the promoter of peace during his life, might have bequeathed a great legacy of peace by his death? Might they not hope that, by his death and by the solemn communion of parties that took place on the occasion of his funeral, he had left peace even to the politics of his own country?

In this chastened mood a kind of political moratorium was accepted by all parties. There was to be a Constitutional Conference of eight members, four Liberals and four Conservatives, to seek an agreed solution of the problem of the relationship between the two Houses. Its meetings began in June and continued till November. Their secrecy was scrupulously preserved. Parliament stood adjourned and politics stood still. Public attention had to be satisfied with the developments of the new science of 'aviation' and with the Crippen case. The Session of 1910 proved to be the shortest since 1865, the year of the death of Lord Palmerston.

At first the hopes of all alike were set upon the Conference. 'It is', wrote a detached observer, 'more than a striking testimony to the respect and affection in which the late King was held. It is more even than a welcome device for settling an acute and barren controversy. It may be the herald of a new and vital piece of machinery in the British constitution.'[1] The 'vital piece of machinery' could not be at that date very closely defined, for the secrets of the Conference were well kept, but there is no doubt today that the plan under discussion was the constitution of a Joint Committee of both Houses to arbitrate in case of con-

[1] *Round Table* (first issue). November 1910.

flict between them. This for 'ordinary' legislation. For constitutional measures, among which would be included any amendment of the terms of the Union of Great Britain and Ireland, a Referendum was proposed.

Though both these proposals presented well-nigh insuperable difficulties there was, beyond doubt, a deep desire, shared by men of goodwill in all parties, to lift great controversies out of the ruts of organized rancour. And yet, as the funeral solemnities receded and the light of common day reasserted itself, it could not fail to become apparent to the clear, if short-sighted, vision of practical politicians, that the Conservatives had much to gain from the Conference and the Liberals nothing at all. A Conference could only strengthen the constitutional status of the House of Lords, which was just what none of the parties of the Coalition desired. On the other hand the policy enshrined in the Veto Resolutions had behind it a parliamentary majority of well over a hundred, and there was no reason to suppose that a second general election would seriously impair that majority. After the passage of the Parliament Bill would come the old Liberal policy of Home Rule—the Irish would see to that. It might not be altogether palatable to the British electorate, but there was also Mr. Lloyd George's new Liberal policy of national insurance with more 'rare and refreshing fruit' to follow for the parched lips of the People. These were sound electoral speculations. Why not get ahead with them? To be sure, there was Ulster; but if anyone thought of Ulster in the autumn of 1910 he did not think very much of it. Of course, if all that was going to happen in Ulster had been foreseen, different counsels might have prevailed. But man is not a foreseeing animal; if he were, not only this chapter but all other chapters of his history would have been different.

The Conference announced its failure, without offering any explanations, in November. Parliament was dissolved and the country proceeded to another election; not since the time of the first Reform Bill, eighty years before, had there been two elec-

The Parliament Bill

tions in one year. The issues were plain enough. On the Liberal programme was the Parliament Bill with Home Rule, but also National Insurance, behind it. Mr. Lloyd George and Mr. Churchill, at that date Mr. Lloyd George's closest ally and always a hearty spender of public money, offered alluring sketches of insurance for invalidity and sickness, pensions for widows and orphans, costing four millions 'at first'. On the Conservative programme was reform of the House of Lords, Tariff Reform, —and the Referendum! This last was an afterthought and, no doubt, an unwise one. It had made its first appearance as part of the scheme for the reform of the House of Lords which Lord Lansdowne, the official leader of the Conservative peers, had put forward as his party's alternative to the Liberal 'Veto' policy. According to the Lansdowne proposals, 'major differences' between the two Houses were to be settled by a direct vote of the whole people. Liberals were at once challenged to consent to submit their prospective Home Rule Bill to a 'referendum' of this kind. They could not but demur, and suggest that Tariff Reform, and in particular food taxes, should be submitted to the same arbitrament, and Mr. Balfour light-heartedly assented. It was perhaps a small matter for the moment that ardent tariff reformers once more revived their suspicions of their leader's faith in the programme of his party. What mattered much more was that the Conservatives had once again revealed themselves as the party of reckless innovation. They had allowed the House of Lords to reject a Budget, and now they offered, as an unconsidered trifle, a measure which would revolutionize the normal workings of the constitution far more fundamentally than any curtailment in the powers of the House of Lords. Once more the 'party of progress' could claim to be also, in contrast with the newest 'Conservatism', the party of constitutional propriety.

The results of the election were singular, and yet entirely logical. The political events of 1910 had been, on the balance— nothing; and the result of the election was to leave the relative strength of the parties entirely unchanged.

The Parliament Bill

The stage was set for the grand constitutional engagement in the spring and summer of 1911. There was the majestic advance of the Parliament Bill through all its stages in the House of Commons towards its crisis in the House of Lords. It ought to have been very interesting, but there was a general agreement among observers that the country did not find it so. 'Despite the high quality of the debates, public opinion in the country, so far as it could be gauged, remained entirely unmoved. The country was not angry; it was not pleased; it was not impressed; it was not even bored, for the very good reason that it had never listened.'[1] How different the parallel occasion eighty years before, when the mobs had cried 'The Bill! the whole Bill! and nothing but the Bill!' when the obstinacy of the Peerage had brought the country to the verge of revolution. Was it that ordinary people refused to consider the supposition that the Lords would put up a fight to the finish? Was it that popular attention was absorbed by other interests—the coronation, the current Anglo-German crisis, all the sports, crimes, and frivolities which filled the popular newspapers? Had we become a complete democracy only to cease to be a genuinely politically minded people?

However that might be, the Conservative party did their best to secure an exciting finale. In July the Lords, who had spent the first part of their session over an academic scheme for the reform of their own body by the introduction of elected members, returned the Parliament Bill drastically amended. Where were those 'guarantees' which Mr. Asquith had promised to secure from the King before he went a second time to the country? He had said no more about them, which might mean that he had not got them. Those who reasoned thus did not know their Prime Minister; Mr. Asquith had said nothing about them for the very good reason that there was no reason why he should say anything and every reason why he should not. If the House of Lords had accepted the logic of the December election, the

[1] *Round Table.* August 1911.

The Parliament Bill

King's name need never have been dragged into the controversy. The Lords had not accepted it, and it had become necessary for him to play his last card, which happened to be the ace of trumps.

'Dear Mr. Balfour,' began the letter which appeared in the newspapers of July 21st, 'I think it courteous and right, before any public decisions are announced, to let you know how we regard the political situation.' After saying that the Government could not accept the Lords' amendments, the letter proceeded: 'In the circumstances, should the necessity arise, the government will advise the King to exercise his prerogative . . . and his Majesty has been pleased to signify that he will consider it his duty to accept and act on that advice. Yours sincerely, H. H. Asquith.'[1]

After this Mr. Balfour and Lord Lansdowne were in favour of allowing the Bill to pass, but many of their former colleagues in office were not, and a large body of Conservatives who wanted a fight to the finish found a leader in the aged Lord Halsbury, who had been Lord Chancellor in Victorian times. They were nicknamed 'Ditchers' in reference to the last ditch in which William of Orange had once expressed his willingness to die; Mr. Balfour's group were the 'Hedgers'. Another name for the 'Ditchers' was the 'Diehards', and this has survived for use on many subsequent occasions.

So the new peers might have to be created after all, and indeed Mr. Asquith had the list of some 250 possible candidates drawn up—a fact unknown to the general public until twenty years later. Only once in the past, in Queen Anne's reign, had peers actually been created in a batch for the avowed purpose

[1] We are told that it was by King George's own express desire that Mr. Asquith delayed no longer this explicit announcement. The King had been vexed by persistent rumours in Tory cricles that 'the whole thing was a *brutum fulmen*, not meant for use but to terrify, and expressly desired that the announcement should be made in the most authentic terms'. (Lord Morley in conversation with Sir Almeric FitzRoy, as recorded in the latter's *Memoirs*, p. 460.)

of securing the passage of a measure through the House of Lords. There were twelve of them, and an insolent inheritor of ancient titles had asked them if they voted through their foreman, like a jury. No popular use seems to have been made of this story in 1911, but there was a good deal of amused speculation. Would the new peers pay for their titles at the usual rate, or would mass production entail a fall in prices? In the former case, it was computed that the creation of five hundred peers would endow the Radical party funds with a sum of twenty-five millions sterling. On July 25th there was a noisy demonstration in the House of Commons, and 'many newspapers considered it worth their while to give the Constitutional Crisis type almost as large as they were giving to the airmen's race round England for the *Daily Mail* prize of £10,000.'[1] Very different was the atmosphere at Westminster where Mr. Balfour declared that Mr. Asquith had 'arrogated to himself powers possessed by the Republican dictator', that he had 'trampled on the Constitution and dragged the Crown in the dust', and much more to the same effect and of the same intensity. A curious vein of vehemence was from time to time apparent in Mr. Balfour's subtle composition, and, since he had taken his stand with the 'Hedgers', he could only unpack his heart with words.

To the very last the result in the House of Lords was uncertain, for no one could predict the exact numbers of the 'Hedgers', the 'Ditchers', and a third section who out-hedged the 'Hedgers' by declaring their readiness to vote for the Bill they hated rather than suffer, by its defeat, an invasion of new peers. Many undoubtedly left their votes to be determined by the course of the debate, which was held on August 10th-11th, two of the hottest days of a very hot summer.[2] The Government's intentions, in the event of defeat, were kept in the dark until

---

[1] *Round Table.* August 1911.

[2] On the first of these days the thermometer at Greenwich proclaimed a record of 100 degrees, but Sir Edward Grey, who disliked sensationalism as much as Mr. Asquith, tells us that he never believed that reading.

The Parliament Bill

the second day of the debate when Lord Morley read a statement which had been approved by the King. If the vote
went against the Government, 'His Majesty would assent to a
creation of peers sufficient in number to guard against any possible combination of the different parties in Opposition by
which the Parliament Bill might be exposed a second time to
defeat.' After reading this crucial sentence a second time, Lord
Morley pointed its moral: 'Every vote given against my motion
will be a vote for a large and prompt creation of peers.' So the
worst was true; but was the worst enough to cool the courage of
the 'Ditchers'? The Archbishop of Canterbury, as might have
been expected, and Lord Curzon, as few would have expected,
spoke strongly in favour of submission, and the Government
carried their measure by seventeen votes—one hundred and
thirty-one to one hundred and fourteen. Thirty-seven Conservatives and thirteen bishops gave their votes with the majority; the
noble army of 'Hedgers', under Lord Lansdowne, voted in
neither lobby.

Many obvious remarks may be made in criticism of the Parliament Act. By what it did and by what it left undone the
Government, it may be said, admitted that there ought to be a
Second Chamber, admitted that the House of Lords was the
wrong sort of Second Chamber, and admitted that they had no
clear ideas as to what the right sort of Second Chamber would
be. The clause which left to the Speaker the decision as to what
was, and what was not, a Money Bill, and in consequence immune from interference, thrust an invidious duty upon an
official whose invidious duties were already sufficiently numerous, and whose reputation for independence of party ties was
second only in importance to the reputation of the King himself.
Moreover subsequent Speakers' decisions on this subject made
it probable that the Budget of 1909 would not have secured the
certificate of immunity. It would have been found to contain
other things besides finance. Again, the system of a suspensive veto
for ordinary legislation was bound, if it was put in action, to entail

wearisome repetitions in the work of the House of Commons. It was, as Mr. F. E. Smith remarked, the principle of the Bellman in *The Hunting of the Snark:* 'What I tell you three times is true.' The sessions of 1912-14 staggered under the burden of these repetitions. Three controversial measures were designed for procedure under the Parliament Act. Of these one missed the first passage and fell out; a second reached the Statue Book and died there; only the third, the measure disestablishing the Welsh Church is alive today as a healthy offspring of the Parliament Act. Even the Welsh Church Act was not technically made law under Parliament Act procedure. The Bill of 1912-13-14 was not put into operation, and another Bill, differing in some of its provisions, was enacted by both Houses in the course of 1919. Since the war, procedure under the Parliament Act has never been attempted, or even seriously suggested.

None the less, the Parliament Act was an effective and a necessary gesture. The House of Lords had come to think that it could act as a permanent Conservative majority, subjecting Liberal measures and even Liberal Budgets to Conservative tests. Among the many things said about Mr. Asquith the hard saying he probably resented least was a comparison between himself and Cromwell. Like Cromwell he had, by his Parliament Act, put a stop to 'that foolery'.

The dethronement of Mr. Balfour from the leadership of the Conservative party may be treated as an appendage to the final struggles over the Parliament Bill; indeed the B.M.G. movement, indicating that Balfour Must Go, was but a corollary of the 'Ditchers' movement for the rejection of the Bill which Mr. Balfour had decided to accept. He was, by general consent, the most distinguished figure in the British politics of his generation, and he inspired in all political circles a degree of personal affection unapproached, it was said, since the death of Charles James Fox. But he was a thoroughly bad party leader—at least so it seemed, for he had been beaten in three successive elections. It was said that he regarded this world as an enigma, and one of his most enthusiastic admirers admits that this world, or the fraction of it contained in the British Conservative party, repaid him the compliment. The best that could be said of him was that he was too big a man for his job; for how could a metaphysician whose best-known book was *A Defence of Philosophic Doubt* be expected to be perfectly sound and unremittingly enthusiastic about a policy of protective tariffs and food taxes? Mr. Balfour approached his abdication, which occurred in November, in a cheerful spirit, not entirely innocent of irony. He had, he said, reached the age of sixty-three, and he had been told that there was a danger, as the years advanced, of a petrifaction of the faculties. He had not himself noticed any of the usual symptoms, but it might be that he was not the best judge of his own case. As for the alleged 'unrest' among his followers, he did not think that at that moment it was 'anything exceptional'.

It only remained to choose a new leader. There was Mr. Austen Chamberlain, his father's son and the chosen representative of his father's policy. He had been Chancellor of the Exchequer in the last years of Mr. Balfour's Government. There was also Mr. Long, the leading representative of the country squires who had for two hundred years given to the Tory party its special character as the party of the Gentlemen of England. Mr. Long had held various offices in all the Conservative Governments since 1886, but the most memorable fact connected with his career was that, a very long time ago, he had extirpated rabies by the compulsory muzzlement of dogs. Mr. Chamberlain represented the new Birmingham Unionism, Mr. Long the old Toryism of the shires; Mr. Chamberlain had been a 'Ditcher', Mr. Long a 'Hedger'. Both represented, in different ways, the hereditary principle; for Mr. Chamberlain was the son of a great statesman and Mr. Long the descendant of innumerable Knights of the Shire.

Between two such candidates it was hard indeed to decide,

The Parliament Bill

and a *tertium quid* was found in Mr. Bonar Law, a Scottish-Canadian iron merchant. His political career had been brief; he had no known ancestors, and it was credibly asserted that he never drank anything stronger than ginger ale, but he had proved himself a skilful and pugnacious debater. Pugnacity was wanted, and Mr. Bonar Law was chosen. Liberals mocked, and someone had the bad taste to parody a petition from the Liturgy for the use of Conservative members. 'Lord have mercy upon us, and incline our hearts to Bonar Law.' But in a very few months Mr. Law was reported to be 'doing very well. His platform utterances have a pleasant pungency, which has already gone some way towards restoring the strength and spirits of the ordinary Unionist elector, who has starved and languished too long upon the milk diet of a philosophy which overlooked the obvious and a dialectic too subtle and delicate for his comprehension.'[1] Poor Mr. Balfour! all seemed over with him. Mr. Law was, at any rate, not too big a man for his job; it was just possible that he might prove big enough.

The year which witnessed the passage of the Parliament Act also saw the disappearance from the streets of London of the last horse bus. Times were changing and we were changing with them.

[1] *Round Table.* March 1912.

CHAPTER III

AGADIR: THE ANGLO-GERMAN PROBLEM

On July 1st, 1911, just when the Parliament Bill was about to enter on its last agonies, a wider world than that of Westminster was startled by the news that a German gunboat, the *Panther*, had appeared off Agadir, or Mogador, an insignificant port on the Atlantic coast of Morocco. The German Government explained that it had been sent to protect German subjects in Southern Morocco, whose safety was threatened by 'local unrest'. This was, of course, a mere figure of speech; it was hardly worth inquiring whether there were in fact German subjects or local unrest in Western Morocco. The *Panther* had been sent to inform the French Government that its diplomacy was altogether too dilatory and too clever; that Germany must know at once what she was to get in Central Africa in exchange for allowing France a free hand in Morocco.

The French had long been angling for the possession of Morocco, which would round off and complete that North African Empire, the development of which had been their pride and their consolation ever since the loss of Alsace-Lorraine. The Morocco clause had been, for France, the all-important clause in the Anglo-French *Entente* Treaty of 1904. The French had recognized the position that the British had secured in Egypt and, in return, the British Government, in view of the declaration of the French Government that it had 'no intention of altering the political status of Morocco' (i.e. its independence), agreed that it 'appertained' to the French Government to 'preserve order' in Morocco, and 'to provide assistance for the purpose of all administrative, economic, financial, and military reforms which it may require'. In other words, France was to swallow Morocco with British approval provided only that her table manners were correct—as they certainly would be, for it was well known that the French were the most expert diplomatists in the world.

Far back in the 'eighties of the previous century, the Great Powers had solemnly undertaken that all partitioning of Africa should be by general agreement, and Germany was therefore within her rights in protesting against this Anglo-French arrangement. In the summer of 1905 the Kaiser had landed at Tangier and had declared that the maintenance of the independence of Morocco was a German interest, as indeed it was, for French political control would certainly throttle the German commercial enterprises which undoubtedly existed in that country. Russia, France's ally, was at war with Japan. England was not her ally, but had recently become her 'friend'; what was such friendship worth? The Tangier coup was the first testing of the *Entente* and, whatever the merits of the Morocco case, it was essential on far wider grounds that the *Entente* should stand the test. It stood it. There was an International Conference at Algeciras, and behind the smoke screen of its pretentious and illusory conclusions the position of France in Morocco remained intact.

Thenceforth the 'political status of Morocco', which France was not to alter, began to alter itself with gratifying rapidity. Germany protested, and there was a Franco-German Agreement, which settled little, in 1909. In the early summer of 1911 the French, on the request of the best people in Morocco, consented to occupy Fez, the capital of the country.

The farce was played out at last. The French government agreed that Germany should receive 'compensation' in French Equatorial Africa. The only, but the all-important, question was 'How much?' It was in order to influence the answer to that question that the *Panther* was sent to Agadir. But the dispatch of

Agadir: The Anglo-German Problem

the *Panther* meant something more than that. It raised once again the question whether the friendship of the greatest naval Power in the world was, in fact, worth anything to her continental neighbour and friend. If France had to accept Germany's terms, the sooner she made friends with Germany and entered 'the German system' the better for her. In that case the Great War, if there ever was a Great War, would be England against Europe.

To understand and justify the brusque English intervention in what had been up to that point a quite normal diplomatic fencing match between two old and equally unscrupulous antagonists, one must get a picture of the Anglo-German situation as it was envisaged in England before the *Panther* and Agadir had ever been heard of. The opening article in the first number of the *Round Table* (November 1910) considers the subject at length, and is typical of its date.

'The antagonism between England and Germany', says this writer, 'is the topic which dominates all others in the columns of the world's press which are devoted to foreign affairs. . . . An overwhelming majority of Germans regard war with England as inevitable. Germanism, they say, must and will prevail, for it is the most vital and the most self-sacrificing of the forces of the day. England, the colossus with feet of clay, lies across her path. The prospect of gaining a new colonial dominion, or winning the first place in the world, is hopeless so long as the British bar the way. They do England the credit of believing that she will not surrender without a struggle, and therefore they believe that war, with all its horrors and sufferings to themselves and to the world, must come. There is a common toast in military and naval circles in Germany: it is "the Day", the day when the myth of England's greatness will be finally shattered by German arms. There is something heroic about this. . . .

'The ultimate aim of the more advanced of Bismarck's disciples is to add to the circle of states dependent on Germany, Denmark, Holland and Belgium, and Switzerland. The pressure

31

of Germany in some of these quarters is already beginning to tell. But the magnetic attraction of the tremendous power in Central Europe is beginning to extend even farther afield . . . Turkey. . . . It is obvious that the small states of the Balkans cannot by themselves withstand the combined pressure of Turkey and Germany. . . .

"Germany's full fleet of *Dreadnoughts* will not be ready until 1918. The time for applying Bismarck's maxims to an active world policy is therefore not yet come. But. . . .'

Exactly. And when the *Panther* went to Agadir, Sir Edward Grey informed the German ambassador that 'our attitude could not be disinterested with regard to Morocco'. To this information the Germans made no reply. Nearly three weeks passed and on July 21st, in the ordinary routine of his office, Mr. Lloyd George had to address the bankers of the City of London at their annual feast. In the course of his speech he said: 'It is essential in the highest interests, not merely of this country, but of the world, that Britain should at all hazards maintain her place and her prestige among the Great Powers of the world. I would make great sacrifices to preserve peace. But if a situation were to be forced upon us in which peace could only be preserved by the surrender of the great and beneficent position Britain has won by centuries of heroism and achievement, by allowing Britain to be treated, when her interests were vitally affected, as if she were of no account in the Cabinet of nations, then I say emphatically that peace at that price would be a humiliation intolerable for a great country like ours to endure.'

As Mr. Churchill told us long afterwards, 'the Chancelleries of Europe bounded together.' The ultimatum owed its peculiar effectiveness to the fact that it had come from the mouth of Mr. Lloyd George, notoriously the leader of the pacific and anti-naval section within the Liberal Government. Germany was smitten in the house of her friends, and the German ambassador was soon afterwards recalled because he had not warned his Government that Mr. Lloyd George had turned over a new leaf.

Agadir: The Anglo-German Problem

This was hardly fair to the German Ambassador, for no one knew it, not Mr. Churchill himself. Probably Mr. Lloyd George had not known it for many hours, and subsequently, indeed, the leaf fluttered back again and the author of the most famous of Guildhall speeches was once again protesting against 'building navies against nightmares'. There were, indeed, many in England who thought that Mr. Lloyd George had over-acted his new part, and that he had better have left the ticklish business to the Prime Minister or Sir Edward Grey. Sir Edward's own memoirs dispose of this criticism. The speech was Mr. Lloyd George's own idea, but Sir Edward Grey had approved it. 'I welcomed it. The effect was much greater than any words of mine could have been.'

No doubt the effect was great, but perhaps it is necessary to prove that the dramatic intervention was really necessary. Was there, it may be asked, any real danger that France might be losing faith in the efficacy and reality of the *Entente*? She had not asked us to intervene in this or any other manner. The convincing reply to these surmises is to be found in the fact that at that moment M. Caillaux was Prime Minister of France. M. Caillaux was the one French statesman of the first rank who honestly disliked the *Entente* and preferred a policy of conciliation with Germany. Unknown to us, and also to his own foreign office, M. Caillaux had been during these very months pursuing with Germany negotiations of a most capitulatory character. His fall, which followed the disclosure of these negotiations at the end of the year, marked the rejection of his foreign policy and the recovery of the *Entente*. Subsequently, at the end of the war, M. Caillaux was convicted of treasonable activities and sent to prison.

The Germans were extremely angry, but they were not prepared to face a war, and they proceeded to execute a diplomatic retreat. Owing to the British intervention, they got less than they deserved on the merits of the Franco-German dispute, in Equatorial Africa. France had secured Morocco in exchange for a few trivial concessions, and the first steps towards what was intended to be a great German African Empire were blocked: —perhaps in the interests of Africa, but certainly in the interests of the balance of power in Europe.

So the war scare blew over; and it is a curious but undeniable fact that, though anxieties continued to multiply at the Foreign Office, the man in the street was less worried about the prospects of European war during the three years between Agadir and Sarajevo than during the three years preceding, the years that had begun with the impassioned demand for eight *Dreadnoughts*. Perhaps the reason was that the man in the street, with his strictly limited capacity for worry, had more to worry about at home. Perhaps he felt that the recovery after Agadir proved that these war scares were matters of bluff. He recalled that on at least two occasions in the 'nineties we had been reputedly on the verge of war with France, and he drew from the passing of the German war scare the inference which accorded with his desires. He had been much impressed by Norman Angell's *The Great Illusion*, first published as a short pamphlet under a rather different title in 1909. This was the most widely read and persuasive of all the handbooks of pacifism; even King Edward VII read it, and he seldom read anything that was neither official nor amusing. The argument was that a modern war could never be made to pay its costs, even to the victors. It did not directly advance to the fallacy that there would therefore be no modern war, but it suggested, because its author assumed, that the Governments and peoples of the Continent were more swayed by economic reason than proved to be the case.

But the British Government knew too much to put its money on Mr. Angell, and one of the first consequences of Agadir was an immediate revision of our war plans, as a result of which Mr. Churchill succeeded Mr. McKenna at the Admiralty. The reasons for this change were unknown outside officials circle at the time, but there is no secret about them now. Mr. McKenna had been an irreproachable servant of the Admiralty, but he had not been its master. The war plans of the Admiralty were the work of the professional sailors; they involved a close blockade of the German ports and the retention of our Expeditionary Force in England during the first phase of the war—several months perhaps—so that, after the modern Trafalgar had been fought and won, the Force might be landed afterwards wherever the first round of the fighting showed that its intervention would be most effective. The War Office, on the other hand, envisaged the immediate despatch of our Expeditionary Force to the main seat of war in northern France or Belgium, and Mr. Haldane declared that he could not continue responsible for the War Office unless the Admiralty plans were changed. Mr. Churchill was sent to change them.

But the possibilities of conciliation were not yet exhausted. In January 1912 Sir Ernest Cassel, an eminent financier with relations on both sides of the water, was sent on a secret mission to try the ground. Would not Germany accept British superiority at sea if Great Britain undertook to give favourable consideration to whatever colonial ambitions Germany chose to offer for discussion? Sir Ernest Cassel received a kind reception but was unable to obtain any light on German colonial ambitions; they did not seem to want colonies and they could not reduce their naval programme. In fact they were just about to increase it. Mr. Haldane's public mission to Germany followed: he brought back a proposal that both England and Germany should undertake to observe neutrality in the event of either being forced to engage in war with one or more European Powers. This formula, though apparently laying equal obligations on both parties, would in effect have tied our hands while leaving those of Germany free; for there was no likelihood of our feeling called upon to enter a European war unless Germany had already become a belligerent. In other words Germany might begin a war with France or Russia or both; that was the contingency that all parties had in their minds; but it was quite inconceivable that we should begin a war with Austria. The proposal was therefore rejected by the Cabinet.

Mr. Haldane, however, brought back with him a confidential copy of the new German Navy Law, and with this in his pocket Mr. Churchill delivered, in February 1912, a speech in Glasgow which, followed by another speech in the House of Commons, gave a very welcome definition to our own naval policy. In the first years of the Liberal government we had reduced our programme in the hope that Germany would respond. She had on the contrary increased her efforts to overtake us, and in fact would have done so in a very few years but for the sudden reversal of policy marked by the 'We want eight' agitation of 1909. Henceforth, said Mr. Churchill, we should regulate our programme mathematically by that of our rival, building three ships to every two of hers; the more Germany built the more we should increase our margin of superiority. This was satisfyingly plain and Mr. Churchill, whom no one had taken very seriously as an aristocratic understudy to Mr. Lloyd George, became at once a national leader.

One result of Mr. Churchill's arrival at the Admiralty was the initiation of 'conversations' with the French naval authorities, similar to those which had been going on for some years between the military leaders in both countries. As a result of the naval conversations the whole of the French battle fleet was transferred to the Mediterranean, leaving our own North Sea fleet, augmented by our Mediterranean fleet, as guardians both of our own and of French security in the Channel. On paper this arrangement committed us to nothing in the sphere of policy, but there is no doubt that it greatly added to the weight of our moral obligation to support France in any war with Germany.

Mr. McKenna's lot was much less enviable than that of Mr. Churchill; he had to exchange the exhilarating task of building the greatest navy in the world for the sordid problem of administering enforced nourishment to hunger-striking suffragettes.

Agadir: The Anglo-German Problem

It was no more than a fortunate coincidence that the three weeks' interval between the arrival of the *Panther* at Agadir, and the ultimatum delivered by Mr. Lloyd George in the Guildhall, was marked by an event of great importance to our naval security. The Anglo-Japanese Treaty was renewed for ten years on July 13th, 1911. That treaty, first negotiated in 1902, had served many purposes; it had enabled Japan to attack Russia in 1904 and to drive her out of Manchuria and, while retaining Port Arthur for herself, to return the province to China; but its principal utility to us was that it enabled us to economize our naval power by concentrating it in the North Sea. Figures speak for themselves. In 1901 we had five battleships and thirty-three cruisers in the Pacific; in 1910, no battleships and nineteen cruisers. Japan undertook the guardianship of all our interests in Eastern waters on the condition (there is of course always a *quid pro quo*) that we supported the Japanese occupation of Korea. That was, in effect, the substance of the treaty as renewed in 1911.

Australia had expressly assented to the renewal of the treaty, but she was not entirely satisfied about it. Indeed the problem of imperial naval co-operation was beset with difficulties. As the Dominions grew to nationhood their capacity to contribute to the naval power of the Empire increased; as the German menace developed into a race in naval armament, the need for their contributions increased yet more rapidly; but the very consciousness of nationhood in the Dominions placed obstacles in the way of the most effective method of contribution. The best naval opinion, speaking with the voice of every authority from Admiral Mahan, the great American naval historian, to Mr. Churchill, declared that the unity of the fighting force was the only true strategy. Russia had lost to Japan on sea because she had kept half her fleet in the Baltic and half in the Far East; if both halves had been in either place she might have won her war. Yet the contribution of either money or ships to the 'British' navy was scouted by all the Dominions, except New Zealand, as 'tribute',

37

comparable with the notorious Stamp Act which had lost (or was supposed to have lost) the old American colonies.

During the sudden naval scare of 1909 a grandiose project had been launched for the creation of a Pacific fleet, built up of British, Australian, New Zealand, and Canadian contributions. Australia built her fleet unit, hoping that it would form part of a Pacific navy equal to the naval power of Japan. Everywhere else this scheme had been not merely abandoned, but forgotten. There was, indeed, no sense in it; it ignored, and might have imperilled, the cardinal fact of the Japanese Alliance. The patriotism of the Dominions was beyond question, and their ships, especially the ships of Australia, played an invaluable part in the outer regions of the naval activities of the Great War. But the German battle fleet could be kept in its place only by the efforts of the British battle fleet—and the British taxpayer.

CHAPTER IV

MILITANT LABOUR AND THE INSURANCE ACT

By the gift of the gloriously hot and dry summer of 1911 Providence might seem to have designed for her Englishmen an interval of ease and genial contemplation. But though God proposes, man disposes. Never had there been such alarums and excursions. No sooner was the Agadir crisis over and the Parliament Act consigned to the Statute Book than a sporadic crescendo of strikes culminated in a two days' stoppage of almost the whole of the railway system. Nothing of the kind had ever happened before; what were we coming to? We were, in fact confronted with a new social philosophy and a new conception of the uses and possibilities of trade unions. The 'General Strike' was waiting round the corner, though for various reasons it waited fifteen years.

The opening years of the century had been a quiet time in industry, much quieter than the middle 'nineties. The reasons for this quiescence cannot be considered here, but it is to be noted that the quiet period began to come to an end as soon as the Trades Disputes Act of 1906, relieving trade unions from irksome legal responsibilities in cases of damage incidental to strikes, was placed on the Statute Book. It was to secure such an Act as this that the Parliamentary Labour Party had fought the 1906 election and won its fifty seats. The Liberal government had, after some hesitation, accepted the Labour policy in this matter and the Lords had illustrated their broadmindedness, or perhaps their inclination towards Disraelian ideals of Tory Democracy, by admitting the dubious measure to the Statute Book.

39

Militant Labour and the Insurance Act

But such a measure as this, though it removed obstacles, could not inspire action. New industrial ideals were flooding in from abroad, in particular from the Syndicalists of France. There had long been in England large bodies of trade-unionists, and small bodies of revolutionary socialists; now for the first time the ideas of revolutionary socialism were making their way into the rank and file of the trade unions. 'Direct Action' was the war-cry of the moment; it meant the use of the strike weapon on a national scale, reinforced if necessary by physical violence, in order to secure the nationalization of industries. Early in 1912 during the great strike in the coal mines, these ideas were starkly proclaimed in a pamphlet entitled *The Miners' Next Step*, by two Welsh miners, one of them A. J. Cook, afterwards famous as the principal author of the General Strike of 1926. The writers of this pamphlet attacked the very conception of the State. Their aim was to cripple 'capitalism' by reiterated strikes and to in-augurate on its ruins a new system in which each industry would enjoy complete democratic self-determination, being ruled by the workers within it. Just as the Home-Rulers said 'Ireland for the Irish', so the syndicalists said 'The mines for the miners, and the railways for the railwaymen'. This pamphlet was suppressed as indiscreet by the trade-union authorities, and its policy was severely criticized by the leaders of the political Labour move-ment, Mr. MacDonald and Mr. Snowden; none the less, the spirit of Direct Action, vaguely stimulating the outlook of thou-sands of workers who would have recoiled in distrust from its ultimate implications, was behind the three great strikes and the dozens of lesser strikes of 1911-13.

Unrest on the railways had flared out in 1907. Mr. Thomas and others were engaged in trying to weld the whole body of railwaymen, hitherto organized in trade unions representing their different crafts, in one great industrial union. The em-ployers would not have it, and Mr. Lloyd George, then at the Board of Trade, successfully intervened with an offer of Railway Conciliation Boards. The strike of August 1911 was due to the

40

failure of these Boards. Public sympathy was not on the whole with the men. So far as could be understood—and the general public is seldom enabled to understand the real issues in an industrial dispute—the men had broken an agreement. It was also widely believed that the Companies had patriotically given way on certain points in order to terminate the strike, simply because the Government had informed them that we might be at war with Germany in forty-eight hours.

The coal strike, which lasted more than a month in the spring of 1912 was a more impressive demonstration. There had been unrest in the mines ever since the limitation of hours by the Eight Hours Act of 1908 had been found to carry with it a reduction of earnings. The miners concentrated on the case of hewers working in 'abnormal places'. Hewers were not paid wages, but piece-rates dependent on the amount of their output. Why, it was argued, should the hewer's earnings suffer if he happened to be employed on an abnormally difficult seam, where an average expenditure of energy produced less than an average result? They demanded that piece-rates should be protected by a minimum wage, below which, whatever his output, no hewer's weekly earnings could fall. The owners resisted, and what began as a Welsh strike quickly spread over all the coalfields. A million men were involved, and the strike was only terminated by a Coal Mines Minimum Wage Act, hastily rushed through Parliament. The Conservative party, disapproving both of the strike and of the only apparent means of ending it, refrained from voting on this measure.

The lessons of the coal strike may have been obvious, but they were not the less important. For one thing, the community was found to possess greater powers of resistance than had been supposed. A community which, without widespread hardship, could stand a complete cessation of coal-production throughout an English March, could clearly stand a great deal. But it was also noted, with surprise and apprehension, that the class who suffered most directly, namely the workers in industries which themselves stood idle owing to lack of coal, displayed no resentment, indeed much sympathy, with the miners. Was not this a convincing proof that the talk about the class-conscious solidarity of the wage earners in the coming class war, which many had inclined to dismiss as the verbiage of 'un-English' agitators, was not all verbiage by any means?

The claims of the miners had been comprehensible enough, and they evoked a great deal of sympathy. The great strike of the summer of 1912, on the other hand, that in the London Dockyards, was involved in mystery. What was apparent was neither statistics nor arguments but sheer hatred, a hatred so sincere that one had an uneasy feeling that it must be justified. Ben Tillett, standing before the crowd of his followers on Tower Hill and uttering his prayer: 'O God, strike Lord Devonport dead'—was not he a sign of the times? The writer in the *Round Table* certainly thought so.

'This dock strike', he says, 'is one of the strangest phenomena that have occurred in recent times. Its motives are wrapt in obscurity. . . . The incoherent orator has not explained the matter to us any more than the dumb crowds at the dock gates. All that we can be sure of is that there is something which stands very much in need of explanation. He must be a very superficial observer who does not see something very solemn and moving in this profound upheaval. Occurrences in the mean streets of London during the past ten weeks have been apt to strike us as purposeless and squalid; are they perhaps manifestations, none the less, of the same spirit which, as we look back, appears so sublime at Valmy, but which is still an unread riddle after a hundred years? One fact is clear enough—between the leaders of men whose spirits are disturbed in this fashion, and a cabinet intent upon reforming the Irish Constitution, disestablishing the Welsh Church, and amending the law as to the registration of voters, there is a great gulf fixed. To the Labour party it may appear as the gulf separating reality from unreality.'[1]

[1] *Round Table*. September 1912. The battle of Valmy was the first victory

Militant Labour and the Insurance Act

About this time people began to realize that the new King and Queen were striking out a line of their own. They took tea with a miner's wife in South Wales; they visited the mines and industries of Yorkshire, and soon afterwards the railway works at Crewe and the potteries of the 'Five Towns' near by. These visits, one felt, were no mere sightseeing; they were less expressions of pride in the triumphs of industry than of homely friendliness for the simple folk on whose daily work the triumphs of industry depended. If the politicians were out of touch with the things that really mattered, were not the King and Queen doing what they could to redress the balance?

On these lines, at any rate, the general public began to form their picture of the new King. It was a long time before the outlines of that picture became very precise and perhaps the details were never very elaborately filled in. Perhaps most of us never, at any stage of the reign, got much further than a rhymester whose simple verse is said to have given much pleasure to Queen Mary. There was an old lampoon on 'The Four Georges' which had ended with the couplet:

'When George IV from earth descended,
Then, Heaven be thanked, the Georges ended.

This rhymester added four more lines:

'Say not so, my ancient friend,
Times may change, and times may mend:
In George the Fifth at length you see
How good a King a George may be.'

King George had not, we supposed, the dominating personality and the flair for European politics of his father: he had not his grandmother's astonishing shrewdness of wit and force of will: but he was a good sportsman, a hard worker, and a thoroughly good man who set himself to help his country in all kinds of ways, all the better pleased, no doubt, if his services were un-

---

of the raw levies of the French Revolution, which matured into the armies of Napoleon.

obtrusive and unadvertised. The great Victorian tradition of British monarchy was safe in the hands of this, its third, generation.

A superior person might think, perhaps, that all this did not much matter, that a perfectly constitutional king was nothing more than what Americans call a rubber stamp. To reason thus would be to show great ignorance alike of human nature and of history. Anthropologists tell us that the earliest discernible kings were even more devoid of political power than the most constitutional of modern sovereigns. They were figures of magic and awe, surrounded by the pomps of superstition, symbols of their people's unity but not rulers of its destiny. It was only at a later stage that kings, just because they were held to be divine, accumulated mundane powers of legislation and leadership in peace and war. Ages passed, and what history had given history began to take away. Kingship passed through the stages of Agamemnon and Augustus Caesar, William the Conqueror and Louis Quatorze, and was now becoming something much more like what it had been in the very beginning. English monarchy had long been approximating towards a perfectly 'constitutional' ideal, yet even Victoria, as everyone knew, had been a strong partisan at times, and her partisanship had exercised an incalculable influence on the course of party politics. In George V the long approximation of the Crown towards an absolutely central position might be at last completed. A devout Gladstonian could not approve wholeheartedly of Queen Victoria; in George V we had a King whom all factions of his never-so-quarrelsome subjects could honour without reservations. He exactly fitted our National Anthem. More than any of our sovereigns since Queen Elizabeth he was 'mere English'. The traces of German accent, recalling the Hanoverian origin of his family and renewed by the long series of his predecessors' German marriages were in him at last, the ninth generation since George I, extinct. His Queen was an English princess; he had seen service in what had been, since the days of Drake, the most national of the professions. His father had been 'the uncle of Europe' and as much at home in Paris as in London. King George cared nothing for Paris, but had paid official visits to India, Canada, Australia and South Africa. Better still, perhaps, in one whose life work was to represent the average twentieth century Englishman, he thoroughly enjoyed a cup-tie final at the Crystal Palace.

Indeed he was no mere King from *The Golden Bough*. He was a symbol, but he was a person as well. The symbol inspired awe, and he never did anything which could mar his symbolic dignity; but only the person could inspire affection, and we liked to think of him as a very homely person. Mr. Page, the American ambassador and no admirer of the king-species, was delighted and half surprised to find that King George and he could 'chat like two human beings'. King George, he found, was an emphatic and vivacious talker, fond of emphasizing his remarks by pounding the table, and enjoying nothing so much as a good story. 'He talked about himself,' says Page, 'and his position as King. "Knowing the difficulties of a limited monarch," he said, "I thank heaven I am spared being an absolute one." '

The period of the great strikes, which extended with short intervals from the summer of 1911 to the summer of 1912, was also marked by the controversies and agitations that beset Mr. Lloyd George's Insurance Bill, the idea of which he had, it is said, brought back from Germany, when he visited that country in 1908. Bismarck had been the pioneer of State industrial insurance, and Mr. Lloyd George described the German system as 'superb' soon after his return to England. There were, to be exact, two Bills, one establishing Unemployment Insurance for the engineering and building trades, the other establishing a general system of Health Insurance which covered 14,000,000 persons. The two Bills together constituted the longest and most complicated piece of legislation that had ever confronted Parliament, surpassing the record previously held by Gladstone's

Militant Labour and the Insurance Act

second Irish Land Act. Unemployment Insurance was not made general until after the Great War, and received comparatively little attention at this time. The Health Insurance scheme was the principal interest in 1911 and 1912. The Bill was introduced in the spring of 1911, to provide a counter-attraction to the Parliament Bill, but the main Parliamentary battle over it was fought in the autumn session of that year; premiums became payable on the first of July 1912, and medical benefits could be claimed on the first of January 1913. Not until the last of these dates was safely passed could the author rest from his labours and enjoy the satisfaction of assured achievement.

The general plan of the Bill was easily comprehended. The weekly premiums were to be shared by the insured person, the employer, and the State, that is to say the ordinary taxpayer; the benefits went entirely to the insured person, who thus got ninepence worth of benefit for a fourpenny contribution to the premium. 'Ninepence for fourpence' was Mr. Lloyd George's slogan. It seems harmless, and it was superficially accurate, but it provoked intense irritation, perhaps because, after 'Limehouse', anything from Mr. Lloyd George's lips was assumed to be vicious.

The Conservative party had expressed themselves as 'in principle' friendly to the Bill, which might mean much or little; as it became plain that the scheme would encounter exasperated opposition from many quarters outside political circles, friendliness 'in principle' dwindled to vanishing point. Many began to hope to extract from the Insurance Bill their revenge for the Parliament Act.

Opposition was bewilderingly diverse. To begin with, about one-third of the persons to be insured were already insured through friendly societies and trade unions. The national scheme was to take over and work through these existing institutions just as the Education Act of 1870, which established the national education system, took over and worked through the existing 'voluntary' schools. There was friction here because the friendly

46

societies and trade unions wanted better terms than Mr. Lloyd George had intended to give them. Secondly, there was a conflict with the socialists and the Labour members in the House of Commons who objected to the contributory element in the scheme and wanted the medical benefits to be as free a gift as the Old Age Pensions—wanted, in fact, 'ninepence for nothing'. There were the mistresses of well-conducted households, conservative femininity who resented the indignity of 'stamp licking' as symbolical of an unwarrantable intrusion of 'officials' into their domestic affairs. These found spokesmen to their taste among the genuine individualists, who opposed, on principle, every intrusion of State control, every enforced surrender of the right to do as one pleased with one's own. Last, and most formidable, were the doctors, embattled in the British Medical Association, who demanded a drastic revision of the conditions under which their services were to be given.

Sectional opposition kept Mr. Lloyd George busy long after the Act was on the Statute Book, but his 'Liberal Insurance Committee' organized meetings all over the country to confound opponents and convince sceptics. He was 'assailed as no Minister has ever been assailed in my time', and no doubt he thoroughly enjoyed it and looked forward to more battles in the same campaign. 'I can see the Old Age Pension Act, the National Insurance Act, and many another Act in their trail descending, like breezes from the hills of my native land, sweeping into the mist-laden valleys, and clearing the gloom away until the rays of God's sun have pierced the narrowest window.'

The Health Insurance system continued to incur unfriendly criticism for some time after it had come into full operation. In part this was due to the occasional jolts and jars inevitably incident to the starting of an extremely complicated machine; in part to the strong feelings excited by the personality of its author. Those who disliked Mr. Lloyd George—and they were by no means all of them Conservatives—were determined to believe the worst about his principal achievement. But in course of time complaints died down and the system was accepted as an immense contribution to the health and well-being of the working classes. When in 1933 the system 'came of age', and a complimentary dinner to its author gave occasion for retrospection the only criticism was that it did not go far enough; that the wives and children of the insured workers ought to be brought completely within the scheme of insurance.

A great deal of the credit for the success of the scheme should go to the men in charge of its administration during its first years, and in particular to their chief, Sir Robert Morant, one of the greatest Civil Servants of his generation. Sir Robert Morant had, during the previous ten years, been in charge of the Board of Education. While politicians were raising the unprofitable dust of sectarian controversy Sir Robert Morant was building up the Secondary School system inaugurated by the Education Act of 1902, and introducing free meals for the necessitous and free medical inspection into the elementary schools. He brought the same qualities to the administration of national health insurance.

One of the 'narrow windows' of Mr. Lloyd George's apocalyptic vision was pierced by a clause in the 1911 Budget which allotted a salary of £400 a year to every member of the House of Commons. In giving salaries to its members the House was only falling into line with practically all the other Parliaments of the world. There had been a time in the distant past when members, or at any rate some members, were paid by their constituencies. The poet Andrew Marvell, member for Hull under Charles II, is said to have been the last of these. But that was long ago, and for the last two centuries it had been assumed that a member of Parliament would be a man of substance, and that his parliamentary duties would absorb but a small part of his time. Neither of these assumptions was any longer valid; a wage-earner M.P. could not perform his duties without a salary and, unless he received a salary from the State, he must receive it from his supporters. It was wrong that a constituency should be invited to choose between Mr. A. who would and could represent them for nothing, and Mr. B. who could not do so. The matter had not, however, been decided on its abstract merits, and the clause in the 1911 Budget is part of a rather longer story.

Labour members had been financed from trade-union funds until, in 1909, a Mr. Osborne, who was both a trade unionist and a Liberal, secured a judgment to the effect that such payments for political purposes were illegal. The Labour party demanded that the Government should introduce legislation reversing the Osborne judgment, but a simple reversal was refused, and payment of members was a device for shelving the question. It did not solve it, for the Labour party needed political funds for many purposes besides the salaries of its successful candidates, and in 1912 a Bill was passed into law which enabled the trade unions once again to levy contributions from their members for political purposes, provided that such contributions constituted a separate fund, and that those members of the trade unions who did not wish to subscribe were enabled to contract out of doing so. The Labour party was not altogether satisfied. It anticipated more extensive 'contracting out' than actually occurred; but it had to be content with what the Liberals would give it.

Throughout the three years which intervened between the Osborne judgment and the passage of this measure, the Labour party was perforce a somewhat humble suppliant on the doorstep of the Liberal Government. Indeed the Left Wing of Liberalism had for the time being entirely eclipsed the self-styled leaders of 'Labour' in the House of Commons. Whether they had given the quietus to syndicalism was not so certain, but syndicalism unmistakably waned in the years before the war. This revolutionary movement envisaged Trade Unions acting in defiance of the State and aiming at its destruction, but the Insurance Act, docilely accepted after all, bound the unions all the closer to Whitehall, by making them the channel through which the insurance system could be most conveniently operated. The unions drew increased membership from the fact that workers joined them in order to insure through them rather than through the Post Office.

Another dissolvent of syndicalism was the beneficent activity of a distinguished Civil Servant, Sir George Askwith, whose name used to crop up at this time whenever a grave industrial dispute had to be settled. One of the commonest causes of industrial irritation was the unskilful drafting of industrial agreements. It was the art of Sir George Askwith not only to secure a cessation of industrial hostilities but to draft industrial treaties in terms calculated to secure a lasting peace. But perhaps after all syndicalism never established roots in England. It was Welsh; it was Irish, as became apparent when Jim Larkin's strike of the transport workers paralysed Dublin; it inflamed the Clydeside; it was acceptable all along the 'Celtic fringe' but not among those who were, rightly or wrongly, supposed to be descended from the Anglo-Saxons.

But if syndicalism faded out of the industrial picture, the prospect of gigantic strikes certainly did not. In the early months of 1914 the three biggest unions, the miners, the railwaymen, and the transport workers, organized their Triple Alliance for concerted action. Very strange reading, in the light of after events, is the speech delivered by Mr. Lloyd George on 17th July 1914, a week before the Austrian ultimatum to Serbia. His audience was the City bankers at their annual dinner. The occasion was, in fact, the third anniversary of his famous warning to Germany during the Agadir crisis. In this speech Mr. Lloyd George dwelt at length on the danger inherent in the synchronization of an Irish civil war and a Triple Alliance strike. That something worse than either might be synchronized with both did not occur to him. 'In the matter of external affairs,' he said, 'the sky has never been more perfectly blue.'

CHAPTER V

THE HOME RULE BILL (1912), AND
WELSH DISESTABLISHMENT

It was scarcely possible that Liberals should look forward with enthusiasm or without apprehension to the session of 1912. There was to be an Irish Home Rule Bill, a Welsh Disestablishment Bill, and an Electoral Reform Bill, intended to take the final step towards a complete male democracy. One sometimes assumes that that step had been taken by the Act of 1884, but in fact, owing to the complications of a franchise based on residence, only seven and a half of the twelve million adult males were Parliamentary voters, and half a million of them, fortunate occupiers or possessors of property in more than one constituency, enjoyed a plurality of votes, and the practice of spreading the election over a period of nearly three weeks enabled the more active of them to record votes in various constituencies. Indeed the popular purpose of the Bill, so far as any of it was popular, was to abolish plural voting. So there were to be three first-class contentious measures in one session. John Bright's homely aphorism about the impossibility of driving three omnibuses abreast through Temple Bar was heard again, though Temple Bar was no longer to be seen. Others, happily gifted with a memory for dates, remarked that Mr. Asquith was crowding into one year an 1886, an 1869, and an 1884.[1] Still more to the point was the remark that Mr. Asquith was staging another 1893. The session of 1893, which had run on well into 1894, had been the last, the longest, and the most disastrous in

[1] These were the dates, respectively, of Gladstone's measures of Home Rule, Irish Church Disestablishment, and Electoral Reform.

Gladstone's career. Gladstone, 'an old man in a hurry', had introduced in that year a Home Rule Bill, flanked by several other contentious measures, and had lost them almost all. The country had turned in relief to eleven years' Conservative government.

Mr. Asquith was also in a hurry, not because he was an old man but because he had sentenced himself to three years' hard labour under his Parliament Act. Each of these measures would be rejected by the House of Lords—and quite reasonably, or what, one might well ask, was the procedure under the Parliament Act intended for? Of the five possible sessions of the present Parliament the first was gone, and it would be most unsafe to reckon that the fifth would ever be reached. If each of these three measures was to become law, each and all must now 'catch the first boat'. Moreover none of them could safely stand without the other two. The existence of the Liberal government depended upon the maintenance of a very loose Parliamentary coalition. English and Welsh Nonconformist Liberals demanded the Welsh Bill; without it they would not vote for Irish Home Rule, which in their hearts they distrusted. The Labour party cared very little for either the Welsh or the Irish measures but insisted on electoral democracy. As for the Irish, it was notorious that they were in British politics for nothing but for the measure of their own emancipation. And so—the triple programme. It was easy to remark that not a single one of its items made any contribution whatever to the solution of those problems of poverty and social maladjustment on which the welfare of the community really depended.

As for Home Rule, it might seem to those who knew nothing about it to be a simple matter of righting an ancient wrong, but hardened politicians who knew all about Gladstone and Parnell, and could not foresee the Irish Free State, were well aware that the production of a satisfactory scheme of semi-self-government —that is what Home Rule meant before the war—was about as easy as squaring the circle. Before Gladstone introduced his first

Home Rule Bill (1912)—Welsh Disestablishment

Bill he had appealed to the Conservative leaders to co-operate with him in framing an agreed, an all-British, solution. That appeal had been rejected, for sound electoral reasons, and the Conservatives had committed themselves to a policy of mere negation. Mr. Balfour, in his last speech before laying down his leadership of the Conservative party, had declared that all schemes of Irish Home Rule were 'dreams of political idiots'. Was that altogether wise? Mr. Asquith was about to introduce a Home Rule Bill. Could his worst enemy hold that the phrase 'political idiot' was a very felicitous description of him?

In any case the first demonstrations in Ulster in the autumn of 1911 were felt to be premature and rather ridiculous. Their leader was not an Ulsterman at all but a lawyer—another of these lawyers!—from Dublin. Ulster seemed to suppose that the Pope, whose existence had long been forgotten in England, would use Home Rule to persecute Irish Protestants. It was announced that Protestant Ulster would refuse to obey any Parliament that should be established in Dublin, and would set up a provisional government of her own. After all, nothing could well happen before 1914. If Ulster was already in a tearing passion by the autumn of 1911 she would have relapsed into the reasonableness of exhaustion long before the fatal date. These were English views; but Englishmen do not understand Irishmen, either the Ulster sort or the other sort.

Almost exactly a year later the Ulstermen repeated this performance, with the addition of the signing of a solemn Covenant of resistance, evidently modelled on the famous National Covenant of the Scottish Kirk which had been the beginning of the downfall of Charles I. This time the impression created in England was entirely different. This time nobody laughed. And yet, what had happened?

Early in the year Mr. Asquith had introduced his Home Rule Bill, and it had been subjected to prolonged debate. Everyone who cared about such matters was now familiar with the constitution of the proposed Irish Parliament; with the long and complicated list of subjects which were excluded from the control of that Parliament; with the arrangements for giving Ireland a partial control over her customs duties; with the curious distribution of responsibility for Irish administration between the Irish and the Imperial authorities; with the method of calculating the 'transferred sum' from the Irish to the Imperial exchequer; with the important financial matters which were to be left over for decision by a Joint Exchequer Board, hereafter to be established; with the circumstances under which Ireland would retain sometimes forty-two and sometimes sixty members in the British House of Commons. They asked themselves whether all these ingenious arrangements would satisfy Ireland; would they also maintain Imperial supremacy? would they, in fact, 'solve the Irish problem' and bring to an end the agelong and intolerable friction between the two countries? Only the very sanguine were prepared to give an affirmative answer. Even those who wished well to the Home Rule Bill as a bold and honest attempt to provide a solution could not deny the force of Mr. Balfour's fundamental criticism. The Bill, he said, seeks to establish 'a national Parliament without national powers'. Nor could they deny the difficulty of meeting his dilemma. 'If', he said, 'Ireland is a nation, what right has Great Britain to supremacy?'

What was a nation? A modern Irish poet had offered a definition in blank verse:

'What is a nation but a multitude
United by some god-begotten mood,
Some hope of liberty or dream of power?'

If unity was necessary then Ireland certainly did not fall within A.E.'s definition, for there was Ulster—not to mention the Southern Unionists who, being for the most part men of substance, were perhaps congenitally immune from 'god-begotten moods'. To Ulster the Liberals offered safeguards—every conceivable safeguard. But on this subject Mr. Bonar Law had

spoken words as true as they were, for Liberal Home Rulers,
inconvenient. All the experience of history, he said, had proved
that one democratic Parliament cannot impose permanent
limitations on the powers of another democratic Parliament.
And as if to justify his assertion Dublin had just inscribed be-
neath its statue of Parnell his own prophetic words: 'No man
has the right to set a boundary to the march of a nation. No
man has the right to say to this country—Thus far shalt thou go
and no farther. We have never attempted to fix the *ne plus ultra*
to the progress of Ireland's nationhood, and we never shall.' Mr.
Redmond, in his oration at the unveiling of the statue, had made
no allusion to the legend inscribed on its base; but Mr. Redmond
was a very tactful man. Mr. Redmond might alter his tone; he
had often altered it already; or Mr. Redmond might find himself left behind by his followers. Mr. Arthur Griffith, for example, had concluded an ironical exposure of the inadequacies
of the Home Rule Bill with the sentence: 'If this be Liberty, the
lexicographers have deceived us.' But of course Mr. Griffith was
a crank and represented no one but a handful of mad poets and
disgruntled schoolmasters who composed his society of *Sinn Fein*.

As for Ulster the Liberals had already come very near admitting that they did not know what to do about it. Equally
ominous was the fact that Mr. Bonar Law knew perfectly well
what he, for his part, was going to do. He gave his unqualified
and official blessing to the prospective Ulster rebellion. It was
perhaps unfortunate that the leader of the British Conservative
party was no impartial judge of the Ulster case, for he was himself an Ulsterman by descent. His father had emigrated from an
Ulster manse to New Brunswick ten years before the future
statesman's birth, but acts of private benefaction proved that
the old family home in which he had never lived was very near
Mr. Bonar Law's heart.

The plain man would have liked to give both parts of Ireland
all that they wanted, or seemed to want. Let Southern Ireland
have Home Rule and let Ulster remain within the Union. We

know that something like this was to be, after a series of events inconceivable in 1912, the final solution. A private member of the Liberal party did in fact suggest the exclusion of the four predominantly Protestant counties of Ulster in a speech delivered during the 1912 debates, but his idea received no encouragement from any quarter. Quite apart from the Ulster boundary question, it would have satisfied neither Irish party. Both asserted that Ireland was one and indivisible and both desired to impose their solution on the whole of it. For one must remember the curious fact that, though the Conservative leader was an Ulsterman, the Ulster leader was not. Sir Edward Carson was a Dublin Unionist lawyer, who had accepted from the Ulster members a formal invitation that he should lead their group and conduct Ulster's case against Home Rule. His acceptance of the brief is wholly to his credit, for he took no fee; indeed he voluntarily sacrificed for it both an exceedingly lucrative practice at the English bar and his prospect of succession to the leadership of the British Conservative party. But that does not alter the fact that the ultimate object of his work for Ulster was less to secure Ulster's exclusion from a Home Ruling Ireland than to use Ulster's opposition to smash Home Rule. His leadership rendered indefinitely remote the prospects of the kind of settlement which events after the Great War showed to be inevitable.

Meanwhile the Home Rule Bill went its way and completed its first passage in January 1913. It was of course rejected at once by the House of Lords. There seemed nothing to be done but to wait and see.

The Welsh Bill pursued the same course to the same end, and provoked rather more violent language than the Irish Bill, perhaps because it was, after all, a less serious matter, perhaps because Mr. Lloyd George was involved. He had been a full-blooded Welsh Nationalist long before he was a Liberal statesman, and in the Welsh nonconformist society of his boyhood the Anglican establishment used to be denounced, as a matter of common form, with all the apparatus of apocalyptic Billingsgate which seventeenth-century Puritans had applied to the Church of Rome. The English Church interest was mobilized in opposition to the Bill with a thoroughness and efficiency which disgusted some of the greater men among its servants. Mr. Smith, afterwards Lord Birkenhead, not content with his role as 'Galloper Smith' in the army of Ulster, was among the foremost champions of the Welsh Church and a speech in which he declared that the Bill had 'shocked the conscience of every Christian community in Europe' drew a refreshingly contemptuous little poem from the pen of Mr. Chesterton:

> 'It would greatly, I must own,
>   Soothe me, Smith!
> If you left this theme alone,
>   Holy Smith!
> Talk about the pews and steeples
>   And the cash that goes therewith!
> But the souls of Christian peoples . . .
>   Chuck it, Smith!'

The Bill deprived the four Welsh dioceses of a part of their endowments, devoting the money to educational and other purposes, and formed the dioceses into a united self-governing Church under an Archbishop of Wales. The measure, or rather one like it, became law almost unnoticed by the general public in 1919, and it is generally held to have proved an unqualified success. Such, at least, was the judgment expressed by the Archbishop of Wales in an article contributed to the *Times* in 1923. The disestablished Church feels a new pride and confidence as a genuinely Welsh institution, and its relations with Welsh Nonconformity have been marked by a friendly spirit of co-operation impossible so long as every vigorous Welsh nonconformist was a foe to the establishment. As the Archbishop wrote: 'Few, if any, now desire a return to the old order.'

CHAPTER VI

THE SEX WAR

The third member of the Government's legislative trio, the Franchise and Registration Bill, fell out by the way under very singular circumstances. In the autumn of 1911 Mr. Asquith had given a solemn promise that this Bill should be so drafted as to admit amendments giving votes to women, and that, if any amendment of this character was carried on a free vote of the House, he would accept it as an integral part of the Government's policy. It was on the strength of this promise that a private member's Women Suffrage Bill was rejected on its second reading in the course of the session of 1912. That session lasted on into the new year, and the fateful day arrived on January 23rd, 1913. There were three alternative amendments, one of which would have enfranchised women on the same terms as men and created a female majority on the electoral registers; the second would have given the vote to women householders and the wives of householders on attaining the age of twenty-five; the third would have given the vote only to women householders in their own right. An immense amount of care and pains had been given to the drafting of these amendments in such a way that each of the three policies should enjoy fair play and no favour. One was to be moved by a Conservative, one by a Liberal, and one by a Labour man. But first of all an amendment had to be carried deleting the word 'male' wherever it occurred in the Bill. This was entrusted to no less a person than Sir Edward Grey who, unlike Mr. Asquith but like the majority of his Cabinet colleagues, was a supporter of the women's cause.

The Sex War

It is, however, a rule of Parliamentary procedure that an amendment entirely altering the character of a Bill is 'out of order'. A Bill so amended, it is held, would become in fact a new and different Bill and would have to start its whole Parliamentary career afresh from the beginning. This being so, an opponent of women's suffrage now asked the Speaker whether, in fact, a sex suffrage amendment was not thus 'out of order' as applied to a Bill which, on the face of it, was merely concerned with the mechanism of the existing male franchise. The Speaker assented, and Mr. Asquith's 'solemn promise' proved a hoax.

It is always easier to believe that great men, especially great politicians, are knaves than that they are fools. Mr. Asquith was the greatest living master of Parliamentary tactics. He was an avowed opponent of women's suffrage. Could one really suppose that what was plain to the Speaker had not been equally plain to him from the first? could one really doubt that his tongue had been anywhere but in his cheek when he gave his 'solemn promise' fifteen months before, and that it had remained there ever since? So argued heated champions in their very natural exasperation, but it need hardly be said that Mr. Asquith's personal character rendered their suspicions entirely untenable. The Prime Minister was as much surprised by the Speaker's ruling as was Mrs. Pankhurst. Nor is it necessary, in acquitting Mr. Asquith of dishonesty, to convict him of stupidity on this occasion. The law, as Lord Chancellor Clarendon said long ago, is an admirable mystery, and Parliamentary law not least so. If Mr. Asquith had been Speaker, as of course he could have been had his ambitions lain in that direction, he would have given a different ruling from that of Speaker Lowther, and no one can say whether, if there were an appeal from the Speaker's ruling to the Day of Judgment, he would find his ruling upheld.

None the less, the women may be excused for finding in this incident a crushing exposure of the stupidity of man-made politics. It opened at once a new phase in their campaign.

The Women's Suffrage agitation is not only one of the most

important features of the years before the war, it may also be regarded as the most interesting, just because it is unique. There have, both before and since, been constitutional crises, Irish rebellions, and industrial upheavals, but never before had we seen anything like the 'Suffragettes' and we may hope that we shall never see anything like them again.

Discussion of Women Suffrage Bills in the House of Commons can be traced back to the times of Gladstone and Disraeli, but the thing remained as academic as Irish Home Rule in the hands of Isaac Butt until a Parnell of the suffrage arose in Mrs. Pankhurst. Parliamentary procedure is a mystery to all ordinary people, but it is well known that it can be used by its experts to block the advancement of any measure, however generally desired and desirable, that has not the official support of the Government. Since no Government was ever agreed on the suffrage question, that question was always at the mercy of the experts, chief among whom was Mr. Labouchere, who revealed an interminable fecundity of speech on such subjects as the inspection of verminous aliens or the rear-lighting of vehicles whenever a women's suffrage measure was waiting its turn. It was after hearing one such exhibition by Mr. Labouchere in 1904 that Mrs. Pankhurst, supported by Mr. Keir Hardie, the forerunner and first leader of the Labour party, founded the Women's Social and Political Union. The purpose of Mrs. Pankhurst's society was not to preach to the people—there had been enough of that—but to frighten the Government. Like Parnell before them, they would make the lives of politicians a burden and a nightmare until their demand was granted.

They began with a spirited campaign of heckling at the meetings of Liberal Cabinet ministers during the election of 1906, and three months afterwards they made their first little essay of the new tactics within the House of Commons. The usual Women's Suffrage Bill was up for debate, and it was, as usual, going to be 'talked out'. The ladies grew anxious, and just before eleven o'clock they began to protest, and cries of ''Divide,

The Sex War

Divide." rang out from behind the grille, through which, as the
Members looked up in astonishment, little *Votes for Women* banners were seen to be thrust. At once the police rushed in and
pulled the ladies out, and the House rose amid angry murmurs.
Friends and enemies alike regretted the disturbance.'[1] Shortly
after this the Prime Minister, Sir Henry Campbell-Bannerman,
received a deputation. Sir Henry was the possessor of a rather
pawky Scots humour, and he was in his element on this occasion.
He told the ladies that their arguments were 'conclusive and
irrefutable', that he agreed with every word they said, but that
he was going to do nothing about it. So he could only advise
them 'to go on pestering', and to exercise 'the virtue of patience'.

In order to carry out as effectively as possible the first part of
Sir Henry's advice Mrs. Pankhurst's Society (the W.S.P.U.) was
organized on what, by an anachronism, one may call Fascist
lines. All authority was vested in four persons, Mrs. Pankhurst
and her daughter Christabel and Mr. and Mrs. Pethick-Law-
rence; the members of the society were to do whatever their
leaders told them. The principal activities of 1906-1910 were
'technical assaults' such as the breaking of shop windows and
the slapping of policemen's faces. The older suffrage societies
disapproved, but the results were undeniable, and the short
Parliament of 1910 gave unwontedly serious consideration to a
measure of limited women's suffrage—votes for women who
were householders in their own right—known as the Conciliation Bill because the various sections of the women's movement
agreed to give it, for tactical purposes, their unreserved support.
Most women suffragists favoured a more sweeping policy, but
all friends of the movement had been persuaded to concentrate
on this, as the thin end of their wedge. The old male jokes were
no longer aired and the Bill secured its second reading by over
one hundred votes. And then Mr. Lloyd George, a notable supporter of the cause, denounced their Bill as undemocratic! The
rejoinder was an unprecedented demonstration at Westminster

[1] *The Cause* by Ray Strachey, pp. 299, 301.

on the day of the dissolution of Parliament (December 1910). One hundred and fifty-three women were arrested.

The years 1911 and 1912 witnessed a steady crescendo of what was now commonly called 'militancy'. One laughed when women spent a night out under the stars in order to boycott the census of 1911; one was annoyed when their attacks on public property led to the closing of the British Museum and other august institutions; but one did not know what to think when, in 1912, the 'suffragette' prisoners (somehow the word 'suffragette' had come into use as a synonym for militant suffragist or a member of the W.S.P.U.) took to hunger striking. They could not be released, and they could not be allowed to die; but 'forcible feeding', was, by all accounts, a very objectionable proceeding. Some said that these suffragettes were ruining the cause, converting its friends into enemies. But most of those who said this had always been enemies. Mr. Lansbury challenged the assertion by resigning his seat and standing for re-election as a suffrage candidate. He was defeated by eight hundred votes, but nothing except Mr. Lansbury's sporting character had been demonstrated, for many other questions inevitably entered into the contest for his seat.

It was a commonplace to say that the women were not the only militants. What else but militancy was Ulster's threat of armed rebellion, or the avowed intention of the extremer trade unionists to cripple the industrial system by reiterated strikes? Had not the very doctors themselves, decent, kindly folk, been threatening a refusal of their services under the Health Insurance Act? How had we got ourselves involved in this nightmare of anarchy? Where had it begun? So far as one could make out it had begun with the staid nonconformist Passive Resisters of 1902.

Such was the position at the time of the fiasco of the suffrage amendments to the Government's Franchise Bill. The Bill was dropped—a sympathetic gesture perhaps, but it is not surprising that organized violence and hunger striking redoubled. The

The Sex War

Government's only positive contribution to the problem was the once notorious Cat and Mouse Act which became law in April 1913. Under this Act suffragette prisoners who endangered their health by hunger striking could be released and rearrested as soon as they had nourished themselves back to health. One hundred and eighty-two women suffered under this measure in the remainder of the year. At the end of it Mr. McKenna, the Home Secretary, made the grim surmise that the W.S.P.U. selected women of delicate health for their more serious offences in the hope that some of them would die under the treatment. It is likely enough, for Mrs. Pankhurst and her devoted disciples believed themselves to be at war and were eager to suffer its utmost rigours. One of them chose death in its most sensational form by throwing herself in front of the horses on Derby Day. She was given the most spectacular funeral that London had witnessed since that of King Edward.

And so on, until the outbreak of the Great War cut short this, as it cut short the Irish, melodrama. Ordeal by fire became the favourite form of offensive. Houses, pavilions, grandstands, stations, hotels were burned wherever they were found to be unoccupied. A church was burnt to the ground, another was damaged by a bomb, a bomb was found under the Coronation Chair in Westminster Abbey, famous pictures were damaged in public galleries. No one can say how the story would have ended. There seems no doubt at all that the volume of public support and sympathy among women of all classes, who had hitherto regarded the movement with indifference, was vastly augmented. What the man in the street, who would decide the next election, thought, cannot be known. Perhaps he did not know himself. He was certainly very much worried about it; he was worried about many things.

CHAPTER VII

FOOD TAXES AND MARCONI SHARES

The Parliamentary session of 1913 was generally agreed to be the dullest within the memory of man. Mr. Balfour, discussing the decline of the House of Commons, said that events had 'greatly destroyed the House of Commons' own interest in itself', and added that 'directly the House of Commons ceases to be interested in itself, no human being is likely to be interested in it'. Mr. Balfour, as a political philosopher, ranged widely in search of causes over the whole period since 1874 when he had himself first entered the House; but a special cause for the dullness of the session of 1913 was apparent to everyone. Under the rules of the Parliament Act it would have to repeat the performance of 1912. 'There will be a considerable amount of walking round in the division lobbies. The closure will work with the regularity of a piston rod. If any of the Bills be amended in a single particular, it will become automatically dead. So, as nothing can possibly be changed, perhaps the less said the better. More talking by Ministerialists will not help the Government, nor will more talking by the Opposition much hinder the Government. The work, therefore, that lies before the House of Commons at the present time is certainly arduous, and it may be necessary; but it is not such as will ever be undertaken without disgust by intelligent and self-respecting men.'[1]

Whatever shame and dishonour there might be in this state of affairs was placed to the discredit of the Government. But it was a curious fact, often observable in our Parliamentary history but

[1] *Round Table*. June 1913.

never more than at this time, that what was lost by the Government did not seem to be gained by the Opposition. Indeed, some said that the strongest security of the Government was like that claimed by Charles II at the time of the Popish Plot, when he cheerily remarked to his brother James: 'Nobody would kill me in order to make *you* King!' What was wrong with the Conservative party? Clearly not its opposition to Liberal policy. The answer must be found in its presentation of Conservative policy. These were years of abounding economic prosperity, and at such a time the demand for tariffs can never be made to seem very urgent. The Conservative party could hardly, at this time of day, return to free trade, but there was one item in its official protectionist programme which nearly all Conservative candidates agreed, in private, in regarding as a millstone round the neck of the party. This, needless to say, was the food taxes.

Taxes on the importation of foreign foodstuffs had been the very first plank in the programme of Joseph Chamberlain's Tariff Reform Campaign of 1903. He advocated an Imperial *Zollverein* or customs union—what in post-war controversy was called Empire Free Trade—as the only effective means of securing the object nearest his heart, namely the closer union of the Empire. His mind was not set on the protection of British agriculture but on the conciliation of Dominion governments. Canada already offered in her tariff system certain 'preferences' to British manufactured imports. Only by offering similar 'preferences' to colonial foodstuffs could we give Canada a *quid pro quo*, and encourage both her and the other Dominions to go a great deal further in the extension of their favours to British goods. Mr. Chamberlain was quite candid in describing his policy of taxing foreign foods as involving an economic sacrifice —only a temporary sacrifice, one hoped—for a far grander immaterial ideal. The bottom was knocked out of this policy when it became plain that the Dominions had no intention of approaching the problem in the same spirit. They did not intend to make any sacrifices. They put their own welfare first, and the promotion of imperial unity a bad second. A good deal of the Chamberlain philosophy of empire they regarded with profound distrust. They did not expect us to make any economic sacrifices on their behalf and they were certainly going to make none on ours.

Meanwhile Chamberlainism had developed into a general programme for the protection of home industries. 'Dumping' became the key-word: 'retaliatory duties' which would force protected foreign countries to discuss with us a mutual lowering of tariffs made a general appeal, in so far as any part of the Conservative Protection policy ever made a general appeal before the war. But the food taxes remained in the programme, though the profound hostility of the urban electorate was not balanced by any enthusiasm in the agricultural constituencies. The agricultural labourer was more convinced that the food taxes would increase his expenses than that they would lead to an increase in his wages, nor was the farmer interested in a measure which was expressly intended to encourage his most dangerous competitor, the food grower in the dominions.

All these points and many others were discussed with candour and elaboration in all Conservative circles throughout the autumn of 1912. Mr. Bonar Law had been accepted as leader on the understanding that he was a convinced 'whole-hogger', as the phrase was in those homely days, and he had declared that, if his supporters decided to abandon the principles for which he stood, he would ask them to accept his resignation. None the less, facts are stubborn things, and Mr. Law's speech at Rood Ashton in December was awaited with tense interest. 'For nine years', said Mr. Law, 'we have kept the flag flying and, if there is any sincerity in political life at all, this is not the time, and I at all events am not the man, to haul down that flag.'

But perhaps it might be flown at half-mast. Mr. Law continued: 'If our countrymen entrust us with power, we do not intend to impose food duties. What we intend to do is to call a conference of the colonies to consider the whole question. . . .

66

Food Taxes and Marconi Shares

We are told that the colonies have made no offer, that they do not wish such an arrangement. If that is true, no food duties will be imposed in any circumstances. (Cheers.) We do not wish to impose them. (Cheers.) I hope it will be possible—I think it may be possible. . . .' On the surface of the thing a Colonial Conference had been substituted for Mr. Balfour's unfortunate Referendum proposal, but actually the food taxes were dead. The Conservative press, from the *Times* to the *Daily Mail*, made sure of that.

There only remained the question whether Mr. Law would resign. He was not the kind of man to cling to office after the sacrifice of his principles, and had not his principles been sacrificed? The Liberals, having few sources of pleasure in their own affairs, had extracted the maximum of satisfaction from the food-tax comedy. They hoped Mr. Law would resign, and no doubt that decided all good Conservatives in a resolve that he must stay. The Liberals did not like him, and that was the best evidence that he was a good leader of opposition—'offensive' in both senses of the word. A 'memorial' expressing the confidence of all sections of the Conservative party in Mr. Law's leadership was prepared and presented to him. He accepted it and consented to stay. The Conservative party had not nailed their flag to the mast, but they had at least nailed their leader. There had been some rather ludicrous episodes, but everyone had behaved very well, especially Mr. Austen Chamberlain who might, if he had wanted, have secured on this occasion the leadership he missed on the retirement of Mr. Balfour. Above all, the party programme had been relieved of its worst item.

No one understood better than Mr. Lloyd George the declining prestige of official Liberalism, and he was not one who would stand idle and resourceless on the deck of a sinking ship. Parallels were often drawn at this time between Mr. Lloyd George and Joseph Chamberlain. Both were sanguine adventurers in politics with an innate addiction to 'unauthorized programmes'.

Food Taxes and Marconi Shares

The phrase had first been applied to the programme of social reforms, including the once famous 'three acres and a cow', with which Chamberlain had tried to popularize Gladstone's party in 1885. Gladstone had smothered it under Home Rule and Chamberlain had gone out into the wilderness. Eighteen years later he had played the same trick on his new associates with Tariff Reform. People pointed out that Mr. Lloyd George's relation to Mr. Asquith was much the same as had been Joseph Chamberlain's relation to Mr. Balfour, the dynamic over against the static, or, if you preferred, impudence chafing under the weight of dignity. That the energy generated by the People's Budget should be exhausted in turning the rusty wheels of Home Rule seemed a sad waste of motive power, as indeed it was. Mr. Lloyd George had, one may presume, a good deal of sympathy with the Direct Actionists when they described the House of Commons as the House of Pretence and a good deal of contempt for the political Labour party who seemed to get no further than throwing cold water on their own Direct Actionists. He knew better. He would give them a Land Campaign.

What was wrong with the land? According to Mr. Lloyd George it was 'shackled with the chains of feudalism. We have got to free the people from the anxieties, the worries, the terrors that their children may be crying for bread in this land of plenty. . . . You have no notion in the towns of the pagan thraldom that stifles liberty in our villages. The squire is God; the parson, the agent, the gamekeeper—these are his priests; the pheasants, the hares—these are the sacred birds and beasts of the tabernacle.' Mr. Lloyd George's knowledge of pheasants became suspect when he described them as destroying a crop of mangold-wurzels. Perhaps his squire was as mythical a beast as his pheasant. The picture seemed to be taken from a handbook about France before the French Revolution. Mr. Lloyd George instituted a Land Enquiry, but its reports seemed to be open to the same objection as those of Henry VIII's enquiry into the condition of the monasteries. The enquirers found what they

68

had determined to find. Official Liberalism was uneasy and Conservatism derisive. The plan seemed to be to cure a class war in industry by starting another class war in agriculture, the principle of the counter-irritant as exemplified in pre-scientific medicine, when doctors cured gout in the feet by burning holes in their patients' thighs.

None the less Mr. Lloyd George had always hitherto been a good judge of his own career. It may be that, had everything gone according to plan, he would have split the Liberal party and carried away most of it with him, overthrowing Mr. Asquith and annexing in the process most of the Labour party, which had certainly not yet secured any very firm anchorage. There were rumours that he had once already tried to form a new 'national party' at the time of the Constitutional Conference, and had made approaches to several Conservative politicians with that end in view. However, things did not go according to plan. While the Land Campaign was in full swing, its author found himself involved in a cloud of suspicion. He was accused of dishonest dealings in the shares of the Marconi Company.

It is difficult to tell the Marconi story at once fairly and briefly, for its details are complicated and upon those details, it might be asserted, a fair judgment should depend. None the less, the attempt must be made. To omit it, either as sordid or as unimportant, would be indefensible. The public was greatly interested, and quite rightly too, for few questions are more important to a community than the question whether its chosen leaders are, in fact, honest men.

On March 7th, 1912, the Post Office provisionally accepted a tender from the Marconi Company for the installation of a chain of wireless stations throughout the Empire, and the chief terms of the tender were immediately published in the press. The Government did not ask the House of Commons for a final ratification of the agreement until the following October, and during the intervening months wild rumours had been circulating to the discredit of various members of the Government,

Food Taxes and Marconi Shares

including Mr. Lloyd George. The origin of these rumours was, no doubt, the fact that the Attorney General, Sir Rufus Isaacs (afterwards Lord Reading) was the brother of the managing director of the Marconi Company. It was asserted that Sir Rufus and some of his political colleagues had used their inside knowledge of the Government's intentions to make large sums of money by the surreptitious purchase and sale of Marconi shares. In the course of the October debate Mr. Lansbury made allusion to these rumours, and all the Ministers implicated rose in turn and made categorical denials. These denials were accepted by all reasonable men, and there seemed to be an end of the matter.

Early in the next year, however, Sir Rufus Isaacs and Mr. Samuel, the Postmaster General, had occasion to bring a libel action against a French paper, *Le Matin*, on account of an article imputing gross corruption in Marconi transactions, and in the course of his evidence Sir Rufus stated that, though he had bought no shares in the English Marconi Company, he had, in fact, bought shares in the American Marconi Company a few days after the tender of the English Company had been accepted and its terms published. Some of these he had sold to Mr. Lloyd George and another Minister; all three of them had made a slight loss on their transactions.

Once again ugly insinuations began to fly about. Why had these facts been kept back when the Ministers had made their statements in the previous October? How close was the connection between the two Marconi Companies, as illustrated by the comparative prices of their shares? The English company had a large holding in the American company. This fact would not, of course, in itself make the American shares rise as a direct consequence of the successful tender of the English company, but the contract with the British government, regarded as a first-class advertisement for the Marconi patents and system, could hardly fail to improve the position of the American company as well as the English. A Select Committee of the House, appointed to

70

Food Taxes and Marconi Shares

investigate the merits of the contract, was still sitting, and before this the implicated Ministers now gave evidence.

When the Committee came to report on the 'scandal' its members were most unfortunately unable to agree. In fact they seem to have approached their problem not as men of honour investigating a charge of dishonour but as party politicians briefed to blacken, or to whitewash, the characters of certain other party politicians. The Chairman of the Committee, Sir Albert Spicer, himself a Liberal, had prepared a Report which exonerated the Ministers from all real charges of corruption, stating only that they had been unwise, both in their American investment and in their failure to mention it in their speeches of the previous October. This might well have satisfied the Committee, but the Liberal majority would not have it so. They reported that the Ministers had done all things well. Accordingly, the Conservative members also produced their own report, in which the faults and follies of the transaction were sharply emphasized.

It was, from every point of view, a most regrettable result, but even now all might have been put right by the debate on the Report in the House of Commons, if the three Ministers could have risen superior to their whitewashers and frankly admitted that the purchase of the American shares had been wrong and that they regretted it as a fault. But they did nothing of the kind. They expressed regret for the transaction only because, owing to the wickedness of a wicked world, it had got them into trouble. Mr. Asquith defended them with his customary loyalty. Mr. Balfour made one of the best speeches of his career, retelling the whole story with sympathy and candour, and seeking to guide the House towards a unanimous conclusion which would in fact express the judgment of all sensible men. There had been a Conservative resolution 'regretting the transactions of certain Ministers' and a Liberal amendment accepting the statements of the Ministers, and 'putting on record its reprobation of false charges which have been proved to be wholly devoid of foundation'. 'We entirely agree', said Mr. Balfour, 'with the substance of the amendment moved by the learned gentleman opposite. Do honourable gentlemen opposite agree with the substance of our resolution? If that is so, by the mere process of running the resolution and the amendment together, you may obtain complete unanimity.' But the tone and character of the statements already made by Sir Rufus Isaacs and Mr. Lloyd George (the third Minister had resigned, and had left the country) made this solution impossible, and the House, like the Select Committee, proceeded to register a party vote. Perhaps this flagrant abuse of the party system was the worst, as it was happily the last, incident in the whole story.

As for Mr. Lloyd George, the long ordeal over, he was quite himself again. At a luncheon given in his honour he made what his friends described as 'a splendid fighting speech', comparing himself to a modern Saint Sebastian, plucking the arrows from his quivering flesh and hurling them back at his persecutors. A month later he had realized that the whole Marconi agitation had been a deliberate conspiracy 'to overthrow democratic government'.

CHAPTER VIII

THE BALKAN WARS

The Turkish Empire seemed to be falling to pieces at last. The Sick Man's dissolution had begun as soon as the last of the old despotic Sultans, Abdul-Hamid, had been deposed in 1908 by the 'Young Turk' Committee of Union and Progress. Austria, supported by Germany and in defiance of Russia, in defiance also of the international compact known as the Treaty of Berlin, had at once proclaimed annexation of Bosnia and Herzegovina. In 1911 Italy had gone to war with Turkey for the conquest of Tripoli. In the autumn of 1912 the Balkan League of Serbia, Bulgaria, Montenegro, and Greece had entered on a swiftly victorious campaign which seemed likely to sweep Turkish rule out of Europe altogether, unless perhaps Turkey managed, with or without European intervention, to retain Constantinople and Gallipoli with the control of the Straits.

The Balkan peninsula was notoriously the storm centre of Europe, and pessimists had long been saying that a Balkan war must inevitably bring a European war in its train. In fact the destiny of the Turkish Empire was inextricably entangled with that of the Austro-Hungarian Empire, the factor common to both being the Serbs, or, as we now say, the Jugoslavs.[1] There were Serbs in the Kingdom of Serbia; Serbs, mixed up with Bulgars, Greeks and Albanians, in the Turkish provinces of Macedonia and Albania; and Serbs, seven million Serbs, Croats, and Slovenes, a majority of the Jugoslav race, in the southern

[1] Jugoslav mean Southern Slav, and includes the kindred peoples called Serbs, Croats, and Slovenes.

73

parts of Austria and Hungary. The success of the Balkan Allies would not only block Austrian aspirations to Albania and Salonika; it would also stimulate the grave unrest among the Serbs in Austria and Hungary.

Behind Austria was Germany. Bismarck had once said that all the affairs of the Balkans were not worth the bones of one Pomeranian grenadier, but such was not the Kaiser's opinion. He and his advisers were set on the policy popularly summarized as Berlin-Baghdad. A great German statesman, Marschall von Bieberstein, who might, it was said, have been Chancellor if he had been a Prussian and not a Badener, had secured for Germany a preponderance in Turkish affairs such as had belonged to England in the distant days of Lord Stratford de Redcliffe. German enterprise had built the Turkish railways and munitioned the Turkish armies. The Baghdad railway was cutting its way through the Taurus mountains, rapidly extending itself along the Tigris towards Baghdad, Basra and the Persian Gulf. German control should, in a few years, extend, through Austria and Turkey, from the ports which looked out towards London to the ports which looked out towards Bombay. There was one little gap in the chain, occupied at the crossing of the Danube by the independent and violently anti-Austrian Kingdom of Serbia. German strength and Austrian weakness alike demanded the extinction of that kingdom. The victory of the Balkan League would double its size and strength.

By December the Balkan armies had victories and conquest enough to force Turkey to an armistice and a discussion of terms. The belligerents met in London, at their own request. It was soon discovered that the Turks were willing to satisfy the claims of Serbia, Montenegro and Greece, but not those of Bulgaria whose armies had won the principal victories and whose claims lay, for geographical reasons, nearest to Constantinople. The war was renewed, but the League fell to pieces. Greece, Serbia, and Roumania attacked Bulgaria; Turkey regained Adrianople, and the Treaty of Bucharest, in the summer of

The Balkan Wars

1913, merely registered the results of force as revised by the results of treachery. Serbia and Greece, successful in their use of both weapons, had done very well.

Since the fate of Constantinople was no longer in question the interest of the Great Powers concentrated on Albania. Austria and Italy were both concerned that this Adriatic province should not go to the Serbs, and Russia could not allow the Serb claims to fail for want of advocacy from her. Sir Edward Grey proposed a Conference, and it sat in London from December 1912 to August 1913, Sir Edward presiding and the five continental Great Powers being represented by their London Ambassadors. The chief problem before the Conference was the delimitation of the frontier between an enlarged Serbia and a newly created State of Albania, the protégé of Austria and Italy. The points at issue were the allocation, on either side of the frontier, of obscure villages of which no one had heard before or was ever likely to hear again. There was within this Conference a general will to peace animating all its members, and in consequence peace was secured.

It would not be extravagant to claim for this obscure and forgotten Conference an honourable place in the ancestry of the League of Nations. When, less than a year after its conclusion, another Austro-Serbian crisis arose out of the murder of the Archduke Francis Ferdinand, Sir Edward Grey suggested that the same Conference, or one like it under another chairman in another capital, should be assembled. The refusal of his suggestion by Germany was in fact the decision that precipitated the Great War. Later on, when Colonel House visited England as the special envoy of President Wilson, Sir Edward retold the story and pointed the moral. The war would have been impossible if such a Conference had been accepted as the recognized international procedure. Colonel House was impressed, and recorded his impressions to President Wilson. No doubt several other lines of thought led Wilson to his advocacy of a League of Nations, but this was one of them, and not the least important.

75

The Balkan Wars

War on the Albanian issue had been avoided, but the general situation was not relieved. The menace of war grew blacker than ever. The German Army Bill of 1913 foreshadowed measures which would raise the peace strength of the German army from under 700,000 to nearly 900,000. The causes alleged were the growth of pan-Slavic hostility to Germany as a consequence of the Balkan Wars, but there were reasons for thinking that the terms of the Army Bill had in fact been decided before the Balkan Wars began, and were due to the progressive recovery of Russia from the Japanese War and the Revolution of 1906. France responded with a measure to increase her own peace establishment; but a significant difference was observed between the French and the German measures. Germany, with her abundant and rapidly growing population, had only to tighten up her short-service system, by cutting down the generous exemptions hitherto granted. France, having already cut down every exemption, could only increase her establishment by lengthening the period of compulsory service from two to three years.

There were many who now thought a great European war inevitable, but even those who did not go so far were prepared to admit that a war was a very practical possibility and to consider what it would involve. Those who faced the problem had little difficulty in concluding that Belgian neutrality would be violated. 'It may be regarded', says a writer in the *Round Table* of June 1913, 'as a practical certainty in the event of war. Some years ago the Germans completed a series of detraining stations on their railways close to the Belgium-Luxemburg frontier. These miles of sidings deal with no traffic in peace time; they can only be meant to teem with troops in war. An advance across Belgium and Luxemburg, north of Verdun and south of Maestricht, turns the French frontier fortresses and leads direct on Paris.'

What would Belgium do? 'Unable to protect herself unaided, no wonder Belgium wishes to sit on the fence and to side with the winner. . . . A British expeditionary force would probably decide Belgium to throw in its lot with France, with the result that, for every British soldier landed, a Belgian would be found fighting by his side.'

Thus we discussed these things: statesmen and high officials of the Admiralty and the War Office weighing and pondering every detail, elaborating every technicality; journalists and pamphleteers roaming vaguely and at large, exploring avenues of terrific hypotheses. The ordinary man had little idea of what the statesmen and the officials were doing, but he read what the journalists and pamphleteers had to say, and as he read he struggled to repress his natural incredulity. Were these ghastly follies really possible?

Lord Roberts, the best-loved soldier in the British army, who had won his Victoria Cross in the far off days of the Indian Mutiny, certainly thought that war was both possible and probable. For some years he had been preaching to crowded and anxious audiences, up and down the country, the necessity of 'national service', which meant in effect some form of conscription. The force of his argument was strengthened when it was known that the Territorial Army, established by Mr. Haldane in 1907 as an essential part of his military system, after rising to nearly its projected 300,000 in 1910, had since then fallen in numbers, and was still, in 1912, shrinking. But neither the Government nor the Conservative Opposition accepted the national service policy of Lord Roberts, and they had behind them the considered judgment of the Imperial General Staff of professional soldiers in the War Office. Even if national service had been politically feasible, which it was not—the electorate would certainly have rejected it—the introduction of such a system would have temporarily upset all our military arrangements. It might have made us stronger in the end; for the time, for an all-important interval, it would have made us weaker. So at least we were told, though the fact that a vast volunteer army was afterwards raised and trained while the Expeditionary

The Balkan Wars

Force was fighting in France, seems to refute this argument. However, Lord Robert's crusade never came within the circle of practical politics.

The navy had almost passed out of the range of controversy since Mr. Churchill's speeches in the spring of 1912. There remained the Air Force, about which no one thought much before the war. Blériot had flown the Channel in 1909, and the first non-stop flight from London to Paris had been accomplished in 1911. In the same year the Army Estimates contained their first provision for aeroplanes—five aeroplanes! On the Estimates of 1913 there was the first considerable debate on air defence, for the existence of the German Zeppelins had become a matter of general interest and anxiety. Colonel Seely, on behalf of the War Office, ridiculed the notion that these monsters could do any damage to life or property, and his assurances seem to have encountered little criticism. Flying machines of all kinds were regarded as scouts attendant on armies, not as weapons of offence. Our own Air Force consisted, at the time of the 1913 debate, of three squadrons, which were to be increased to five.

In the same year the general public was excited by the performances of a French airman, Pégoud, who could fly upside down, and gave exhibitions of 'looping the loop'. Very few can have realized that in these apparently useless circus feats lay all the possibilities of aircraft as fighting machines; that out of the 'accidents' of the pioneers was to be developed the normal tactics of air warfare.

In the spring of 1912 there had occurred a catastrophe, entirely unconnected with all other causes for anxiety abroad or at home, which for a brief period eclipsed them all. The White Star liner *Titanic*, the largest and most luxurious vessel ever yet launched upon the seas, had struck an iceberg on its first crossing and had sunk with a loss of over sixteen hundred lives. Enquiry revealed that the supply of boats for use in case of

The Balkan Wars

accident had been altogether inadequate and that the difficulties involved in launching them from a vessel of such gigantic bulk had not been adequately considered. Another curious fact which became known was that the salary of the chief cook was larger than that of the captain of the ship—a fact symbolic, one might say, of an age intent on luxury and indifferent to safety. It was indeed all too easy to draw morals from the sinking of the *Titanic*. The very name, borrowed from the giants who made war on the gods and, piling mountain upon mountain, were themselves buried under the ruins of their erections, suggested that hubris which is followed by nemesis. At the time, the moralists pressed the lesson that the products of triumphant science were, after all, edged tools and that, carelessly used, they destroyed their users. From the triumphs of the shipyard to the triumphs of the arsenal was an easy transition. Today, our retrospective Jeremiahs, painting in lurid colours the Belshazzar's Feast of the last pre-war years, moralize upon the *Titanic* and its watery grave as a symbol of the old civilization itself and the gulf into which it was about to plunge.

It is wiser to draw no morals and seek no symbols. The loss of the *Titanic* was simply an accident, like the hundreds of little accidents, involving the loss of a life or two, which befall unnoticed by all except those whom they immediately concern, every day of the year. It would have happened just the same even though there had been no class war, no sex war, no threat of rebellion in Ulster, no prospect of oncoming Armageddon.

CHAPTER IX

INDIA

'No one who writes of India at the present time can avoid the reflection that conditions are changing under men's eyes with a rapidity unknown to previous generations.' Thus, in his opening sentence, the writer of the *Round Table* article on India for December 1912. Ten years later so ponderous a platitude could hardly have been tolerated, but it was paradox enough for 1912. 'We have been challenged to recognize, and we have recognized,' says the writer, 'that in our management of India the people of India must henceforth take an increasing share. It is time that we defined our ideas; that we knew more clearly what it is that India wants, and how far and by what stages we are going to assist her to get it. Ten years ago few people would have asked such questions. India in 1902 had an autocratic government serene in its conviction. . . .'

Lord Curzon had no doubt been both autocratic and serene, and with his retirement in 1905 the 'period of efficiency' came to an end, to be followed by the 'period of experiment'. Agitation against the partition of Bengal, political crime and political boycott, demands for colonial self-government, were met by the scheme of Reforms devised by Lord Morley, as Secretary of State, and Lord Minto, as Viceroy, in 1909. These Reforms were the last word in British concession to Indian demands before the Great War. Generally speaking, they introduced the principle of representative institutions on a very limited and artificial scale, but they did not give the representative bodies thus created any control over the British executive. Lord Morley repudiated the suggestion that his scheme 'could be said to lead directly or indirectly to the establishment of a Parliamentary system in India'; if such had been its character he would, he said, 'have nothing at all to do with it'. He believed, in fact, that the Indian demand was for prestige rather than power, and that it would be satisfied by the former without the latter. Up to a point he was justified by the result, for his reforms were accepted with expressions of gratitude such as have greeted none of the far more generous and genuine 'reforms' of later dates.

Thus it was in a mood of old-fashioned geniality that we could afford to contemplate India, in the spring of 1911, preparing for the King-Emperor's Durbar. 'Native India is on tiptoe with suspense. It awaits the coming of its monarch with something of the fervour of Messianic expectation. Queen Victoria's proclamation after the Mutiny, her personal interest in her Indian subjects, her kindly messages in times of trouble, and her employment of Indian servants invested her with almost divine reverence in the eyes of millions. King Edward succeeded easily to the regard in which his mother was held. The elder generation could recall his journey through India as Prince; all men knew him as the Peacemaker and accepted him confidently as the perfect embodiment of the tranquil and prosperous ruler which is the East's political ideal. Of King George much less is known. That he will be welcomed with immense enthusiasm is certain, but it will be tinged with enquiry too. The imagination of the people is profoundly stirred by the knowledge that for the first time an English King is about to set foot on his Indian possessions. They feel that India can never be quite the same ordinary place again. Some blessing, some miracle, is expected to show that the son is indeed his father's successor, and to leave an abiding mark of his momentous coming. Every detail of the ceremony will be scrutinized by thousands, curious to draw from it some inference as to the Sovereign's personal temperament or taste. For instance, the abandonment of the elephant procession at Delhi has been rather a shock to many. But the instinctive

India

disposition was to find some explanation which would commend itself to Indian minds. One learned maulavi wrote a long letter pointing out that, because the mahout turns his back upon the rider, it was customary in the past for Rajas to employ holy Brahmins as their mahouts, but that elephant driving was little practised in Europe, and very probably the King-Emperor had found difficulty in securing "a saintly bishop well versed in the art" to steer his imperial beast through Delhi streets.'[1]

We have let this quotation expand itself at length because, take it for all in all, we shall not look upon its like again. It belongs, morally and intellectually, to the same phase as Lord Dufferin's delightful despatch to Queen Victoria, describing the Indian celebrations of the first Jubilee;[2] it is separated by a moral and intellectual gulf from the *Round Table* Indian article of only nine months later and from the articles on the same subject in all subsequent issues.

What exactly happened? The Durbar went off excellently. Even the 'miracles' were duly forthcoming in the shape of the transfer of the Imperial capital from Calcutta to Delhi, and the annulment of Lord Curzon's well-meant but intensely unpopular partition of Bengal. But evidence soon came to hand that the grant, in the Morley-Minto Reforms, of Indian elective majorities on the Provincial Councils was not accepted in the spirit in which it had been given. Mr. Gokhale, the most prominent Indian Nationalist leader and hitherto accounted a Moderate of unimpeachable loyalty, was preaching the adoption of 'Irish' tactics of obstruction which would reduce Provincial government to a standstill, and compel the British authorities to grant 'full provincial autonomy'. But this 'Indian Heptarchy' of Mr. Gokhale's excited more derision than alarm.

Then came the attempted assassination of the Viceroy, Lord Hardinge, in December 1912. There had been assassinations in India before, but this attempt produced a different and pro-

[1] *Round Table*. March 1912.
[2] *Letters of Queen Victoria* 1886-1890, p. 277.

India

founder impression. It was obviously not the crime of an isolated fanatic. Had we not gone too far and too fast? Our educational system based on English classics which glorified a Liberty inapplicable to India, had been our first and fundamental mistake. Now we had given India sham Parliaments, which provided a sounding-board for the windy rhetoric of every professional sedition-monger. 'We have provided a beautiful procedure for keeping council debates more or less within the limits of relevancy, reason, and decorum; but we have never calculated on, or provided for, the effect which the exhibition of such war in heaven may have upon the minds of admirers in much lower regions.'[1]

The moral drawn by this writer was plain enough to him. We ought to address India in the following terms: 'This crime strikes at the very root of the privileges you enjoy. Both you and we desire their continuance, but you desire it most. . . . We notify to you and to India in general that on the day that the next political murder is attempted, every legislative council, every shred of representative institutions, and every district and municipal board in India, will be suspended.'

Brave words, but mere words. Such a policy never succeeds, and the Government was wise enough not to adopt it.

[1] *Round Table*. March 1913.

CHAPTER X

FINALE: FROM ULSTER TO BELGIUM

Home Rule had been dull enough in 1913 but nothing could prevent it from being quite painfully interesting in the following year. It was the third passage. Apart from some strictly political crisis, of the coming of which, under Mr. Asquith's dexterous management, there was no sign whatever, the Bill would become law. In that case, unless Sir Edward Carson was a sheer buffoon, there would be a rebellion in Ulster, in fact an Irish civil war, with the British government on one side and the British opposition on the other.

One of the least of the difficulties, though no small difficulty, in the way of compromise was the fact that each of the British political parties regarded the other as being in a state of moral turpitude. The Conservatives held that they had been the victims of a trick. The election of December 1910 was not fought on the policy of Home Rule; the subject was not so much as mentioned in Mr. Asquith's election address. Mr. Asquith and the Liberal party in general did not, it was said, really believe in Home Rule. They had sold their souls and their policy to the Irish Nationalists because, as a result of the figures of that election, they could not otherwise secure their revenge for the rejection of the Budget. They were going to force on the Statute Book a revolutionary measure for which they had no mandate whatever.

Against this the Liberals could, and did, retort that everyone knew that Home Rule was part of the Liberal programme. It had been part of that programme since 1886. As for the charge about putting measures on the Statute Book without any popular mandate, it was untrue, or (alternatively, as lawyers say) it came ill from the Conservatives who, when in office, had again and again used a docile House of Lords to enact any measure, good or bad, that happened to strike their fancy. Anyhow, it ill became the Conservative leaders to discuss the niceties of political propriety when their hands were prospectively dripping with the blood to be shed in the Ulster rebellion. Polite society was rent in twain, and Duchesses made sure before accepting dinner invitations, that no member of the Liberal Government was going to be present. Walter Page, just arrived as Ambassador from the United States, was astonished and frankly horrified. 'Somehow', he wrote, 'it reminds me of the tense days of the slavery controversy before the Civil War.'

Yet the British are a compromising people. The root of the trouble was that both British parties had bound themselves, hand and foot, to the leaders of the rival Irish factions; and, it may be added, the leaders of the Irish factions were in bondage to their followers.

The Ulster position seemed paradoxical enough. 'It sounds absurd', says a writer in the spring of 1914, 'that men should regard the Union Jack as the symbol of a party creed and sing the National Anthem as a prayer for the discomfiture of their fellow countrymen.'[1] Yet this was the strong point of the Ulster position. They were 'loyalists'; their objection was to union with a community which notoriously contained a large percentage of people who hated the very names of England and the British Empire. There was much force in the contention of a letter-writer to the *Times* who called himself Pacificus, and was believed, rightly or wrongly, to be Mr. F. S. Oliver, a strong Imperial Federationist and author of a powerful biography of

[1] Oddly enough this seems, in fact, to have been the original significance of the National Anthem, if those scholars are right who say that it was composed by Jacobites in exile and that its 'gracious king' was the King across the water.

Finale: From Ulster to Belgium

Alexander Hamilton, the architect of the American Union. 'Conceivably', said Pacificus, 'we may divorce Ulster as Henry VIII divorced Queen Catherine; but we cannot thereupon marry her to another bridegroom against her will. No, not even if we secure her interests under the most advantageous marriage settlement which the ingenuity of lawyers can devise.'

In fact Ulster had driven the Irish Nationalists to allow the Liberal Government to try the policy of partition, and Mr. Asquith made his formal offer to Ulster in the House of Commons on March 9th, 1914. His plan was that each of the Ulster counties, Belfast and Londonderry being treated as separate counties, should ballot for itself whether it should be excluded from the Bill. Any county in which there was a majority in favour of exclusion should be excluded for six years, at the end of which time it should automatically come within the jurisdiction of the Irish Parliament.

The offer was not a large one, and Sir Edward Carson rejected it, nominally on account of the time limit but actually quite as much on account of the appeal to the popular vote. There were nine counties in Ulster, of which three, Donegal, Monaghan and Cavan, had large, and two, Tyrone and Fermanagh, had small, Nationalist majorities. Londonderry would also probably vote for inclusion within Nationalist Ireland. Self-determination by counties would, in fact, partition Ulster itself. What though there was an unarmed majority of Nationalists in five counties? Did not the Covenanters in those very counties possess 'thirty battalions of volunteers and a regiment of horse, organized and well supplied with arms—in all thirty thousand strong?'[1]

Ten days later extraordinary news arrived to the effect that the great majority of the British officers of the cavalry brigade stationed at the Curragh, in Ireland, had resigned their commissions rather than run the risk of fighting against Ulster. Headlines featuring 'The Army versus the People' leapt into

[1] *Round Table*. March 1914.

prominence on Liberal hoardings. It turned out that these re-
signations were the result of a deplorable misunderstanding, a
chapter of accidents, and the officers were reinstated. Colonel
Seely, the Minister for War, then committed an error in the
opposite direction by issuing an order on discipline in which he
asserted that the Government 'had no intention whatever of
using this right' (i.e. military discipline) 'in order to crush
political opposition to the policy or principles of the Home
Rule Bill'. There was a violent outcry from the Nationalists and
the more stalwart Liberals. Colonel Seely had to go and Mr.
Asquith, imperturbable as ever, took over the office of Secretary
of State for War in addition to his other duties. He was still
holding this office in August, when he made way for Lord
Kitchener.

The Curragh incident was in March. April also provided its
sensation—the gun-running at Larne. Far back in 1907 the
Liberal Government had allowed the Arms Act to lapse. This
was an old Gladstonian 'Coercion Act' of 1881, which gave the
Government complete control of the importation, sale, and
carrying of arms, and it had been renewed every three years for
a quarter of a century. In 1907 Mr. Redmond asked that it
should be dropped, and the Government in an ecstasy of ami-
ability had acceded to his request—to the astonishment and
dismay, some say, of Mr. Redmond who had made the request
only to satisfy his extremer adherents. So Ulster had had no
difficulties in the matter of arms until December 1913 when the
importation of arms was suddenly prohibited by proclamation.
It was now for the Covenanters to illustrate the value of the
proclamation. On the night of April 24th-25th, the Larne coast-
guard was decoyed, telegraphic communication interrupted,
and along guarded roads 25,000 rifles and 3,000,000 cartridges
were conveyed to secret points of distribution. These munitions
came from Germany.

In May the Home Rule Bill completed its passage through
the House of Commons.

Finale: From Ulster to Belgium

But before these events of the spring an entirely new factor had intruded itself upon the calculations of embarrassed statesmen. Nationalist Ireland had acquired its own army of Volunteers. These Volunteers were, like their rivals, an Ulster inspiration. Their origin is traceable to a private gathering of certain anti-Carsonite Ulster Protestants at Ballymoney in October 1913. These Ulstermen were unconnected with, and indeed contemptuous of, the Irish Nationalist party with its Roman Catholic traditions and Parliamentary habits. They maintained the secular republican traditions of Wolfe Tone, an Ulster Protestant whose aim had been to establish an Irish Republic with the assistance of the French Revolution. Sir Roger Casement was a leader in this group, and he got into touch with Professor John MacNeill of Dublin University, another Ulsterman, learned in the glorious and mythical history of ancient Ireland. MacNeill summoned a meeting in Dublin in November, issuing a manifesto which called Irishmen to arms to 'maintain the rights and liberties common to all the people of Ireland'. 'A plan', it was said, 'has been deliberately adopted by one of the great English political parties, advocated by the leaders of that party and by its numerous organs in the press, and brought systematically to bear on public opinion, to make the display of military force and the menace of armed violence the determining factor in the future relations of this country and Great Britain.' Therefore, if Irishmen 'fail to take such measures as will effectually reject this policy, we become politically the worst degraded population in Europe and no longer worthy of the name of a nation.' Ireland was compelled in self-respect to arm, and the occasion which compelled her to do so was 'not altogether unfortunate'. Nor should the Volunteers be regarded as a temporary formation to meet a passing crisis. 'The Volunteers will form a permanent element in the National life under a National Government.' This implied defiance not of Ulster but of the Home Rule Bill itself and the Redmondites, *soi-disant* Nationalists, who supported it and declared it sufficient for Ireland; for under the provisions

Finale: From Ulster to Belgium

of the Bill the Irish executive would have no forces other than the police at its disposal.

Response to this appeal was quite as satisfactory as its authors hoped, and in the course of the ensuing ten months the Nationalist Volunteers had 150,000 enrolled, passing the total of their Ulster rivals. But they fell far short of Ulster in equipment, and the arms proclamation of December, forbidding to them the free trade in arms of which Ulster had for two years taken full advantage, seemed a measure specially designed for Ulster's benefit. But on the whole the leaders of the volunteers displayed little animus against Ulster. Ulster had shown the way to nationhood in manly defiance of Westminster politicians. Casement, always eccentric, idolized Carson (whom he had never met) and played with the idea of offering him the crown of Ireland. On one occasion he called for 'three cheers for Carson' at a recruiting meeting in Cork—after which, however, he had to withdraw very hastily from his audience.

Mr. Redmond disliked the new Volunteers only less than the old ones. Under his guidance Irish nationalism had pursued without deviation a strictly constitutional line. Standing on the margin of a future when everything, in Ireland as elsewhere, was to be settled by force, he had maintained intact his childlike and rather pathetic faith in the efficacy of Parliamentary majorities, in the combinations of political intrigue. It was dignified but, like so much that is dignified, old-fashioned. Carson rather than Redmond represented the spirit of the new Ireland that was to make a hero out of Michael Collins. By June Mr. Redmond decided that he must give the Volunteers his official blessing; indeed he thrust it upon them with something of the tone of an ultimatum. Henceforth the majority of the controlling committee would be nominees of the Parliamentary Nationalist party. None the less, the Volunteers were not his Volunteers, and neither now nor later did he control them. They were, in fact, the beginnings of the Irish Republican Army of Sinn Fein.

So rival Irish armies were arming side by side. They seem to have got on together well enough. They were known to have sometimes pooled their funds to buy targets whereon to practise the markmanship they would subsequently exercise on one another. When this information reached England, British Liberals and British Conservatives alike may have felt forced upon them a reluctant admission that the Irish are all one and that the British do not understand them and never will.

In one respect the rapid development of the Nationalist Volunteers improved the prospects of peace, for they forced the Ulstermen and their British Conservative backers out of the merely negative attitude they had hitherto maintained, compelling them to realize that, whatever Ulster might claim for herself, she could not claim to dictate the political future of the rest of Ireland. In other words, just as the arming of the Ulster Volunteers had driven Mr. Asquith to offer partition, so the arming of the Nationalist Volunteers might dispose Ulster to accept the offer, or at least to consider whether the offer might not become acceptable in an amended form. In these circumstances an Amending Bill, embodying the proposals which Sir Edward Carson had rejected on March 9th, was introduced in the House of Lords on June 23rd. The debate turned on the extent of the area to be excluded from Home Ruling Ireland. Lord Lansdowne asked for the exclusion of all the nine counties of the historic Province, even though in three of them (Donegal, Monaghan, Cavan) the Nationalist majorities were over seventy-five per cent. No doubt he had been briefed by Sir Edward Carson who on July 12th, the annual festival of Ulster oratory, stated his case for himself: 'Give us a clean cut, or come and fight us.'

In these circumstances, on the very eve of apparent civil war, the King summoned a Conference. Like the Constitutional Conference of 1910 it contained eight members, but this time four were Irish, two Ulstermen and two Nationalists. Like the Constitutional Conference it failed, but its failure, instead of being spread over five months, was compressed into four days.

Finale: From Ulster to Belgium

It failed to reach agreement on the boundary question, the crucial issue being whether Tyrone and Fermanagh, the two Ulster counties in which the Nationalist majority, though indisputable, was small, should or should not be excluded. The nature of the problem was precisely the same as that with which Sir Edward Grey's Conference of Ambassadors had wrestled only a year before, when drawing the frontier between Serbia and Albania. But Sir Edward had been more fortunate in the composition of his Conference; it did not contain two Serbians and two Albanians but consisted entirely of persons who had probably never set foot in either country.

The Conference failed on July 24th. On July 26th the Nationalist Volunteers carried through their first great exploit in gun-running, at Howth. The arms were successfully landed, but two or three people were killed as a result of the intervention of British troops. On July 28th Sir Edward Grey made his statement in the House of Commons concerning the Austrian rejection of Serbia's reply to her ultimatum demanding satisfaction for the murder of the Archduke at Sarajevo. On July 30th, when the Amending Bill, as amended in the House of Lords, was to be debated in the House of Commons, Mr. Asquith rose and proposed its indefinite postponement, and Mr. Bonar Law, on behalf of his party, assented. A week later *Punch* had a picture of Sir Edward Carson shaking hands with Mr. Redmond, and underneath the legend 'One touch of Potsdam makes the whole world kin.' In the course of his famous speech of August 3rd, the speech that committed us to the war, Sir Edward Grey spoke of Ireland as 'one of the few bright spots'.

It was not really quite so bright as it appeared.

In February 1914 the German Foreign Secretary had publicly declared that the relations between England and Germany were 'very good'. It was perfectly true. The German Government was desperately anxious to secure British neutrality in the coming war, and had given a warm welcome to Sir Edward Grey's proposals for a general settlement of points of controversy between the two countries. Sir Edward was working towards a treaty for the elimination of sore spots, such as had preceded and made possible the *ententes* with France and Russia, and in fact such a treaty was only awaiting final ratification in August 1914. The most important points concerned the extension of the Baghdad railway and the preservation of British interests in the Persian Gulf, and the proposed settlement of these was regarded as entirely satisfactory to both parties. The settlement was achieved because both parties wanted it, Sir Edward working for peace, and the Germans clearing the ground for war.

That the war was coming was well enough known in certain circles in Germany and Austria. Mr. Asquith, in his book *The Genesis of the War*, quotes the statement of the American Ambassador at Constantinople to the effect that Francis Joseph, Emperor of Austria-Hungary, had said on May 14th: 'The Central Powers cannot accept the Treaty of Bucharest as definitely settling the Balkan question: nothing but a general war can bring about a suitable solution.' Francis Joseph may not have said those words on that day: the evidence for them, though as strong as that for a good many facts of history, is not such as would be admitted in an English Court of Law; but that they substantially represented the situation is beyond all doubt. The position was that the new Serbia and the Austro-Hungarian Empire could not continue to exist side by side. Austria must either destroy Serbia or expect to see the Serb provinces pulled out of her own Empire. There is every reason for thinking that the war party in Austria had determined on a Serbian War even before the Archduke was murdered at the end of June. The murder supplied the pretext, for the repute of certain Serbian politicians in high places was not such that an assumption of their guilt would lack plausibility. Perhaps the Archduke's murder was part of the Austrian plan: certainly the police arrangements for his protection in Sarajevo, a notorious centre of Serb hostility, seem to have been deliberately inadequate.

Finale: From Ulster to Belgium

So we see things today—so clearly that it is hard to believe that they were not as clear at the time. But it seems to be established that only two British newspapers sounded a note of alarm directly after the murder of the Archduke on June 28th, the *Morning Post*, and an obscure organ of Labour called the *Daily Citizen*. Nearly a month of false calm intervened before the Austrian ultimatum, and that month was three-parts gone when Mr. Lloyd George, in his speech to the bankers of the City, called for economy in naval and military expenditure on the ground that the international sky had never been 'more perfectly blue'.

The Austrian ultimatum of July 23rd was itself almost a declaration of war. Germany had backed Austrian policy up to this date and beyond it. She only began to waver after July 27th when she became convinced, by the British Admiralty orders to the British fleet, that Great Britain would come into the war at the very beginning. That, at least, is Mr. Churchill's view. From that date onwards Germany made half-hearted efforts to draw Austria back, but she had already gone over the precipice and dragged Germany with her.

When we say Austria, and Germany, we mean the groups of persons who from time to time secured the control of those erratic vessels. The governments of Germany and Austria were called despotisms, and the advantage of this kind of government is supposed to be that the despot speaks with a single and authoritative voice. In actual fact, unless the despot is a Napoleon or a Bismarck, this is not so. The German system was rightly described as 'chaos at the top'. If the German Chancellor, Bethmann-Hollweg, had ruled Germany in the sense in which Mr. Asquith and Sir Edward Grey ruled England, there would probably have been no war. But he did not. He did not control the Kaiser. The Kaiser was controlled by military and naval advisers, and with these, since they were not officially 'the government', no foreign government could deal. This is the essence of 'militarism', a state in which soldiers control where they ought to serve.

Finale: From Ulster to Belgium

This militarism was rooted in Prussian history. In transferring the old Prussian despotism, thinly disguised, to the new German Empire of his creation, Bismarck had set up an anachronism and he did well to express, in his old age, bitter regret for what he had done. This anachronism could only maintain its authority over one of the most intelligent nations of the world by proving the necessity of its existence. It had to prove to the ever growing millions of Germans who voted for the Social Democratic party that their country was ringed round by enemies, and that only by trusting the soldiers could Germany maintain her position. The German Imperial despotism pursued a diplomacy of 'mailed fists' and 'shining armour' because only by maintaining the insecurity of the European situation could such a despotism be secure at home. The only convincing proof of the need of militarism was Bismarck's proof—war and victory. No doubt, for the Prussian monarchy of 1914, war was a gamble—world power or downfall. But 'no war' was not a gamble; it was downfall to a certainty. Sooner or later the Hohenzollerns were bound to go the way of the English Stuarts, unless they could prove their title by the sword.

These opinions are not in fashion today. Today it is the fashion to say that the war was due to the 'general situation'; that we were all to blame. During the war every conceivable devilry was attributed to the Germans, and we are now reacting in the opposite direction; we realize that it was a mistake to insert a controversial clause about war guilt in the Treaty of Versailles; we have a very natural and proper desire to let bygones be bygones, and to be good friends with the post-war German Republic; we are very ready, in the interests of international charity, to cultivate a certain woolly-mindedness about the causes of the Great War. But the fact remains. Germany and Austria were the authors of the war. The alteration of the policy of none of the other Great Powers would have prevented the war. The alteration of the combined policies of Germany and Austria would have prevented it.

94

Finale: From Ulster to Belgium

That admirable man Mr. Walter Page, American Ambassador in London, was greatly impressed by America's oncoming responsibilities as the greatest World Power, and by the need for Anglo-American co-operation. America had almost every virtue except diplomatic good manners. Let her acquire this virtue also, and the British Empire would eat out of her hand. These reflections were reported to Colonel House, and his immediate reaction was to ask, why not Germany too? If anyone ever had diplomatic good manners it was the Colonel himself, and in the summer of 1914 he came over to try them out on England and Germany. He would persuade England and Germany to make friends. He went first to Germany in May, where he found the military oligarchy in absolute control, but secured his coveted interview with the Kaiser who talked at length about the Yellow Peril. Then he came to England where he got nothing that would have justified his returning to Berlin. After the outbreak of the war he wrote: 'Just think how near we came to making such a catastrophe impossible! If England had moved a little bit faster and had let me go back to Germany the thing could, perhaps, have been done.'

Mr. Page answers: 'No, no, no!—no power on earth could have prevented it. The German militarism, which is *the* crime of the last fifty years, has been working for this for twenty-five years. It had to come. . . . We've got to see that this system doesn't grow up again; that's all.'

On July 25th the Serbian reply to the Austrian ultimatum was received and rejected. On the 26th Sir Edward Grey launched his proposal for an international conference, which was rejected by Germany on the following day. On that day the Cabinet was still, in Mr. Churchill's words 'overwhelmingly pacific. At least three-fourths of its members were determined not to be drawn into a European quarrel unless Great Britain herself was attacked, which was not likely.' On this point Sir Edward Grey remarks, 'If there had not been an anti-war

95

Finale: From Ulster to Belgium

group in the Cabinet, there ought to have been.' They represented the predominant opinion at that date, not only of the Liberal party but of the nation. Indeed nowhere was opposition to British intervention in arms more forcibly expressed than in the principal headquarters of the City of London. But this pacifism of the majority of the peace party in the Cabinet was not unconditional. On July 29th Germany tried to secure England's neutrality by a guarantee that she would not in the event of victory annex an inch of French soil in Europe, only certain French colonies; and the proposal was immediately rejected. Rejected also was a proposal to secure our neutrality provided that the German fleet refrained from entering the Channel and attacking French ports. Gradually the issue fixed itself on Belgium.

As late as July 28th both Lord Kitchener and Mr. Churchill expected that Belgium would consent to whatever terms Germany offered as the price for the free passage of her troops through Belgian territory. Lord Kitchener and Mr. Churchill took the line that Belgian neutrality was a European as well as a Belgian interest, and that, even though Belgium sold the pass, we were bound, both morally, by reason of our friendship with France, and also in our own interests, to defend it. What degree of national assent this plea would have won we do not know. Happily Belgium solved for us our own problem. On August 2nd, when Germany was at war with Russia and was obviously on the eve of war with France, the King of the Belgians addressed his appeal to King George. It united, with insignificant exceptions, both the Liberal Cabinet and the nation.

When Sir Edward Grey rose in the House of Commons on the afternoon of August 3rd, to tell the story of the most honourable failure in the history of our foreign policy, and to point its unescapable moral, he had the great bulk of his audience with him at every stage of his grave and unadorned argument. It was very fortunate that such a task should have fallen to such a man. He was something more than an unquestioned exponent of that

Finale: From Ulster to Belgium

national and continuous foreign policy, unswayed by the swing of the party pendulum, which Queen Victoria had inaugurated when, by Lord Salisbury's advice, she insisted that Lord Rosebery should take charge of the Foreign Office in Gladstone's 1886 government. Sir Edward was the heir of Lord Rosebery, whose Under-Secretary he had been. He was equally the heir of Mr. Balfour and Lord Lansdowne, the authors of the Japanese Alliance and the French *Entente*, whose policy he had made his own in 1906. But he was more than this. He was the most universally respected figure in British politics. The policy that he had followed through nearly nine years of unexampled difficulty was one that might have been mistaken at this point or at that, but no one could suppose that at any point it was a policy of which one should be ashamed. It was of incalculable importance that Sir Edward Grey, and no other, was there to tell us that we had got to go to war.

PART II

THE EPIC

1914-1918

CHAPTER XI

1914

There is at all times a discrepancy between the appearance of things seen at the time and their reality—if it is indeed reality—as analysed in retrospect. Be politics ever so frank and diplomacy ever so open, even so the picture formed in the mind of the most acute and persevering student of the daily press will not be quite the picture presented by the subsequent historian, with all the once secret documents open before him. Thus a divided duty confronts the historian. He has to reveal the secret history, for that is the real history, through which alone effects can be traced to their causes. But if he is to give a true impression of the times of which he writes he must also tell the story as it misleadingly unfolded itself to those who participated in it; for it is the appearance and not the reality of things which makes its impact upon the public, and creates that public opinion which, in turn, is itself a reality and a part of the real history. In ordinary times of peace the discrepancy between appearance and reality is so slight that one is hardly conscious of it. The essential facts are open to the inspection of those who have the wits and will take the trouble to inspect them. If it were not so we should indeed have reason to despair of democracy. But during the Great War appearances and realities were poles asunder. The belligerent governments may be likened to players in a game of cards which they had never played before, gambling for life itself on behalf of the nations which had sent them to the card table. They could not show their cards to their supporters without at the same time showing them to the players on the other side. The nations watched the fall of the cards and the taking of the tricks, but, not seeing the hands, they could form only the most incoherent ideas of the quality of the play or of the probabilities of the result. It is very difficult for us to-day, with impressions of 'the real war' derived from innumerable books, to recreate in our minds the war experience of the men and women of 1914-1918.

The fundamental experience was, it need hardly be said, the fact of war, over and above any and all of its strategic vicissitudes. 'Your King and Country want you.' For the men who went to serve in the fighting forces, a complete break with all that had hitherto given meaning and purpose to life, a new departure with as likely as not no return; for those who stayed behind, the aching anxiety, the waiting for news, until perhaps news came that there would be no more news. I am unable to write anything worthy of this theme. I pay it the tribute of silence, and the tribute implicit in the title I have given to this part of my book. For the greatest of all epic poems is a tale of war, of battle and wounds and death, and love that is stronger than death: Hector's last good-bye to Andromache, with their child in her arms: Achilles mourning the death of his friend: Priam seeking his son's body for burial. . . .

There was one form of anxiety that troubled us surprisingly little—the fear that we should be beaten. Perhaps those despised persons, the writers of the old-fashioned schoolbook histories, deserve some of the credit for this. They had presented to the young a picture of English history as an endless succession of wars, which the English always won in the end, except—and note this important exception—when it was 'a good thing' that we should be beaten. It was 'a good thing' that we failed to subdue our American colonies in the eighteenth century. Hence Saratoga and Yorktown. Apart from these the well-conducted British schoolboy would know of no British defeats between the Armada and the present day. It would certainly not be 'a good thing' that we should be beaten by Germany, therefore history,

as learnt at an impressionable age, had indicated in advance the
only possible conclusion to the Great War.

But to go back to August 4th, 1914. The first impact of the
war upon the ordinary person was, no doubt, a bewilderment
bordering upon sheer vacuity. The curtain was rung down on
the Unfinished Melodrama, for the sufficient reason that persons
outside had thrown a bomb into the theatre. One had no idea
what was to happen next.

The first piece of war news was the appointment of Lord
Kitchener as Secretary of State for War, announced on August
5th. The Prime Minister had himself taken charge of the War
Office during the last months of the Irish crisis, and it was obvious that he would now relinquish the post. The *Times*, then
owned, like the *Daily Mail* and many other papers, by Lord
Northcliffe, had published a leading article entitled 'Kitchener
or Haldane?' exalting the soldier at the expense of the lawyer,
and the announcement of Lord Kitchener's appointment followed: apparently a striking illustration of the value of our great
patriotic newspaper millionaire. In fact, however, he had been
appointed before the Northcliffe article saw the light of day.
Lord Kitchener's appointment reassured the public as nothing
else could do. He had long enjoyed, and in many ways deserved,
a unique reputation throughout the British Empire as a strong
silent superman. Lord Roberts, now in old age, might be more
loved, but Lord Kitchener was esteemed as the incarnation of
sheer efficiency. He was more than a man; he was a legend: his
appointment converted the Liberal Government into a National
Government at a single stroke, without any of the drawbacks
that would have been involved in a coalition of Liberals and
Conservatives who only a week before had been denouncing one
another as traitors. Four days later he issued his first appeal—
for 100,000 men, whose term of service was to be 'three years or
the duration of the war'. Lord Kitchener, we soon knew, had
said that it would be a long war. How did he know that? All the
experts had concluded that a European war under modern con-

ditions must inevitably burn itself out in about six months.
Indeed the bases of Lord Kitchener's forecast remain a mystery
to this day. The prolongation of the war was due to the formation of an entrenched and flankless western front, which Lord
Kitchener certainly did not foresee; he has frankly recorded the
fact. Perhaps his famous forecast was less a forecast than a wise
determination to err on the safe side. Whatever it was, however,
stroke of luck or stroke of genius, it confirmed the unanimous
impression that Kitchener was a Great Man—which was just
what we needed. Carlyle's theory of democracy as a game of
'Hunt the Hero', and when you have found him, obey him, is a
very good theory for war time.

Once the first spasm of bewilderment was over we settled
ourselves down as calmly as we could to wait for news. Had the
army crossed to France? It was disconcerting to find that we did
not know. And if the movements of the army were concealed
from us, what else might not be concealed also? Most people
seem to have assumed that the first great event would be a naval
battle in full force in the North Sea. We had no news of this
Trafalgar. Had it been unaccountably posponed, or——? the
alternative was more than thought could bear. The earliest real
war news was Belgium—'Plucky little Belgium' was the phrase
of the moment, an irritating phrase in retrospect, but there was
still something adolescent, something 'sporting', faintly reminis-
cent of old Kruger days, about our outlook in those first very few
weeks. We were to be stiffened into seriousness soon enough.

Liége fell on the 15th. On the 18th we had news that the main
portion of the British Expeditionary Force had landed in France
without loss. Then we heard that the French were driven back
in Lorraine, and that the Belgian Government had withdrawn
to Antwerp. The Germans were in Brussels on the 21st, and
Namur, a fortress of immense reputation, had fallen on the 24th.
Two days later came accounts of the burning of the Library of
Louvain. Meanwhile Belgian refugees were reaching the Channel ports with their lamentable tales. Suddenly we realized the

Germans in a new and terrible light. Our enemy was not as other enemies had been—the French, for example, whom we had fought so often in old days without ever ceasing, so it was said, to like and respect them. The Germans were enemies of civilization, fiends of hell; their warfare had no limits, knew no obligations. An evil thing had been allowed to grow up in the very centre of Christendom—Prussianism; there could be no peace worthy of the name until Prussianism had been utterly swept from off the face of the earth.

So we felt at the time, and we need not regret it now. Subsequent investigation proved that the facts of German outrage were very much in accordance with the spirit, if not always the letter, of those first reports. Indignation, hatred of Prussianism gave a new and deeper significance to our determination to fight the thing out whatever the consequences. It is of course also true that these emotions, carried over into 1919, gave a cloak to motives of vengeance and made more difficult a wise and just settlement after the war. It is also to be remembered that these emotions found very little echo in the fighting line. I remember talking to an officer home on leave shortly after the execution of Nurse Cavell, which more than any other single event roused anti-German passions in England. This officer took a deplorably cynical view of our outburst. 'You're still trying to make Tommy hate Fritz,' he said, adding, 'but of course he never will.'

And then amid the news of German atrocities in Belgium came the news of overwhelming German victories. The retreat from Mons had begun on the 23rd but we knew nothing of it till the 30th when the French forces, with the British on their left flank, were revealed in full retreat across northern France. The French Government withdrew to Bordeaux. Paris was as good as lost.

But when things seemed at their worst we heard that the Russians were coming to the rescue. They were being landed in the north of Scotland, hurtled through the length of Great Britain in an unending series of express trains and across the

Channel in an unending series of transports. There must have been some who remarked that this route was not the obvious one, but they were doubtless answered by something about minefields. For the evidence was overwhelming. Russians were actually seen at Leith, at Berkhamsted, at Eastleigh. They called hoarsely for vodka at Carlisle, and placed roubles in the penny-in-the-slot machines at Durham. They acknowledged small services with a courteous 'Thankovitch!' and—most convincing of all—stamped the snow off their boots on railway platforms. When the Russian rumour was discredited the rationalizers were ready with their explanations. Someone had spoken of *rushing* troops to the front, or of troops from *Ross-shire*; perhaps some Anglo-Saxon had heard Highlanders speaking Gaelic and drawn inferences; it may be that some official person had mentioned Mr. Churchill's proposal to bring Russian troops round to the western front, and that his hearers had assumed that the thing was already done and spread the good news.

Our faith in a Russian deliverance survived the Russian rumour. They would save us on their own front if not on ours. Long after the disaster of Tannenberg, of which we knew nothing, amateur authorities confidently asserted that 'the Russian steam roller' would grind forward over prostrate hosts of Germans and enter Berlin before Christmas. It was, of course, not altogether pleasant that the two most civilized peoples of Europe should be rescued from the clutches of German militarism by the hordes of a semi-oriental despot, but we had hardly time to think of that.

The Russian rumour was not dispelled before we had more substantial reasons for a renewal of hope. In the second week of September the German advance was miraculously stayed along the Marne. A retreat began. We realized almost at once, it seems, that here had been fought one of the decisive battles of the world, and, oddly enough, we were right. The long-considered German plan for the destruction of the French armies in a six weeks' campaign had broken down. From that date onwards the Germans, like the rest of us, had to improvise.

But the retreat did not extend very far. Forty miles back the Germans had, with really incredible forethought, considering that victory seemed within their grasp, prepared a line of defence behind the river Aisne. So the battle of the Aisne began.

The Allies supposed that the Germans were merely fighting a rearguard action, but they were to be disappointed. Newspapers started enumerating the days of the 'battle of the Aisne'—the fifth day, the tenth day, and so on. They must have given it up after a time, for in a sense the battle of Aisne went on until the general advance in the last months of the war. The Aisne became the central section of the western front.

Since the German line held firm the only thing to do was to outflank it. So began a series of movements in which each side extended its lines to right and left, each seeking to overreach the other. Both failed, and the lines ultimately extended from the Belgian coast, just short of Ostend, to the Swiss frontier—the line of the western front. Nothing perhaps brings back the war so vividly to those of us who were fated to stay at home as the sight of that too familiar line upon a map.

At the beginning of October the fall of Antwerp was imminent. It was delayed a few days by the sudden arrival of Mr. Churchill, the First Lord of the Admiralty, with a brigade of marines and two newly formed brigades of naval volunteers. Antwerp fell, and a part of the British force accidentally strayed into Holland and was interned. Mr. Churchill's Antwerp venture was much derided at the time, but it has been argued that the few days' postponement of the evacuation of Antwerp, which it undoubtedly secured, made all the difference to the battle for the Channel ports. The retention of the German force in front of Antwerp may have enabled the Allies to extend beyond Dunkirk a line which might otherwise have failed to cover Calais. October was filled with the battles that stabilized the northern section of the front, our own strained attention being fixed upon the desperate struggle for the retention of Ypres.

That ancient and lovely city to whose looms English wool merchants had taken their wool in the Middle Ages, the only Belgian city not in German hands, remained in its ruins the trophy of the British army. In later years the British forces, growing from thousands to millions, extended far to the south, but Ypres remained, and remains, central as a prize of sacrifice and a shrine of dedication.

The Germans had not won the war, but they had secured and retained what would enable them to prolong it; the great industrial area of Belgium, with a population that could be forced to serve their needs, half the coal-bearing country of northern France, and the iron mines of Briey and Longwy in French Lorraine. The loss of these things to France could only be made good in the workshops of England and America.

This much of the war we understood in that first autumn. We also understood that the Russians, though beaten along the Baltic coast, had won immense victories against the Austrians, and had occupied the whole of Galicia with its oilfields. Next spring, it was understood, they would occupy the vital industrial area of Upper Silesia and filter through the passes of the Carpathians into the corn-bearing plains of Hungary. Turkey had joined the enemy, and the Australian and New Zealand volunteers were retained in Egypt to guard the Suez Canal. On the whole we were exceedingly optimistic and nothing heartened us more than the magnificent response to the call of battle from every part of the British Empire, not least from India, where there had been so much unrest and sedition. The Germans had always said that the British Empire would be proved a pretence in time of war, and though we had disbelieved them we had not felt altogether certain of our ground. In discussions about military preparedness at Imperial Conferences the attitude of Dominion statesmen had often struck us as unpleasantly detached. Sir Wilfred Laurier had declared in 1911 that Canada would not hold herself bound to take part in any and every war in which the British Government might choose to involve itself.

The German outrage had swept all that away. Whatever the caveats and cavillings of peacetime politicians, the hearts of the peoples of the Empire beat as one.

As for the naval warfare we were only not satisfied because from the navy we expected everything. We commanded the seas, and absolutely denied their use to the commerce of the enemy. State insurance against maritime risks, starting at six per cent, had fallen to one per cent, and on that modest premium there was a considerable profit. The raid on German naval bases at the end of August, known as the battle of the Bight of Heligoland, had been a magnificent achievement, and though the German raiders who had shelled Hartlepool and Scarborough were not caught, criticism of the failure of the police was swallowed up in indignation of the conduct of the criminals. In the middle of September there was a gasp of horror and dismay when three cruisers, the *Cressy*, *Hogue*, and *Aboukir* were sunk by a single German submarine in the North Sea. The *Cressy* and the *Hogue* were sunk because they closed in on the sinking *Aboukir* to pick up its survivors. The loss of life was appalling—fourteen hundred men, but the loss of the ships was a trifle, we were assured, for they were already practically obsolete. They were indeed historic ships, the first 'battle-cruisers' ever launched—in the year after Queen Victoria's second Jubilee; but in the development of naval construction 1898 was ancient history.

During the early months of the war the German Pacific squadron was at large. One of its cruisers, the *Emden*, did a good deal of damage in Indian waters before it was caught and destroyed by an Australian cruiser, the *Sydney*, in November. The main German contingent crossed the Pacific and destroyed the British Pacific squadron at Coronel off the coast of Chile. A month later it was itself destroyed by a British squadron, sent out to hunt it down, off the Falkland Islands. Thus by the end of the year the last enemy warships were swept from the surface of the seas. The future of the enemy submarines was uncertain but gave at present no particular cause for anxiety. Naval warfare under modern conditions was to the ordinary man an almost metaphysical mystery. What happened on land, in the blood-sodden trenches of Flanders, was all too tragically obvious. What was not plain was how the Grand Fleet controlled the oceans of the world from a place of concealment in the Orkney Islands. We knew that the fleet was in daily and hourly communication with the Admiralty by means of wireless, but not till after the end of the war did we know that the Admiralty intercepted and decoded the wireless orders of the enemy.

At home every town and village had its 'War Help' organization, but it was not easy to find useful work for more than a small fraction of those who were eager, as the phrase was, to 'do their bit'. The first big piece of civilian war work was entirely unexpected, the reception, distribution, and entertainment of the Belgian refugees. There were ten thousand arrivals before the middle of October. English hosts only too often had cause to regret the complete futility of the teaching of French in English schools, and were reduced to communicating with their guests in a jargon pleasingly described by Mr. Wells as 'entente cordiale'. As time passed the Belgian refugees seemed to disappear from view. Some returned to Belgium; many more made homes for themselves and found employment in England 'for the duration'.

There was indeed one service, so easy that it hardly ranked as a service, which was asked for from the first. At the beginning of the war there was a general fear that the country would soon be face to face with widespread destitution. The situation was so unprecedented that everyone began to economize. Peace industry slackened off alarmingly before war industry had begun to get into its stride. The rate of unemployment for August was three times that of July. In these circumstances the Prince of Wales's Fund was instituted and several millions immediately subscribed. But never was a forecast more completely falsified. By the end of the year unemployment had vanished, and the

Fund was left with nothing to do. Its resources were eventually handed over to the Red Cross Society for the service of the wounded.

But if England was not yet wholly at war as she was to be long before the end, the whole country was full of soldiers—Kitchener's armies. A million had joined up before the end of November, and the success of the voluntary system, says a writer in the *Round Table* for December 1914, had been 'a surprise even to its own most enthusiastic advocates'. There were at present far more soldiers than rifles available for their use. But some of the drawbacks of voluntary enlistment were already apparent. 'Many an employer', says the same writer, 'is able to use a press gang of his own, and appeals made to employers to put pressure on their employees naturally and rightly arouse the suspicion of the working class.' Further, 'the unseemly appeals to patriotism and emotion by means of advertisements and brass bands' did not help to solve the problems of the business man in genuine doubt whether he would be more useful at home or at the front. 'Business as usual' was still a potent and indeed a patriotic slogan. We had not got the scale of the war, and of our own part in it. We still thought in terms of ancient history, of the Napoleonic wars for example, when England's part had been to supply a supreme navy, a small army, and an infinite amount of financial and commercial backing. People complained, and rightly, that the government did not give any clear leading in these matters; but indeed the government did not as yet see much further into the future than anyone else.

But if most of us could as yet do very little about the war, we could think of little else, and a literature sprang into existence to cater for our needs. The first of all the war books was the official White Book, published by the British Government, with astonishing promptitude, on August 5th. It contained the correspondence of the British Foreign Office with the governments of the other Great Powers during the thirteen days between the Austrian ultimatum to Serbia and the British ultimatum to

Germany—one hundred and fifty-nine documents in all, without comment and without expurgation. It was a fascinating study, and, what was more important, extremely reassuring. It was impossible to resist the impression that, at every turn in the complicated story, the course pursued by our government had been at once wise and honourable. We were further reassured when, some weeks later, the German Government produced an equivalent record in which commentary and expurgation were the principal features.

The White Book was also exceedingly instructive, and unofficial persons hastened to continue our education. Six Oxford tutors collaborated in a work entitled *Why we are at war*. Books already extant, such as *The Anglo-German Problem* by Professor Sarolea, suddenly became best-sellers. It is perhaps characteristic of England just before the war that the best short book in English on the prospects of Anglo-German war was written not by an Englishman but by a Belgian serving as Professor of French in a British University; and that his book, published in 1913, attracted no notice until after the war had begun. In such books as these we mastered the policy of Bismarck and discovered wherein it had differed from that of his successors. We dissected the anatomy of the Dual Monarchy, and distributed Germans, Magyars, Czechs, Slovaks, Poles, Ruthenes, Italians, Croats, Serbs and Slovenes over the 'racial map' of what Mr. Lloyd George happily described as a 'ramshackle empire'. Our researches into the war mind of the enemy brought us to the English translation of Bernhardi's *World Power or Downfall*, and some even went so far as to peruse the works of Treitschke and Nietzsche.

But what mattered now was less why we were at war than whether we were winning it. Here the articles of Mr. Belloc, published weekly in a hitherto obscure periodical called *Land and Water*, became our principal resource. Official war news was fragmentary and obscure, but, just as Euclid was able to erect the whole edifice of his geometry on the basis of a very few axioms, so Mr. Belloc could spin out of a very few facts a succession of detailed strategical expositions. Mr. Belloc is a master of many styles, but for the purpose of these articles he rightly rejected all but one; he was always frigidly scientific, laboriously logical. We accepted him as our strategical Sherlock Holmes, and he assured us that, whatever superficial appearances might suggest, the Allies were getting the best of it. He made a great point of 'wastage' and of elaborate calculations of German casualties in relation to those of the Allies—estimates which were reasonable enough on the facts at his disposal but must have been shockingly wide of the mark.

Another weekly anodyne of a very different description was provided by the leading articles in the *Times Literary Supplement* by Mr. Clutton Brock, a well-known literary critic, afterwards published and very widely circulated under the title of *Thoughts on the War*. These were lay sermons, very beautifully written and exactly right in tone and temper. One of them was translated into French by the order of the French Government and read aloud in all the *lycées* of Paris. Those, on the other hand, who liked their sermons to be heretical got what they wanted in Mr. Bernard Shaw's *Commonsense and the Great War*. The most striking feature in this aggravating essay was the writer's depreciation of the Russians. Mr. Shaw assured us that the "steam roller" was a broken reed, that the western democracies would have to win the war by their own efforts and energies; that, if they could not do so, they would lose it—a forecast as remarkable in its way as the more famous forecast of Lord Kitchener about the war's duration. At the time it struck us as not only offensive but silly. We pinned our faith in Russian valour and were rapidly discovering the Russian virtues. Russia might, like Prussia, be a despotism, but how admirable was the Russian *moujik*, especially as described by Mr. Stephen Graham. 'The *moujiks*', he told us, 'are sociable and brotherly; they do things together, sing together, pray together, live together. They like meeting together in public places. They like great parties at marriages and

funerals; they like to wash themselves together in the public
baths. They are more public than we are, less suspicious, less
recluse. They do not shut themselves in; their doors are open,
both the doors of their houses and the doors of their hearts.'
There was certainly something very attractive about the Russian
moujik in 1914.

But none of the war books of the first autumn gave us the facts
which fill the first chapter of any subsequently written history of
the Great War.

For many years before August 1914 the leading military experts of France and Germany had been devoting their energies
to the selection and the elaboration of war plans. As a result the
French chose a plan which proved wrong in army organization,
wrong in strategy, and wrong in tactics, a plan which led with
appalling swiftness to disaster just not quite irreparable. The
Germans adopted a plan which would, in face of the French
plan, have won their six weeks campaign against France outright, had they not at the last minute flinched from their own
resolves and destroyed the balance of their own carefully calculated dispositions. To say this is not to say that the French and
German experts were unintelligent; quite obviously, keen competition and ruthless selection must have brought to the leadership of both the great military organizations men of exceptional
intellectual quality. None the less, it must be said that these
men were, in the strictest sense of the word, incapable; they
were not capable of grappling successfully with the task that
confronted them. The men were not small, but the task was
immeasurably big. The men proved incapable of the task.

All through the war the same impression recurs; the impression of mistake after mistake, failure after failure, on both sides.
Even victories entailed such embarrassing consequences that
they were hardly distinguishable from defeats. Students of industrial organization tell us that combinations and amalgamations of more than a certain magnitude lose efficiency, not be-

cause the principle of amalgamation ceases beyond a certain point to be theoretically productive but because beyond a certain point no general manager or board of directors is humanly capable of mastering all the problems involved. So it is in war. Generalissimo is supposed to be the superlative of general; confronted with the magnitude of his impossible task, the superlative only emphasizes his impotence.

Early in 1911 General Michel, who was at that time marked out to command the French armies in the event of war, concluded that the Germans would come through Belgium; he also concluded that they would use for their initial attack not only their twenty-one active army corps but also the greater part of the twenty-one reserve corps which it was known they intended to form on general mobilization, a force in all of over 2,000,000 troops. He laid his plans accordingly, plans which involved placing the strongest part of the defence along the comparatively unfortified Belgian frontier, and drawing upon his reserves to an extent which would raise the French army on mobilization from 1,300,000 to 2,000,000 men. During the Agadir crisis Michel's plans were considered and rejected. He resigned. Joffre was installed in his place, and the French plans were elaborated on assumptions the opposite of those of Michel. A French army of only 1,300,000 was ready to confront German forces which exceeded two million, and the weight of the French forces was thrown into entirely abortive attacks upon the German defences in Alsace and Lorraine. These mistaken plans had to be entirely recast in the middle of August, but even so the notion still prevailed that attack was the best defence, and the French forces were hurled against the enemy over the Belgian frontier. What followed was the worst disaster of the war for France. Civilian opinion at the time inclined to measure that disaster geographically; it saw the French armies rolled back from Belgium to a line running east and west from Paris to Verdun. The geographical aspect was important, but much less important than the loss of men. With insane gallantry, as if the magazine rifle and the machine gun had never been invented, the French dashed themselves against the enemy. In twenty days they lost over 600,000 men, two-thirds of whom—dead, permanently disabled and prisoners—would never again rejoin the colours. The French losses were far greater than the German, whereas the later history of the war showed that, when attack and defence were conducted with equal skill, the attackers lost anything from twenty to eighty per cent more than the defence.

The initial errors of France were on a colossal scale. It was her fate

'To suffer woes which Hope thinks infinite,
To defy Power which seems omnipotent.'[1]

But she was also

'To love, to bear; to hope till Hope creates
From its own wreck the thing it contemplates,
Neither to change, nor falter, nor repent.'

The German plan bore the name of Schlieffen, who had made it and was dead. Its execution fell to his successor, Moltke, who may have owed his position more to the fame of his uncle, the victor of 1870, than to his own merits, and was already in declining health. The general idea of the Schlieffen plan was an overwhelming sweep through Belgium of forces weighted on their right, or outermost, flank. The Germans should have swung round the French armies and rolled them up. The German left was to be lightly held and to give ground if heavily attacked; French success in that region would only add to the general embarrassment of the French defence.

One would like to think that the Schlieffen plan was spoiled by the resistance of the Belgians; but it was not. Schlieffen had included arrangements for meeting Belgian resistance and also

[1] Between these two lines the reader of Shelley will realize that a line has been omitted: 'To forgive wrongs darker than death or night'. It still remains for post-war France to rise to the full stature of Prometheus.

for a British force of 100,000, and at the date of the fall of Namur the German advance was still ahead of its scheduled time-tables. What spoiled Schlieffen's plan was the irresolution of Schlieffen's successor. Moltke could not bear to allow the French advance in Lorraine; he strengthened his inessential left at the expense of his all-important right; he allowed too many troops of good quality to be detained by Antwerp and Maubeuge; he suddenly concentrated on an attempted 'Sedan' around Verdun; he also withdrew four divisions—and from his right wing—and despatched them to East Prussia where they arrived too late for the battle of Tannenberg. By all these divagations Moltke proved that he lacked the courage of his, or rather Schlieffen's, convictions. His right, thus denuded, lacked just what it wanted of sweep and weight. The result was that his advance led not to overwhelming victory and 'World Power' but to the Marne—and ultimate 'Downfall'. Moltke, having lost the war, retired, and made way for Falkenhayn.

The battle of the Marne conformed, we are told, to the ideal Napoleonic type. Napoleon used to stretch one of his enemy's flanks until a gap appeared in his line of battle, and then thrust through the gap. But Napoleon's battles were the product of a single comprehending mind, whereas the Marne was the product of many minds none of which clearly comprehended how it was contributing to the general result. Galliéni, the Governor of Paris, secured Joffre's permission to attack the outer flank of Klück's army on the German right. Klück was drawn outwards into battle with Galliéni and the British advanced through the gap which unexpectedly opened between Klück and Below. But Mr. Churchill also played a part. On August 26th, ten days before the battle began, he had dispatched 3000 marines to Ostend with orders that their presence should be given the fullest publicity. When the battle was in its opening stages the German High Command announced 'The news is bad. . . . The English are disembarking fresh troops continually on the Belgian coast. There are reports of a Russian expeditionary force in the same parts. A withdrawal is becoming inevitable.' We know from other sources, says Captain Liddell Hart, that the 3000 marines had grown in the German Command's imagination to 40,000 and that the Russians were said to be 80,000. Perhaps after all it was 'the Russians' who saved the western front.

By the end of 1914 it was plain that the Germans had been prevented from winning the war as and when they had calculated on winning it. More could not be expected as winter darkened over the embattled plains. When spring came it would be our turn.

CHAPTER XII

1915

It is clear enough in retrospect that the fatal year in the life-time of our generation was not 1914, or 1919, but 1915. The event of 1914, the outbreak of the Great War, was bound to come and it was best to get it over. It had been predestined since 1870. The Germans had created a system in Central Europe which involved the piling up of ever greater armaments by Germany and by all her neighbours. There was no way out save through an explosion in which all Europe was to be involved. Similarly, if the explosion of 1914 had been rendered inevitable by forty years of armed peace, so the treaties of 1919, with all their legacy of financial woe, were rendered inevitable by four years of war. Four years of war had reduced every belligerent to a state of exasperation in which healing and recuperative measures were out of the question. By the end of 1918 the war had achieved such a grip on the minds of the belligerents that the war mind inevitably dominated the statesmanship of the peace treaties. 1914 and 1919 were each predestined by their immediate pasts, but 1915 might so easily have been, indeed so very nearly was, quite different from the 1915 we have to chronicle. In 1915 the Allies might have won the war; or, if that is too bold, they might have confined it within limits where it was faced with a prospect of early extinction. A peace conference in 1916 would have been confronted with comparatively simple problems; its result might well have been the blessings and not the mockeries of peace. But it was not to be.

Trench warfare, along four hundred miles of flankless trenches stretching from Switzerland to the sea, presented a baffling problem. Ever since the Franco-German War tactical theory had ruled out the frontal attack as suicidal. Since that date the machine gun had been invented, and the Germans, unlike the other belligerents, realized and exploited from the first its deadly defensive uses; it increased tenfold the strength of the argument against frontal attack. And yet what tactics other than frontal attack were possible? Therefore—frontal attack. The argument was uncomfortably like that of an old cartoon at the expense of General Buller in Boer War days: 'War under modern conditions is impossible, is it? Very well, I will make war under ancient conditions.' In the first winter of the war the dividing line was between those who knew that they were baffled and those who did not. 'I don't know what's to be done,' said Lord Kitchener to Sir Edward Grey; 'this *isn't* war.' Sir John French, on the other hand, was full of confidence, and so apparently was Joffre since, as Sir John told Mr. Asquith, he was equipping himself with a complete apparatus for bridging the Rhine.

Some of those who stood back at a certain distance from the embattled trenches looked further afield and took longer views. Let it be granted, they argued, that the frontal attack with existing weapons and existing tactics was impossible. What remained? Two possibilities: a new tactic with new engines of war which would baffle the machine gun, flatten out the barbed wire, and ride over the trench, and a new strategy which would sidetrack the Western Front and defeat the enemy elsewhere. The first line of argument led to tanks, smoke screens, poison gas. The second line of argument led to Gallipoli. Behind both lines of argument was the resourceful brain, the inexhaustible energy of Mr. Churchill.

Mr. Asquith recorded in his diary under December 29th, 1914: 'I have had two very interesting memoranda today on the war; one from Winston and the other from Hankey, written quite independently but coming by different roads to very simi-

1915

lar conclusions. Both think that the existing deadlock in West and East is likely to continue, and W. points out that the flanking movement we urged on the French a month ago is much more difficult now that the Germans have fortified, line by line, almost the whole of Belgium. The losses involved in the trench-jumping operations now going on are enormous and out of proportion to the ground gained. When our new armies are ready, as they will be soon, it seems folly to send them into positions where they are not wanted and where, in Winston's phrase, they will "chew barbed wire" or be wasted in futile frontal attacks. Hankey suggests the development of a lot of new mechanical devices, such as armed rollers to crush down barbed wire, bullet-proof shields and armour, smoke balls etc. But apart from this both he and W. are for finding a new theatre for our new armies. Hankey would like them to go to Turkey and in conjunction with the Balkan States to clear the Turk out of Europe. Winston, on the other hand, wants, primarily of course by means of the navy, to close the Elbe and dominate the Baltic. He would first seize a German island, Borkum for choice, then invade Schleswig-Holstein, obtain naval command of the Baltic, and thus enable Russia to land her troops within ninety miles of Berlin. . . .[1] There is here a good deal of food for thought.'

The lot of inventors is proverbially a hard one. A tank, superior in design to the tanks which fought in 1916, was invented in 1912. The design was sent to the War Office, and, duly pigeon-holed, was unearthed after the war, the file bearing the simple comment, 'The man's mad.' As soon as the war began tank experiments of a partial and tentative character began also. It was necessary not only to invent the machine but to convince both the War Office and Headquarters in France that it would be useful, and of these tasks the latter was the more difficult. Mr. Churchill was the only person in high executive office who was prepared to put his money on tanks from the first; actually

[1] This was a scheme of Lord Fisher's; its author seems ultimately to have agreed with other naval authorities that it was too risky to be practicable.

he put £70,000 of the nation's money on the experiment, acting without the authorization which would certainly have been refused him. When he left the Admiralty in May 1915 he persuaded Mr. Balfour, his successor, to allow the continuation of the experiments. As a result 'Mother Tank' gave a first exhibition of her prowess in the presence of the King, Lord Kitchener, and other great ones, in January 1916.

The closely related problems of chemical warfare, smoke screens and poison gas, had also a pre-war inventor behind them, the celebrated Lord Cochrane, a Nelson born just too late for Nelson's career, who gave his services to Chile in its war of independence against Spain in the years following Waterloo. Cochrane had offered his inventions of poisonous and blinding gases to the British government at the time of the Crimean War, and they had been rejected. His grandson now offered them to Lord Kitchener who suggested that, as they were the inventions of an Admiral, they had better be passed on to the Admiralty. Experiments with smoke were actively pursued. Gas was rejected as contrary to the laws of war until the Germans made their gas attack in the second battle of Ypres, April 1915. The German gas attack furnishes convincing proof that the German professional soldier was as sceptical and unreceptive of the contributions of science as his opposite number on the Allied side. The first German gas attack was utterly perfunctory, without forethought and without reserves; it was not exploited, it was simply tolerated as a new-fangled fad. The Germans added one more count to the moral indictment against them, without securing any military compensation. They sanctioned a new instrument of destruction by which, before the end of the war, they lost many more lives than their enemies. Indeed, so long as the gas attack retained its primitive form, the gas cloud being emitted from cylinders and carried across to the enemy by the wind, the chances of gas were all against the Germans, for in western Europe winds from the south and west are much commoner than those from the opposite quarters.

The new tactics could hardly, under the most favourable circumstances, have secured decisive results in 1915. They depended upon the perfecting of engineering and chemical inventions, followed by the construction of plant for manufacture in bulk. Moreover tactics are the sphere where the last word is with the professional soldiers, and the professional mind is slow to accept novelties, well knowing that ninety-nine novelties are follies and forgetting that the hundredth is wisdom. The new strategy on the other hand did not depend upon invention, nor was it at the mercy of a professional *non possumus*. There was, indeed, nothing new about the new strategy, for it was the strategy by which half the wars of history had been won, and its application depended on the final judgment not of soldiers but of statesmen. The argument was put into a nutshell by Mr. Churchill: 'In any hostile combination, once it is certain that the strongest power cannot be directly defeated itself, but cannot stand without the weakest, it is the weakest that should be attacked.' For 'certain' one should, no doubt, read 'probable', for it could not be said to be 'certain' that the Allied armies could not in 1915 break the German front in the west—not until they had tried to do it.

The story of the Dardanelles and Gallipoli remains an almost intolerable tragedy because again and again a decisive success, altering all subsequent history, could have been secured if only a little more pressure had been exerted, if only a little less time had been wasted. Truth is stranger than fiction, and the accumulated succession of avoidable misfortunes that wasted the new strategy of 1915 surpasses the perversities of fate exhibited in the most morbid of the novels of Thomas Hardy.

The possibilities of diplomacy in the Balkan area were apparent from the first day of the war. Serbia, Bulgaria and Greece had combined against Turkey only two years before. They then had quarrelled over the spoils of victory and their ambitions were left incompletely satisfied. If only they could be induced, with the addition of Roumania, to forget their mutual feuds and combine again, in co-operation with the Allies, they could fulfil all their desires at the expense of both Turkey and Austria-Hungary. Serbia, was, of course, in the war from the beginning, indeed from a few days before the beginning. The others were nervously watching each other, and watching also the progress of the war. They would come in, jointly or severally, on the side which they expected to win. As Sir Edward Grey said, the best, and almost the only, effective argument of diplomacy in war time is military success. Roumania wanted Transylvania at the expense of Hungary; Bulgaria wanted Thrace at the expense of Turkey; Greece wanted a great many things, also at the expense of Turkey. On the other hand Bulgaria wanted a Macedonian province at the expense of Serbia, and the Serbs, with a fatal obstinacy which equalled their courage, refused to surrender an ill-gotten gain even to avert the hideous ruin that was to befall them at the end of 1915; and Greece would not attack Turkey unless she could be sure of the alliance or at least the neutrality of Bulgaria. Nothing would induce these States to combine except a conviction that the western Allies were throwing their weight decisively into the scales of war in the Balkan peninsula. As early as September 1st, 1914, Mr. Churchill adumbrated plans 'for the seizure by means of a Greek army of adequate strength of the Gallipoli peninsula, with a view to admitting the British fleet to the Sea of Marmora'. But, for the reason already given, Greece would not move.

But Mr. Churchill was not the only amateur strategist in the Cabinet with an Eastern policy. At the beginning of the new year Mr. Lloyd George, acting in agreement with M. Briand in France, proposed the landing of 600,000 troops at Salonika or on the Dalmatian coast, to attack Austria through Serbia. There was a great deal of discussion of a plan on these lines in the first winter of the war, but where were 600,000 men to be found? On January 21st Mr. Asquith wrote in his diary: 'There are two fatal things in war. One is to push blindly against a stone wall; the other is to scatter and divide forces in a number of separate and disconnected operations. We are in danger of committing both blunders.' We were.

But perhaps, if only a diplomacy of sufficient 'push and go' were employed, the Balkan prize could be carried off without the 600,000. Mr. Asquith again, on February 26th: 'Lloyd George is anxious to go out as a kind of extra ambassador and emissary to visit Russia and all the Balkan States and try and bring them in. Grey is dead opposed to anything of the kind.'

The decisive argument for an Eastern offensive of some kind was a despatch from the Grand Duke Nicholas, commander-in-chief of the Russian armies, asking for a British demonstration against the Turk in order to relieve Turkish pressure on Russia in the Caucasus. This tilted the scales in favour of the Dardanelles rather than Salonika. Lord Kitchener said that he could spare no British troops for the undertaking. At the same time Lord Fisher, the First Sea Lord, Mr. Churchill's senior naval colleague at the Admiralty, suggested that the Dardanelles could be forced by a squadron of obsolescent battleships, useless for fighting Germans, whose total loss would subtract in no way from the margin of British naval preponderance in the North Sea. Lord Fisher suggested much else, no doubt, at the same time, but Mr. Churchill's attention was riveted on this proposal. His naval experts at home and Admiral Carden in the Mediterranean both agreed that a naval attack, even though unsupported by troops, was perfectly feasible. Naval opinion was, at this stage, unanimous, and on January 28th the War Council of the Cabinet formally endorsed the plan. Mr. Balfour, already a member of the War Council though not yet of the Cabinet, enumerated its advantages. 'It would cut the Turkish army in two; it would put Constantinople under our control; it would give us the advantage of having the Russian wheat, and enable Russia to resume exports; it would also open a passage to the Danube; it was difficult to imagine a more helpful operation.' To this one must add that it would enable the Allies to send urgently needed munitions into Russia. Sir Edward Grey said that 'it would finally settle the attitude of Bulgaria and the whole of the Balkans'.

On February 19th the naval squadron began its attack. Operations, frequently postponed owing to bad weather, were continued for a month. Then Admiral Carden fell ill, and his successor declared against resuming them. There is absolutely no doubt today, on the post-war evidence of the enemy, that the naval squadron was already nearly through with its task, and that if the operations had been resumed they would have been completely successful. This naval squadron would have passed through into the Sea of Marmora, and Constantinople would have been at its mercy.

The naval attack could have succeeded without military collaboration. It was undertaken, as an admittedly speculative venture, because troops were refused. But before it was abandoned troops were found to be available in ample numbers after all. Greece was ready and anxious to come in as soon as the naval attack convinced her that the Allies meant business. A Greek army would have assured success. It was vetoed, on March 3rd, by the insane jealousy of Russia, who regarded the Greeks as rival claimants to Constantinople. 'Russia', says Captain Liddell Hart, 'would not help even in helping to clear her own windpipe. She preferred to choke rather than to disgorge a morsel of her ambition. And in the end she was choked—the verdict should be *felo de se*.'

Meanwhile the British government was wrestling with the problems of the British force for Gallipoli. 150,000 newly trained troops could have been made available by March but they could not act effectively, it was agreed, without the 29th division, the last available division of the old regular army. Could the 29th division be spared from the Western Front? And now Lord Kitchener was himself the battlefield over which the claims of East and West were fought out. He succumbed to the Easterners on February 16th, withdrew his consent on the 19th, gave it again on March 10th, but the division was sent out with its equipment so ill arranged for active service, that it had to be taken to Alexandria and re-embarked before operations were possible. Thus the immortal landing at Gallipoli was postponed until April 25th. By that date the Turks had 42,000 men on the peninsula; a month earlier they had only 14,000. The story of the second attack, at Suvla Bay, is the same—too late. On that occasion, August 7th, the Allied forces were 120,000, but so were the Turks. All the troops available on August 7th could have been made available by July 7th, when the Turks had only 75,000. Even so, the Suvla Bay offensive failed by the very narrowest margin, and owing to the most astonishing mistakes.

When at the end of the year the Gallipoli army was withdrawn without loss the British public heaved an immense sigh of relief. They were right to do so, for the military expert, a convinced Westerner, who was sent out to report in favour of withdrawal, had anticipated a loss of thirty or forty per cent of the troops involved. But there is reason to think that even in December a combined naval and military effort—for the naval command had changed again, and the new commander begged to be allowed to attack—would have carried through to a triumphant conclusion. Meanwhile Russia had been defeated, Bulgaria had joined the enemy, and Serbia had been overwhelmed. In these depressing circumstances the Salonika scheme was taken up again. A large army, ultimately half a million men, was assembled in front of Salonika, where, for the next two years and eight months it served no very obvious purpose. The Germans spoke of it as their largest and cheapest internment camp.

It is idle to elaborate the might-have-beens. On the Western Front the Allies staked and lost pounds to secure pennies; in the East, in 1915, they boggled over pennies when the reward would have been pounds. It is difficult to resist the conclusion that Turkey would have been driven right out of the war; a single blow at the heart in 1915 would have accomplished a result eventually secured by the laborious and circuitous campaigns of

Palestine and Mesopotamia in the following years. The united Balkan States and a replenished Russia would have been hurled upon Austria-Hungary and the German eastern front.

The only modern war which, on strategic scale, bears even a remote resemblance to the Great War was the war of North and South in America. The points of the compass are reversed but otherwise the parallel, though exceedingly rough, is apt enough. The American Civil War was not decided on the front where the greatest forces were packed within confined spaces in Virginia; it was won by wide sweeping movements from the Mississippi, 'from Atlanta to the sea'. The South held firm in Virginia until it was taken in the rear, on the line of least resistance. The Great War was to be won along the line of the greatest resistance.

But Gallipoli was not entirely without result. It hastened, if it did not cause, the entry of Italy. It also involved the exclusion of Mr. Churchill from executive office, and the formation of a Coalition Government.

When the war began the Conservative leaders pledged their support to the war measures of the Liberal Government, and loyally they kept their word; but it was inevitable, as soon as Liberal war measures furnished material for legitimate criticism, that the critics should seek to gain the ear of the Conservative leaders. It was equally inevitable that the Conservative leaders should then recollect—if indeed they had ever overlooked the fact—that theirs was traditionally the warlike and 'patriotic' party, bound by the closest of social ties with the professional heads of the fighting services; they could also claim that the Conservative party was the largest single party in the House of Commons, for the Liberal government owed power to a coalition of parties. Yet frank criticism and discussion across the floor of the House of Commons was impossible; the facts could not be revealed to the enemy. There was, of course, the possibility of a secret session; but this would be a novel and obviously dangerous experiment, and it was not tried until very much later.

From the beginning of the war the possibility of a Coalition, or National Government, had been discussed. Some in each party favoured the idea, but the leaders, Mr. Asquith and Mr. Bonar Law, were both against it. If one took a superficial and atomistic view, it was obvious that the twenty ablest statesmen were not all to be found in one party. But a Government is something more than the sum of its members; it is a team. A coalition would not be a team; at any rate, with Ulster episodes only a few weeks old, it would not start as a team. Mr. Asquith's government, by the inclusion of Lord Kitchener and the unofficial co-operation of Mr. Balfour, had already acquired a quasi-national character; its intentions were generally recognized as worthy of the spirit of the nation. It was best to wait and judge it by its performance.

In these circumstances, in a war in which every belligerent made repeated and disastrous mistakes, the collapse of the Liberal Government, sooner or later, was inevitable. Its actual fall, in May 1915, was due to the actions of two great, but very differently placed, professionals, Lord Fisher and Sir John French. Either alone would have brought down the Government; the *coup de grâce* happened to come from Lord Fisher.

Lord Fisher is generally esteemed the greatest figure in our naval history since Nelson. He first held high office in the Admiralty in 1885, and he had done more than anyone else to create the navy which now controlled the oceans of the world. Not only had he built the ships, but he had modernized naval education which, until his day, had clung to the Nelsonian methods as staunchly as the public schools had clung to the classical curriculum. Both the Navy and the schools had been afraid of 'science'. Lord Fisher changed all that. He was a man of genius within the limits of his profession, and, outside those limits, wildly eccentric. He had constantly urged on his old friend, King Edward VII, a plan for 'Copenhagening' the German fleet, i.e. destroying it in its harbours without declaration of war. When the air raids began he suggested that we should shoot an interned German civilian as a reprisal for every British non-combatant killed from the air. One of the sources of his confidence in ultimate victory seems to have been a conviction that the British nation was descended from the Lost Ten Tribes.

Lord Fisher had retired from the Admiralty in 1910. Mr. Churchill brought him back as First Sea Lord in the first autumn of the war, at the age of seventy-four. It was a bold experiment, and it proved a mistaken one. He was too old. He seems to have rendered no service that could not equally well have been discharged by his juniors, and he was active for mischief as no one else would or could have been. On the Dardanelles expedition he blew first hot and then cold. Indeed, he found that he could not cope with the youthful energy and overwhelming argumentative powers of Mr. Churchill. He contrasted his position with that of Lord Kitchener. Why should Lord Kitchener be in the Cabinet while he, his naval equivalent, was subordinated to a civilian minister? Lord Fisher was always exuberant, and he poured forth his woes to his friends in the Conservative party. He created an intense prejudice against Mr. Churchill as a naval administrator in the minds of men who had never had any reason to love Mr. Churchill as a party politician. At last, on a point of no importance in itself, he resigned. Mr. Asquith was prepared to maintain Mr. Churchill in office—quite rightly if the efficient conduct of the war was the only consideration. Mr. Bonar Law however informed Mr. Lloyd George that his party would not stand it, and would attack the Government. Mr. Lloyd George, seeing at once that the result might be a Conservative Government from which he would be excluded, threw all his weight into the scales in favour of a Coalition which would include himself, and—it could not be helped—exclude Mr. Churchill. Mr. Asquith accepted the inevitable. He reconstructed his Government as a Coalition, with Mr. Lloyd George as Minister of Munitions.

For the 'shells scandal' had been maturing at the same time as the wrath of Lord Fisher. The story is a very complicated one, and it is best to say at once that there was no 'scandal'—the term was part of Lord Northcliffe's newspaper vocabulary. There had already been, under War Office management, an immense expansion of munitions production. No doubt it might conceivably have been greater still. No doubt it was not adequate to the demand. But no government on either side foresaw or could humanly have foreseen the scale of munitions expenditure on the Western Front. At the battle of Neuve Chapelle in March, the first and smallest of the massed attacks of 1915-1917, a very small affair by later standards, on a three-mile front, the British guns shot off as much ammunition as had sufficed for the whole of the South African War. Indeed the demand for shells might itself be criticized as exorbitant; it was based on the tactic of prolonged artillery 'preparation' which gave away the vital element of surprise—a tactic afterwards abandoned in 1917.

None the less there was certainly a shell shortage, actual or in prospect, a need for an expansion of munition production beyond the imaginations of the War Office, but this fact got inextricably mixed up with the grievances of Sir John French, and consequently with party politics. Sir John French had very greatly distinguished himself in the rapid, small-scale operations of the South African War, but he had not the right temperament for 1915. His outlook was curiously unstable, rapidly alternating between extremes of optimism and discouragement. Also he was, almost from the first, on bad terms with Lord Kitchener. Just as Lord Fisher resented his subordination to a civilian, so Sir John French resented his subordination to a fellow soldier. He would, he felt, have been in a stronger position to deal with the Government that employed his military talents if his departmental chief had been an ordinary civilian Cabinet Minister. He, like Lord Fisher, poured out his woes, in person and by deputy, to his Conservative friends.

Lord Kitchener may, or may not, have realized the shortage of munitions, but he was not going to give the fact away for the benefit of the enemy, and, speaking to the brief which he supplied to them, both Mr. Asquith and Mr. Lloyd George declared that there was no cause for alarm. This was too much for Sir John French. He sent his agent to Mr. Lloyd George, and to Lord Northcliffe. This would, no doubt, have brought matters to a head, had they not already been brought to a head by the resignation of Lord Fisher.

The Asquith Coalition Government which followed had one great achievement to its credit, Mr. Lloyd George's mobilization of the engineering industry through the Ministry of Munitions. His achievement in this new office, which he held for a little over one year, established his reputation as a man who could make a vigorous contribution to victory in other spheres besides war oratory and propaganda. Mr. Lloyd George was never a man with any very close grasp of details; he had not, perhaps, the patience or the intellectual conscientiousness for that, but he had in a pre-eminent degree the qualities which he himself described as 'push and go'. He gathered round him some of the foremost business men in the country and let them loose upon our industrial resources with a mandate to mobilize those resources for war purposes. When they met with obstruction Mr. Lloyd George sallied forth in person to deal with it and, by the time he had dealt with it, there was not much obstruction left. But he did more than that. He saw, as in a vision, the scale which military requirements were to assume and, with this vision before his eyes, he utterly pooh-poohed the actual requirements of the War Office. Did they say that two machine guns would be enough for each battalion? Mr. Lloyd George, after a talk with unofficial people who happened to understand machine guns, multiplied the War Office order by sixteen. He took up the Stokes gun, in spite of official discouragement; he gave his support to the tanks.

But Mr. Lloyd George could have gone to munitions in a purely Liberal Government. If we subtract his performance, it is hard to say what is to be put to the credit of this Coalition, and on the opposite side of the account must be set the delay in the reinforcement of the Gallipoli army, which postponed the Suvla Bay landing from July to August—a month too late. This fatal delay seems to have been entirely due to readjustments within the Cabinet; for the new ministers took a considerable time acclimatizing themselves to their work and to their colleagues.

Mr. Lloyd George and Mr. Churchill were the two men in British politics most obviously fitted to render great service in war time—Mr. Churchill by reason of his intellectual grasp of the essential dynamics of war, Mr. Lloyd George because of his imaginative grasp of the scale of human effort which events were going to demand. Both were by nature coalitionists from the start; in their new preoccupations they forgot the very existence of pre-war party politics. Yet Mr. Churchill failed, as conspicuously as Mr. Lloyd George succeeded, in securing the power to which each was, on his merits, entitled. Mr. Churchill, in fact, was no politician. He buried himself in the work of the Admiralty, ignoring alike the appetite of the public for war heroes and the swirl of esoteric factions always eddying round the feet of the holders of high office, but never so much so as in times of war. Mr. Lloyd George, on the other hand, was never so absorbed in the labour of winning the war as to forget either King Demos or Mr. Taper and Mr. Tadpole. He kept in with Mr. Bonar Law and Sir Edward Carson, with Lord Northcliffe and with the millionaire whom he subsequently made Lord Beaverbrook; he re-tuned the lyre of Limehouse, and gave the public just the speeches it wanted. And in doing all these things he was entirely justified.

Lord Fisher had attacked Mr. Churchill and he had gone; Sir John French had attacked Lord Kitchener—but he had not gone, and Lord Northcliffe's attack on Lord Kitchener in the *Daily Mail* raised such a storm of resentment that it was not repeated. None the less, while Mr. Lloyd George's war reputation grew rapidly throughout 1915, so, but much less obviously and perceptibly, did that of Lord Kitchener decline. The public came to realize that they had expected too much; the wars Lord Kitchener had so successfully organized had, after all, been very small affairs; his administrative experience had been exclusively oriental; Christmas 1914 was, it was rumoured, the first Christmas he had spent in England for forty years. He was unfamiliar with the War Office, and did not know how to get the best out of its complicated mechanism: an autocrat by nature and by training, he did not easily adapt himself to the technique of Cabinet procedure where a dozen or a score of minds pool their resources and work together as equals. It seems that the only Cabinet colleague with whom Lord Kitchener's relations were completely happy was Mr. Asquith; for this Mr. Asquith's tact and sympathy deserve full credit, but it may also be that in the Prime Minister he recognized a Commander-in-Chief, and a commander-in-chief was a thing which Lord Kitchener could entirely understand.

In establishing Lord Kitchener at the War Office the British Cabinet had hoped to secure a strategic oracle whose deliverances they could accept without demur. Unfortunately the oracle, like the Delphic oracle, proved ambiguous. Lord Kitchener never definitely declared his mind in the controversy between the Eastern and the Western schools of thought. We have seen the effect of this on Gallipoli. As regards the West, in July he entirely concurred with the decision of the British and French governments that there should be no further offensives that year on the Western Front, but in August he allowed himself to be persuaded by Joffre and Foch to sanction the most ambitious British offensive yet undertaken. The result was the battle of Loos, the first battle in which 'Kitchener's armies' played a great part and also the first battle in which a smoke screen was used: a battle in which we suffered 60,000 casualties, more than three times the losses of the Germans and gained— nothing. The inception of this battle was opposed by Sir William Robertson, Chief of the Staff to the Expeditionary Force, and by Sir Douglas Haig, who was to be in charge of it. Its only

ardent supporter among British officers of high rank was Sir
Henry Wilson, an extremely ambitious and talkative soldier
with a reputation for 'brilliance'. Wilson's judgment generally
coincided with that of the French commanders, with whom,
indeed, he could converse fluently in their own language.

The double disaster of Loos and Gallipoli marked the real end
of Lord Kitchener's supremacy. Before the end of the year Sir
William Robertson was brought back from France and appointed
Chief of the General Staff, with direct access to the Cabinet; he
became, in fact though not in name, an extra Cabinet minister
in control of strategy, Lord Kitchener retaining control of military administration. It was in this sphere from the first that
Lord Kitchener's incomparable service to his country had been
rendered. He had foreseen a long war, and had raised the new
armies. To secure the adequate training of his armies he had
resisted, as only he could have resisted, the demand from Headquarters in France that every available resource of the old army
should be brought into the fighting of the first winter and spring.
Long before Mr. Lloyd George had got into the saddle of his
war-horse Lord Kitchener taught the British people what the
war meant and what was expected of everyone fit for active
service. No civilian could have done this, and no other soldier.
His armies are his memorial, armies which Sir Henry Wilson
had described in his diary as 'Kitchener's ridiculous and preposterous army of twenty-five corps', which 'is the laughing stock
of every soldier in Europe . . . under no circumstances could
these mobs take the field for two years. Then what is the use of
them?'

By a curious coincidence Joffre, the great figurehead of French
military effort, suffered a curtailment of his authority at almost
exactly the same time as Lord Kitchener. His mistakes had been
many, the misfortunes of the French armies under his command
enormous, but mistakes and misfortunes, if only the scale is vast
enough, can afford a basis for a great reputation. Joffre had
become the personification of the French will to victory, and to

deprive him of his command would have had a demoralizing effect upon the French nation. He was therefore promoted to a post of such elevation that the armies were no longer within his reach, and the conduct of the French military effort on the Western Front was entrusted to Castelnau. Sir John French was also, at the end of the year, relieved of his command and succeeded by Sir Douglas Haig who, as Commander of the British First Army, had distinguished himself on every occasion on which he had been engaged. Sir Douglas Haig had a more powerful mind and a more phlegmatic temperament than his predecessor.

It is curiously difficult today, for those who lived through the war, to realize how very gradual was its subjugation of the old peacetime outlook, how tentative its first incursions upon the use and wont of peacetime daily life. Memory, it has been well said, selects for retention the beginnings and the ends of things. We remember the intense excitement of spectators watching the breathless drama of the first three months—from Mons to the first battle of Ypres; we remember the grim struggle of a nation all at war, amid food shortage and coal shortage, during the last year; we tend to forget the long middle period between the first excitement and the final tension, a period filled with a long and tedious succession of confusing dislocations. The first part of this middle period fills 1915. In March of that year it was still necessary for a writer in the *Round Table* to confute with patient argument the view that 'we should wait and see whether the exhaustion of German finances, or the strangling effect of the economic blockade, will not save us from the need of further military measures'. The writer does not at this point mention 'the Russian steam roller', but it was still the chief source of popular miscalculation. On no subject was the gulf between instructed opinion and public opinion so wide. Instructed opinion, within the British Cabinet, already knew by December 1914, that the Russians, by firing as many shells per day as they could produce in six weeks, had practically disarmed their own forces, and that a vast Russian defeat was almost inevitable in the spring of 1915.

The Russian débâcle began at the end of April, a week after the first gas attack at Ypres, and the crowded month of May contained the 'shells scandal', the formation of the Coalition Government, and the sinking of the *Lusitania*. This last event stirred the passions of war as nothing had done since the first Belgian atrocities, for the public mind drew a very sharp distinction between what was inevitable and legitimate in war and what was classed as sheer barbarism. There were 'Lusitania riots' in the poorer quarters of all large towns wherever aliens still carried on their businesses. After these riots the volunteer Special Constables were provided with caps, the first item in what ultimately became a complete uniform. Their plain clothes, it was said, had exposed them while discharging their duties to the onslaughts of the regular police who were unable to distinguish them from the patriotic hooligans. There may be an element of truth in this; if there is not, it may serve as a typical example of the kind of humour that was extracted from the novelties of war time.

The opening month of the war had witnessed, not only a suspension of party politics but also an industrial truce. The trade-union leaders, without awaiting any definite understanding with the employers, abandoned 'for the duration' the use of the strike weapon. But prices soon began to rise and, without some clear lead from the Government, it was not easy to see what was to happen to wages. The railways were under Government control from the first, and the railwaymen, whose pre-war wages were extremely low, negotiated the first war bonus before the end of 1914. But this did not apply to other industries, and Mr. Asquith's speech on the subject of prices and wages in February was deemed exasperatingly aloof and fatalistic by the world of labour to whom it was addressed. Mr. Snowden summarized the Prime Minister's message to the wage earner under three heads:

'First, that the state of things, however bad it might be, is not so bad as it was expected to be in the sober judgment and well-informed knowledge of people six months ago. The second point was that, bad as things might be, there was a time in the history of this country when things were quite as bad; and the third point was that if the poor people of this country who are suffering from the present high price of the necessaries of life would only continue to starve until June, it was possible that some relief might be afforded to them.' There immediately followed an 'unofficial' strike of munition workers on the Clyde. The Government issued an ultimatum ordering the men to return to work and referred the dispute to official arbitration: the strikers stayed away from work until some days after the expiry of the ultimatum, and the arbitrators awarded the men a somewhat larger advance of wages than their employers had offered.

There was a complex of questions at issue. In the first place there was the elementary fact of the standard of living, which would fall to starvation level in view of the rapid rise of prices unless wages kept pace with prices. Secondly there was the demand for 'equality of sacrifice'. Certain classes of employers were already making enormous profits, and examples of such were given a wide publicity in the press. Business men in the Government, such as Mr. Runciman, could not imagine employers of labour following any policy except the traditional one of selling their goods at the highest price obtainable. 'If they find offers coming along week by week at increased prices,' he said, 'it is more than we can expect of human nature that they should refuse these offers made to them. All business men are anxious to get the largest amount they can for what they have to sell. This applies to every section of the community, employers and employed alike.' It did not apparently occur to Mr. Runciman that these doctrines of the 'economic man' condoned the full use of the strike weapon.

A third element in the problem was that the government was beginning to demand the complete reorganization of the engineering industry and ultimately of every other industry which ministered to the needs of the war. The war required both that every available man should join the army and also that industry should yield an unprecedented output of munitions in addition to whatever might still be necessary in the way of production for ordinary purposes. This could only be accomplished by the abandonment of an immense body of 'trade union conditions', customs of trade painfully elaborated by generations of trade unionists. Tens of thousands of people, particularly women, to whom trade unionism meant nothing, were clamouring for munition work. Their admission to the factories, in other words the 'dilution' of trade-union labour, was absolutely necessary if anything like the munition production now envisaged was to be secured. But the trade unionist owed a divided duty, to his country and to his class, and he was genuinely confused by the conflict of loyalties confronting him.

In March 1915 the Government Committee on Production proposed that the trade unions should accept both compulsory arbitration and the abrogation of trade-union restrictions, on condition that the Government should pledge itself to restore the *status quo* at the end of the war. This was accepted under the name of the Treasury Agreement, by all except the miners; the engineers accepted on condition that the Government undertook to limit the profits of their employers. In July this agreement was given the force of law by the Munitions of War Act.

The force of law was soon to be tested in South Wales. An old agreement terminated, wage disputes between employers and employed developed unpromisingly, and the Government extended the application of the Munitions Act to the Welsh coalfield, by Order in Council. Thereupon 120,000 Welsh miners went on strike and remained on strike for a week. 'The strike', says the writer in the *Round Table*, 'came as a shock and a disappointment, and even with a sense of stinging shame, to the public at home, and its effect on the world at large must have been even more pronounced.' It proved that, even in war time, law could not enforce compulsory arbitration in Great Britain. The 120,000 miners had all rendered themselves liable to terms of imprisonment, instead of which they secured practically the whole of their demands and returned to work unpunished. Mr. Runciman, within a month or two of his defence of unlimited competition, introduced a Coal Prices Bill restricting the price of coal.

Mr. Lloyd George muddled valiantly through the labour growing-pains of his new ministry. He was not always wise, but he was ultimately triumphantly successful. At one stage he suddenly declared 'Drink' to be the greatest enemy, greater than the Germans, and forced upon a sceptical Cabinet the consideration of schemes for total prohibition or, alternatively, the nationalization of the drink trade. His 'plain talks' on the deficient patriotism of trade unionists were warmly applauded in the cheaper organs of the capitalist press, but they were neither accurate in their facts nor fair in their conclusions. In fact Mr. Lloyd George's natural inclination towards tirades seemed to be developing dangerously in new directions. 'I never believed what he said about the rich,' someone is reported to have said, 'and I see no more reason for believing what he now says about the poor.' The *Round Table* had no affinities with Socialism or the Labour party, but it expressed a good deal of frank sympathy with the Labour unrest of 1915. 'The real answer of the trade unionist, when he is taxed with not keeping his side of the bargain, is that the State has not been scrupulous about keeping the other.' The State, in the person of Mr. Lloyd George had promised—first, the restriction of the profits of employers, so that the new conditions 'should not work out to the enrichment of individual capitalists but entirely to the advantage of the State'; secondly, the restoration of trade-union customs after the war; thirdly the state control of wages. Of these terms the State had taken only partial and inadequate steps to fulfil the first and the third, and the fulfilment of the second was widely regarded as impossible.

None the less, with many jolts and imperfections, an enormous mobilization of industry in the service of, and under the control of the State was accomplished. In July 1915 a procession of 30,000 women, organized by the suffrage societies, paraded the streets of London with banners inscribed 'We demand the right to serve.' The rain poured down upon them all day, and one newspaper described it as 'a touching sight'. By the end of the year they were serving. 'Today', says a writer in the *Round Table* for March 1916, 'we have all grown used to women ticket collectors, women police, women volunteers . . . the women engaged as unskilled workers in the munition factories have displayed such zeal and skill, and have so strikingly justified the reorganization of labour that the Ministry of Munitions is using every effort to persuade their male fellow workers to allow their numbers to be increased.'

As the year 1915 advanced and the problem of the factories passed over from the field of political controversy into the field of administration, another question, that of conscription, took its place. In the first place, was it necessary? Three million men had come forward freely, but by the summer of 1915 the number of voluntary recruits was dwindling; soon the wastage would exceed the supply; the defeat of Russia and the probability of ultimate failure at Gallipoli opened a prospect of an indefinite prolongation of the war. Granted, then, that conscription was desirable, was it possible? Intense pride in the unparalleled achievement of the voluntary system combined with a deep-rooted prejudice against 'militarism' to render conscription extremely unpopular with the politically minded leaders of the working class. The Trade Union Congress, assembled at Bristol in September, while wholeheartedly supporting the war policy of the Government, carried with an equally close approach to unanimity a resolution 'emphatically protesting against the sinister efforts of a section of the reactionary press in formulating newspaper policies for party purposes and attempting to foist upon this country conscription, which always proves a burden to the workers, and will divide the nation at a time when absolute unanimity is essential'.

The Trade Union Congress is at all times a very imperfect representation even of the trade unionists for whom it professes to speak, but the feeling against conscription was undoubtedly widely and deeply cherished. It was useless to point out to working men that conscription was not merely an engine of Prussian oppression, that the free democracy of France had accepted it for generations. As likely as not, the opponent of conscription was thinking of France as much as of Germany; he remembered the recent occasion when M. Briand had broken a railway strike by calling the strikers to the colours as reservists. Moreover it was widely expected that if we once adopted conscription, we should fail to get rid of it at the end of the war, as indeed we might if the war had ended indecisively.

None the less the pressure for conscription as a military necessity grew stronger as the year passed into autumn, and if there was a popular case against it there was also a popular case in its favour, since the demand for 'equality of sacrifice' could be turned not only against 'profiteers' but still more cogently against 'shirkers' who, for whatever private reason of their own, elected to stay at home in safety while others fought their battles. Mr. Asquith and most of his Liberal colleagues held out against conscription till the end of the year, supported by Lord Kitchener; on the other side were most of the Conservatives and Mr. Lloyd George. A last effort to revive the voluntary system was made by a special Recruiting Campaign directed by Lord Derby. Its results were disappointing. Lord Kitchener and Mr. Asquith gave way, and a Bill for the conscription of bachelors was carried by overwhelming majorities. This was a half-measure which abandoned the voluntary principle without satisfying the conscriptionists, and was ill received alike by the married and the single. It was a measure which said '*you* have got to go and fight for *my* wife.' So, at least, a married man described it at the time. Whatever its demerits, it strengthened the demand for equality of sacrifice and made easy the progress towards full conscription which came in May 1916.

1915 had been a year of bitter disappointments but it had at last brought the whole nation into the war.

CHAPTER XIII

1916

The strategy of 1915 had been a story of conflicting purposes and wasted efforts. At the beginning of 1916 there were at any rate no conflicting purposes. M. Briand, who for the moment was Prime Minister of France, had coined the phrase 'unity of front'. The Allies had to learn a lesson from their enemies, namely to treat the war on all fronts as a single whole. Preparations were made for simultaneous and co-operating onslaughts, on an unprecedented scale, by British and French, Italians, and Russians. Russia's munitions could not be replenished nor the new British armies fully ready until midsummer; till then all fronts would act on the defensive. The Franco-British contribution would be 'the battle of the Somme', not the mainly British battle afterwards undertaken, but a far larger affair. In all this there was no new strategy, no new tactics; it was simply the old strategy and the old tactics pressed to the utmost limits of human endurance. Mr. Churchill would have liked to try the Dardanelles again, but he was by now completely discredited and had gone as a soldier to the Western Front.

These Allied plans were thrown out of gear by the German plans. Falkenhayn resumed the German offensive in the west for the first time since the battle of the Marne, and filled the first half of the year with a series of assaults upon Verdun. It was a purely local offensive, designed not to secure any dramatic 'victory' as the term would have been understood in former wars, but to wear out the French army. Falkenhayn, like so many of the military men opposed to him, accepted the theory of 'attrition'; he believed that the war could be won by 'killing Frenchmen', and unlike the attritionists on the Allied side he conducted his attacks in such a manner that he killed more of the enemy than of his own men. He secured this result partly by improved technique and partly by his choice of Verdun as his battlefield. Verdun was a historic trophy, a fortress with a tradition reaching back to the days of Charlemagne; in front of Verdun the French could not give ground, and giving ground was, roughly speaking, the only alternative to giving lives. In front of Verdun, from February to June, the French suffered 460,000 casualties to the German 280,000, and this battle marked quite definitely the end of the period in which the French bore the major part of the burden of the Western Front; thenceforth that burden was to fall upon the British.

Thus the Somme battle, opening on July 1st and continuing on a diminishing scale far into the autumn, was something very much smaller than the battle which had been planned. None the less, it was far the greatest battle ever undertaken hitherto by British arms; it was the great event for which Kitchener's mighty army of volunteers had been trained. 'Never before', says Sir James Edmonds, the compiler of the Official History of the Military Operations of the Great War, 'had the ranks of a British army on the field of battle contained the finest of all classes of the nation, in physique, brains, and education. If ever a decisive victory was to be won it was to be expected now.' Lord Kitchener himself did not live to see the armies which were the supreme creation of his career put to their supreme test; he had, a few weeks before, gone down with the *Hampshire*, which struck a mine off the Orkneys when taking him on a mission to Russia.

The result of the opening attack on July 1st was a shattering disappointment to high hopes. The casualties were appalling, 20,000 dead in one day, and the impression made on the enemy's lines quite inconsiderable. The battle was renewed on a smaller scale, and prolonged far into the autumn. The Germans sacrificed a considerable amount of ground—very wisely, as an alternative to greater sacrifice of men, but the verdict of failure, pronounced after the first onslaught could never be reversed. Indeed the whole battle, as seen in retrospect, was wrongly conceived. The most damaging of all elements in warfare, the element of surprise, was entirely neglected. The Germans knew exactly when and where the attack was coming, and their defensive system surpassed in strength anything ever seen before in the history of war. The tactics of the attack were far too simpleminded and, in a word, amateurish. It was a trial of strength between the greatest amateur army and the greatest professional army in the world, the latter enjoying all the advantages of defence; and the professionals had the best of it. Moreover the British artillery preparation was found to have yielded disappointing results, because much of the ammunition proved to be defective. The enemy's positions were afterwards found, says Sir James Edmonds, to be 'littered with unexploded British shells'. Mr. Lloyd George's Ministry had done wonders in the way of production, but his hustling methods had led, as professionals in the War Office always foretold, to some sacrifice of quality for the sake of quantity.

In fine, valour was not enough. Yet let it not be said that valour was in vain. The incredible bravery of the new British armies produced a profound and never forgotten impression upon the enemy. Never again, German historians have since recorded, did the German rank and file fight as confidently and as resolutely as they fought before the Somme. It is obvious enough today, however, that the same result could have been secured with much less expenditure of life. The cemeteries of the Somme, like the cemeteries of the Crimea, are a tragic witness to the fact that bravery is commoner than brains. There was no reason except official incredulity and obstructiveness why the battle of the Somme should not have been a tank battle.

It was not a tank battle; none the less, tanks were used, as an afterthought and a desperate expedient, and the day of their

appearance in the field, September 15th, 1916, is a landmark
not only in the history of the war, but in the history of War itself
—equal in significance to the first use of cannon. Though few in
number and used at haphazard and without their proper tactics,
they managed to achieve remarkable results. A single tank,
followed by two companies of infantry, cleared a mile of trench
and took 370 prisoners, apart from numerous killed and wounded,
with a loss to the British of only five men. The apostles of the
new tactics were appalled to see their fifty tanks taken from
them and thrown into battle in this heedless manner. They
wanted to keep the tank in reserve until a surprise attack, with
tank tactics instead of the self-defeating artillery preparation,
could be staged with several hundred tanks. They were quite
right; none the less, as it happened, no harm was done. The
Germans learnt nothing from their first experience of the engine
which was to be the principal military instrument of their defeat.

Brusilov's Russian offensive against the Austrians opened a
month before the battle of the Somme, on a two-hundred mile
front. Though a very light attack by western standards it sufficed
to break a very fragile defence, and achieved sensational results,
advances measured by scores of miles, prisoners by the 100,000.
Once more, and for the last time as it happened, the pathetic
Russian 'steam roller' was trotted out, and disgruntled clubmen
contrasted Brusilov's results with those of Sir Douglas Haig.
The Russian offensive inevitably petered out when the Germans
had brought down their troops from the north, and before the
end of it Brusilov had lost a million prisoners. This, the last
great military effort of Russia, relieved the pressure on Italy; it
also tilted the diplomatic balance in Roumania.

If the Roumanian Government had entered the war at once,
when Brusilov's offensive was in the first flush of its success, the
Roumanian armies, though little more than a militia of infantry-
men with few machine guns and no trench-mortars, might have
swept along with the Russians all over the Hungarian plain,
with incalculable results on the policy of the Austrian Govern-

ment, and on the prospects of the war. Indeed it might be said that, for about a week in the first half of June, the decisive theatre of the war was the council chamber of the Roumanian Cabinet. But here, as in Gallipoli a year before, the verdict must be—too late. The Roumanian politicians must first drive a series of bargains, securing them all that they wanted in the way of military support from Russia and Salonika, all that they wanted in territorial loot as the reward of victory. As a result they entered the war several weeks after their chance was gone. Germany, thoroughly alarmed at the prospect of losing Roumanian corn and oil, which she had purchased in large amounts so long as Roumania remained neutral, decided that the new enemy must be conquered at once, and put forth what, in view of all that had gone before, was an amazing effort. It was at this date that Hindenburg and Ludendorff took control of the German military machine and, as events proved, of the German civil government also. Falkenhayn was sent against Roumania. He and Mackensen, the commander of the assault on the Russians in the spring of the previous year, fell upon the two wings of the Roumanian army, and rolled it up into the extreme northeast of Roumanian territory. The addition of another nation to the Alliance had meant nothing but an extension of the territory under German control.

Earlier in the year there occurred the mysterious battle of Jutland, the only occasion during the war when the rival Grand Fleets, on which such infinite labour and skill and money had been expended, came within speaking distance of a Trafalgar. The encounter occupied some hours of the afternoon and evening of May 31st, and the events of those hours have furnished food for argument for as many years in naval circles. Since the subject bristles with technicalities it will be best to say nothing about it—unless it be this: that it is probably a mistake to claim Jutland as a 'moral victory', and to trace to the events of that night the ultimate demoralization of the crews of the German fleet. Within twelve weeks of Jutland, on August 19th, the

German fleet made another bid to draw the British fleet into an ambush of mines and submarines, but caution this time avoided decision by so wide a margin that the episode has been almost entirely forgotten. Jutland was, in result, entirely negligible.

From May onwards conscription was in full force, and the local tribunals on which fell the duty of deciding appeals for exemption found themselves confronted with a long succession of difficult and distressing cases. Claims to exemption on industrial or economic grounds were merely difficult; it was extremely hard for a committee of local worthies to decide whether in fact the services of A or B of military age were essential to the continued existence of the shop or farm on which he was employed. The distressing cases were those of the so-called conscientious objectors. The intention of the Act had been that those who could prove 'conscience' should be exempted without any pains or penalties. But what is conscience? in what does it differ from mere opinion? and in any case how could it be proved? It was soon plain that to accept 'conscience' on the mere assertion of the objector would offer altogether too strong a temptation to cowardice. In the result, practically all who could not prove membership of the Society of Friends, and even a considerable number of those who could prove it, were treated as non-conscientious and, after refusing military service, sentenced to penal servitude for the remainder of the war. It was easy to denounce this policy as a breach of the principles of liberty of thought and religious toleration; it was less easy, indeed impossible, to answer the argument that, human weakness being what it is, the State had to confront those who refused to risk their lives on its behalf with an alternative almost equally grim. Among those who served sentences on Dartmoor were certainly some saintly and heroic souls. Some, who could have avoided military service with impunity on medical or other grounds, deliberately courted imprisonment; it was not from such as these that complaints of the Government's policy came. Nor was the total number of the 'conscientious' objectors such as to have any military significance.

The opening day of the battle of the Somme may, in retro-spect, be regarded as disastrous. It was certainly the most ex-pensive single day in the whole war, if cost be measured in the lives of British soldiers. Mr. Churchill bluntly describes it as a catastrophe, adding that 'the extent of the catastrophe was con-cealed by the censorship and its significance masked by a con-tinuance of fighting on a far smaller scale'. Very different was the impression produced on the British public at the time. Not only had the censorship removed half the facts; the newspapers had filled in the gaps with their own rosy imaginings. 'During the last two months', says a writer in the *Round Table* for Sep-tember, 'a noteworthy change has come over the people of this country. . . . This silent revolution is the reaction upon Britain of the great advance. It is a change strangely compounded of the spirit of hope and the spirit of sacrifice—of the sense of com-ing victory and the ache of personal loss. We know now that the Empire and what it stands for are saved, that the old country will "carry on" for generations to come. But we know too that for tens of thousands life has henceforth lost much of its personal meaning. . . . How can we best bear our testimony to the spirit in which they died?'

The article from which these sentences are taken is entitled 'Reconstruction'. The word was very much coming into fashion: there was actually to be a Ministry of Reconstruction in a few months' time, a Ministry dedicated, while the war was still un-decided, to the wholesome and exhilarating task of building castles in the air. We began to envisage a post-war world. In early days, when the war was still expected to be short, the post-war world was expected to be simply the pre-war world *minus* 'Prussianism'. Now, as we realized the breadth and depth of the gulf separating the two eras of peace, we realized also that the post-war world would be fundamentally different, and we were confidently determined that it should be immeasurably better. It was curiously easy to suppose that it must be so. War can easily be represented as a surgical operation performed upon an unhealthy body-politic, and by the extremity of our suffering we measure the scope of the benefits which we expect to accrue when the operation is over. The war was already securing, through the complete cessation of unemployment and the immense amount of overtime work, as also by the immense amount of wage earning undertaken by hitherto unpaid sections of the population, a marked rise in the standard of working-class living. That must be maintained. More important still the comradeship and goodwill of all classes in the trenches must be carried over into the post-war world of industry. No one had written more strikingly on this theme than Donald Hankey, a younger brother of Sir Maurice Hankey, one of the first champions of tanks and soon to be Secretary of the War Cabinet. Donald Hankey, himself a victim of the Somme offensive, had chosen to enlist in the ranks rather than avail himself of a commission, and had written from the trenches a series of articles for the *Spectator* subsequently published under the title of 'A Student in Arms'. Donald Hankey's picture of 'The Good Captain' who always thought of himself as the servant of his company, exactly expressed the new ideal of what the captain of industry ought to be. 'The Two Nations' of Carlyle and Disraeli, rich and poor ever at war with one another, must find a reconciliation in that post-war world which was to be. It seems incredible, does it not, that anyone outside the pulpit should have enlarged upon so Utopian a possibility; yet there is abundant evidence of it in the ordinary journalism of the latter half of the war.

The leaders of organized Labour approached the problems of Reconstruction from their own sectarian angle. The Trade Union Congress carried unanimously a resolution in favour of the nationalization of all vital industries. That might mean many different things. More concrete were the suggestions offered by the President, Mr. Gosling, in his presidential address. After declaring that the Government must not 'allow unemployment to be prevalent', he continued:

'But we hope for something better than a mere avoidance of unemployment and strikes. We are tired of war in the industrial field. The British workman cannot quietly submit to an autocratic government in the conditions of his own life. He will not take "Prussianism" lying down, even in the dock, the factory, or the mine. Would it not be possible for the employers of this country, on the conclusion of peace, to agree to put their businesses on a new footing by admitting the workmen to some participation, not in profits, but in control? We workmen do not ask that we should be admitted to any share in what is essentially the employer's own business—that is to say, in those matters which do not directly concern us. We do not seek to sit on the Board of Directors, or to interfere with the buying of materials or the selling of the product. But in the daily management of the employment in which we spend our working lives, in the hours of beginning and ending work, in the conditions of remuneration, and even in the manners and practices of foremen with whom we have to be in contact, in all these matters we feel that we, as workmen, have a right to a voice—even to an equal voice, with the management itself. Believe me, we shall never get any lasting industrial peace except on the lines of industrial democracy.'

These were the counsels of a moderate and highly respected trade unionist. Their fundamental weakness was that they did not, in fact, amount to industrial democracy. 'Industrial democracy', says a writer in the *Round Table* for December 1916, 'implies a far more fundamental revolution than Mr. Gosling appears to realize. Democracy in industry carries with it the same implications as democracy in government. It means that Labour must shoulder the whole responsibility. Industry is one indivisible whole and, in the long run, the final responsibility for it must rest in one set of hands. The capitalist can no more be responsible for one half of the business and Labour for the other half than Cabinet and Opposition can each control a separate share of public administration. Industrial democracy can only mean that the management will be appointed by and responsible to Labour, who will thus be responsible not only for interest on the capital it borrows but for liabilities undertaken, orders given, and for the whole complicated process of buying, producing, and selling from start to finish. According to Mr. Gosling, Labour is anxious to avoid shouldering this responsibility. So long as that is so, the capitalist must continue to be responsible for the conduct of industry, and Labour must work under his direction.'

Along such lines as these capitalists and anti-capitalists continued to argue the problems of the reconstruction of industry in the post-war world, until the post-war world itself arrived and interrupted their discussions.

On September 2nd the first Zeppelin was brought down on English soil. This was to prove very nearly the end of Zeppelin raids, for our aircraft was henceforth too much for these unwieldy monsters, and German air raids thenceforth were the work of aeroplanes. There were in all fifty-two Zeppelin raids over England, the first in January 1915 and the last before the end of 1916, and fifty-seven aeroplane raids, half of which, including the most destructive raids, were in 1917. The total casualties of all the air raids was 1400 killed, and 3400 injured, rather more than half the total being the work of the aeroplane raids.

Air raids were not, intrinsically, an important feature of the war, and the amount of damage done to munition works was surprisingly small. One wonders whether, according to the laws of probability, the Germans were rather unlucky in this matter. There was in the Ministry of Munitions a large-scale map of the Woolwich area marking the places where all the bombs had fallen round the arsenal; none ever fell inside it. It hardly needs saying that, for the population at home, the air raids enjoyed a prominence out of all proportion to their intrinsic importance. The streets were darkened every night, and any householder who forgot to pull down his blinds was lucky to get off with no more than a police warning: he might quite possibly find himself suspected of communicating with the enemy. Schools and other institutions on the East Coast found themselves compelled to migrate inland. Problems of air defence against these raids long baffled the experts and furnished the agitator with material for charges of inefficiency. At a Hertfordshire by-election in the spring of 1916, a certain Mr. Pemberton-Billing, standing as an independent candidate with a programme of 'better air defence', secured a sensational majority and became at one stroke a hero of the ultra-popular press. The Zeppelin was conquered, but no completely satisfactory defence against the raiding aeroplanes was ever worked out.

1916 was the first year with 'summer time'. Mr. Willett had pressed his simple and ingenious idea upon an uninterested and mildly contemptuous public for many years. It needed a world war with its demand for the economizing of everything, including lighting materials, to persuade us to take him seriously.

Before the year 1916 had reached its dismal and depressing conclusion, with Roumania wiped out and the Somme offensive brought to a standstill, Mr. Asquith fell from power and Mr. Lloyd George took his place. The intrigues which led up to this event were exceedingly complicated. Many forces converged to produce a result which was till the last moment unexpected, although in retrospect it seems broadly inevitable. Chief among them were the journalistic activities of Lord Northcliffe, the ambitions of Mr. Lloyd George, and the apprehensions of Mr. Bonar Law; the solution of the tangle should be set down to the credit—if it is credit—of Mr. Aitken, of whom hardly anyone outside the inner circles had heard at that time, though he afterwards became well known as Lord Beaverbrook.

The eclipse of the journalist in the first months of the war had been of brief duration: before many months were over the journalists became, owing to the abeyance of party politics and free political debate, the leaders of the national opposition. As such they enjoyed formidable powers, for the government could not defend itself against their attacks without giving information to the enemy. Among these journalists Lord Northcliffe was easily pre-eminent, and it was a curious and unfortunate accident that during the war years, and only a very short period before and after, the *Times* should have belonged to a man who rose to fame and wealth and power by way of *Answers*, the *Daily Mail*, and the *Daily Mirror*. Lord Northcliffe was a genius in his own line, which was manufacturing and marketing the dangerous commodity which is ironically called news. He had a genius for this as Lord Leverhulme had a genius for manufacturing and marketing soap. His interest was 'good copy' and his field was the exploitation of the passions of war time. With this end in view he had hounded Lord Haldane out of public life. It mattered not at all that Lord Haldane had organized the Expeditionary Force; he had once made some remark about Germany being his 'spiritual home', referring to the fact that he was a disciple of the classical German philosophers. The public wanted a villain, and Lord Northcliffe offered Lord Haldane for the part; consequently when the Conservatives entered Mr. Asquith's Government in 1915 they insisted that Lord Haldane should cease to be Lord Chancellor. For this and many other reasons Mr. Asquith detested Lord Northcliffe: he ignored his importance, and refused to feed him with useful titbits of information about the war. In revenge Lord Northcliffe undertook to bring down Mr. Asquith as he had brought down Lord Haldane. By all the devices of which he was a master he created the impression that Mr. Asquith's continued tenure of office was the principal obstacle to the winning of the war; and over against Mr. Asquith the man of 'wait and see' he set up Mr. Lloyd George the man of 'push and go'.

Since Lord Kitchener's death Mr. Lloyd George had been at the War Office, and there he found the discharge of what he, perhaps rightly, conceived to be his responsibilities hampered

1916

at every turn by the abnormal powers granted to Sir William
Robertson as Chief of the General Staff. Sir William Robertson
was one of those whose whole energies were concentrated upon
the Western Front. Mr. Lloyd George had from the first made a
special interest of Salonika, and when Roumania entered the
war he was determined that the Salonika Force should break
into activity and co-operate with Roumania. Sir William
Robertson blocked his way. Mr. Asquith supported Sir William
Robertson, and it became apparent that Mr. Lloyd George
could only get over the obstacle in his path by deposing Mr.
Asquith. But here he was on very problematical ground, for the
Conservatives in general upheld soldiers against civilians, and
some of Mr. Lloyd George's public outbursts against the incom-
petence of military management were ill received in Conservative circles.

Mr. Bonar Law occupied a somewhat undeterminate position
at this time. Accepting the Colonial Office at the time of the formation of the Coalition, he had never held the position in that
Government to which, as leader of the Conservative party, he
might have thought himself entitled, but, being singularly free
from personal ambition, he had probably not resented the fact.
He attached, however, very great importance to the maintenance, for post-war purposes, of an undivided Conservative
party and, when we remember the fate that actually befell the
Liberal party, anxiety on this score cannot be accounted unreasonable. At the moment the Conservative party was seriously
threatened with schism by reason of the activities of Sir Edward
Carson. There is no reason for supposing that Sir Edward Carson had any great gifts for statesmanship, but he was, like Mr.
Lloyd George and unlike both Mr. Asquith and Mr. Bonar Law,
a salient personality. With the glamour of Ulster behind him,
with that grim, intensely carnivorous countenance, he had the
air of an Elizabethan buccaneer. Sir Edward Carson had left
the Coalition towards the end of 1915, because it had failed to
give adequate support to Serbia, and had since become the

156

leader of an ultra-patriotic Opposition. Early in November he divided against the Government on a motion respecting the disposal of enemy properties in Africa, and secured an alarmingly large number of Conservative members for the Opposition lobby. After this debate Mr. Bonar Law came to the conclusion that Sir Edward Carson must be got back into the Government, but Mr. Asquith, having already had experience of Sir Edward as a colleague, would not hear of it.

It was at this point that Mr. Aitken lent his services in bringing Mr. Lloyd George, Sir Edward Carson, and Mr. Bonar Law together, and thenceforth the story becomes altogether too complicated. The secret operations of the four principals were accompanied by an anti-Asquith barrage from the press, but there seems to be no doubt that most of the leading Conservatives, other than Mr. Bonar Law and Sir Edward Carson, were looking forward to the exclusion from office, not of Mr. Asquith but of Mr. Lloyd George himself. On this point Lord Beaverbrook's narrative is quite explicit. Finally, however, when the ground had been fully prepared, Mr. Lloyd George resigned office. Thereupon Mr. Asquith resigned. The King sent for Mr. Bonar Law who, as prearranged, failed to form a Government, and advised His Majesty to send for Mr. Lloyd George.

What followed was the establishment of a 'new Government' in a sense much more fundamental then the term usually bears. The organization of the supreme executive was entirely transformed. The old Cabinet was abolished and its place taken by a War Cabinet, consisting of only five or perhaps five and a half members. The five were relieved of all departmental duties and would thus be able to concentrate their entire energies on winning the war; their names were Lord Curzon, Lord Milner, Sir Edward Carson and Mr. Henderson, and of course the Prime Minister himself. Sir Edward Carson's position needed no explanation for those who were aware of the recent intrigues, and Mr. Henderson was included as the representative of Labour.

The presence of the two noble Lords occasioned a shock of mild surprise, and it was remembered that in his unregenerate days the new Prime Minister had described the pair of them as 'prancing proconsuls'. Perhaps their merit was that they were not 'professional politicians', for the popular press had taught its public to regard very unfavourably almost all persons who could be thus described.

The half-member of the War Cabinet was Mr. Bonar Law, Chancellor of the Exchequer and Leader of the House of Commons. 'You cannot run a war with a Sanhedrim,' said Mr. Lloyd George. 'That is the meaning of the Cabinet of five, and one of its members doing sentry duty outside, manning the walls and defending the Council chamber against attacks while we are trying to do our work inside.' But it is easier to understand the function of Mr. Bonar Law if we discard these rather surprising metaphors and seek precedents from past history. Both the Pitts, when engaged in organizing victory, had relied on Parliamentary managers for the maintenance of their political position; the elder Pitt employed the Duke of Newcastle and the younger Pitt employed Henry Dundas. Mr. Bonar Law was a much better man than Newcastle or Dundas; he was one of the most skilful Parliamentarians of his day. He had, indeed, played his cards extraordinarily well. The new Government was in effect a Conservative Government with numerous temporary adjuncts for war purposes. After the war was over the temporary adjuncts —including the Prime Minister himself—could be discarded at will, and the Conservative party would remain in possession of the field.

The other temporary adjuncts besides the Prime Minister were the new Ministries of Food, Labour, Shipping and National Service. These, and also some of the old ministerial posts, as well as a host of secondary departments and controllerships were entrusted to business men. Careful compilation proves that the new Government contained representatives of railways, textiles, hardware, coal (wholesale and retail), chemicals, newspapers, oil, margarine and sugar.[1] The Ministry of Munitions had been a big-business crew, skippered by the little Welsh wizard; the new Government was a more august adaptation of the scheme of the Ministry of Munitions. It would be easy to prove that there was in all this a large element of window-dressing; in many cases a change of names advertised to the public changes which had in fact been carried out under the direction of Mr. Asquith. But to say this is not to condemn. Good advertisement is essential to success in business, and Mr. Lloyd George's inaugural performance acted on the drooping spirits of the nation at large like a brass band on tired troops.

Mr. Asquith's retirement terminated the longest Premiership since Lord Liverpool, a hundred years before. Press and public had treated him with cruel injustice, but though his management of affairs never fell below his own high level of dexterous competence, he was by no means a great war minister. Perhaps he was already too old and tired when the war began. It was his misfortune that he deferred too much to naval and military opinion on naval and military questions, for their counsel was seldom unanimous and often unprofitable. Perhaps what many of us would like to think his merits were demerits for the task he had to undertake. Balliol had made him, and he was always too Balliol for a Northcliffized and half-Americanized democracy. Lord Grey writes of him: 'Asquith took no trouble to secure his own position or to add to his personal reputation. When things were going well with his Government he would be careful to see that any colleague got the credit, if he were entitled to it, without regard to whether any credit would be given to or left for himself. On the other hand, if things were going badly he was ready to stand in front and accept all responsibility: a colleague who got into trouble was sure that the Prime Minister would stand by him. These qualities are happily not unique, but Asquith possessed them in a rare degree.'

[1] E. T. Raymond, *Mr. Lloyd George*, p. 221; to whom also I owe the happy simile of the brass band at the end of the paragraph.

This is a very noble testimonial. As a testimonial to personal character it could not be bettered. But, as a Prime Minister in war time, was Mr. Asquith altogether wise or right to give full play to his instinctive and selfless chivalry? A nation at war imperatively calls for the illusion of a superman as hero-leader. Cavour once said something to the effect that in order to lead his country through the crisis of war to victory he had to play the part of a great rascal. Mr. Asquith was not a great rascal and nothing would make him one. Mr. Lloyd George was in almost every respect the opposite of Mr. Asquith. He eagerly took personal credit for everything to which he could lay claim, and shifted discredit on to other shoulders. He assiduously built up his own legend. We need not like his performance, but perhaps we ought to be grateful for it.

Lord Grey (he had accepted a peerage in the summer of 1916) left office at the same time as Mr. Asquith, having held the Foreign Secretaryship for a longer continuous period than any of his predecessors, eleven years to a day. He too had lost credit during the war. He was blamed, quite unreasonably, for the failure of our diplomacy in the Balkans. He was also blamed for what was esteemed his weakness in the enforcement of the blockade in his relations with neutral America. In this sphere he had in fact rendered services of inestimable value to the Allied cause, but the subject of Anglo-American relations previous to America's entry into the war has been held over until the next chapter.

CHAPTER XIV

1917

The year 1917 was dominated by three events of transcendent significance, the German attempt to starve us out of the war by means of U-boats, the entry of America, and the Russian Revolution. Of these events the second was the result of the first, but the third was unconnected with either of the other two. The Germans announced that they would sink all Allied and neutral commerce at sight on January 31st. America entered the war on April 5th; the Russian Revolution began on March 8th. The Germans reckoned that the new submarine policy would bring in America, but they also reckoned, and rightly, that a year would pass before American armies could play an important part in the fighting, for the United States were practically an unarmed nation when President Wilson declared war. The Germans hoped to starve Great Britain out of the war within that year, and they came within a measurable distance of succeeding. They adopted the submarine campaign because, after their experience of Brusilov in the Carpathians and the British on the Somme in the previous summer, they despaired of winning the war by purely military methods. But suppose the Russian Revolution had been foreseen by them, or had broken out two months earlier, and enabled them to transfer to France their Eastern armies at the beginning instead of at the end of 1917. Presumably they would not have embarked on their submarine campaign, and America would not have joined the Allies; and what then?

Today, in retrospect, we see the entry of America and the

Russian Revolution as items on opposite sides of the Allied war accounts, the gain of the former rather more than balancing the loss of the latter. It is, therefore, very curious to recall that in the spring of 1917 both items were set down on the credit side. This was but a further instalment of the Russian legend. Something was wrong with Russia, we could clearly see. The fault could hardly lie with our old friend the Russian *moujik*; it must therefore lie with his Government. Sinister tales of Rasputin, Stürmer and Protopopoff gained currency. Russia was being held back by the pro-German proclivities of the camarilla centring round the Tsaritsa. 'When it became evident', says the *Round Table* for June, 'that the natural instincts on which the Holy Alliance and Bismarck's league of autocrats had once been founded were again asserting themselves in the *entourage* of the Tsar, when it was discovered that certain of his ministers had even contemplated a treacherous bargain with the German Government, the Russian people rose, and, the army being with them, achieved the most sudden and sweeping Revolution in history. . . . In the course of three days the largest State in Europe and the third largest in the world became a democracy.' This was the style of every English newspaper at the time, and Mr. Lloyd George expressed no more and no less than the feelings of the nation when, in his message to the first Prime Minister of Revolutionary Russia he declared that 'the Revolution whereby the Russian people have based their destinies on the sure foundation of freedom is the greatest service which they have yet made to the cause for which the Allied peoples have been fighting since August 1914'. One thing at any rate was clear to the writer in the *Round Table*: 'Free Russia can never come to terms with absolutism. She can no more make peace with the Kaiser than she can restore the Tsar.'

The notion that the Russian 'democracy' was clamouring, like the *Morning Post*, to 'get on with the war' was of course pure delusion. The Russian people, and more particularly the rank and file of the Russian armies, wanted above all things to escape

an agony the purposes of which were quite beyond their comprehension. They surrendered themselves, before the end of the
year, to the tender mercies of the Bolsheviks simply because the
Bolsheviks alone promised immediate peace on any terms obtainable. Nothing at all was to be the contribution of Russian
revolutionary armies to the Allied cause, but it was by no means
unreasonable to expect profit from the spread of revolutionary
infection among the peoples of Austria and Germany. In May
the Austrian Government was persuaded to summon the
Reichsrat, which had been prorogued since before the war
began. The result was such an outburst of nationalist clamour
from Czech, Serb and Polish deputies that, after six weeks tur-
moil, the Reichsrat was prorogued again. Even in Germany the
Kaiser promised a reform of the Prussian franchise, and invited
the leaders of the political parties, including the Majority (i.e.
moderate) Socialists to a conference with himself; in spite of
which the Reichstag, in July, carried by a majority of one hundred votes a resolution which, in England, would have been
equivalent to a vote of censure of the Government. In fact, in
the summer of 1917 the first premature and abortive rumblings
of the Austrian and German revolutions were distinctly audible.
But the Governments steadied themselves and kept the saddle
for another sixteen months.

When the war began almost all Americans, from President
Wilson downwards and including ex-President Roosevelt, were
agreed that it was no concern of theirs. The old tradition,
linked with the venerated names of Washington and Monroe,
held good; Europe and America were, politically, two separate
worlds—the New World and the Old, the good world and the
bad. The few who displayed violent sympathies with one side or
the other proved, it was said, by that very fact that they were
not hundred-per-cent Americans but hyphenated creatures who
had left their souls behind in the land of their fathers. When
President Wilson urged his countrymen to be neutral in speech

and thought, and not merely in action, he was simply urging them to be true Americans. It might seem as if he was urging them to be indifferent spectators of a struggle between right and wrong; but in such a wicked world who could be right? If Germany was an aggressive and cruel despotism, was not Russia the same, and was not England the apostle of something all good Americans condemned under the name of Imperialism? If one said 'Look at Belgium!' another would reply 'Look at Ireland!' It seemed to us in England an unconvincing retort, but it was good enough for New York and Chicago.

Unfortunately the two worlds were not as separate as theory demanded. If there is one respect more than another in which history repeats itself it is this: that in any war not merely local the belligerent in possession of sea power will seek to injure his enemy by cutting off his sea-borne trade, and will involve himself in controversy, or even conflict, with neutrals seeking to pursue their normal trade with the enemy. An immense body of law and custom regulating neutral rights of trade and belligerent rights of interference—blockade, contraband, and all the rest of it—had accumulated during past centuries, and with each new war new conditions proved the old rules to be out of date. Of all the problems handled by Sir Edward Grey after the outbreak of the war this was at once the most important and the most difficult. He had to stop every German import he could safely stop, and no more. 'Absolute contraband' presented no difficulty. No one supposed, for example, that a belligerent was not entitled to prevent neutrals from sending guns and shells to his enemy, if he could. But copper? rubber? cotton? Sir Edward Grey decided to let through cotton in order to secure the recognition of copper and rubber as contraband. For this he was subjected to a great deal of patriotic abuse, but he was absolutely right, for when, later on, cotton was made contraband, the Germans at once found an efficient substitute for it as an ingredient in explosives.

It was all very well for a writer in the *Quarterly Review* to say

'Some blight has been at work in our Foreign Office, steadily undermining our mastery of the seas.' If the Foreign Office had, by some misfortune, been entrusted to the editor of the *Quarterly Review*, we should not, perhaps, have found ourselves at war with America, for the President who was 'too proud to fight' after the sinking of the *Lusitania* would hardly have been proud enough to fight about cotton, but we should have suffered consequences not much less unpleasant. Congress might have put an embargo on the export of American munitions to England. This was a real threat, though some regard it as bluff on the ground that Americans would not sacrifice a source of abundant profit. But there were other possibilities. For example, the Americans might have sent their cargoes to Germany under the convoy of American ships of war.

Thus began and continued an Anglo-American correspondence which, on the American side, was often exceedingly acrimonious. In the main it was conducted, from America, by Mr. Lansing, Secretary of State, a man of great legal acumen and a perfect exponent of the Wilsonian doctrine of neutrality in word and thought. Indeed the Anglo-American official correspondence of the war period exceeded in bulk the whole of the previous correspondence between the Governments of the two countries since the establishment of the Union, and much the greater part of it was concerned with 'cargoes'.

Sir Edward Grey had, in these his most tiresome labours, two invaluable allies. The first was Mr. Page, the American ambassador. Mr. Page was delightfully anti-German from the very start of the war. 'We did pretty well at the battle of the Marne, didn't we?' he remarked to his principal assistant. 'Isn't that remark slightly unneutral, Mr. Ambassador?' replied Mr. Laughlin, amid 'roars of laughter'. The Page-Grey stories are many, and are deservedly well known. On one occasion, for example, Mr. Page came to the Foreign Office with a long despatch. 'I am instructed', he said, 'to read you this despatch.' He read it, and said: 'I have now read the despatch, but I don't agree with it; let us consider how it should be answered.' Mr. Page was one of the best friends our country ever had, but his notorious lack of neutrality inevitably undermined his influence at Washington.

Sir Edward Grey's other ally was the German U-boat.

When the war began Great Britain had more than twice as many submarines as Germany, but three-quarters of ours were small craft suited only for the protection of our own bases; the Germans had a larger number of 'over-sea' submarines for long-distance cruising. What craft of this latter order could do was complicated by the question what they would be authorized to do. A year before the war Lord Fisher, then out of employment, declared that they would be used to sink unarmed merchant vessels, but neither Mr. Churchill nor his First Sea Lord could bring themselves to believe this. Not until February 1915 was Lord Fisher proved to have been right, when the Germans announced that they would use submarines to destroy enemy merchant vessels in all seas surrounding the British Isles, and warned neutrals that for various reasons it would often prove impossible to distinguish between neutral and enemy vessels.

This first German U-boat offensive falls under Talleyrand's definition as 'worse than a crime—a blunder'. The number of German submarines available was entirely inadequate and by May the attack on British commerce petered out with derisory results. The Government marine insurance at one per cent continued to show a profit all through 1915 and the first three quarters of 1916. On the other hand, the British Admiralty were given a warning, and were able to put in two years hard work on anti-submarine devices of every sort and kind. If the Germans had refrained from attacking merchantmen until their second U-boat offensive with a fleet of three hundred submarines in 1917, it may well be that they would have caught us unawares and starved us out.

However, the first U-boat offensive had one enormous achievement to its credit: it sank the *Lusitania*, and started the

American Government on another famous correspondence.

There were many Americans besides Mr. Page who not only hoped but expected that the *Lusitania* tragedy would bring America into the war. In private conversation Colonel House declared: 'We shall be at war with Germany within a month.' But President Wilson would not have it so. He was 'too proud to fight'. The phrase, with its affectation of moral superiority, strikes a European as unfortunate, but it represented a perfectly defensible policy. War is the worst way of settling disputes. Nothing could bring the dead of the *Lusitania* back to life. If one admits the assumption that the war itself, the causes for which the Allies were fighting, did not make a moral demand on American intervention, then the President was quite right in seeking by diplomacy rather than by war to prevent the further loss of American lives. His diplomacy was assisted by the proved inadequacy of the German submarine offensive at that stage of the war. The correspondence, peremptory on the American and evasive on the German side, punctuated from time to time by occasional sinkings of ships with further loss of American lives, lasted almost exactly a year, and terminated in the '*Sussex* pledge' in May 1916. After the sinking of the *Sussex*, Germany undertook to sink no more neutral ships on condition that the President would bring pressure to bear on Great Britain to secure the mitigation or suspension of the British blockade of Germany.

President Wilson repudiated the condition, but it was not altogether out of harmony with the policy he had by this time set before himself. His object was not to mitigate the blockade, but to force a conclusion of the war and the establishment of a League of Nations. To this policy he publicly committed himself in an address to the American League to Enforce Peace on May 27th, an address in which, once again, he emphasized his neutrality by declaring that he 'was not interested to search for or explain the causes and the objects of the war'. There was no time to be lost, for the Presidential election was due in November. He had already despatched Colonel House to England and Germany in pursuit of this policy.

Colonel House's attitude was perfectly explicit. Unlike his master he sympathized with the Allied cause, but he believed that Europe, unaided, could never extricate herself from the toils. The war would, if left to itself, go on till both sides were utterly ruined. The Allies must accept a Peace Conference on an American programme. These terms would then be offered to Germany. If Germany accepted them, the war would be over. If she did not, then America should join the Allies in war against Germany. The American programme could not be very sharply defined in advance. Its general intention was embodied in a secret Memorandum drawn up by Sir Edward Grey and Colonel House and subsequently endorsed by President Wilson, in which the following sentences occur:

'Colonel House expressed the opinion that, if such a Conference met, it would secure peace on terms not unfavourable to the Allies; and, if it failed to secure peace, the United States would leave the Conference as a belligerent on the side of the Allies, if Germany was unreasonable. Colonel House expressed an opinion decidedly favourable to the restoration of Belgium, the transference of Alsace and Lorraine to France, and the acquisition by Russia of an outlet to the sea, though he thought that the loss of territory incurred by Germany in one place would have to be compensated to her by concessions to her in other places outside Europe.'

The Memorandum was an agreed definition of the American offer; it implied no acceptance of the offer by Sir Edward Grey and, in fact, the British Government made no use of it. Its policy would have been entirely abhorrent to the French and it was impossible, at the time of the battle of Verdun, when the military efforts and sacrifices of the French had, up to date, so enormously exceeded our own, to pursue a policy which would certainly suggest that we were weakening in our resolve to carry the war through to victory. Moreover we were profoundly convinced that the decisive defeat and overthrow of the German military machine was essential to the future peace of the world. In any case, was the American a firm offer? Did President Wilson really mean to make good his undertaking to join the Allies 'if Germany was unreasonable', and even if he meant it, would he be in a position to do so? American opinion was still overwhelmingly pacifist. Wilson might fail to secure re-election. Again, what would America do as an ally that she was not already doing, to her own profit, as a neutral? The United States had practically no army; even if they decided to raise an army, it would take them a long time to do it. Meantime as the Germans would have no more to hope or fear from America, they would at once resume unrestricted submarine warfare on all merchantmen visiting British harbours, and the Allies might well lose thereby more than they gained. Finally, the British Government realized that effective prosecution of the war depended above all things on an undivided will, and it was felt that an elaboration of 'peace talk' in 1916 would be psychologically enervating.

Thus when President Wilson stood for re-election in November he was thoroughly out of sympathy with the Allies. He stood as 'the man who kept you out of the war'. Senator James of Kentucky amplified this definition. 'Without orphaning a single American child, without widowing a single American mother, without firing a single gun or shedding a single drop of blood, he has wrung from the most militant spirit that ever brooded over a battlefield the concession of American demands and American rights.' The Republican party did not venture to put forward any of their war candidates against him: they chose Senator Hughes, whose programme was as neutral as Wilson's. The election, like so many American elections, was Tweedledum versus Tweedledee. Wilson was re-elected by the narrowest majority in American history. He at once resumed his series of exhortations to the warring world, taking 'the liberty of calling attention to the fact that the objects, which the statesmen of the belligerents on both sides have in mind in this war, are virtually the same'.

But the control of events was passing out of the President's hands. This, the last dove of peace to issue from the American ark, had been anticipated by the German 'peace offensive' of December 12th. 'In a deep moral and religious duty towards this nation and beyond it towards humanity, the Emperor now considers that the moment has come for official action towards peace.' The terms proposed were not designed for acceptance but for refusal—a refusal which would furnish a pretext for the renewal of unrestricted submarine activity. In January the German Government announced that all sea traffic within the war zone would be stopped by every available means after February 1st. The German ambassador was immediately dismissed from America. For two months more a futile effort was made to avoid actual hostilities, in spite of frequent losses of American lives at sea and the publication of German intrigues with Mexico. At last, on April 2nd, the President declared that 'the world must be made safe for democracy' and on April 5th Congress pledged all the resources of the States to the active prosecution of war. It was a war against Germany, but it was not, in President Wilson's mind, a war in alliance with 'the Allies'. They were only a little less bad than the Germans.

President Wilson brought America into the war in order to meet the German submarine attack on American ships. Subtle and cynical persons say that he was driven into the war by American financiers who were determined that England and France, America's debtors, should not be allowed to go bankrupt. But once in the war the President let loose a swarm of new idealisms. Nothing could reconcile them with his previous idealisms, and moreover they proved too much. If America was fighting for her own interests he was right to wait until her own interests were vitally endangered, and of that she was her own judge; but if she was fighting to make the world safe for democracy, then the argument for intervention in April 1917 had been equally valid in August 1914.

But these are unkind thoughts, and no one in the England of 1917 entertained them. President Wilson's English reputation was transformed in a single night. His past was scarcely even explained away; it was forgotten. The man whom *Punch* had cartooned as Pecksniff was henceforth recognized as the weightiest exponent of the Allied cause.

Once America had come in, the war-weary armies in France knew that, if they could hold on into 1918, the man power on their side would be increased by as many millions as the circumstances might require. Without this knowledge France might quite conceivably have collapsed after the fiasco of Nivelle's offensive. However, American man power was an assurance for the future; it was in other departments that the new Ally, or 'Associated Power', brought immediate relief. One of them was finance; there had come a real danger that the British pound would fail to maintain terms with the American dollar. If the Germans had not tried to stop the inflow of American supplies, they might have stopped of their own accord because there was no more credit to pay for them. Another department was the blockade. Now that America had ceased to be neutral she had lost all interest in 'the freedom of the seas' and other 'ideal' aspects of neutral rights. Mr. Balfour, who had succeeded Lord Grey at the Foreign Office, went over to America to discuss these and other questions. Mr. Polk of the State Department seems to have met him more than halfway. 'Mr. Balfour,' said Mr. Polk, 'it took Great Britain three years to reach a point where it was prepared to violate all the laws of blockade. You will find that it will take us only two months to become as great criminals as you are!' In other words, British sea power could now at last be used to enforce a rigid exclusion from Germany of everything Germany wanted to import. Neutral states in contact with Germany, such as Holland, were 'rationed', and allowed only such imports as were assumed to meet their own requirements.

1917

German U-boats had brought America into the war, but it was still possible that they would drive England out. That April of the American entry was, in fact, the most alarming month. The total of tonnage sunk was nearly double that of either March or February, reaching the appalling figure of 800,000 tons. One ship out of every four that left the British Isles that month never returned. If things had gone on at that rate for a few months more, we should have been starved out. But they did not. The loss-of-tonnage figures fell almost as sharply as they had risen, and from September onwards averaged about 300,000 a month until August 1918, after which date the U-boat attack was slackened off. The number of German U-boats sunk in the last two years of the war was 130, which just about balanced the German rate of construction, the numbers on active service in each month ranging between 140 and 115.

These last figures show that it was not chiefly by destroying U-boats that we met their attack, but by rendering the attack itself abortive. The famous Q-ships or 'mystery ships' are, for obvious reasons, better remembered today than any other anti-submarine devices, but the Q-ships belong in the main to 1915 and 1916. Our methods of defence were many and various. One was to arm all merchant ships with guns. The U-boat's favourite method of attack was to come to the surface and fire its gun, but if its intended victim had a gun, it had to stay under water and fire a torpedo, of which submarines could carry only a small supply. More effective still was the convoy system, whereby merchant vessels travelled in groups, guarded by destroyers and directed by wireless information from the Admiralty. Ship-building was speeded up, and within the first quarter of 1918 the world output of new ships overtook and passed the monthly total of destruction. Emergency agriculture, producing wheat on land which had been down as grass since the 'seventies and converting patriotic tennis lawns into potato patches, increased our island food supply as well as bringing a flicker of prosperity to British farmers, and the same food supply could be made to go further by voluntary abstinence, supplemented as time went on by a more and more rigorous system of rationing.

The Ministry of Food was fortunate in securing and retaining a deserved reputation for efficiency. Its personnel illustrated the co-operation of parties in the national cause, for its chief, during the greater part of its existence, was Lord Rhondda, a Welsh coalowner once notorious as a doughty opponent of the miner's trade union, and his Under-Secretary and successor was Mr. Clynes, a leading member of the Labour party, the first, in fact, to win marked distinction in an executive position. Under these leaders the ministry extended the control of fixed prices and rationed supplies over an ever-widening range of foodstuffs, beginning with milk and sugar, and soon including butcher's meat. Housekeeping became a finer art than ever before.

Food is one of the few subjects in which everyone is interested, and very few aspects of the war came home so universally to men's 'business and bosoms' as food shortage and food economy. It was a source of infinite exasperation and innumerable jokes. In connection with a subject so homely the gravest facts occasioned merriment, which may have been inappropriate but helped to relieve the mental strain. 'Anti-waste' campaigners estimated that the people of Great Britain wasted 9380 tons of bread every week, and deplored the newly discovered biological law that navvies could not eat crusts. Certainly 'anti-waste' activities achieved wonders. The fat collected from the refuse of army camps not only provided sufficient soap for the Army, Navy, and various Government departments but also 18,000 tons of glycerine for ammunition. Bitter and unresolved controversy raged round the question of pet dogs; should they eat or should they be eaten? Perhaps it was a dog-lover who sought to turn aside this food offensive with the proposal that we should consume the Zoo.

In October 1916, when the battle of the Somme was dying down, the French succeeded in recapturing Douaumont, the

most famous of all the forts lost to the Germans during the battle
of Verdun. The attack had been rehearsed with exceptional
care, certain tactical surprises were introduced in the handling
of the French artillery, and the changes and chances of the
weather favoured the assault. It was an unexpected and exceedingly heartening achievement, and it had far-reaching consequences. The French wanted a new commander-in-chief, and
M. Briand offered the post, over the heads of many better known
and more experienced commanders, to Nivelle, the hero of
Douaumont. Nivelle took command in France within a week of
Mr. Lloyd George's accession to the Prime Ministership in England. They met. Nivelle spoke perfect English and they became
fast friends. The Prime Minister, hitherto an Easterner and a
sceptic as regards the orthodox tactics of the Western Front,
became an ardent supporter of Nivelle's projected offensive,
more ambitious than any that had preceded it; it was at this
date also that he began to interest himself in the idea of uniting
the control of the French and British armies under a French
generalissimo.

Nivelle's plan was formulated very early in the new year. A
combined French and British attack, the French in Champagne
and the British on the Somme would win the decisive battle; of
that he seemed extraordinarily confident. But Ludendorff, who
had now, in partnership with Hindenburg, assumed supreme
control of the German armies, also had a plan, and its execution
at the end of February put Nivelle's arrangements out of gear.
Ludendorff withdrew the German armies on a sixty-mile front;
to the newly prepared Hindenburg line. Half the line of Nivelle's
projected battle had ceased to exist. In its stead was a new line,
protected by the wide strip of desert which the retreating German armies had left in their wake. No Englishman who followed
the war in the newspapers at home can ever forget the bewilderment and delight which greeted the news of the German
retreat; but it created a very different impression on instructed
minds. Ludendorff had executed a masterly withdrawal, dis-

locating the plans of his enemies and securing an almost impregnable position from which he could watch the experiment of the U-boat offensive.

Meanwhile M. Briand had fallen from power, and his successor, supported by the most eminent French soldiers, urged Nivelle to hold his hand. Nivelle's original plan had in any case to be drastically revised, and the imminent entry of America into the war was adduced as a further reason for delay. But the new commander was incurably optimistic; he was determined to attack on the Champagne front, even though the British supporting attack had to be far away at Arras, at the other end of the Hindenburg line. His attack fell in April, and its result was worse than failure. There followed widespread mutinies. The secret of those mutinies was wonderfully well kept; most of us in England knew nothing about them till after the war. Indeed Pétain, who took over Nivelle's command, succeeded in pulling the French armies together again without further mishap. But absolute and irrevocable disaster had only been avoided by a narrow margin; and for the remainder of 1917 it would have been risky to expose the French armies to any severe strain. The British armies had to carry on the war of the Western Front and keep the Germans busy till the French recovered.

There followed, then, for us what was perhaps the most distressing period of the whole war. True, there were two brilliant successes, the capture of the Vimy Ridge in April, and of the Messines Ridge in June. Vimy Ridge first demonstrated the effectiveness of gas shells in paralysing the enemy's artillery, and the Canadians played a memorable part in the victorious assault. The capture of the Messines Ridge has been described as 'almost the only true siege-warfare attack made throughout a siege war'. The feature of the attack was the simultaneous explosion of nineteen great mines containing 600 tons of explosives and involving the tunnelling of 8000 yards of gallery. But Messines was followed by the long agony of Passchendaele, officially called the third battle of Ypres, where the attack struggled on week after week in appalling conditions, for the artillery bombardment destroyed the drainage system on which the fenlands east of Ypres depended. No British battle has been condemned so unsparingly by the critics as this of Passchendaele, and not least by Mr. Churchill. Yet it was not fought altogether in vain. In October the Austrian armies, stiffened by a few German divisions, delivered an assault upon the Italians which drove them back on Venice, and came within a measurable distance of driving them out of the war. If Ludendorff could have spared more troops for the Italian front, Germany might well have dealt with Italy as she had dealt with Russia. 'It is', writes Mr. Churchill, 'a valid though inadequate claim on the part of the British High Command that the continuous pressure on Passchendaele played its part in influencing the German war mind. The almost inexhaustible resources of the British attack, its conquering of superhuman difficulties, its obstinate commanders, its undaunted troops, the repeated destruction of the German front lines, the drain—half ours, but still frightful—on German resources, all riveted the eyes of Ludendorff on the Western Front.'

And then, as though in ironic comment on the orthodox inferno in Flanders, the tanks were at last allowed their chance, and for the first time since the beginning of the war the church bells of England were rung in acclaim of victory. At Cambrai, on November 20th, 381 tanks attacked at dawn, without any warning given to the enemy by preliminary bombardment. The whole German trench system was penetrated in a few hours on a six-mile front, 10,000 prisoners and 200 guns were captured, at the cost of less than 1500 British casualties. The victors were as unprepared as the vanquished; reserves were not available to exploit the success, and the later stages of the battle were marked by a German recovery. But that was comparatively unimportant. At last the tank had justified itself. Cambrai was a rehearsal for August 8th, 1918, which, as Ludendorff acknowledged, was 'the black day of the war'.

The battle of Cambrai, in spite of its dubious ending, undoubtedly brightened the prospects of the Western Front as envisaged by the ordinary newspaper reader at home; and the Americans were coming—at least we supposed they were, though there was a good deal of talk at this time about the dilatory character of American methods, and it was alarming to hear that 'in official circles at Washington the end of the war is put five years hence'.[1] That was pessimism indeed: on the other hand it is astonishing to find that we still had hopes of Russia. 'There is a doubt', says the *Round Table* for December 1917, 'as to whether Russia will be able to reorganize her partly demoralized army so that an unequivocal military decision may be possible in 1918.' These words must have been written in October, just before the Bolsheviks occupied Petrograd and overthrew Kerensky's wavering régime; when they appeared in print Russia was already out of the war.

1917 had also brought with it remoter triumphs. The conquest of the greatest of the German colonies, East Africa, was completed after a tough struggle against a gallant enemy and a variety of tropical impediments, and General Smuts, who had commanded the British, South African and Indian forces in that campaign, was now serving as an extra member of the War Cabinet in London. In the spring Sir Stanley Maude had entered Baghdad, and in December General Allenby entered Jerusalem. These campaigns, each of which would have counted as a first-class war at any time in the Victorian age, were inevitably dwarfed both by their own remoteness and by the scale of events near home. The siege of Kut, for example, and the failure of the relieving expedition in the spring of 1916 was, by all standards of measurement, a larger event and a more painful tragedy than the siege of Khartoum and the death of Gordon. Yet the latter event is an outstanding episode in Victorian history; its tale has been told again and again and is familiar to 'every schoolboy', whereas the agony of Kut was soon lost to view in the swirl of

[1] *Round Table*. December 1917.

events. The appalling scale of things deadened our sensibilities and we felt, perhaps, as Edgar did when the deaths of several minor characters were announced in the course of the last Act of *King Lear*: 'These are but trifles here.' We should hardly have felt so, had we known of the ghastly experiences of the Kut garrison after its surrender.

At home the increasing rigours of war and its various 'shortages' were accompanied, though perhaps hardly mitigated, by the promissory notes of Reconstruction. 'We seem definitely to have entered', says the *Round Table* for June, 'upon a period of revolutionary change. Legislative projects which, according to pre-war standards of political action, it would have taken years or even decades to prepare are now being carried through Parliament, almost as a matter of course, in the space of a few months.' Mr. Fisher, the Oxford tutor whom Mr. Lloyd George had made President of the Board of Education, introduced a Bill which, besides providing many excellent and expensive improvements in the existing elementary and secondary systems, ordained compulsory part-time education for all young persons between the ages of fourteen and eighteen. This rather sensational clause never became operative. Another Bill extended the franchise for men and granted the franchise on the same terms to women over thirty. The electorate was in effect doubled and its character radically changed, but no one really minded: it was accepted as inevitable.

Once the idealization of the prospective post-war world had begun there was no stopping it. In particular, two delusive prospects fascinated the optimists of 1917, the unification of the Empire and the unification of capital and labour in industry. So large a measure of united effort was achieved under the stress of war that it seemed intolerable that all this co-operation should end with the conclusion of the stress that had produced it.

One of the first acts of Mr. Lloyd George's War Cabinet was to invite the Governments of the Dominions and India to a

special Imperial War Conference. The Prime Minister's invita
tion stated that 'for the purpose of these meetings your Prime
Minister will be a member of the War Cabinet'. The distinction
between the Imperial War Conference and the Imperial War
Cabinet remained somewhat blurred. In May Mr. Lloyd George
announced that 'the Imperial War Cabinet was unanimous that
the new procedure had been of such service not only to all its
members but to the Empire that it ought not to be allowed to
fall into desuetude'. The Imperial War Conference unanimously
accepted a resolution that there should be a special Constitutional Conference, which should meet as soon as possible after
the cessation of hostilities.

Idealism in industry was the special province of the Committee on the Relations of Employers and Employed, appointed
under the chairmanship of Mr. Whitley (afterwards Speaker of
the House of Commons) by the Minister of Reconstruction. The
Whitley Report recommended the establishment, in all well-
organized industries, of Joint Industrial Councils with equal
representation for trade unions and employers' associations.
There were to be General Councils for each industry, with
District Councils and Works Committees acting under their
authority. The main business of these Councils was not to be
the fixing of wage rates and other matters normally settled by
collective bargaining, but the co-operation of employers and
employed in promoting industrial efficiency and industrial welfare. In fact, the Whitley Report was a bold effort to meet the
demand of the trade unions, as expressed in a speech of Mr.
Gosling's already quoted, for 'a share' in the management of
industry. The Government accepted the Report, and submitted
it to a number of employers' associations and trade unions for
their considered opinion. These opinions were, according to
official summary, 'overwhelmingly in favour of the adoption of
something on the lines suggested by the Report'.

There was already in existence a good deal of organization
designed to bring together representatives of employers and

employed in various industries. In the best-paid and best-organized industries such organization, entirely voluntary in character, dated back to 1870 or thereabouts. In 1909 the Trade Boards Act had created statutory conciliation boards, with power to enforce their decisions regarding wages and conditions of work, in certain sweated industries, and this Act was after the war extended to cover about forty trades with over a million workers. The need for conciliation boards was, therefore, neither at the top nor at the bottom of the industrial scale but in its middle reaches, and here the Whitley movement produced valuable results. The Government led the way by establishing Whitley Councils for its own employees, and in all about seventy Whitley Councils were set up in various industries hitherto without any recognized conciliation system, and more than half these Councils are still in action. But they have been little more than wage boards, like the conciliation boards already existing in other industries. As industrial parliaments, striking out new lines and introducing a new spirit into industry, a spirit which would secure the retention of the advantages claimed for 'capitalism' while adding the advantages claimed for 'socialism', as a new departure pregnant with beneficent consequences, the Whitley Councils have disappointed their founders.

After a year of comparative quiet in 1916 organized Labour was once again becoming very restless and there was a widespread strike in the engineering industry in May. The ostensible causes of the strike were trivial; the real cause was the irritation of nerves jaded by fatigue. The phrase 'fed up' came into popular use at about this time, and it exactly described the state of mind prevalent in the factories. 'Many men', said a leading official of the Ministry of Munitions, 'after nearly three years excessive labour are nerve-tired. The strain has begun to tell on them and things that in ordinary times they would have settled by ordinary means are now made the occasion for rash and extreme action.' Bitterness was directed much less against the employers than against the State by whom the employers were controlled. Multitudinous regulations, most of them necessary, some merely vexatious, were lumped together as 'Prussianism'. There was discontent about the restrictions on the sale of liquor, about 'profiteering', about the application of Compulsory Military Service Act, whereby some were taken and some left. In some areas where new industries had sprung up and new populations aggregated, bad housing was a very real grievance. No doubt the hardships of war in the munition field were the merest trifles in camparison with what other men, morally no better and no worse, endured in the battlefield; but army and workshop have very different traditions. Mutiny was indelible disgrace, whereas strike was common form.

The Labour unrest of the last two years of the war found its organ of expression not in the officials of the trade unions, many of whom were in Government employ, but through shop stewards. Before the war the very name of shop stewards had been unknown to the general public, as it is again unknown today, but they had existed in many industries as minor officials, elected by the trade unionists in each shop or factory for the performance of a variety of routine duties. When the war began and the trade unions proclaimed an industrial truce, these noncommissioned officers of the trade-union army began to step into positions of local leadership vacated by their officers. Moreover, there arose side by side with the old type of shop steward who was simply a minor trade-union official, a new and much more significant type, men elected by a local group of workers to fight for what they conceived to be their wartime rights, quite independent of the trade-union organization. This new shop-steward organization revealed the notorious inability of working men to select representatives who will really represent them. The vast bulk of working men in munition factories may no doubt have been 'fed up', but they were on the whole as loyal to the Government in its determination to win the war as any other section of the community. A great many of their chosen representatives, the new shop stewards, were, on the other hand, extremists or pacifists enamoured of the Russian Revolution, and ambitious to use their power to bring the war to an immediate end on any terms available. The proof of this is the fact that, after the war, many of the more prominent shop stewards passed over into the British Communist movement.

There was a great deal of talk about 'pacifism' in the last winter of the war, especially in ultra-patriotic circles. It is bewilderingly difficult to ascertain how much pacifism there was in the country; indeed the term 'pacifism' itself, especially when used as a term of abuse, was not susceptible of exact definition.

There were, to begin with, the strict 'pacifists' who disapproved of the war because they disapproved of war itself under any conceivable circumstances. The number of these was always small, and many even of the small body who had disapproved of the declaration of war in 1914 soon ceased to be pacifists, either because after events made them realize their mistake or because they held that, once the war had been begun, it must be resolutely pursued. No doubt this body of pacifists was somewhat enlarged after the publication by the Russian Bolsheviks of the inter-Allied Secret Treaties. These treaties were, indeed, unpleasant reading. Their justification was that, without them, the alliance could not have been built up and held together. The Italian treaty was the most notorious; it promised Italy many things to which Italy had no right, simply because without these promises Italy would not enter the war in May 1915. The full defence of the Secret Treaties must be grounded on the admission that war is a bad business: if the war was just and necessary, and victory essential, then any diplomatic instrument which furthered the purposes of the war is also justified. The fulfilment of all the Secret Treaties would have been a lesser evil for the world than the victory of Germany. None the less, the revelation of the Secret Treaties seemed to some superficial minds to prove that the boasted 'idealism' of the Allied cause was mere hypocrisy. Thus the number of the stricter pacifists was perceptibly increased.

At the other end of the scale, people were called pacifists who were not pacifists at all, simply because they thoroughly disliked, and openly expressed their dislike of, Mr. Lloyd George's methods. Just as Mr. Asquith's statesmanship had been too quiet and refined for popular taste, so that of Mr. Lloyd George offended the smaller public which appreciates reticence and dignity. The *Round Table* was never even accused of pacifism, but it had a sharp word to say on this subject. 'Much of the propaganda carried on under Government auspices', says a writer in the issue of March 1918, 'is not only unworthy of its professed cause but a source of direct and unmistakable injury. Occasional lapses of geography and good taste in Ministers may be passed over. Harmful abroad, they are taken at their true worth at home. But the disheartening effect produced by the effusions of paid writers and speakers trained in the school of pre-war party warfare cannot be so easily discounted. . . . The recent appointment of Lord Beaverbrook, a Canadian millionaire, otherwise little known to the public, to a very responsible position as Minister in charge of Propaganda cannot help exciting the reflection that this obvious lesson has not yet been learnt by those in authority.'

In the spring of 1918 Lord Northcliffe and his brother Lord Rothermere joined Lord Beaverbrook as members of the Government. These appointments were strongly criticized in the House of Commons, and Mr. Lloyd George defended them rather quaintly by saying that they were the best men he could find. This payment of Danegeld to the proprietors of the sensational press was an alarming development, and one did not know where it would end. There was, for example, Mr. Horatio Bottomley, editor of *John Bull*, the hero of hundreds of recruiting meetings, and esteemed in thousands of humble homes as a greater prophet of patriotism than Lord Northcliffe himself. However Lord Rothermere did not hold his office of Air Minister for very long. His resignation was a source of amusement as well as relief, for it took effect two days before the affairs of his department were due to be debated in the House of Lords.

Midway between the genuine pacifists and those who, in no sense pacifists, incurred the charge because they criticized Mr. Lloyd George, was a considerable but vague and fluid body of opinion, which inclined to think that the possibilities of what President Wilson had called 'peace without victory' had never been given a fair chance. Was it quite certain that a bold and generous peace offer would not secure such a response from the German people as to compel the German Government to accept it? would not a peace so secured, even if it fell short of our original intentions, be better for the world in the end than an indefinite prolongation of the war? Was there not an irrelevant and deplorable element of mere lust for vengeance in the demand that the German army must first be decisively defeated in the field? Could it ever be so defeated, and if so, when?

Such views as these found expression in unexpectedly high circles when Lord Lansdowne, once Foreign Secretary in Mr. Balfour's Government, published his famous letter in the *Daily Telegraph*, at the end of November 1917. Lord Lansdowne's letter was guarded and ambiguous, but he committed himself so far as to say that 'some of our original desiderata have probably become unattainable'; he expressed the opinion that the difficulties in the way of an early and satisfactory peace were 'not insurmountable', and that, if Germany was assured that we did not intend to subject her to vindictive and penal terms, 'an immense stimulus would probably be given to the peace party in Germany'.

The Lansdowne letter brought this peace movement into the open, and its reception proved that the nation was overwhelmingly against it. It was felt to be, even if unconsciously, the manifestation of a spirit quite other than that which it professed; to be in fact what the French called 'défaitiste'. Mr. Lloyd George spoke for the nation when he said, in immediate reply to Lord Lansdowne: 'The danger is not the extreme pacifist. I am not afraid of him. But I warn the nation to watch the man

who thinks there is a halfway house between victory and defeat.
. . . Victory is an essential condition for the security of a free
world.' The nation refused to believe that complete victory was
not within the capacity of the Allied Powers, now reinforced by
America; and it refused to believe that anything short of the
complete defeat of the German armies would ensure the overthrow, in Germany itself, of the military domination which had
made Germany an intolerable menace to the world.

Among the supporters of the Lansdowne movement there
were many who were influenced by unworthy motives—failure
of nerve, lack of courage, dislike of prolonged and increasing
discomfort. There were also many unworthy motives, it must be
admitted, on the other side—sheer hatred, the desire to have the
enemy at one's mercy and to inflict upon him an unprecedented
punishment. But if we agree that the motives of those who were
determined to go on were in the main heroic and admirable, it
should also be allowed that the better motives on the other side
were neither unreasonable nor unpatriotic. It is quite impossible
to dogmatize on the might-have-beens of history, quite impossible to say what would have been the result of a resolute effort
for peace, emanating from the British Government, at the end
of 1917, or whether that result would have given us a better
post-war world than that which we are now fated to enjoy.

CHAPTER XV

1918

As the war entered on its final phase it achieved a sudden simplification. It was no longer a question of what we ought to do, but whether we could do it. The three middle years—endless years they seemed—had been years of entrenchment at the front and altercation everywhere else: should we fight here or fight there, fight this way or fight that way? From March 21st onwards until November 11th there was obviously only one stupendous thing to be done.

The outline of the story is simple enough. For the first time since the Western Front had stabilized, the Germans had a clear numerical majority over the Franco-British forces—a preponderance of about five to four. They owed this preponderance in part to their victory over Russia and the consequent transference of German troops from east to west; in part also, as critics of our orthodox tactics have since emphasized, to the long series of our wasteful offensives from Neuve Chapelle to Passchendaele. Between March 21st and midsummer the Germans made three tremendous assaults on widely separated sections of the Allied front, the first and second against the British, the third against the French. All three swept right over the opposing systems of defence as no Allied offensives of the previous three years had ever done, except, on its own small scale, the tank attack at Cambrai. The first German attack might have pierced to Amiens and produced a complete separation of the British and French armies. The second, in the north, might have driven through to the coast, cut off the northern section of our armies, and deprived us of our main line of communication through Calais and Boulogne. The third might have cut the French in two and secured Paris. Each of the three attacks was stayed after a desperate week, and the Germans were left with three enormous 'bulges' to defend, the embarrassing consequences of partial success. Meanwhile the Americans were pouring into France at a rate, so we were told, of one American every five seconds, day and night.

In July the Germans delivered a fourth attack, against the French on the Reims front. It failed, and Foch's counter-attack, with immense numbers of small tanks, began. The British attack on the Amiens front, a tank attack of unprecedented dimensions, opened on August 8th. From that date onwards Allied offensives followed in rapid succession, now here and now there. The enemy were never given time to recover. We had them on the run. We advanced up to the line of the previous winter: we crossed it: the retreat became general and continuous.

And then things began to happen in places whose existence we had, since March 21st, almost forgotten. The Salonika front came to life, and Bulgaria was out of the war. General Allenby made a superb northward drive through Palestine and Syria; the Mesopotamian army advanced from Baghdad to Mosul, and Turkey was out of the war. Austria crumbled before the Italian advance. Meanwhile the first rumblings of the German Revolution were audible; the new German Government appealed to America and President Wilson was booming his Fourteen Points across the Atlantic. It was the end.

Why did the Germans succeed in breaking through the reputedly impregnable Western Front on March 21st?

The problem may be approached from either side, German success to grasp, or British failure to hold. On the German side were new artillery and infantry tactics, involving the element of surprise, the same tactics as had secured the German recovery at Cambrai—not tanks, for the Germans never realized the significance of that master key of modern war until it had defeated them. There was also on their side the fickle element which plays so large a part in war as in sport, the luck of the weather. On the morning of the 21st, the defence was blinded by a curtain of mist.

But these things were not all. When we turn from the German success to the British failure we confront an extremely unpleasant subject. There had long been complete lack of confidence and cordial co-operation between the British Prime Minister and the Commander-in-Chief of the British armies. They were no doubt an ill-matched pair; on one side an ecstatic and voluble Welsh rhetorician, a man of slapdash genius, a brilliant amateur of war who, without ever bothering to grasp the elementary grammar of the science, yet often struck out undeniably brilliant ideas in the sphere of the higher strategy; on the other side a phlegmatic and extremely inarticulate Lowland Scot, intensely professional in outlook, confident in the mastery of his art which had secured for him the foremost place, without a rival, among the members of his own profession in his own country. It may be said—indeed it must be said—that Sir Douglas Haig was unduly slow in recognizing the significance of tanks. In that matter he erred with all the rest of the higher commanders on both sides. In all other respects his professional competence was immaculate. It is probably true to say that he made fewer mistakes than any other commander, British or French, on the Western Front.

Being unable to penetrate the mind of Sir Douglas Haig and unwilling to face the consequences of removing him from his command, Mr. Lloyd George set himself to get round the obstacle. An inter-Allied Executive Committee at Versailles with uncertain powers of general control over operations on the Western and Italian fronts was created in January. This committee seemed designed to encroach upon the functions of the Chief of the Imperial General Staff, and Sir William Robertson, always a staunch supporter of Sir Douglas Haig, was dismissed, his place being taken by Sir Henry Wilson. More serious than this, Sir Douglas Haig had been persuaded, in fact compelled against his own better judgment, in face of the combined pressure of the British and French Governments and the French Higher Command, to take over fourteen additional miles of the Western Front. To those who measured in miles, the extension might seem reasonable, for the British front was not much more than one-third of the stretch from the sea to Switzerland. But practically half the German army was already concentrated on that third, and German reinforcements from Russia were being steadily drafted in the same direction. Finally, in spite of this extension of the British line, the War Cabinet refused to reinforce Sir Douglas Haig from England. On March 21st 800,000 Germans attacked 300,000 British; on the same day there were 300,000 trained troops at home, which might as easily have been in France. Mr. Churchill, back in office again and Minister of Munitions, had protested, but in vain. Mr. Lloyd George was afraid that, if Sir Douglas Haig was given the troops, he would waste them in 'another Passchendaele' before the Americans arrived. In order to make sure that their commander should not attack, the British Government starved his resources for defence.

After the blow had fallen, these troops were of course hurried into France. General Gough, the commander of the weakened front which had been overwhelmed, was relieved of his command. Sir Frederick Maurice, Director of Military Operations at the War Office, was also dismissed. He had published a statement impugning certain figures given by the Prime Minister. Mr. Asquith called for an enquiry in the House of Commons. A confused debate followed, in which Mr. Lloyd George laid stress on the unsuitability of such discussion in the very crisis of the war. The 'Maurice debate' marked the final cleavage in the Liberal party. Every member who supported Mr. Asquith on this occasion was marked down for destruction in the 'coupon' election after the Armistice.

Why was it that the attack, having succeeded so far and overwhelmed the prepared position of the defence, was not able to push right through and succeed altogether? A sufficient answer would be that, under modern conditions, an attack inevitably loses impetus as it advances: as it presses forward into conquered country it loses touch with its own long, elaborated system of roads and railways on which its supplies of ammunition depend. If the retreating army maintains its defence, the defence will eventually find itself equal to the weakening attack.

But this general answer can be supplemented. A new use was found for aircraft. Captain Liddell Hart writes: 'When the British front broke in March 1918 all the available fighter squadrons, French as well as British, were concentrated to strike at the advancing enemy. Their overhead counter-attacks during this crisis were an important factor in stemming the German onrush, and one that has been inadequately recognized.' In the 1914 numbers of *Land and Water*, where Mr. Belloc published his widely read military appreciations, a certain Captain Blin Desbleds used to advance daring theories of the possibilities of aircraft. One of his articles was entitled 'The Vertical Battle'. At last the vertical battle was staged.

There is a story that the first time Foch saw an aeroplane he said: 'That is good sport, but for the army the aeroplane is worthless.' The Italian campaign of 1911 in Tripoli had demonstrated the value of aircraft as scouts, but in the first months of 1914 the British army was apparently the only one to make efficient use of its aeroplanes, forty-four in number. One air reconnaissance discovered the initial attempt to outflank the British army at Mons, and another, a fortnight later, brought the first news of the changing direction of Kluck's army before the battle of the Marne. Rival air scouting led to air fighting, and the duels of single planes developed into the duels of organized squadrons. The machine gun succeeded the rifle as the weapon of the air. The story of the war in the air is not only a record of well-nigh incredible feats of arms but also a record of steady and rapid development, mechanical and tactical, on both sides. For brief periods the Germans shot ahead and acquired air supremacy; during the greater part of the war air supremacy was with the Allies. But it is probable that neither side ever fully exploited the possibilities of aircraft in wrecking the enemy's communications.

But there was yet another reason for the breakdown of the German offensive after it had penetrated the British lines. Many a victorious army in the good old days was demoralized by the loot of victory, and so it was now. The half-starved German armies entered a land of milk and honey—and alcohol, left behind in abundance by the retreating British armies. They were demoralized by the good things set before them; they were demoralized also by the discovery that they had been fed with lies by their own Government. They had been told that the German U-boats had reduced the British to a destitution more desperate than their own, and here was convincing proof to the contrary. It may well be that the captured loot of that last week of March first convinced the rank and file of the German armies that they could never win the war.[1]

An immediate result of the disaster of March 21st was the establishment of 'unity of command' under Foch. Of this event a very misleading conception was formed at the time. At last, it was supposed, Mr. Lloyd George had overcome the obstinacy of Sir Douglas Haig, and had forced upon him a French superior. At last the Welsh wizard and the French Napoleon had come together over the head of the British general. The true story was very different. The proposal, in fact, originated with Sir Douglas Haig. His original orders, given to him personally by Lord Kitchener more than two years before, had been to 'keep united with the French at all costs', and now the French commander-in-chief, Pétain, declared his intention of breaking with the British and withdrawing eastwards to cover Paris. Fresh from his interview with Pétain on March 24th, Sir Douglas Haig telegraphed to Lord Milner, then Secretary of State for War, and

[1] On this subject Captain Liddell Hart, *The Real War*, pp. 427-9, gives striking evidence by quotation from a German war diary.

Sir Henry Wilson to come over immediately. They had, in fact, already started. Lord Milner went to Paris and saw Clemenceau, who had recently become Prime Minister of France. Then followed the famous meeting at Doullens at which it was Sir Douglas Haig who insisted that Foch should be given control over the whole of his own and Pétain's armies. It was the French, not the British, commander who was overruled in the interests of a united action.

On April 9th the second German assault broke through on a narrower frontage, just south of Ypres, and the battle of the Lys began before the battle in front of Amiens was ended. Three days later Sir Douglas Haig issued to his troops the unforgettable order: 'There is no course open to us but to fight it out. Every position must be held to the last man. There must be no retirement. With our backs to the wall and believing in the justice of our cause, each one of us must fight on to the end.' The simple statement and exhortation had the greater force as coming from one of the least dramatic of great men, a man who had coined no epigrams, sounded no clarion calls, and indeed taken no pains to impress his personality on the army or the nation.

The two battles covered the last ten days of March and the whole of April. Together they constituted the severest ordeal that the British army has ever endured. By the end of these six weeks one quarter of the British troops in France on March 21st were killed, wounded, or prisoners. And yet by June the British forces on the Western Front were stronger again than they had been on March 21st. Reinforcements had been poured in from home, from Salonika, from Palestine. As for munitions, the enormous losses of the week, March 21st-28th, were all incredibly replaced by April 6th. By the last year of the war the Ministry of Munitions had become a well-oiled machine of enormous productivity, the largest industrial organization ever created. Easter fell early that year, and the Minister issued instructions that, in a long list of factories, there should be no cessation of work during the Easter week-end. The only unfavourable response came from some groups of factories not included in the list, where the workers felt that, since they were not also asked to sacrifice their holidays, their efforts were being disparaged.

At home, the month of April was filled with rather hectic debates on 'man power'. A new Conscription Bill was carried, extending the age limit of military service and bringing Ireland within the sphere of conscription. Neither of these measures made any positive contribution to our military resources, and the second of them produced a storm which threw Ireland irrevocably into the arms of Sinn Fein, thus providing the 'Aftermath' with one of its principal problems. There was a drastic 'combing out' of industrial workers, 50,000 men being taken from the coalmines, a very well justified measure, even though it lowered the temperature in many homes in the ensuing winter —the winter of the Armistice and the influenza. Much more productive, however, than the exploitation of any home resource was the appeal to President Wilson to send all the troops he could as quickly as he could, without waiting for formation in complete and autonomous American armies. President Wilson responded nobly to an appeal which certainly involved a sacrifice of American national pride, and from that moment onwards the Americans began to flow in. Nearly 2,000,000 arrived before the Armistice, and well over a million took part in the fighting.

After the British battles had died down there ensued a pause of nearly a month, and on May 27th the blow fell upon the French in Champagne. Once again, and for the last time, the Germans scored a dramatic, but local and incomplete, success.

Many authorities maintain that by his three 'victories' in the spring of 1918 Ludendorff lost the war. He threw away the German advantage in numbers, for his casualties were nearly fifty per cent in excess of those of the Allies. He greatly extended the length of his lines, and threw away the advantages of well-prepared and carefully chosen positions. He should have stood his ground and waited for the Allies to repeat their performances of previous years. Again, a similar line of argument reaches the conclusion that, in the latter part of the year he could and ought to have effected a withdrawal to the comparatively short line extending north and south from the south-eastern corner of Holland to Verdun, and again awaited the onslaught of the enemy. But in fact Ludendorff had no choice in the matter. Other than military factors were involved. It may be that if one regards war, absurdly, as an affair of armies fighting as it were *in vacuo*, the German army could have secured a stalemate, though the development of the tank renders this very doubtful. But wars are between nations, and the German nation was crumbling under the stress of the blockade. Sea power, which inevitably fills so small a space in any brief account of the activities of the war, was none the less the finally deciding factor. America decided the war against Germany when she gave Great Britain permission to enforce an absolute and throttling blockade. It was not that the German people were physically starved to death, though many of them came uncomfortably near it. Partial starvation was enough. It altered the minds of the German people, and on the minds of the German people the continuance of the war ultimately depended.

We must take a last glance at England in war time before proceeding to the turn of the tide and the final stages of the war. It may be a brief glance, for very few new features appeared in 1918. For the man—and the woman—who stayed at home 1918 was a continuation of 1917 with all its features intensified.

The standard rate of income tax, which had been one and eightpence at the beginning of the war, three shillings in 1915, five shillings in 1916 and 1917, rose to six shillings in the pound, where it was to remain until 1922. An immense revenue was also derived from the Excess Profits Tax which was intended to skim off five-sixths of business profits due to war conditions. None the less there was an immense apparent prosperity, in which Capital and Labour each participated in their own degrees, a 'fungoid prosperity' no doubt, for which we should have to pay somehow or other, on the outbreak of peace. From an economic standpoint the prospect of peace was as alarming as the prospect of an indefinite continuation of the war. For the present however 'profiteers' abounded; some of them declared themselves quite honestly ashamed of the fortunes they had made and could not help making. Fortunes were as unavoidable in the industrial field as wounds and death in the field of battle. Wage earners, too, were much better off than they had ever been before, not because wages soared high above their pre-war relationship to prices—this in the main they never did—but because overtime work and the earnings of womenfolk added up an unprecedented family income. Stories, often true and often ill-natured, of the grotesque extravagance of wage earners were retailed amid much head-shaking in middle-class circles. Certainly the war achieved for the working classes standards of dress and food from which they have never consented to go back. Sound incomes in working-class homes and food rations for all combined to secure that 'for the first time in the history of England the necessaries of life are distributed with some reference to social justice. . . . Far fewer families in the British Isles failed to get not only a full but even an extravagant Christmas dinner in 1917 than in 1913.'[1]

If it needed a world war to secure everyone a good Christmas dinner, it also needed a world war to make the British farmer confess that he was doing fairly well. In 1918 he was at the apex of his brief prosperity. Four million extra acres were growing corn, the acreage under potatoes had increased 50 per cent in two years even though this calculation excluded the potatoes grown on 800,000 new allotments. The food situation was well in hand: we were getting accustomed to a variety of 'substitutes' at first regarded as inedible, and the Food Controller was promising, in June, an improvement in the quality of war bread.

On the surface, life was not only prosperous but extremely gay. When the war began the theatres had been deserted. Many

[1] *Round Table*. March 1918.

felt disinclined for that sort of thing; others felt that, whatever
their inclinations, it was indecent to amuse oneself when others
were 'at the war'. This early war-puritanism was broken down
by the soldiers home on leave. They wanted to have a good
time, and it would not be a really good time unless their friends
and relations shared it with them. Thus organized amusement,
like the press, soon emerged from its 1914 eclipse. By the end of
the war everyone was in war work, and everyone was consequently entitled to a good time. Charlie Chaplin arrived, and
soon achieved a celebrity equal to President Wilson. Certainly
no Americans had ever before made such an impression on the
British public as these two.

No chapters in the social history of war time are so important
as those which concern the new activities of women, with the
moral and psychological consequences involved. Something has
already been said of the invasion of munition industries by
women workers from 1915 onwards. They had, of course, found
scope for war service in nursing from the very beginning of the
war. The new feature of 1917-18 was the development of auxiliary corps of uniformed women, attached to the army, the navy,
and the air service, the W.A.A.C. the W.R.N.S. and the
W.R.A.F. The titles behind these letters can be deciphered by
the studious: actually they were called the Wacks, the Wrens,
and the Raffs. Their purpose was to perform, within the fighting
organizations both at home and at the front, all kinds of duties
which are as well, or better, done by women than by men. The
'Wrens' were the pioneer service. Their director ranked as an
admiral, and naval officers were required to salute all W.R.N.S.
officers, who were to acknowledge such salutes by 'a bow and a
smile'.

The picture of 1918 at home would not be complete if one
omitted the Coventry strike. It is a singular illustration of the
anfractuosities of the Labour mind that 12,000 workers in aircraft factories should have struck work about virtually nothing
just when the Allied advance was about to begin. The point at

issue was the so-called Embargo. In order to ensure the best possible distribution of engineers, the Ministry of Munitions had published a list of about a hundred firms which were forbidden to take any more members of the A.S.E. (Amalgamated Society of Engineers) into their employ, because other firms were in fact handicapped by a shortage of these skilled men. There was, as usual, a misunderstanding. The 12,000 in Coventry struck because they regarded the Embargo as a step towards the 'conscription of industry'. The strike collapsed when the Government announced that all who did not immediately return to work would forfeit their 'cards' and render themselves liable to immediate recruitment for the army.

The tide turned with Foch's counter-attack in the Second Battle of the Marne, in the middle of July. The British joined in on August 8th in front of Amiens. The British attack, with 450 tanks, was a masterpiece of surprise, every kind of device being used, with success, to persuade the Germans that the blow would fall elsewhere. Ludendorff's remark, to the effect that August 8th was 'the black day of the war' is well known. Another German commander said: 'It was not the genius of Marshal Foch that beat us but "General Tank".' It is impossible to give any definite order of precedence to the various factors which combined to ensure the Allied victory—tank tactics, unity of command under Foch, and the American reinforcement. There were also, as has already been said, other factors not military, the blockade breaking down the German national will behind her armies. If at the time popular propaganda, always in search of a superman, overstressed the personal contribution of Foch, it would be wrong to go to the other extreme and depreciate him. He manipulated the distribution of his reserves and the incidence of his successive onslaughts with consummate skill. Not the least proof of the greatness of the man was his readiness to accept the suggestions of others, and particularly of Sir Douglas Haig. It was Haig, it seems, who convinced Foch that the attack could and therefore ought to be pushed right on to final decision before the end of the year. In 1914 a British soldier was the first to proclaim that the war would be long; almost exactly four years afterwards another British soldier was the first to realize that its remainder would be short.

This opinion was not shared at home. At the end of July Sir Henry Wilson submitted to the Cabinet a detailed examination of the military position, leading up to six conclusions, the third of which states that 'July 1919 should be kept in mind as a date for the opening of the main offensive campaign', and in his diary of the same date he records that Mr. Lloyd George, Lord Milner and General Smuts, with the other Dominion Premiers (except Hughes of Australia) 'are of opinion that we cannot beat the Boche on the Western Front'. As late as the end of September Sir Douglas Haig was cautioned from home against excessive expenditure of force in his attack on the Hindenburg line. The Home authorities were still afraid of 'another Passchendaele'.

With such views prevailing in the highest quarters it is not surprising that the general public was slow to realize what was in store for it. We were, perhaps, determined not to fool ourselves once more with hopes of speedy victory. It has been said that 1918 was the only year of the war in which most Englishmen did not expect the war to end. At first we visualized these advances as no more than a return to the old front through which the Germans had broken in the spring. The first event to open our eyes was the Bulgarian armistice of September 29th. Here indeed was something quite unmistakable and irrevocable, the surrender of one, even though the smallest, of the four enemy Governments. Only a fortnight before, the heterogeneous forces, French, British, Greek, Serbian and Italian, which maintained the Salonika front, weakened by disease and ill supported by artillery, had set themselves in motion against the mountainous frontier of Bulgaria. The Bulgarian forces under Mackensen could have defended their positions had they wished to do so, but they refused to fight. Intelligence received from France convinced them that Germany had lost the war.

News of the Bulgarian armistice reached Ludendorff just as the general Allied offensive was breaking through the Hindenburg line. It broke his resolution. Four days later, by his instructions, the newly appointed German Chancellor, Prince Max of Baden, appealed to President Wilson for an immediate armistice. But President Wilson was not to be hurried. For another five weeks war raged on. Turkey collapsed; Austria-Hungary resolved itself into its racial elements; the German fleet mutinied; the Kaiser abdicated, and all the other petty royalties of the German Empire vanished into space. It was more than victory: it was chaos.

The first Armistice day was celebrated in what might be supposed to be the proper manner: immense crowds thronged the streets, and the sound of revelry was heard far into the night. But all that was superficial, and soon over. The Armistice marked a cessation, a vacuity, and at first nothing more. The nation was overtired, underfed, just exhausted. A surprisingly large number of people were either sickening for or recovering from influenza. Statistics no doubt can prove that 1918-19 was not far the coldest autumn and winter of modern times, but shortage of fats and shortage of coal combined to make it seem so. The dawn of the post-war world was a very grey and chilly dawn. We sat shivering round very small fires—in our overcoats, to economize coal —and wondered what would happen next. War had stopped; but would peace come, and what would it be like?

PART III
THE AFTERMATH
1918-1922

CHAPTER XVI

PEACE AT HOME
THE BOOM YEARS 1919-20

Three days after the Armistice announcement was made that a general election would follow with the least possible delay. The campaign filled the month before Christmas, and the result was announced on December 28th—478 Coalitionists, 59 Labour men, mostly solid trade unionists who had supported the war, and only 27 Asquithian Liberals. The greatest victory in the field had been followed by the greatest victory in the ballot box.

Much righteous indignation has been expended on this 'Coupon Election'. One is almost led to suppose that it was the fount and origin of all the misfortunes that followed, that the fruits of victory, potentially so 'rare and refreshing' on November 11th, were transformed into Dead Sea apples by a month's tournament of vulgar oratory. Exactly a year after the election Mr. Keynes published his *Economic Consequences of the Peace*, a book important not only by reason of its intrinsic merit but also because, as the first sustained attack, at once popular in style and profound in argument, upon post-armistice policy, it exercised an enormous influence on public opinion. Mr. Keynes declared that the election was 'an act of political immorality', implying that its sole purpose was to secure Mr. Lloyd George and his colleagues a further lease of power, before they became entangled in the controversies of peace, international and domestic.

But an election, an immediate election, was inevitable. It was inherent in the logic of democracy. Indeed—and this fact seems

to have been almost completely forgotten—an election at the
end of 1918, when the new register including the women over
thirty was ready, had been widely forecasted and advocated at
a time when it was assumed that the war would be still in progress. In the *Round Table* of September 1918 we read: 'It is
generally expected that the new register will be completed this
autumn and that a general election will be held before the close
of the year. The arguments against a wartime election are obvious . . . but there is a widespread feeling that a House of
Commons which was elected four years before the war can no
longer adequately fulfil the object of its being. . . . It is imperative that the conclusion of the war and the settlement of the
terms of peace should be controlled, as far as this country is
concerned, by a body which truly represents the new spirit and
the new purposes of its people.' The writer goes on to say that a
victory for Mr. Lloyd George's Government may be confidently
expected, and that such a victory ought to improve its character, by delivering its leader from what was at present his worst
temptation, namely, a tendency to look for support to the magnates of the popular press rather than to the people's accredited
representatives.

Argument that the election could have been postponed until
some unspecified condition which we may call 'the crisis of
peace' was over, is based upon two unwarranted assumptions:
the first, that the game of democracy can be played with reservations, and the second, that 'the crisis of peace' would prove
to be a period of limited and brief duration. The only logical
alternative to an immediate election would have been a dictatorship 'for three years or the duration of the Aftermath'.

As for the much derided 'coupon', it also lay in the logic of
the facts. The facts, from the point of view of party politics, were
that the war had been carried to a triumphant issue by the
Conservative party, acting in co-operation with a number of
individuals who had broken loose from the other parties. The
Conservatives were not prepared to allow seats to be won with-

out a contest by any non-Conservative who had not proved himself a dependable supporter of the Coalition. To such candidates letters of approval, over the signature of Mr. Lloyd George and Mr. Bonar Law, were issued. Outside mining constituencies and a few other Labour strongholds these 'coupons' proved, in fact, a fairly safe passport to acceptance by the electorate.

When we pass to the programme and the electioneering tactics of the Coalitionists we are on more debatable ground. One would like to be able to think that these politicians, for whom we hold no briefs, were the villains of the piece. One would like to think that, in spite of the daily guidance of Lord Northcliffe and Lord Beaverbrook and their underlings, the electorate of November 1918 was capable of responding to wise, generous, and idealistic counsels of a peace of forgiveness and reconciliation, which would staunch the wounds of war and start a re-united world on a course of mutual co-operation. Mr. Keynes provides what he truly calls 'a sad, dramatic history' of the moral decline and fall of the Coalition statesmen, from the moderation of their first movement down to the frantic yells of 'Hang the Kaiser' and 'Make Germany pay for the whole cost of the war', the *allegro furioso* with which their electioneering symphony concluded. He suggests that this decline and fall was prompted only by the press and by the party organizers. Mr. Churchill may not be a wiser man than Mr. Keynes but he had the advantage, as a witness, of having fought the election. By his account the electorate was frantic from the start. Plato's Beast was unchained, and his keepers had to humour him unless they were prepared to be devoured. For that fate they were certainly not prepared, and it must be admitted that a statesman with a different sort of courage from that of Mr. Lloyd George might have insisted in his election speeches, and compelled his colleagues also to insist, on the fact that the terms of the Armistice had set definite bounds to the damages we were entitled to claim from Germany. This he did not do, and the omission was to cost him dear. But saving clauses and cautionary qualifications have never been in Mr. Lloyd George's line, and to expect them of him in December 1918 would be to ask for something outside the range of his character.

In fact the Armistice election was an inevitable testing of democracy, in which it was almost inevitable that democracy should fail. The result was, of course, deplorable. It cheapened England in the eyes of Europe and America. It involved Mr. Lloyd George in a hundred embarrassments when, resuming once again the role of statesman, he pleaded for moderation and good sense at Paris. It provided England, during four years that were to be packed full of industrial crises and social problems, with the wealthiest, the least intelligent, and the least representative House of Commons since Waterloo. Mr. Keynes asked a Conservative friend who had known previous Houses, what he thought of the new House. 'They are a lot of hard-faced men who look as if they had done very well out of the war,' said Mr. Keynes's friend.

The first problems confronting the Government were the correlatives of those which had confronted the Government of 1914 —the outbreak of peace, demobilization in the widest sense of the word. To get out of the war was almost as difficult as to get into it, and its problems had, in spite of window-dressing Ministries of Reconstruction, been much less carefully prepared in advance. The War Book compiled by Mr. Asquith's Government in advance of 1914 might be criticized, no doubt, as inadequate in view of the event, but it was a veritable encyclopaedia compared with the Peace Book available in 1918. And there was this further difference. On the outbreak of war people quite understood that they must do what they were told; indeed the common and well-grounded patriotic complaint throughout the first half of the war was that the Government did not do enough commanding. Conversely, however, the ordinary man's idea of demobilization was that he should henceforth, with the least possible delay, be set free to do whatever he liked, the

Government ensuring that the consequences of his free action would be as agreeable as they ought to be.

This was not understood by those who had prepared the official scheme for the demobilization of the armies. The idea of the scheme was that men should be released in the order dictated by the needs of industry. It was unfortunate that those whom industry wanted most were generally the very men whom industry had, during the war, most reluctantly let go, the men, that is, whose military service had been shortest. The rest were to wait, mitigating the boredom of inactive service with liberal and vocational education. The result was a succession of mutinies. Mr. Churchill, having already set in motion the demobilization of the munition factories, was hurried across to the War Office, when he scrapped his predecessor's scheme, and set to work demobilizing at the rate of 50,000 a day, priority being given to length of service and number of wounds. Thus the armies melted away—though they could not be allowed to melt away altogether. Post-war requirements, during the 'transition period' were estimated at 900,000, and this number was secured, partly by retaining in the army the last six months' conscripts, who had seen no active service, and partly by offering drastically improved pay to those who would enlist in the post-war army.

The war had extinguished unemployment, and peace was expected to bring it back on an unprecedented scale, with the armies and munition factories pouring their millions on to the streets. The unemployment insurance scheme inherited from pre-war days, a somewhat experimental appendix to the Health Insurance Act of 1911, was a very modest measure. It applied only to a very few trades, such as engineering, and the benefits were only seven shillings a week. The Government now promised to prepare a complete scheme of contributory unemployment insurance. Meantime, and to fill the gap before the new measure could reach the Statute Book, all unemployed ex-soldiers and ex-munition workers were to be entitled, without contribution, to a weekly 'dole' of twenty-five shillings. In January 1919 two-thirds of those entitled to this donation were said to be drawing it, but what followed was one of the few pleasant surprises of the post-war years. Industry absorbed practically all that was offered it. Though about 4,000,000 men were demobilized from the fighting forces the number of the unemployed exactly a year after the Armistice was only 350,000 and throughout the greater part of 1920 it was much less than that. Indeed one may say that for two whole years—until the last month of 1920—there was, practically speaking, employment for all. Before the post-war slump came the post-war boom. All the world bought what it had been unable to buy during the war, whether it could afford it or not. Prices and wages pursued one another upwards in a 'vicious circle', as though unaware that the war was over.

There was very little unemployment in 1919, but it would be a mistake to suppose that all were quietly and contentedly busy. The strikes of 1919 surpassed all previous records. By the end of June more days' work had been lost through strikes than in the whole of any pre-war year, and by the end of the year the number of days' work lost reached the astronomical figure of 32,000,000. In other words, an average of over a hundred thousand men had been on strike every day of the year.

It is easy to find half a dozen good reasons for the post-war epidemic of strikes. Psychologically, the workers had not yet settled down to an accepted routine after the war adventure; nor were they prepared to settle down to a routine which was not a great improvement on anything they had known before the war. Spokesmen of the Government had promised 'a land fit for heroes to live in'—this had become one of the stock phrases of the day. Well, the heroes were back in industry, ready and waiting: where were their new habitations? Nor should it be supposed that the phrase about 'a land fit for heroes', though a theme of bitter mockery among the intellectuals of labour, was not accepted at something near its face value by the rank and file who first voted the Coalition Government into power and then proceeded to render its life a burden. Economically, the war had proved—what had it proved? No one knows whether anything is proved in the sphere of economics. But at least the war displayed possibilities of extravagant expenditure undreamed of before 1914. If it was possible for the State (that mysterious abstraction) to spend seven millions a day on killing Germans, what could not now be spent on making the British workman happy?

Then there was Russia. It is very difficult to trace the influence of the Russian Revolution on British working-class opinion. Few certainly enrolled themselves as Communists, but there can be little doubt that the fact of Socialism established and in action, in the seat of one of the Great Powers, powerfully influenced the aspirations of organized Labour. A Trade Union Memorandum of 1919, signed by Mr. Henderson as Secretary of the Labour party and by Mr. G. D. H. Cole as Secretary of the Labour Research Department, declared that 'the fundamental causes of Labour unrest are to be found rather in the growing determination of Labour to challenge the whole existing structure of capitalist industry than in any of the more special and smaller grievances which come to the surface at any particular time. . . . It is clear that, unless and until the Government is prepared to realize the need for comprehensive reconstruction on a democratic basis, and to formulate a constructive policy leading towards economic democracy, there can be at most no more than a temporary diminution of industrial unrest, to be followed by further waves of constantly growing magnitude.'[1]

[1] In 1887 Friedrich Engels, the friend and disciple of Marx, had predicted 'a war of unexpected duration and violence', launched by 'Prussia-Germany' in which 'eight or ten million soldiers would kill one another', and 'scrape Europe as bare as a swarm of locusts'. The result would be 'irremediable disorganization of our artificial system of commerce, industry, and credit, ending in general bankruptcy . . . crowns rolling by dozens on the pavements and no one found to pick them up: general exhaustion, and conditions out of which the working class will finally achieve victory'. This forecast was rescued from a forgotten pamphlet and published by Lenin in 1918.

Peace at Home: The Boom Years 1919-20

These were brave words, designed to arrest attention and to secure the widest publicity: but they faithfully represented the spirit of organized Labour in 1919, and that spirit must have been fairly pervasive to persuade so cautious and practical a negotiator as Mr. Thomas to declare that those he spoke for 'stood unalterably for the ownership by the State of the mines, railways, and the means of inland transport'.

But it is possible to find an adequate explanation of the strike epidemic outside any questions of high industrial policy. In ordinary times the organizations of employers and employed in each industry are in continuous contact, and each side knows that the current conditions of work and wages represent fairly accurately the balance of power between their respective forces. Moreover, prices are stable and consequently the real value of the wages is assured. At the end of 1918 none of these conditions existed. For four years the normal processes of collective bargaining had been suspended, and wages fixed by Government departments. In consequence, when the embargo on strikes was removed, neither party to the industrial struggle knew its own strength or the strength of its opponent; it had no reason for supposing that the existing arbitrary wage represented the balance of industrial forces, and, with prices continuing to rise, it had no means of valuing those wages in relation to any particular standard of living. In fact the Government, envisaging widespread unemployment, had anticipated an industrial offensive from the employers against the continuance of war wages, and had hurried through Parliament a Wages Temporary Regulation Act making the standard rates of wages legal minima for six months. But 1919-20 produced a boom instead of a slump, with the consequence that industrial aggression came from the side of the workers, and the Wages Act lost significance.

To describe even a representative selection of the post-war strikes would be an undertaking out of scale with the rest of this book. Public interest and anxiety concentrated on the activities of the miners and the railwaymen, partly because their unions involved respectively a million and half a million workers, partly because a strike in either industry paralysed the industrial life of the country; and partly because these unions together with the transport workers had bound themselves together in a Triple Alliance. Whenever any one of these three unions was in trouble the Triple Alliance was supposed to be in readiness just round the corner, and a strike of the Triple Alliance would in effect be the 'General Strike'—even in pre-war days the bogy of the bourgeoisie and the aspiration of class-conscious proletarians.

Yet the Triple Alliance was not, in intention, a machine for organizing the 'General Strike' as understood by revolutionary socialists. It was something much less ambitious. The idea of it had arisen out of the experiences of 1911 and 1912. In the course of those years the railwaymen, the miners, and the dockers had each undertaken strikes at different periods, with unsatisfactory results, and each strike had inflicted serious losses on the other two industries. The plan of the Triple Alliance was originally no more than that, on some subsequent occasion, the three great industries should present their respective demands and take action on them simultaneously. Oddly enough, as it must seem to the outsider, this practical and promising plan was never put into execution. Each union went ahead along its own lines and at its own time and then looked around in expectation of a 'sympathetic' strike. But the sympathetic strike had never been within the terms of the Alliance, and cries of 'Traitor!' were beside the point.

The Triple Alliance began promisingly enough with the issue of simultaneous ultimatums in January 1919. The miners demanded full wages from State funds for unemployed miners; the reduction of the working day from eight hours to six; a thirty per cent advance on present earnings, other than war wages, which were to be continued, and the nationalization of all mines and minerals. The railwaymen demanded that all increases given as war bonuses should be converted into permanent

wages; an eight hours' working day with double pay for overtime, etc.; and the transport workers made demands similar to
those of the railwaymen. The miners' programme was obviously
of an altogether different order of magnitude from those of the
other unions, and under the leadership of Mr. Smillie and Mr.
Hodges, both of whom were at that time among the extremists,
they proceeded to ignore their allies and gave notice of a strike
for March 17th. The Government replied with the offer of a
Commission, the Sankey Commission, which was to produce an
interim report on hours and wages in March and a final report
on the nationalization issue not later than June. The miners
consented to suspend their strike notices until they had seen the
interim report.

The members of the Sankey Commission were selected on a
novel, and as it proved mistaken, principle: the principle generally deemed appropriate to Peace Conferences but abandoned
by the great Peace Conference which was assembling in Paris at
this very time. Each of the belligerents, miners and mineowners,
was invited to nominate three commissioners, and the Government added three theoretical socialists on the side of the miners
and three industrial magnates on the side of the employers.
There remained the choice of the 'neutral' chairman. Real
neutrals are proverbially hard to find in war time. What the
Government wanted was such a chairman as President Wilson
would in his own estimation have been if, in accordance with
his 1916 plans, he had kept America out of the war to the end,
and then imposed himself on both exhausted belligerents as the
organizer of peace. Actually the choice fell upon Mr. Justice
Sankey; he was professionally accustomed to weighing evidence
with impartiality, but he was also known, to Mr. Lloyd George
and the miners though not to the general public, as a man in
sympathy with the Labour movement. Indeed he subsequently
became Lord Chancellor in a Labour Government.

Only by a miracle could a Commission so constituted have
produced a unanimous report. None the less, the upshot was

interesting. The Interim Report (or Reports) appeared punctually on the day advertised. The three miners and the three socialists combined to advertise their unfitness for negotiation by merely recapitulating the demands of the miners' ultimatum. The three mineowners conceded an increased wage of eighteen pence a day and the reduction of hours from eight to seven. The three independent industrialists joined with the chairman in proposing an increased wage of half a crown a day and the progressive reduction of hours to seven, and at a later date to six 'provided that the economic condition of the industry should prove able to stand it'. But the Chairman went further, and declared that 'even upon the evidence already given the present system of ownership and working stands condemned'. This was quite outside the questions of hours and wages to which the Interim Report was supposed to be confined. It was, no doubt, intended as an indication to all concerned that the Chairman's final Report would make at any rate some advance in the direction of nationalization.

The Government at once announced its acceptance of this Report, and, after discussions prolonged over nearly a month, the miners did the same.

When the final Reports appeared the Chairman, supported by the three miners and the three socialists recommended a scheme of nationalization for the whole mining industry. The mineowners, supported by two of the industrialists, favoured the retention of the present system, with trivial improvements. The remaining industrialist, Sir Arthur Duckham, proposed an elaborate scheme which may have combined the advantages of both systems but was unacceptable to the supporters of either. The Government was now in a quandary. Mr. Lloyd George had used words which suggested that the final Sankey Report would be accepted as a basis for immediate legislation, but it was quite certain that neither his colleagues nor his majority in the House of Commons would consent to nationalize the mines on the advice (for that was what it amounted to) of a single

High Court Judge. The Government could only reject the Report, and offer in its stead a diluted version of Sir Arthur Duckham's scheme, which was at once rejected by the miners. But no strike followed. There had already been a Yorkshire miners' strike, arising out of certain details of the wage award in March, with unsatisfactory results. The miners, having got a part of what they wanted in wages and reduced hours, contented themselves with appealing to the Trade Union Congress which, in September, called upon the Government to nationalize the mines, threatening in the event of its refusal to 'take steps' to compel it to do so. This was the least the Trade Union Congress could do in the circumstances, and for all practical purposes it amounted to nothing. The Sankey Commission had performed the useful purpose served by so many diplomatic conferences: it had tided over a crisis.

The same purpose was served in a wider industrial sphere by the abortive and forgotten experiment of the National Industrial Conference. February 1919 was marked by an absolute pandemonium of major and minor strikes and the Government 'wisely conceiving', as the writer in the *Round Table* has it, 'that the only way of clearing the air was a full and frank discussion of the industrial situation by both sides', convened a National Industrial Conference to which over a thousand representatives of employers and employed were invited. The Triple Alliance and the Amalgamated Union of Engineers refused their invitations, as did a few employers, but with these exceptions the Conference was fully representative. After listening to an appeal for common action and a united front in the style of the Prime Minister's best war speeches, the Conference appointed a Joint Committee of employers and employed, which reported in favour of a general eight-hour day and a general minimum wage. It also recommended the establishment of a permanent National Industrial Council of 400 members, elected in equal numbers by organizations of employers and employed, with a Standing Committee of fifty members, to be recognized by the Government as an official consultative authority on industrial relations. To all this the Government offered its 'immediate and sympathetic consideration'. What followed, however, was neither immediate nor sympathetic; there were doubts, hesitations and pain on both sides, in fact a sustained *diminuendo*, prolonged into the year 1921. But long before its final dissolution the Joint Committee of the National Industrial Council had lost all claims to the attention of the general public.

Yet it served a useful purpose in steadying industrial nerves during the first year after the war, and the same purpose was served in a different fashion by the abortive police strike of August 1919. In London barely five per cent but in Liverpool more than half the police came out on strike without notice. Rioting and looting ensued, and soldiers were called in to restore order. The strikers were everywhere dismissed and forfeited their pensions, with the general approval of the public. A line had to be drawn somewhere.[1]

Meanwhile the negotiations between the railwaymen and the Railway Executive Committee through which the Government continued its wartime control of the railways, had been pursuing a quiet course. There was a general realization that railwaymen had been underpaid before the war. Their post-war demands were practical, businesslike, and moderate, and entirely in character with the statesmanlike reputation of their leader, Mr. J. H. Thomas. The railwaymen were receiving, in addition to their admittedly inadequate pre-war wage, a flat-rate bonus of thirty-three shillings a week, and it had been

[1] Exactly a month later there was a police strike in Boston. The Police Commissioner of the city discharged the strikers, and began to recruit a new force. The President of the American Federation of Labour was unwise enough to send a public protest to the Governor of Massachusetts. The Governor replied, equally publicly, that there was 'no right to strike against the public safety by anybody, anywhere, anytime', and on the strength of this remark he became a national hero overnight and prospective President of the United States. He has been described as 'an insignificant, sour-faced little man', and his name was Calvin Coolidge.

agreed that this bonus should remain in force until the end of 1919. Negotiations concerned the permanent rates which were to come into force in 1920. Satisfactory terms for the engineers and firemen had been negotiated with their own union, the A.S.L.E. and F. in August. There was every reason to suppose that terms for the less well paid and more numerous grades comprised in the N.U.R. would follow on the same lines. There was therefore good cause for surprise as well as dismay when the country found itself plunged, without warning, into a nine days' railway strike at the end of September. In fact this strike, more obviously than most strikes, should never have been allowed to take place, and the Government must bear the greater share of the blame for it.

Negotiations were in the hands of Sir Auckland Geddes, whose brother, Sir Eric, had been one of the supermen of the Ministry of Munitions. The Geddes brothers had held a variety of Cabinet offices under Mr. Lloyd George and indeed were the most conspicuous examples of his talent for discovering statesmen outside the ranks of those who had served apprenticeship in the House of Commons. In his dealings with Mr. Thomas's Union Sir Auckland proved himself both dilatory and niggardly. The tendency of all recent wage awards had been a levelling up of the difference between the more skilled and less skilled grades within each industry. This tendency may not have been altogether wholesome, if one takes a long view of the needs of industry, but this was not the occasion to reverse it, and the railwaymen of the N.U.R. had every reason to expect terms at least as good, in relation to their pre-war wages, as those conceded to the engineers and firemen. The terms proposed were, in fact, distinctly worse. They were, generally speaking, one hundred per cent above pre-war level, though the official cost of living index was one hundred and fifteen per cent above that of 1914. True, it was at the moment falling, though it was destined to rise again sharply in 1920. This offer Sir Auckland declared to be 'definitive' which was presumed to mean 'final'. After a further week of conferences, the strike was declared. No such paralysis of national transport had ever been known in England before.

Mr. Thomas made no appeal to the forces of the Triple Alliance. Indeed the leaders of Labour in other industries exerted themselves, with his full approval, to bring about an ending of the strike and a resumption of negotiations between the railwaymen and the Government. Negotiations were in fact resumed after the strike at the point where they had been broken off, and resulted in the satisfactory sliding-scale agreement under which, with minor modifications, railway wages have been regulated ever since.

A railway strike inconveniences the public more immediately than any other, and during their nine days' venture the railwaymen suffered what the *Round Table* calls a 'hailstorm of public execration'. When the facts came to be known, the handling of the dispute by Sir Auckland Geddes met with general disapproval. And yet, since new rates could not come into operation in any case until the end of the year, could not Sir Auckland have been brought to reason by less drastic methods? Mr. Lloyd George denounced the strike as 'an anarchist conspiracy'. It might more accurately be called an outburst of temper. It may be that Mr. Thomas lost his temper; more likely, he realized that only by a well-calculated display of temper could he hold his associates together and retain control of them. Labour was in an explosive mood. There was a minority who believed, with Mr. Cole, that the war between nations must be followed by the war between classes; there were more who believed that the Coalition Government owed its power to a fraudulent election, that it misrepresented the country, and that a well-calculated industrial act of war might bring it down and install Labour in its place. It was the fashion at this time to comment on the political significance of the immense growth of trade unionism. In 1910 there had been only two and a half million trade unionists, in 1914 four million, in 1918 six and a half, a number still rising to the peak of eight and a quarter millions touched in 1920. In these circumstances Government officials negotiating with organized Labour had need to be firm, but also tactful and sympathetic. Sir Auckland had thought it enough to be firm.

The railway strike also proved, and the lesson was not forgotten in the General Strike six and a half years later, that the time for an effective railway strike was past. The Government, putting to new uses the powers it still enjoyed under the Defence of the Realm Act, organized every kind of volunteer effort, with the result that there was nowhere any perceptible food shortage. With each day of the strike emergency transport, whether on the railways themselves or on the roads, increased in volume. 'Motor transport', says a writer in the *Round Table*, 'is at present far too costly to compete with railway transport; but it has proved its capabilities as a substitute in emergency, and the railwaymen's claim that they could paralyse the community in twenty-four hours has lost its virtue.'

The year 1920, with industry booming and prices still soaring, produced a plentiful crop of strikes, few of which presented features of permanent interest. The industrial novelty of the year was the attempt to control the country's foreign policy by means of a political strike threatened by a group of trade-union leaders who called themselves the Council of Action.

Modern conditions had blurred the distinction between the use of the strike weapon as a means of bringing pressure upon industrial employers and its use as an argument in political controversy. It was not merely that such demands of organized Labour as nationalization, or even the enforcement of a legal minimum wage, asked for Parliamentary legislation and were thus political as well as industrial. The fact that basic industries, like the mines and the railways, still continued to be in many respects controlled by Government departments as a consequence of the war meant that the Government itself was a principal party in the negotiations, and a principal object of the

218

strikers' coercive methods. Further, even without this compli-
cating factor, nation-wide strikes in basic industries, unknown
in the nineteenth century, but commonplaces of the twentieth,
were in fact directed against the whole community, whose life
they were intended to paralyse. The Trade Union Congress had
come to think and to speak of itself as 'the Parliament of Labour'.
Mr. Williams of the Transport Workers' Union assured its delegates that 'you who have sprung from the loins of the common
people are infinitely more representative of the aims and aspirations of the democracy of this country than the House of Commons'. In this exalted mood it was but natural that the Trade
Union Congress should feel itself called upon to veto any policy
of which its members disapproved.

In the summer of 1920 the British Government was engaged
(as related elsewhere) in its attempt to extirpate the so-called
'murder gang' of Sinn Fein; it was also supplying munitions to
Poland in her war with Bolshevik Russia. Organized Labour
disapproved of both these activities and a meeting of the Trade
Union Congress, specially summoned for July, passed two resolutions, one calling upon the Government to change its policy,
and the other recommending the trade unions to prepare for
action. The result of the latter was formation of the so-called
Council of Action, a kind of Labour Cabinet for the emergency
in view. There is reason to believe that there was, from the first,
a large element of bluff in these proceedings, and that the wiser
heads who had voted for the resolutions were much relieved
when circumstances made it possible to ignore them without
sacrifice of consistency. Sinn Fein, as might have been expected,
contemptuously rejected the Labour proposal of Dominion
status, and in Poland the Russian victories quickly proved that
the question at issue was no longer the right of Russians to their
Revolution but the right of Poland to its existence. So the Council of Action felt no call to act.

A three weeks' strike in the coalmines in October and November 1920 must be recorded as the last industrial manifestation of

the post-war boom, already at that date hastening to its close. Though the miners had not got nationalization they had been in all other respects favoured by fortune. The British coal industry had been enjoying an unprecedented export trade owing to the destruction of mines in the battle area of France, and the post-war demoralization in the German coalfields, one of which, Silesia, was the subject of a prolonged boundary dispute. Prices for home and foreign markets were still fixed by the Government, and we had, in fact, been profiteering riotously at the expense of our foreign customers, particularly our late allies, the French. Exorbitant prices for British coal in the foreign market subsidized the British consumer and swelled the miner's wage. In the autumn of 1920, when the domestic price at pit head was 36/7 per ton, the export price was 115/-. The strike in the autumn of 1920 arose over the distribution of this booty between the miners, the owners, and the home consumers, the miners making the novel claim to control not only their own wages but the price of the commodity produced by their labour. The result was a temporary settlement, to last until the end of March 1921. By that date the situation was to be transformed in a manner undreamt of by the negotiators of 1920.

Meanwhile not much progress had been made with the programme of social reform which should fulfil the post-war aspirations of all those who felt that the blood and tears of fifty months should receive a better recompense than the mere beating of the enemy. Much of the thought on this subject was based, like most muddled thinking, on false analogy. The war had quickened up the pace of progress in every department of mechanical science; surely it would be found to have quickened up in a corresponding degree the progress of social betterment. In his election speeches Mr. Lloyd George was confident on this point. An analysis of his speech at Wolverhampton on November 23rd yields such points as—slums must go; the land must be cultivated to its full capacity; a systematic effort must be made to bring back the population to the countryside; and 'inhuman conditions and wretchedness must surrender like the German fleet.'

If little progress was made in the months that followed, a reason for that could be found in the fact that the activities of post-war Europe and post-war industry gave the Government little leisure for calm meditation upon schemes of social reform. Early in the new year the Prime Minister found himself engaged in 'fighting Prussianism in the industrial field as we fought it on the Continent of Europe'. In August he closed the first session of the new Parliament with a typically metaphorical appeal for national unity. 'Navigation is difficult and dangerous. Some seek to help; some lie prostrate and weary. Some try to upset the boat, either because they dislike the steersman or want to steer themselves, or because they prefer some crazy craft of their own. With a clear eye and a steady hand we will row through into calmer and bluer waters, but we must know where we are rowing. The Government have done their best to give a direction. Let all, who will, man the boat and save the nation.'

Substantial beginnings of constructive work were certainly made. There was, for example, the shortage of working-class houses, officially estimated (and as it proved greatly underestimated) at 350,000 houses. In the chaos of post-war economic conditions it was impossible for private enterprise to build these houses on terms which would enable working-class families to rent or buy them. Dr. Addison, a Liberal Coalitionist and a trusted lieutenant of Mr. Lloyd George in many stages of his career, was let loose on this problem with immediate results. The Addison scheme of assisted housing, subsidized in part by the central and in part by the local exchequers, soon supplied every town in the country with a new working-class suburb in which both the architecture and general lay-out of the houses contrasted favourably with the products of Victorian private enterprise. The Addison scheme turned out to be extravagantly expensive, but, in a phrase of the day, it 'delivered the goods'.

No field of reconstruction was, it may be presumed, nearer the heart of the Prime Minister than the maintenance and the permanent establishment on an extended scale of wartime prosperity in agriculture. Like the Victorian Radicals and Socialists of his boyhood, whose ideas he imbibed and never outgrew, he had a passion for the problem of the land, and believed that it lay at the root of all social evils. Hence the extravagant denunciation of landlords which marked his Budget speeches in 1909 and 1910. The Corn Production Act of 1916 had fixed prices for corn in the interests of home food production. It also fixed a minimum wage for farm labourers and established Wages Boards in every county. Were we now to let agriculture slip back into poverty and decay? In one of the best and sincerest of his speeches, a speech quaintly described by the *Spectator* as 'more than a milestone', the Prime Minister answered the question with an emphatic negative, and an Agriculture Act of 1920 consolidated and enlarged the wartime measures for the maintenance of agriculture as an industry of national importance.

But over against the popular demand for social reform arose another demand, equally insistent, for national economy. 'Antiwaste' became the favourite slogan of the newspapers. Every social reform added so many millions to the burden of the taxpayer, and it was painfully apparent that the expenses of the war, quite apart from the service of the war debt, had not ended with the Armistice. The deficit on the national balance sheet for the year 1919-20 amounted to the appalling figure of £473,000,000 though the whole apparatus of wartime taxation was still in action. Estimates of expenditure for the following year amounted to nearly £1,300,000,000 and some of the items in that total are a striking revelation of the difficulty of getting clear of wartime subsidies. There was a railway subsidy £23,000,000; a coalmines subsidy, £15,000,000; a bread subsidy, £45,000,000; a housing subsidy, £25,000,000; Ministry of Munitions, £65,000,000. All these and other items could no doubt be plausibly explained, even the expenditure of the Ministry of Munitions, which was generally supposed to have ceased to exist; but the point was, that neither all nor most of these expenditures could be afforded.

The Government admitted the whole case for economy, but it got little help from its critics in the way of constructive suggestions. The popular press denounced all waste in general and each economy in particular. The Labour theorists recommended a 'capital levy' to raise an enormous lump sum, which some wished to devote to the extinction of the war debt and others to the financing of social reforms. As for the House of Commons, 'nothing', says the *Round Table* of December 1919, 'can more clearly prove the shallowness of the financial knowledge of the present House than their complete inability to debate in any effective manner the Government's financial resolution.'

What made the situation so peculiarly menacing was that every financial authority knew, and reiterated with every degree of emphasis, that worse times were ahead. The booming trade, the soaring prices, the unprecedented export trade, gilt-edged securities at eight per cent and wages which a Victorian artisan would have thought munificent in heaven—these things were not going to last. Indeed those who marked the slight decline in wholesale prices which followed the summer of 1920, suspected that the end was very near.

CHAPTER XVII

PEACE AT HOME: THE SLUMP 1921-1922

The Cassandras of finance had prophesied truly. The bubble of prosperity was in act of bursting. Unemployment, which had been under 200,000 in the summer of 1920, rose to 700,000 by the end of the year; by March 1921 it stood at 1,300,000, by June it was well over 2,000,000; falling in the autumn, it nearly touched 2,000,000 again at the end of the year; thereafter it fell slowly towards 1,400,000, a figure which it had not quite reached at the end of 1922. The new Act establishing the principle of contributory insurance for nearly all industries except agriculture, came into operation in December 1920, in time to bear the brunt of the demand on its resources, much too late to accumulate the capital from which the demand could have been met. Thus the Insurance Scheme was, from the Treasury standpoint, a bankrupt concern from the start.

Demand, especially foreign demand, was exhausted. It could only be revived by a lowering of British prices, and that involved a lowering of wages. Wages, measured in money, touched their peak in January 1921, when they stood at 177 per cent above the pre-war level; thereafter they declined steadily to eighty per cent above pre-war level in October 1922. The actual monetary fall, was of course, greater in so far as many of the employed were working short time. The fall in real wages, or purchasing power, was, on the other hand, much less. Indeed statistics seem to prove that, apart from loss due to working short time, there was on the average no fall in real wages at all. Retail prices reached their peak, 176 per cent above pre-war prices, in

224

November 1920; but October 1922 they stood at 73 per cent above pre-war level. But statistics take no account of human nature. If you halve a man's income he will feel poorer, even though you halve his expenses at the same time. He will attribute a part at least of his reduced expenses to his own economy.

That wages were in fact drastically reduced, the statistics already quoted show. In fact the statistics anticipate, in outline, the upshot of the story that has now to be told, and suggest that this upshot was inevitable. There were many, however, who did not think it so in the first months of 1921. If organized Labour had threatened revolution in the green tree, when wages refused to rise fast enough, what would it do in the dry? Would the slump produce the revolution that had seemed not so very far away on several occasions during the course of the boom?

The decisive action of what Labour writers call 'the employers' offensive' was fought over the mining industry. Export prices, on which the coal industry had been battening, fell in the first months of the year from 85/- to 24/- which was 15/- below the British cost of production. At the same time the onset of unemployment brought a sharp contraction of the home market. In these circumstances the Government decided to 'decontrol' the mining industry, to bring to an end at the earliest possible moment its wartime partnership and responsibility. Decontrol had in any case been timed for the last day of August. Faced with a prospect of paying out £5,000,000 a month to maintain the guaranteed wages and profits of the industry under control, the Government suddenly advanced the date of decontrol to March 31st, leaving the owners and miners only three weeks in which to adapt themselves to the bleak prospect confronting them.

The fundamental question at issue between miners and owners, behind all details of wage reductions, was the question of national or district settlements. Before the war each mining area had fixed its own wages. Under control, wages, though varying somewhat from district to district, had been dependent on national agreements, negotiated with the Miners' Federation as a national organization. The miners demanded the maintenance in a new form of the national system, and the establishment of a 'national pool' into which the more prosperous mines would contribute a share of their profits for the maintenance of wages in less prosperous districts. The owners refused, and offered rates of wages district by district. On this issue the strike began on the first day of April.

For the first fifteen days of that month the nation watched with strained anxiety to see if the famous Triple Alliance was at last going to exhibit its powers. The real nature of that Alliance had always, as we have already seen, been wrapped in the darkest confusion. On the present occasion the railwaymen had no quarrel of their own to prosecute, for their wages were anchored to a sliding scale dependent on retail prices. In fact, the decontrol of the railways was carried through a few months later without discord of any kind. None the less the miners and many of the railwaymen and transport workers had accustomed themselves to the idea that the Alliance existed for the purpose of a sympathetic strike, and for such a strike this seemed the appointed time. On April 8th the two 'allies' announced that, failing a resumption of negotiations between the miners, owners, and Government, 'the full strike power of the Triple Alliance' would be put into operation at midnight on April 12th. On the 12th this operation was postponed until the 15th, and on the 15th it was adjourned *sine die*. That was 'Black Friday', which the *Daily Herald* described as 'the heaviest defeat that has befallen the Labour movement within the memory of man'. The pretext for the desertion was a speech made by Mr. Hodges of the Miners' Federation, in which he indicated that the miners might be content to waive their demand for a 'national pool' if they could secure a reasonable wage settlement without it. The executive of the Miners' Federation immediately afterwards repudiated this concession, and subsequently got rid of Mr. Hodges, but the interval between Mr. Hodges's speech and its

Peace at Home: The Slump 1921-22

repudiation was just long enough to enable 'Traitor Thomas' to switch off a policy to which he had no doubt never been more than a reluctantly consenting party. A sequel to these exciting events was a libel action in which Mr. Thomas won substantial damages from an extremist paper which had portrayed him as Judas Iscariot and other historical characters.

The miners' strike dragged on till June, prolonged by the proverbial obstinacy of the miners rather than by any hope of success. It was terminated by the action of the Government which offered a final subsidy to the industry of £10,000,000 payable only if the strike was terminated before a fixed date. The settlement that followed was far too complicated for the comprehension of anyone outside the industry: suffice it to say that the miners were squarely beaten on all points.

Thereafter wage reductions followed in every industry, accepted, as it seemed to outsiders, with a fatalism in curious contrast with the aggressive mood of 1919. Such fatalism was in part the product of weakness, in part of wisdom. When, in the spring of 1922, it began to be possible to survey the results of the débâcle, comment concentrated on the distinction between what were called 'sheltered' and 'unsheltered' industries. Unsheltered industries were those exposed to the full blast of foreign competition, industries dependent on exports, or compelled to compete with foreign imports in the home market. These had fared, for obvious economic reasons, much worse than industries, such as the builders, which were immune from foreign competition. In the unsheltered trades, the wages were down to a point deplorably near the level of the weekly benefits paid to the unemployed. Indeed unemployment relief itself was often inadequate, and part of the burden of maintaining the unemployed fell upon the elected Boards of Guardians entrusted with the administration of the Poor Law. Certain Boards of Guardians in Labour areas, among which Poplar became notorious, conceived ideas of Poor Law Relief which were deemed extravagant by the Government, and legislation was introduced

227

strengthening the authority of the Ministry of Health over the local authorities in this matter. The Government which only three years before had promised a land fit for heroes had now to take care that the land was not made too comfortable for some of the same persons, no longer heroes but paupers.

While employers were beating down wages the Government was busy repealing the more generous clauses in its own very recent legislation. Seldom in politics has there been a spectacle of Philip sober recanting so explicitly the utterances of Philip drunk. The Agriculture Act of 1920, guaranteeing minimum prices for wheat and oats and minimum wages for labourers was repealed as regards prices, though not as regards wages, in 1921. Unemployment benefits, advanced in the spring to satisfy the just claims of Labour, were reduced in the summer of the same year to satisfy the equally just claims of the anti-wasters. The bonuses awarded to civil servants suffered the same fate. The State housing scheme was drastically cut down and its author, Dr. Addison, removed from office: he found his way eventually into the Labour party.

But these measures alone were insufficient to satisfy either financial requirements or popular agitation. The Government, which had lost several by-elections to Labour, began to suffer defeats by anti-waste candidates in the strongholds of Conservatism. Drastic economy all round was needed, and, since neither the House of Commons nor the Treasury knew how to secure it, the Prime Minister had recourse to the expedient that had served him so well in the palmy days of licensed extravagance during the war. He appointed a committee of five big business men under the chairmanship of Sir Eric Geddes to cut down departmental estimates 'with an axe'. The estimates of the spending departments (excluding war pensions) stood at £600,000,000 for the year 1921-22. Changes of policy, such as the abandonment of the agricultural and housing schemes, combined with the fall in prices and wages, had secured a reduction in this figure of £75,000,000. The Geddes Committee was asked to find another £100,000,000 of reductions for the estimates of 1922-23.

The Report of the Committee, a drastic and exhaustive document, proposed economies of £87,000,000, of which £46,000,000 fell on Defence (Army, Navy, and Air Force) and £18,000,000 on education. The Report, it need hardly be said, provoked vigorous protest from all the interests affected by it, the Admiralty in particular mobilizing all its experts in defence of a naval programme which seemed absurd to every unexpert intelligence in the country. In the end the Government accepted and enforced two-thirds of 'the Geddes axe', and balanced its achievement by knocking a shilling off the income tax in the Budget of 1922. This concession was without justification or excuse in the sphere of finance, but it was probably sound in politics, for the 6/- income tax had become an obsession, as an outward and visible sign of the fact that we had not even begun to creep out from under the incubus of the war. 'It is conceivable', says a writer in the *Round Table*, 'that a man would be justified on psychological grounds in taking his wife to the opera in defiance of financial scruples, even though he knew that if he did so his gas bill would have to stand over until next month. By the same reasoning we think it conceivable that "raiding the sinking fund" in this year's Budget was sound policy.'

It was, as it turned out, the last contribution of the Coalition Government, in the sphere of finance, to the task to which their leader had dedicated them, amidst a riot of roseate metaphors, less than four years before. 'Inhuman conditions and wretchedness' had not 'surrendered like the German fleet'. They had proved more elusive enemies.

CHAPTER XVIII

PEACE ABROAD: THE MAKING OF PEACE 1919

The text 'Blessed are the peacemakers' is not applicable to the authors of the Peace Treaties of 1919. The Peace Conference was, throughout the duration of its sittings, the target of every shaft of ill-humoured suspicion and impatience, and the products of its labours have been criticized in every country and from every angle of vision. Of its three most conspicuous statesmen only one, Mr. Lloyd George, escaped almost immediate condemnation by the popular vote of his fellow countrymen. Clemenceau was refused the Presidency of the French Republic because he had not achieved for France an impossible 'security'; Wilson had to watch, from the impotence of his sick bed, the American Senate, under the leadership of his personal and political enemies, repudiating his signature to the Covenant of the League of Nations. 'The soldiers won the war and the statesmen lost the peace'—the shallow epigram crystallized a mood of general disillusion.

It was, from the first, impossible that the peacemakers should give satisfaction. Not only was the impossible expected of them: many impossible things were expected which, even if they had each been possible singly, were in any case incompatible with one another. The peacemakers were expected to organize a new and better world in which war would assuredly be no more—that was impossible in 1919. But they were at the same time expected to organize the world in such a way that, assuming future wars, the victors in the war just over would be ensured against defeat on the next outbreak of hostilities: that, too, was impossible in itself, and it was also incompatible with the other demand.

It is doubtless true that the treaties not only failed to realize the impossible; they fell far short of what was humanly possible even in 1919, and it is easy to show how things might have been better arranged. The Conference might have met at Geneva or at The Hague, in an atmosphere less embittered and impassioned than that of Paris. France might have given to the Conference a statesman less obsessed by the past and more alive to the realities of the future than Clemenceau: America might have sent a President more capable of the arts of negotiation, more alive to the public opinion of his own country, than Woodrow Wilson: it would be possible also to imagine a representative of Great Britain more adequate than Mr. Lloyd George. None the less there is truth in Mr. Churchill's contention that when these statesmen were most right and most wise they were least representative of the general body of their supporters.

In fact, post-war treaties are made in circumstances that almost inevitably entail their inadequacy, and the greater the war the worse the treaty is likely to be. War is so painful an experience that, while it lasts, we console ourselves for our sufferings by persuading ourselves that they will be compensated by all sorts of future benefits. War is a political and social disease, yet we prefer to figure it to ourselves as a kind of surgical operation. We expect to be better when it is over than we were when it began. The benefits of the war were, in fact, expected to be not utterly unworthy of the suffering it had entailed. The soldiers and sailors had done their part by reducing the enemy to complete prostration: it remained for the statesmen by their treaty-making to do the rest. Yet treaties of peace are inevitably made while the passions of war are still rife. Moreover, haste is imperative; the first need is peace, and there can be no real peace till the treaty has been signed. Much of what was expected from the peacemakers should have been recognized to be, what it was, a task for those who came after; for the making of the treaty is not the first act of peace, but the last act of war. The memoirs of Colonel House, one of the most teachable of men, are instructive on this point. He came to Paris on the eve of the Armistice with his head full of all the good things that the common sense and practical idealism of the most intelligent of American statesmen could think of as appropriate elements in a peace settlement establishing a new and better world. By March 1919 he was urging that a quick peace was more important than a good peace 'or there will be no one but the victors left to sign it.' While the victors debated in Paris, the vanquished nations were tottering on the edge of anarchy, bankruptcy, and Bolshevism.

It would be easy to exaggerate the degree of interest felt by the ordinary Englishman in the process and the result of the treaty-making. A small thing near at hand looms as large as a large thing far away, and it may be that the summaries of the Treaty of Versailles obtained fewer careful readers than the summaries of the Sankey Report. Mr. Keynes, passing to and fro between London and Paris, where he held a position as a financial expert in the British Peace Delegation, was forcibly struck by the remoteness of London from the European agony. Englishmen have never quite made up their minds whether their country is part of Europe or not, and their hesitancy on this subject, which results in an inclination to have it both ways, is at the bottom of the mistrust with which they have often been regarded. When we identify ourselves with Europe in peace time, and conduct ourselves as 'Good Europeans', we feel that we are accomplishing a feat at once virtuous and paradoxical, but as a rule we do not think in terms of Europe at all; we think of 'the Continent', and England is certainly not on the Continent. During the war England came right into Europe; that was, indeed, the essence of our contribution. Our sea power bridged the Channel and our manhood crossed the bridge in its millions. With the end of the war we were an island again, cut off by a Channel for all intents and purposes as broad as the Atlantic.

Peace Abroad: The Making of Peace 1919

The work of treaty-making fell roughly into four parts, from the standpoint of the English public. There were the territorial settlements: the League of Nations; the intertwined problems of Security and Disarmament; and Reparations. With the first of these we did not feel ourselves closely concerned, so long as the settlements were in accord with the principle of self-determination. When it appeared that self-determination was inapplicable in detail to many frontier problems where racial groups were inextricably mixed, or economic convenience conflicted with racial demands, we were content that the settlement should be a compromise inclining in cases of doubt to favour the claims of the victors. On the whole the European treaties seemed to satisfy British demands on these points. We supposed, quite rightly, that the actual demarcation of the frontiers was much less important than the spirit in which the post-war Governments regarded their neighbours, and the fragments of their neighbours' nationals that had fallen the wrong side of the line. But British interest centred elsewhere, on the best and on the worst parts of the Treaty with Germany—the League of Nations and the Reparations settlement.

It seems to be sometimes supposed that the Covenant of the League of Nations was the invention of a lonely American autocrat who, supported by a few British and American idealists, imposed upon the European statesmen assembled in Paris a scheme of his own, which was subsequently rejected by his own countrymen. In actual fact the organization of the League and the terms of the Covenant whereby it was established comprise the inventions of many minds, unofficial and official, and represent a compromise between many shades of policy. The first elaborated programme was that of the American League to Enforce Peace, issued in June 1915, but many minds were already at work upon the problem in England, and an article in the *Round Table* for December 1915, reviewing the problem, is worth quotation because it shows how far the ideas eventually

233

embodied in the Covenant had been developed by that early date.

After pointing out that the questions which cause wars are political questions, and that no body of a judicial or arbitral nature can deal with them, the writer concludes that only a political gathering, which he calls the Concert of Nations, will be adequate to the purpose. 'Moreover, this gathering must have three characteristics. It must include leading statesmen of all the Great Powers, otherwise it will fail of its primary purpose, which is to keep before all that they are members of a greater unity, and to ensure that all international questions shall be considered from the point of view of the human whole and not of any national part. It must meet at regular intervals and have a proper constitution. . . . And its constitution must be such that any international question however controversial can be brought before it, in order to establish the principle that every international question has an aspect which concerns all nations, upon which they are entitled to present their views. . . . The essential principle of the Concert is that the members which compose it, while surrendering none of their sovereign independence, recognize that they are partners in a greater unity.' The writer indicates difficulties inherent in the scheme, one of these being 'the relative positions of the Great Powers and the small nations', but holds that these difficulties need not prove insurmountable.

When we turn from unofficial to official origins, an English source may claim priority. From the beginning of the war Sir Edward Grey impressed upon Colonel House, both in conversation and in correspondence, his conviction that the war would never have broken out at all if a Conference of the Great Powers, such as Grey had proposed and Germany refused in the last days of July 1914, had been a recognized and established institution; and that it was absolutely essential to secure the establishment of some permanent machinery of conference after the end of the war. Before President Wilson delivered his address to the American League to Enforce Peace, in which he first publicly com-

Peace Abroad: The Making of Peace 1919

mitted himself to the policy of a World League of Nations, in May 1916, he secured from Colonel House a digest of Sir Edward Grey's views on this matter, and based his speech upon it. After America's entry into the war, more particularly after the speech of January 1918 which included the League of Nations among its 'Fourteen Points', the President was accepted by all those in England who were unofficially working for a League as their foremost champion. Actually, however, the President's views were still in a rudimentary stage. He declared in a letter to Colonel House in March 1918 his conviction that 'the administrative *constitution* of the League must grow and *not be made*; we must *begin* with solemn covenants, covering mutual guarantees of political independence and territorial integrity (if the final territorial agreements of the peace conference are fair and satisfactory and *ought* to be perpetuated). Any attempt to begin by putting executive authority into the hands of a group of powers would be to sow a harvest of jealousy and mistrust which would spring up and choke the whole thing. The United States Senate would never ratify such a treaty.'

In other words President Wilson, eight months from the end of the war, was unwilling to advance any further than a 'solemn covenant' without consequential machinery, on the same lines as the formal renunciation of war subsequently known as the Kellogg Pact. And the reason why Wilson would advance no further was plain. 'The United States Senate. . . .'

Shortly after this the British Government went ahead and appointed a Committee under Lord Phillimore to draw up a constitution for the League, and the President was invited to establish a parallel committee under his own authority. He was greatly disturbed and refused to do anything of the kind. Only under the intoxicating influence of the final advance to victory did the President begin to think himself the master of the American Senate. He allowed Colonel House to draft him a scheme for a League Constitution, and, without taking advice from any of his Cabinet, he issued a letter to the American people asking them to return only Democratic candidates in the biennial Congressional elections which took place a week before the Armistice. The results of the letter were the very reverse of his expectations and when the President reached Europe he had been condemned in advance by the voice of his own country. In Europe he constituted himself the champion of a League constitution almost every idea in which came from a British source, if the term be extended to include General Smuts. Against all suggestions, prompted by scepticism or by haste, that the Conference should make the peace treaties first and leave the League till afterwards, he set his face like flint. Exerting the full force of his personal and official prestige as the ruler of the only Great Power that had emerged from the war with its wealth and energies unexhausted, he forced the Covenant of the League into the forefront of the first and principal peace treaty. The achievement stands out with an august and lonely eminence amidst the mischievous and ephemeral futilities of the Paris settlements. By this one achievement of a career so largely involved in inconsistency and self-deception and soon to close in darkness and defeat, the President had established his right to the reputation Europe had accorded him. But in his own country the fate of such a League as he had sponsored was exactly what he had forecast before the illusion of omnipotence had descended upon him.

English public opinion upon the League was slow to crystallize. It was, of course, condemned outright by those whose views were clearest and simplest and therefore most readily expressed. Visionary internationalists who had no use for anything short of a World Parliament in which all national sovereignties would be submerged as completely as the kingdoms of the Heptarchy had been submerged in a united England had no use for what they regarded as no better than the Old Diplomacy in a Genevan gown. Among such was Mr. H. G. Wells: he derided the League in a scornful pamphlet, and published an *Outline of History* starting from the nebula and ending with the United States of the

World. At the other end of the scale were those who prattled of human nature never changing and that what has been always must be. Neither of these views had much weight behind them. The average Englishman was entirely in favour of the principles of the League. He made no effort to master the details of its written constitution, partly by reason of his natural indolence and partly because his experience of constitutions nearer home had taught him that they never worked in practice in anything like the way in which what had been put on paper seemed to imply. He regarded the thing as an experiment, and an experiment which somehow or other must be made to succeed.

Such an easy-going outlook was natural to an island race, who remembered the British navy and forgot, or indeed had not yet realized, the future potency of aircraft; but it could hardly suffice for the French. The French were obsessed by the problem of their security, and as an insurance of security the Covenant of the League did not impress them favourably. On the contrary they regarded it as a typically flimsy and problematical product of Anglo-American idealism: they accepted it to please their Allies, but they attached very little importance to it. It was not the kind of League of Nations that France had proposed to herself. For the French had prepared their own proposals for the new international régime, proposals which involved the permanent alliance of all members of the League, and the establishment of an international force under its control. With such a League as that, and assuming French control of it, France might have capitalized the profits of victory and ensured for herself a position of almost Napoleonic dominance in post-war Europe. There had been a brief moment in the early days of the Conference when President Wilson wavered in the direction of something like the French plan: but he evidently saw where he was going and retraced his footsteps. Thereafter the French looked elsewhere for security.

Clemenceau demanded the permanent annexation to France of all territory up to the Rhine. It was a traditional French ideal, with an ancestry extending back to the map of Roman Gaul; but it involved an outrageous defiance of the principle of self-determination at the expense of eight or nine million indubitable Germans living to the west of the river. The Anglo-Saxons would not have it, and France had to be content with a fifteen years' occupation of the Rhineland, and the promise of an Anglo-American treaty guaranteeing her against German aggression. The promise was a rash one, for the term aggression eludes definition. This guarantee treaty might have placed us in the position which we had consistently refused to accept during the ten years of Anglo-French *entente* before the war, a position in which France would consider herself morally entitled to our active support in any war with Germany, however provoked. Perhaps it was fortunate that we were not called upon to ratify our promise. The American Senate rejected the guarantee together with all the rest of the product of Versailles, and our undertaking, being conditional on that of America, lapsed with America's refusal. The French, however, felt that they had surrendered their claim to a permanent Rhine frontier in return for a scrap of paper. In fact, security had slipped through their fingers. They were in no mood to meditate upon the fact, so obvious to those who lived outside France, that the only permanent security for France would be the friendship of Germany. The French regarded the Germans as natural and immutable enemies.

Closely connected with security was disarmament. The ideals of the League, the ultimate abolition of war and the fear of war, involved an ultimate disarmament which should embrace all members of a League conterminous with the world. But that was clearly no part of the task of 1919. It sufficed to disarm the vanquished. Conscription was to be abolished in Germany, and the army reduced to 100,000 men, the number deemed necessary for the maintenance of internal order, and the German Government was forbidden to maintain armed forces or fortifications on the left bank of the Rhine or within thirty miles of the right bank. The German navy was to be limited to six battleships with certain minor craft, but no submarines. Here at least was a substantial temporary security for France, but no more. The authors of the treaty very wisely refrained from making any promises, but they expressly stated that the enforced disarmament of Germany would be followed by measures of voluntary disarmament on their own part, when the time was ripe. But who could tell when that might be?

We have been called a nation of shopkeepers, and in the general election of December 1918 we certainly lived up to our reputation. Nothing is so important to shopkeepers as the payment of their customers' debts and no subject, not even the hanging of the Kaiser and the immediate abolition of conscription in England, excited such passionate and frantic interest as the financial damages to be exacted from the beaten enemy. The simplest and surest way of settlement seemed to be to make Germany pay the whole cost of the war. Mr. Lloyd George never went so far as to commit himself to the feasibility of this plan, but before the end of his election campaign he had gone sufficiently far to satisfy most people. He had laid down three principles: first, we had an absolute right to demand the whole cost of the war; second, we proposed to demand it; third, a committee appointed under the direction of the Cabinet believed that it could be done.

The first of these propositions left entirely out of account a very important piece of very recent history, namely the negotiation of the German Armistice. In its correspondence with President Wilson the German Government, faced with the prospect of immediate and overwhelming defeat, had accepted President Wilson's Fourteen Points as defining the general principles on which peace should be made. The President had then approached the Allied Governments and asked whether they were prepared to accept the same Fourteen Points. In reply they objected to one of the Points, which was concerned with 'the

Freedom of the Seas', and proposed an addition to another of them. The Allied statement runs: 'Further, in the conditions of peace laid down in his Address to Congress on the 8th January 1918 (i.e. the speech containing the Fourteen Points), the President declared that invaded territories must be restored as well as evacuated and made free. The Allied Governments feel that no doubt ought to be allowed to exist as to what this provision implies. By it they understand that compensation will be made by Germany for all the damage done to the civilian population of the Allies and to their property by the aggression of Germany by land, by sea, and from the air.' The meaning of this interpretation of, or rather addition to, Wilson's Points is perfectly plain. Not only must Germany pay damages to the countries whose territories she had invaded and occupied. She must also pay for towns and villages damaged by air raids and (a much larger item) for mercantile shipping sunk by her submarines. Germany accepted the Fourteen Points as thus amended and, on the understanding that the ultimate terms of peace would be based on these Fourteen Points, consented to Armistice terms which deprived her of any power of renewing hostilities she might otherwise have conceivably possessed.

It is hardly necessary to argue that, by defining the injuries for which they would demand reparation, the Allies explicitly undertook not to demand reparations for any injuries which did not fall within that definition. If the point were worth arguing, it would only be necessary to state that the terms accepted, with the emendations already mentioned, by both Germany and the Allies were, to be exact, not only the Fourteen Points but everything relevant contained not only in the speech in which the Fourteen Points were embodied but also in a list of subsequent speeches in which the President reiterated and elaborated his programme. It would be easy to find passages in these speeches which forbade any enlargement of reparations beyond those specified in the bond: for example the President said, 'There must be no contributions, no punitive damages.'

Thus Mr. Lloyd George came to Versailles bound by incompatible pledges, his Armistice pledge to Germany and his electoral pledge to his own people. What was to be done about it? What was done would be amusing if it were not also deplorable. A clause was inserted in the treaty, since famous as the War Guilt clause: 'The Allied and Associated Governments affirm and Germany accepts the responsibility of Germany and her allies for causing all the loss and damage to which the Allied and Associated Governments and their nationals have been subjected as a consequence of the war imposed upon them by the aggression of Germany and her allies.' The statement might or might not be sound as a matter of history: it might or might not be wise in policy to compel Germany at the sword's point to give formal assent to a judgment which could only carry weight when endorsed by an impartial posterity; but in itself it was innocent of any connection with reparations.

The next clause, however, reads as follows. 'The Allied and Associated Governments recognize that the resources of Germany are not adequate . . . to make complete reparation for all such loss and damage.' Here was a statement that Germany could not pay a certain claim. It did not state that she was liable to pay that claim, but it could be read as an assumption that she was so liable. It prepared the ground for the next sentence. 'The Allied and Associated Governments, however, require, and Germany undertakes, that she will make compensation for all damage done to the civilian population of the Allied and Associated Powers and to their property . . . by land, by sea, and from the air (i.e. the Armistice terms) *and in general all damages as defined in Annex I hereto.*' Like Gibbon, the Allied and Associated Powers had reserved their finest point for a footnote. The Annex asserted the claim of the Allies to the payment by Germany of all separation allowances granted to the dependants of soldiers during the war and for all pensions and compensations in respect for the injury or death of combatants payable by their Governments now and hereafter.

When the German delegates received the treaty and were given an opportunity of making comment upon it to its authors, they declared that this stipulation was a breach of the terms of the Armistice, and candid opinion in England and elsewhere has not been able to differ from them. Mr. Keynes, whose book on *The Economic Consequences of the Peace* had an immense vogue both in England and America—some even go so far as to say that it played a perceptible part in hardening American opinion against association with her sometime Allies in the League of Nations—does not mince his words on this subject. Writing 'only after the most painful consideration', he says: 'There are few episodes in history which posterity will have less reason to condone—a war ostensibly waged in defence of the sanctity of international engagements ending in a definite breach of one of the most sacred possible of such engagements on the part of the victorious champions of these ideals.'

Mr. Keynes's judgment was in some quarters suspect. Mr. Churchill, for example, styles him 'a man of clairvoyant intelligence and no undue patriotic bias'. But the *Round Table* is as explicit as Mr. Keynes. After recapitulating the Armistice settlement and setting beside it the pensions clause in Annex I of the Treaty, the writer asks: 'How can that be called damage done to the civilian population of the Allies? If the soldier's pension is damage, why not the soldier's pay? And if that, why not the cost of shells and guns, and in fact every expense arising out of the cost of the war? It might be urged that we were entitled to say (before the Armistice) that Germany should pay such expenses. Certainly we were. But we did not say it. It would be ridiculous, if we really intended to make so wholesale and definite a claim, to have done so merely by extending and defining President Wilson's demand for the restoration of invaded territories. We did not do so, and this meaning cannot, in our opinion, honourably be read into the words we used.'

The point is one of extreme importance, not in the sphere of finance where it had no practical importance at all, but in the sphere of morals. By this more than by any other single action the Allied Governments destroyed the basis of their claim to be the builders of a new and better international organization in which Allies and ex-Enemies alike should find their security. The war, which had begun with the tearing up of one scrap of paper ended with the tearing up of another.

As for the financial significance of reparations, experts estimated the sum due from Germany under a strict interpretation of the Armistice terms at not more than £3,000,000,000. This was fifteen times the indemnity claimed by Germany from France in 1871, but it might by optimists be regarded as a practicable sum. Pensions and separation allowances would add perhaps another £5,000,000,000, which was a plunge from the practicable to the fantastic. It was fair to assume that the utmost Germany could pay for the next fifteen years would be £150,000,000 a year. That would pay the interest at five per cent on £3,000,000,000. Meanwhile the £5,000,000,000 for pensions etc. would have risen to £10,000,000,000, bearing interest at £500,000,000 a year. It is unnecessary to pursue these calculations any further. Actually the Treaty named no total sum for Germany's liability, probably because any sum within the most optimistic estimate of Germany's capacity to pay would have fallen far short of popular expectations in Allied countries. The whole business was handed over to a permanent Reparations Commission.

Meanwhile discussion was moving on to the classical dilemmas involved in indemnity payments. Some perhaps recollected that they had discussed the same subject ten years before, when Mr. Norman Angell published his little book, *Europe's Optical Illusion*, subsequently expanded and renamed *The Great Illusion*. Seldom was a book more discussed and less understood. People talked as if Mr. Angell had said that there would be no more wars, and in 1914 they held that he had been proved wrong. What he actually said was that there ought, on economic grounds, to be no more wars because the victors would lose only less than the vanquished. His strongest point was his demonstration of the futility of indemnities, and he put forward grounds for thinking that Germany had lost more than she gained by the indemnity she imposed on France in 1871. Indemnities can be paid only in goods, or services: they can only stimulate the industries of the country which has to pay at the expense of the corresponding industries of the supposed beneficiary. If Germany were ordered to replace from her own shipyards all the British ships sunk by her own submarines, and if she succeeded in doing so, what would become of the British shipbuilding industry? To this simple question economic experts had answers pointing out, very truly, that the problem was not as simple as it had appeared to Mr. Norman Angell. There were an infinite number of points to be considered, and those who attempted to consider them,

'Found no end, in wandering mazes lost'

like Milton's fallen angels engaged on the finer points of theology. The British public came to the conclusion that the whole business of Reparations was an unprofitable bore. We early began to make up our minds that we should get nothing out of it. We were not yet called upon to consider the cognate problem of inter-Allied debts. America, with ostentatious rectitude, claimed nothing from Germany. Some years passed before she pressed her claim to be paid by the Allies with whom she had 'associated' herself.

CHAPTER XIX

PEACE ABROAD: PEACE IN ACTION

1919-1922

Chaos is by definition indefinable, and no plain prose summary can do justice to the state of affairs prevailing over the greater part of central and eastern Europe from the date of the Armistice onwards through the next few years. Political and social revolutions, here successful, there stamped out in blood: a dozen unofficial wars between nations mesmerized by impossible ambitions of predominance and maddened by the propaganda of national hate and national exclusiveness: Governments bankrupt, commerce dwindling to extinction as new tariff barriers blocked old courses of trade, everywhere a standard of living declining towards and often falling into the gulf of famine, with its invariable accompaniments of plague and pestilence. America, wrapped in the mantle of a virtuous prosperity, could afford to shrug her shoulders, to forget that she had ever responded to appeals to 'make the world safe for democracy', and to concentrate her energies on evading the liquor legislation she had just enacted for her own control. We in England, outside the whirlpool but on the edge of it, could not affect so complete an indifference. At one point and another we found ourselves involved. Our interventions were for the most part completely ineffective, illustrating the toughness of the material, the insolubility of the problems with which we were trying to deal— Russia, and Poland, Franco-German relations, and the resurgence of Turkey. The list is not complete, but it will suffice for a chapter.

Peace Abroad: Peace in Action 1919-22

In the sixth of his Fourteen Points President Wilson had de-clared that 'the treatment accorded Russia by her sister nations in the months to come will be the acid test of their goodwill, of their comprehension of her needs as distinguished from their own interests, and of their intelligent and unselfish sympathy'. The demands of the President under this head were 'the evacua-tion of all Russian territory, and such a settlement of all ques-tions affecting Russia as will secure the best and free-est co-operation of the other nations of the world in obtaining for her an unhampered and unembarrassed opportunity for the inde-pendent determination of her own political development and national policy, and ensure her a sincere welcome into the society of free nations under institutions of her own choosing; and, more than a welcome, assistance also of every kind that she may need and may herself desire'.

This was the longest and most explicit of all the Fourteen Points, but it was also the point least in contact with reality, in fact less a point than a flourish. Thirteen months later, in Con-ference at Paris, the President declared that 'Russia was a prob-lem to which he did not pretend to know the solution'. Both he and Mr. Lloyd George had desired a Conference with the Bol-shevik rulers. Mr. Lloyd George had suggested that both they and their Russian adversaries should be summoned to Paris 'in the way that the Roman Empire summoned generals of outlying tributary states to render account of their actions'. The invita-tion was sent, though the meeting place was shifted from Paris to Prinkipo, an obscure island in the Sea of Marmora. Nothing came of this, as might be expected and, methods of conference having failed, the President declared that 'he would do his share with the other Allies in any military measures which they considered necessary and practicable to help the Russian armies now in the field'. It must be considered doubtful whether the President passed his own acid test.

In the year following the Armistice the Bolshevik Government established in Moscow was fighting for its existence, with what seemed very dubious chances of success, against a host of enemies. An independent republic had struggled into embryonic existence in the vast area of central Russia known as the Ukraine. To the south of the Ukraine, Denikin, a Tsarist general, was advancing against both the Ukrainians and the Bolsheviks as a champion of the old régime. In Siberia, Kolchak, master of an immense mileage of the Trans-Siberian railway based on Vladivostok, was advancing on Moscow with the intention of overthrowing the Bolshevik tyranny and giving Russia freedom to settle her own future destinies on a democratic basis. On the Baltic another Russian general, Yudenitch, threatened the Bolshevik outpost of Petrograd. The state of Russia was not that of the established Soviet system with which we have since become familiar. It was much more like the condition of affairs we have since learnt to associate with China. In China we have learnt not to take sides, and indeed we have never been under any temptation to do so. No Chinese Government or pretender represents any principle in which we feel interested, and one is, from our point of view, as good or bad as another. But the Russian anarchy involved, or seemed to involve, all those questions of socialism versus capitalism which were the principal topic of British domestic discussion in the months when Mr. Justice Sankey was meditating upon the nationalization of the mines. To support Denikin and Kolchak seemed, to a large fraction of the British public, to mean embarking upon a wanton assault on the only community that had achieved the Socialist Revolution. On the same side was ranged a still larger body of opinion which demanded no more war in any quarter of the world, for any purpose.

If the question at issue had been—shall we now, in the spring of 1919, intervene in the affairs of Russia on the side of the anti-Bolshevik forces, because we disapprove of Bolshevism?—there could be only one right answer. Many people argued as if this was the question at issue; but it was not. We were already involved in the Russian war, as a part of the Great War. The war on the Eastern Front had not come to such a complete and final end in 1917 as the British public, its attention riveted on the colossal battles of the West in 1918, very naturally supposed. When the Western conflagration was suddenly extinguished one realized that the Eastern fires were still smouldering. It had been, as a matter of war policy, all-important to limit the powers and resources of Germany in Russia. The Bolsheviks made peace with Germany, and thereby every Russian enemy of the Bolsheviks became our potential ally in the war against Germany, a war which no one had expected to reach a sudden ending in the autumn of 1918. Could we desert these anti-Bolsheviks in the midst of their campaigns, which they had undertaken with our encouragement, simply because they were no longer directly useful to us?

Mr. Lloyd George was quite certain we could not. 'It is our business,' he said, 'since we asked them to take this step, since we promised support to them if they took this step, and since by taking this stand they contributed largely to the triumph of the Allies, it is our business to stand by our friends.' So Bolshevism, it seemed, was doomed. 'Such a direct statement from the Prime Minister', says the *Round Table* for June 1919, 'should mean a final blow to Bolshevist prestige in Europe. It now remains for Russia to shake herself free from the malady that has not only ruined her but has been disturbing the peace of Europe for many months past.'

The management of these ill-fated designs fell to Mr. Churchill —as Secretary of State for War. There was no question of sending British armies to Russia: no new armies would have consented to go. The problem so far as British man power was concerned was to extricate the forces already involved. What we could supply was money and munitions. The expenditure involved was not great. The sum of £100,000,000 assessed by enemies of the Russian policy was reached by charging their cost of production against the munitions which we sent to Russia. But these munitions were simply surplus stores of the Great

Peace Abroad: Peace in Action 1919-22

War, with no market value whatever. Nothing, however, could reconcile British opinion to these undertakings, and certainly not the expositions of Mr. Churchill: for whatever might be the case for supporting our allies irrespective of their political principles, Mr. Churchill was certainly fighting Bolshevism, 'that foul baboonery' as he called it. The more Mr. Churchill abused the Bolsheviks the more he obscured the case for the policy of which he was in charge.

There was, however, one corner of Russia where our obligations were beyond controversy. In the spring of 1918 a small British force had been sent to the White Sea regions. Their area of occupation extended over hundreds of miles from Archangel, where the founders of the Muscovy Company had landed in the reign of Edward VI, to Murmansk, the Arctic terminus of the railway along which Allied munitions had fed the Russian armies. These forces were in imminent peril. They had to be first reinforced and afterwards evacuated. All this was accomplished with success, and with comparatively trifling loss, by October 1919.

By the end of 1919 all the anti-Bolshevik leaders had been routed, and those who had always thought our intervention wrong were convinced of their own wisdom. But 1920 brought another Anti-Bolshevik champion into the field in the shape of Poland. Poland, after a hundred and twenty years of partition between the Empires of Germany, Austria, and Russia, had been re-established on the ruins of those empires at the end of the war. Her frontiers on the west and south were controversial but defined, though in Upper Silesia they still awaited settlement by plebiscite. To the east was chaos, and an indication on a map called 'the Curzon line'. The eastern frontier of Poland had been a wide belt of anarchy all through the centuries during which Poland had maintained her existence as an independent kingdom. There seemed to be no good reason, in geography or ethnography, why Poland should come to an end at one point rather than another. Poland felt herself unduly confined by 'the

249

Curzon line' and, in alliance with the shadowy Government of the Ukraine, proceeded to invade the territory assigned by Lord Curzon, as executor of the wisdom of the Peace Conference, to Russia.

British opinion regarded this venture with disapproval. We were tired of breaches of the peace treaties; we were tired of Bolshevik-baiting, and we had begun to suspect Poland as a catspaw of France. English and French views about the future of Central Europe had never coincided except on one point, the necessity of defeating Imperial Germany. With that aim accomplished their divergence began and widened. Poland, we began to understand, was the cornerstone of the French scheme for securing the permanent domination of Europe, a scheme which would not give Germany a chance of recovering her position as a Great Power. The body called the Supreme Council of the Allies, which was in fact the Ghost of the Peace Conference, expressly dissociated itself from this Polish offensive, but in England it was, rightly or wrongly, supposed that the French Government had given encouragement and support. The British Government had certainly not done so, but it was prepared to do business with Poland by selling and transporting munitions. It was in protest against these proceedings that the Trade Union Congress launched their scheme for Direct Action, as described in an earlier chapter.

The Polish advance into Russia proved a complete fiasco, and was followed by a Russian invasion of Poland which reached the outworks of Warsaw.

Perhaps Mr. Churchill and many others are right in fixing on that moment in the summer of 1920 as one of the turning points of history—though we know the turning points of history are not as sharp as the dramatizing habits of posterity are apt to suppose. In 732 Islam confronted Christendom on the central plain of France: Gibbon liked to think that, if the wrong side had won, the Koran would have been substituted for the Bible in the University of Oxford. In 1530 the Turks were battering at the walls of Vienna, having, in the course of the preceding century, pushed Christendom halfway from Constantinople to Calais. Was that action at the halfway house the decisive action? If Vienna had fallen, would a Christendom rent with sectarian strife between Catholic and Protestant and dynastic strife between Habsburg and Valois, have crumbled before the advance of Suleiman the Magnificent? At Warsaw once again the European tradition, call it what you will, impoverished and distracted by struggles compared with which the battles of Habsburg and Valois were children's games, was confronted with the armed power of Communism, claiming to be the herald of world revolution. 'Our next step on the path to world victory', said Trotsky, 'is the destruction of Poland.' What followed was the battle of Warsaw, 'the miracle of the Vistula', which has been called the eighteenth decisive battle of the world, the seventeenth being the Marne. Some say it was won by the Poles, and their remarkable dictator Pilsudski. Others say it was won by the General Weygand, arrived in the nick of time from France. In any case it was won, and Poland was saved.

These events brought to a close the period in Russian relations which opened with the end of the war. Bolshevism had failed to spread beyond Russia but in Russia it had, apparently, come to stay. 'There is clearly no reason', says the *Round Table* for September 1920, 'why we should not deal with the Soviet Government on the ordinary lines on which business is transacted between states, provided that they themselves abide by those rules. For the establishment of such relations there are many practical reasons. Thus Europe generally stands as much in need of Russian grain and raw materials as Russia does of all sorts of things that she can only obtain from outside.' Mr. Lloyd George had also seized upon this point and, in his picturesque way, pointed to 'the bulging cornbins' of Russia. These however proved to be only one more Russian myth. Within a year of this date Russia was entering upon a famine of unprecedented severity, due partly to drought and more to the impossibility of combin-

ing peasant proprietorship of the land with communal ownership of its products.

The treaty, and agreements subsequent to the treaty, had
postponed until May 1921 the settlement—the final settlement as
it was called, with unconscious irony—of Germany's liability for
reparations. Preparation for this event involved the Allied
Governments, sometimes with German participation and sometimes without, in a series of Conferences which together consti-
tute the most intricate and unprofitable chapter in post-war
history. The controversy forced upon public attention the fundamental disharmony between British and French views. From
the British standpoint, the war was over and done with. Germany had been so completely defeated and so drastically punished that she was no longer to be feared. We had no warrant in
history or common sense for regarding the Germans permanently
as natural enemies. What we wanted, on grounds of commerce
and humanity alike, was to expedite by every means in our
power the return to normal conditions, in Europe as a whole
and above all in Germany. We should have liked to cancel every
clause in the treaty which hampered and delayed the return of
the normal. Unfortunately we had been a party to the treaty
and were bound by it—bound to France.

For France the war was not over and done with until it had
been paid for. The fruits of victory must be gathered to the very
last apple on the tree. If they could not be gathered in the form
of reparation payments, they must be gathered in some other
form—sanctions, penalties. France did not look forward to a
restoration of normal conditions, as the term was commonly
understood, namely pre-war conditions. Before the war France
had been at the mercy of Germany—France with her forty
millions of population and Germany with her sixty-five. 'Normal conditions' would restore the natural preponderance of
Germany in Europe. The war had brought a victory complete
beyond all expectations. The whole object of French policy was

to secure permanency, by every available device, for the preponderance France enjoyed over Germany in the moment of
victory. The territorial clauses of the treaty did much, but not
enough. The reparation clauses must do the rest. If Clemenceau's
intelligence was as profound and as subtle as his admirers assert,
he must have watched with the keenest relish as the reparations
demands of the treaty piled themselves up, the British contribution to the exorbitant demand falling no wise short of the French.
He did not claim to be a financier, but he was not a fool. He
knew that these claims could never be met. But what then?
Every German defalcation would justify a French demand for
something worth more than money.

As for the Germans, they felt no obligation, moral or otherwise, to facilitate the payment of reparations. The full sum demanded they could certainly never pay. They would pay no
more than they were obliged, and they had every reason to
think that the Allies would find that the cost and trouble of
extracting debts from an unwilling nation were scarcely repaid by the results.

At Paris in January 1921 the Allies agreed to demand from
Germany payments for forty-two years to a total amount of
£11,000,000,000. In March Dr. Simons, meeting the Allied
statesmen in London, refused the demand in a speech which was
considered to lack both taste and courtesy: he made an alternative offer which amounted to about one-tenth of the Allied
demand. The French were inflexible, and Mr. Lloyd George
gave them his full support. The Allies would occupy Düsseldorf
and two other towns on the right bank of the Rhine. This
measure was, it subsequently appeared, unauthorized by any
clause in the treaty, but in France considerations of this petty
nature were brushed aside. Plans were elaborated for the occupation of the whole of the Ruhr valley, a wealthy industrial
district on the eastern side of the Rhine, and it was plainly
hinted that, once in occupation of the Ruhr, France would not
come out again.

Peace Abroad: Peace in Action 1919-22

This venture was, however, postponed for the time. A second Conference met in London at which both France and Germany agreed to accept a settlement sufficiently plausible to satisfy the claims of dignity and self-esteem. The terms of this settlement were, of course, ultimately unworkable; but for the moment that did not matter. Indeed in August payments of reparations due under this scheme were actually made. In order to make these payments the German Government, having no credits abroad derived from a surplus of exports over imports, sold marks in exchange for foreign currencies. Immediately afterwards the external value of the mark fell fifty per cent. Thus began the famous 'Flight from the Mark', which ruined the middle classes of Germany and rolled the stone of reparations down to the bottom of the hill again. Conferences were held at Cannes, at Genoa and elsewhere, but with nugatory results. In the autumn of 1922 M. Poincaré, who had succeeded the more pliant and internationally minded M. Briand as Prime Minister of France, occupied the Ruhr Valley with French armies. He neither asked for nor received the approval of the British Government. This experiment in the efficacy of sanctions had only begun when the Coalition Government fell from power in October 1922. By that time the German mark stood at 50,000 to the pound.

While reparations were descending into the nether gulf of Central European bankruptcy the cognate problem of inter-Allied debts was beginning to raise its head above the Atlantic horizon.

When America entered the war in April 1917 she entered it as an unarmed belligerent. Her services to the common cause in the field of battle could not become effective until 1918. But there was much that she could do, and did, at once, and among these immediate services was the granting of credits which financed Allied purchases in the United States. The upshot of these financial transactions was that Great Britain emerged from the war owing to the Government of the United States a sum of nearly £1,000,000,000. This was not, of course, the only inter-Allied debt. France and Italy together owed to Great Britain a larger sum than Great Britain owed to America. These powers also owed debts to America, and there were also the vast debts contracted to her Allies by Tsarist Russia and repudiated by the Bolsheviks. As things stood in 1922 all these debts were unfunded: interest was not being paid but was being added to the capital amount, and the creditor was theoretically entitled to demand the immediate repayment of the whole capital sum.

It is easy to see today that all these debts ought to have been cancelled. The moral argument for cancellation is so strong that it should hardly have required the support of the abstruse, though no doubt equally cogent, ratiocinations of high finance. Nations allied in war should be assumed to be ready to contribute to the common cause the full strength of all their resources. In the war against Germany one ally, France, being exposed to the full shock of invasion, contributed far more than her share of the common toll of blood; she had also been forced to provide the principal battlefield, and had suffered the devastation of her northern provinces. Great Britain, serving the common cause less exclusively on the field of fire, and more in the factory and the workshop, contributed less than France to the common roll of honour. There was no means by which we could possibly repay France for her surplus contribution of blood: was it then consistent with human decency that we should demand from France a repayment of our surplus contribution of mere money? As England stood to France in these transactions, so, in a much more marked degree, stood America to all the European Allies.

Unhappily the cogency of this line of argument was vitiated from the first, in the judgment of the principal creditor nation, by the character of the Treaty of Versailles, and more particularly by the reparations settlement. The European Allies, by the terms of a settlement which America stiffly repudiated, set themselves to extract, in disregard alike of mercy and of common sense, the utmost farthing of damages from prostrate Germany. If the European Allies proposed to enrich themselves at the expense of the restoration of the general welfare of Europe, why should America forgo her claims? 'The Allies' had never been, strictly speaking, her Allies. She had entered the war as an 'Associated' Power, and now, the unwelcome Association was over. Let them stew in their own juice—and pay their debts.

As early as the summer of 1920 the British Government had begun to realize that there was very little money in reparations, and that without reparations our European Allies could not, or would not, pay their inter-Allied debts. Mr. Lloyd George wrote to President Wilson in August of that year: 'The British Government have informed the French Government that it would agree to any equitable arrangement for the reduction or cancellation of inter-Allied indebtedness, but that such an arrangement must be one that applies all round.' This was an oblique appeal for American generosity, and it came more than a year too late. President Wilson answered bluntly that the United States Government was not prepared to consent to the remission of any part of the British debt.

The next word lay with America, and early in 1922 the American Foreign Debt Funding Bill received President Harding's signature, authorizing the funding of Allied debts in securities with a maximum currency of twenty-five years bearing interest at a minimum rate of four and a half per cent, and appointing a commission to negotiate with the debtor Governments.

The British reply was, in effect, the statement of policy known as the Balfour Note, though this Note was formally to the address not of our creditor but of our debtors. In the Balfour Note the British Government declared that they would have preferred to forgo all their claims both upon their late Allies and upon Germany by way of reparations. As, however, they had got to pay America they were reluctantly compelled to make claims upon their debtors. They would however claim no more from their debtors than would enable them to pay their creditor. Immediately after the issue of this Note, preparations were made for sending the Chancellor of the Exchequer, Sir Robert Horne, to America to negotiate a settlement with the Funding Commission. But before he could set sail the Coalition fell, and his thankless task devolved upon his successor, Mr. Baldwin.

The Balfour Note was a masterpiece of logical statement, worthy of the pen of one of the most accomplished writers of English prose. Its policy was unquestionably the right, indeed the only possible, policy, but it may well be that the issue of the Note, at that stage in the proceedings, was a profound mistake. It is always right to pursue the right policy, but not always wise to make a manifesto on the subject. The Note all too pointedly indicated to our European friends the character of Uncle Shylock across the Atlantic, and the contrast between Uncle Shylock and magnanimous John Bull. The need of the moment was to secure the most generous settlement possible with America, and the Balfour Note certainly failed to shame the Americans into generosity. Instead, it vexed them sorely, as a proclamation of British self-righteousness. In fact the Balfour Note should have followed, not preceded, the American negotiations; there would have been time enough to inform our debtors of our policy after we had settled with our creditor.

The Peace Conference had doled out treaties, one by one, to each of its defeated enemies. These treaties bore, for purposes of convenience, the names of various historic sites in the neighbourhood of Paris: the Treaty of Versailles for Germany, the Treaty of St. Germains for Austria, the Treaty of Trianon for Hungary, the Treaty of Neuilly for Bulgaria, and lastly, delayed far into the spring of 1920, the Treaty of Sèvres for Turkey. The fate of this last treaty differs from that of all the others. The others were accepted, albeit in sorrow and with anger, by the victims to whom they were addressed, and they remain in essentials part of the public law of Europe today. The Treaty of Sèvres was never accepted and in course of time the Turk, long ago reported the Sick Man of Europe, arose and smashed the Allied arrangements to smithereens. They had to make a new treaty, the Treaty of Lausanne, giving him nine-tenths of what he asked for. The Turk was neither 'sick' nor was he 'of Europe', and his resurgence was a vivid illustration of the rising position of Asia in the scale of the world balance of power. Mustapha Kemal and Mahatma Gandhi had nothing else in common, but both were champions of the East against the West.

During the long interval of twenty months between the Turkish Armistice in October 1918 and the presentation of the Treaty of Sèvres the Allied statesmen assembled in Paris made many mistakes, but none more obviously disastrous than their consent to the establishment of a Greek Empire in western Anatolia (Asia Minor). This was done to gratify the ambitions of M. Venizelos. M. Venizelos was, in the opinion of his admirers, a first-rate statesman, and he had been a vigorous and effective champion of the Allied cause from the very beginning of the war. His strongest supporters at the Peace Conference were Mr. Lloyd George and Lord Curzon, who had succeeded Mr. Balfour at the Foreign Office after the signature of the German treaty. The Italians were against the Greek claims from the first, because they had an eye on parts of Anatolia for themselves. The French were not greatly interested, and most of the Conservatives in the British Government inclined towards a reconciliation with their old friends, the Turks. But Mr. Lloyd George and Lord Curzon had their way and the Greeks landed in Smyrna in May 1919, massacring some of its Turkish inhabitants in honour of the occasion, and extending their power inland to a point beyond that allotted to them at Versailles. It was a mistake, because Greek rule in Anatolia, the central home of the Turks, the only land they still felt to be indefeasibly their own amidst the ruin of their far-flung empire, was the one thing that Turkish pride could not accept. A British protectorate would, by the accounts of observers on the spot, have been accepted with the equanimity of despair, but not the Greeks. The Turks were soldiers, if little else; they accepted the results of war. They knew by whom they had been beaten. They had not been beaten by the Greeks, and they regarded them as an altogether inferior species of humanity.

Constantinople was in the hands of the Allies, who occupied the city and both sides of the Straits. There was a Turkish Government in Constantinople, but it had no power, and no relationship to the events that followed. The Government of resurgent Turkey formed itself at Angora around the personality of Mustapha Kemal Pasha, who had played a brilliant part in the defence of Gallipoli and was to prove himself in the years that followed one of the most remarkable of the Dictators of the post-war world, the compeer of Lenin and Mussolini.

The Allied Powers were still backing Greece against Turkey when, in the autumn of 1920 a series of events in Greece gave them a reason, or an excuse, for revising their intentions. The young Greek king, who had been simply a puppet of Venizelos, died as a result of the bite of a monkey. His death necessitated a general election, which overthrew Venizelos and recalled to the throne the ex-King Constantine who had been dethroned and exiled during the Great War on account of his pro-German leanings. The Allies protested, and withdrew their support from Greece. They offered to mediate between Greece and Turkey, but Constantine, who was as sanguine an imperialist as Venizelos himself, rejected their terms. In the summer of 1921 the Greek armies advanced on Angora, but were brought to a standstill in September after a ten days' battle fifty miles from the Turkish capital.

It was by now painfully apparent to all concerned that the Greeks had, in vulgar parlance, bitten off much more than they could chew. A Greek army, far too large to be maintained for long from the resources of a small state, was wasting away in the middle of Asia Minor. Greece herself was distracted by the feuds of the followers of Constantine and Venizelos. The British Government surveyed the situation for which they were so deeply responsible with dismay: but they knew not what to do and they did nothing. Not so France. The French had never cared about the Greek venture, and the accession of Constantine gave them an adequate pretext for washing their hands of it. France had taken charge of Cilicia and of Syria. In face of the resurgence of Turkish power she wanted to get rid of the former and to secure a friendly understanding over the latter. In fact France wanted Turkish friendship, and the Turks wanted French munitions. In such circumstances bargaining is easy. A French envoy went to the Turkish headquarters, and secret negotiations led, in October 1921, to the Franco-Turkish Treaty of Angora. In view of the fact that France was a party to the Treaty of Sèvres, the Treaty of Angora can hardly be defended, but it can be very easily explained. The Sèvres treaty was dead. To the charge that France was deserting her ally, French public opinion replied that the British were meditating a similar offence against the French in the matter of reparations.

After the Treaty of Angora Greece was doomed, though the blow delayed to fall. In the spring of 1922 the Allies, acting together once again, offered both Greece and Turkey a revised treaty which ceded to Turkey all Anatolia and Eastern Thrace except the cities of Smyrna and Adrianople. This time Constantine accepted, but Mustapha Kemal refused. He had only to wait, and deliver his blow at his own time and in his own way. He attacked the Greek lines at the end of August, and before the middle of September Greek rule in Asia Minor was at an end. Smyrna was sacked and destroyed.

Interest now shifted with a sudden deepening of anxiety to the Straits, to Chanak on the Asiatic shore of the Dardanelles where British, French, and Italian forces guarded the route from Asia into Europe, under the command of Sir Charles Harington, who had been Lord Plumer's second-in-command with what many considered the best of the British armies in France. Each of the three Allies had to decide, and decide at once, what it would do. The consequences of opening the road to the Turks cannot easily be estimated. Constantinople, with its Christian population of three-quarters of a million, might have suffered the fate of Smyrna. The war of Turkish reconquest would certainly have extended far into the Balkan Peninsula. Russia would very probably have co-operated with the Turk by an assault upon Roumania.

The French withdrew their forces to the European shores of the Straits, and the Italians followed them. The British Government instructed General Harington to stand firm. The position was a strong one relatively to the Turkish forces which, after all, had only defeated the Greeks, and there was ample naval support. After a fortnight of tense excitement an armistice was signed, followed by the Treaty of Lausanne in the following year. By that treaty Turkey secured her position as mistress, not only of Asia Minor and of Eastern Thrace but of Constantinople and the Straits. All the ingenious plans for the international control of that unique city and those unique waterways went to the waste-paper basket. The pre-war system might not be the best, but it was the simplest and it would have to do.

On one frontier controversy between Great Britain and the Turkish Government dragged on for another four years. It concerned the vilayet, or province, of Mosul. The city of Mosul itself is the modern equivalent of Nineveh, the capital of upper Mesopotamia, and its name is commemorated in the fabric called muslin. We claimed the vilayet of Mosul on behalf of Iraq, for which we held a mandate under the Treaty of Versailles. Turkey claimed it also. Both parties agreed at Lausanne that the matter should be referred to the League of Nations, which decided in favour of the British claim. Eventually in 1926 Turkey concurred. This, it should be said, is a drastically simplified version of a very complicated series of events.

CHAPTER XX

FREEDOM IN IRELAND 1914-1924

When Mr. Redmond declared in the House of Commons, on the second day of the Great War, that the Ireland for which he spoke would, loyally and without conditions, contribute her share to the military effort of the British Empire, few expressed surprise; but that was only because, by the end of the fortnight which had opened with the Austrian ultimatum to Serbia, all capacity for surprise had been exhausted. There had always been to Englishmen something of the unreality of a nightmare about the preparations for civil war in Ireland. The nightmare had vanished, and Sir Edward Grey was able to describe Ireland as 'one of the few bright spots' in a world dark with oncoming tribulation.

Mr. Redmond had acted on his own responsibility, and his unconditional offer was expected neither by his colleagues nor by the British Government. The offer proved, as we know, illusory, but it was not made in vain. In spite of all that happened afterwards, the immediate service rendered by Mr. Redmond to the Empire was incalculable. He enabled all parties to turn their backs on Ireland and their faces towards the Continent. Whether, even if all had gone as Mr. Redmond hoped and presumably expected, his offer could have secured, after the war, the united and loyal Home Ruling Ireland of his dreams, must remain for ever unknown: for things did not go as Mr. Redmond hoped. Less than two years later Mr. James Stephens, Irish poet and novelist, in his brilliant picture of the Easter Week rebellion, attributed the source and origin of the events of that week to Mr. Redmond's well-intended speech. 'The leader of the Irish party', he wrote, 'misrepresented his people in the English House of Commons. He took the Irish case, weighty with eight centuries of history and tradition, and he threw it out of the window. He pledged Ireland to a course of action when he had no authority to give this pledge and no guarantee that it would be met.' The Irish leader, in Mr. Stephens's view, succumbed to the infection of British patriotism. If he had kept his head and bargained in England's need for Ireland's terms, Ireland would have got her Home Rule at once and England would have got her Irish soldiers. It may be so: though of all kinds of prophecy Irish prophecy is the most gratuitous form of error. But this much is plain. Mr. Redmond's Anglo-Irish patriotism fell tragically between two stools: it failed to reconcile Ulster to union with Home-Ruling Ireland, and it failed to reconcile Southern Ireland to active co-operation with the British Empire at war.

Having made his speech, Mr. Redmond crossed to Ireland and opened his recruiting campaign. The immediate result was the protest of the original members of the Volunteers committee, and the schism of the Volunteers, henceforth divided into two bodies, the National (Redmondite) and the Irish Volunteers. Professor MacNeill and his colleagues denounced Mr. Redmond for having assented to 'the partition of Ireland', and for committing the Volunteers to a programme 'fundamentally at variance with their published and accepted aims and pledges', namely foreign service under a non-Irish Government. This schism, however, did not seem at the time a very serious matter. The professor and the young poets and journalists associated with him were still nobodies in political estimation, and their Irish Volunteers constituted barely one-tenth of the body from which they seceded. Indeed as late as June 1915 Mr. Redmond declared that 'what is called the Sinn Fein movement is simply the temporary cohesion of isolated cranks in various parts of the country, and it would be impossible to say what their principles

Freedom in Ireland 1914-24

are and what their object is. In fact they have no policy and no leader and do not amount to a row of pins as far as the future of Ireland is concerned.'

The recruiting campaign was neither a success nor an entire failure. It made a poor show beside that of Protestant Ulster where the response was as immediate and overwhelming as in England. Ten thousand of the National Volunteers enlisted in the course of the first fifteen months, and it is to be observed that nearly all came from the towns. It was the country districts that turned a deaf ear, and most of Southern Ireland is remote from towns. The refusal to join up was much less due to Anglophobia than to bucolic indifference bred of remoteness; and in England also the agricultural world lagged far behind the urban world in the statistics of voluntary recruiting. Mr. Redmond afterwards asserted that his efforts were hampered at every turn by the indifference, or rather hostility, of the War Office. 'From the very first hour,' he said in the House of Commons (October 1916), 'our efforts were thwarted, ignored, and snubbed. Our suggestions were derided. Everything, almost, that we asked for was refused: everything, almost, that we protested against was done. Everything which tended to arouse Irish national pride and enthusiasm in connection with the war was rigorously suppressed.' Mr. Lloyd George, speaking later in the debate on behalf of the Government, entirely endorsed this indictment, and it may well be true. The Ireland that did not like Home Rulers has always been honourably conspicuous in the higher ranks of the British army—it is only necessary to mention the names of Kitchener, French and Wilson—and it is likely enough that these soldiers stamped upon an intrusion of nationalist sentiment into official recruiting propaganda.

Thus were things moving, or rather thus were they apparently standing still, when everyone was astonished to hear that the City of Dublin had been seized by rebels on Easter Monday, 1916.

It seems that the leaders of the Irish Volunteers had long been of two opinions as to the use to be made of their force. One party, which included Professor MacNeill, held that the Volunteers should be strengthened and equipped by every illegal means until the end of the war, when they could be thrown into the political scales with decisive effect. Others looked forward to an insurrection, with German help, during the course of the war. The latter party had the support of the Irish-American organizations which had been behind every anti-British movement in Ireland since the Great Famine. From these Americans the Irish Volunteers drew indispensable funds and munitions: through them and through the German embassy in Washington was maintained a fitful contact with a somewhat sceptical German Government. Two contingencies alone, it seems, would enable the party of immediate insurrection to force the hands of the professor and his cautious colleagues—the threat that the British Government intended to disarm and suppress the Irish Volunteers, and the certainty of active German co-operation. In the first particular Mr. Birrell, who had been Irish Secretary now for nearly ten years, gave no assistance. He was of the opinion of Burke that, when the enforcement of the law will make people unhappy and actively resentful, it it best not to enforce the law. The difficulty presented by Mr. Birrell's refusal to give provocation was got over by forgery. A week before Easter Alderman Kelly produced a document which purported to be an official circular prescribing measures for the suppression of the Irish Volunteers. Such forgeries were easy, for the offices of Dublin Castle contained plenty of copying clerks in full sympathy with the prospective rebellion. On the day before the production of this forgery, intelligence had arrived that a German ship with a cargo of arms was on its way to Ireland. A couple of nights before Easter Day the German ship was stopped by a British cruiser and scuttled by its crew, and Casement, landing from a German submarine, was captured near Tralee. Casement's confused and tragic story has very little historical importance. His biographer, Mr. Denis Gwynn, holds that

Freedom in Ireland 1914-24

Casement came over not to lead the rebellion but to stop it; that he was of the party which wanted to save up the Volunteers until after the war was over. It may be so, and it does not much matter.[1] After these events the British authorities decided that the Irish Volunteers must be disarmed as soon as possible, but that it could not be done until more British troops had been moved to Ireland. Of this decision the Committee of the Volunteers was immediately informed by its agents in Dublin Castle.

The detail of what followed in the inner councils of the rebel leaders between Easter Eve and the morning of Easter Monday is exceedingly confusing. This much is plain: Professor MacNeill was opposed to the insurrection and issued orders which were intended to make it impossible, after which the young hotheads took control out of his hands. MacNeill's action had a twofold result. It checked practically all insurrectionary movements outside Dublin and thus spoiled whatever chances there may have been of ultimate success: but it also put the British authorities off their guard and increased the element of surprise on which the Dublin rebels depended for staging their five days' wonder.

What was the object of the rebellion? The remarkable fact about its leaders is that so many of them were poets.

> 'A dream! a dream! an ancient dream!
> Yet ere peace come to Innisfail,
> Some weapons on the field must gleam
> Some burning glory fire the Gael.'

That was not written by any one of these poets. It is the work

[1] Casement was taken to England and, some months after the rebellion was over, he was tried and convicted of treason under the Statute of Edward III, and executed. It was, perhaps, an unfortunate circumstance that the duty of prosecuting him fell to the Attorney General, Sir F. E. Smith, who, a few years before, had been threatening to commit treason himself on behalf of Ulster. Only three treason trials have been held in the British Isles during the last hundred years, and the prisoner in each case was an Irishman, Smith O'Brien in 1848, Colonel Lynch in 1902, and Casement. The two former were sentenced to death, but reprieved and subsequently pardoned.

of Lionel Johnson, who died some years before: but it condenses into one magic verse the diffuse aspirations of the Gaelic bards of Easter Week. Perhaps the most notable of them was the schoolmaster-poet, Patrick Pearce. He seems to have had some of the qualities of a great headmaster, for his staff went on working for him when he had ceased to be able to pay their salaries. His was, of course, a Gaelic school, and he hoped some day to lead his scholars in war. He dreamed of martyrdom, of closing the long list of Irish martyrs with one final and sufficient sacrifice, his own. He was, in fact, a very conceited young man. But the decisive influence in favour of immediate rebellion may have come from outside the ranks of Sinn Fein, from James Connolly, the leader of the Dublin Labour movement. Connolly was an older and weightier man, a revolutionist of a very different school. He too saw Red, but his inspiration was not the legends of ancient Erin but the present-day facts of the Dublin slums. He had learnt his creed of violence from the American syndicalists of the I.W.W. (Industrial Workers of the World) with whom he had associated for several years, and he was exactly what eighteen months later we learnt to call a Bolshevik. Why Connolly and his 'Citizen Army' should have involved themselves in a bourgeois nationalist movement is not at first apparent, unless it be that the Dublin strike of 1913 had left them with a feeling of intense bitterness against the Royal Irish Constabulary.

The rebellion was suppressed after five days of murderous street fighting, at the cost of 450 lives, soldiers, police and civilians. There is no doubt at all that the action of the rebels was intensely resented by the overwhelming majority of the population. Writing immediately after the last shots had been fired Mr. Stephens said: 'There is no bitterness against you (i.e. England) on account of this war, and it is entirely due to the more than admirable behaviour of the soldiers you sent over here.' The soldiers were in fact effusively welcomed by all the Irish people with whom they came in contact. And yet, within a very few

Freedom in Ireland 1914-24

years, a retrospect would seem to show the fiasco of Easter Week as the first of a series of events leading inevitably to the Irish Free State. It was not inevitable: few things in history are, but —what happened? What were England's mistakes?

For mistakes were made from the very start. To begin with, for obscure reasons connected with propaganda and the maintenance of Allied morale, the serious nature of the rebellion was minimized: it was treated by the British press, under Government direction, as though it had been no more than 'a sort of street riot', to quote the words of an Irish historian. If deeds had matched words and the rebel leaders had been treated somewhat as Henry VII treated Lambert Simnel, all might yet have been well. On the contrary they were executed, after secret court martials, to the number of fifteen. Sinn Fein was enriched with the blood of its martyrs, and it is hard indeed to imagine what other result the British Government can have expected from the execution of all these desperate and gallant young men. Compared with this it was a small matter that 3000 persons were arrested, some of them entirely loyal citizens, and two-thirds of the number conveyed to internment in Wales:[1] though the figures are an incongruous sequel to a 'street riot'. In fact it had been no street riot but a desperate and destructive act of war which might, if the German cargo had been landed, have involved immeasurable misfortunes to the Allied cause.

As soon as the executions were over Mr. Asquith visited Ireland and conferred with 'representative exponents of various shades of Irish opinion', including some of the imprisoned rebels. He reached the conclusion, to which he gave public expression on his return, that the existing system of government 'had broken down' and that steps should immediately be taken to negotiate a compromise between Belfast and Dublin under which the Home Rule Act of 1914 could be brought into immediate operation. There can be little doubt that Mr. Asquith's visit, together with the policy issuing from it, was a gratuitous

[1] 1400 of these 2000 were released after brief detention.

Freedom in Ireland 1914-24

error. In Ireland, as elsewhere, nothing succeeds like success. Sinn Fein, having already secured the glamours of martyrdom, could now point to the fact that it had succeeded where Mr. Redmond had failed.

It remained for Mr. Lloyd George, to whom the Irish negotiations were entrusted, to complete what his chief had begun. Negotiating with each of the loyal parties separately he compromised both and left them in disagreement with one another. Ulster consented to Irish Home Rule on condition that her six counties were excluded, thereby grievously offending the Unionists of the rest of Ireland. Mr. Redmond accepted Home Rule without the six counties thereby once again branding himself as a 'partitionist'. It then appeared that Ulster understood the exclusion of the six counties to be permanent, while Mr. Redmond understood it to be temporary. In face of this disagreement Mr. Asquith announced in July that the proposed 'settlement' of the Irish question would be abandoned.

From this date onwards the history of Ireland is the history of the Irish Republican movement, advancing under the banner of the hitherto obscure society of Sinn Fein. Before the war Sinn Fein had been nothing but journalism, and enthusiasm for the revival of the Gaelic language, its greatest triumph being the decree of the Senate of the National University that Gaelic should be a compulsory subject for Matriculation. When the war began it penetrated the Volunteers, and fought Redmond for the possession of them. After the British failure to profit by the fiasco of Easter Week it became conterminous with the anti-British movement. Its appeals throve less on their own merits than on the discontent engendered by war taxation and food shortage and the threat of Irish conscription. The Irish peasant was simply uninterested in the war and therefore unprepared to accept its hardships. Sinn Fein traded upon this apathy for its own purpose just as in Russia the Bolsheviks traded on the apathy of the Russian peasant and his longing for an immediate peace. In December 1916 the British Government obligingly gave the movement back its leaders by releasing the six hundred internees. Among these Mr. de Valera quickly made his mark. He had played a prominent part in the Easter Week rebellion, and would probably have joined the martyrs but for the accident that he was by birth an American citizen. The British Government had been almost morbidly anxious to avoid doing anything which could offend America, so Mr. de Valera was spared to fight another day. His knowledge of the wrongs of Ireland was inexhaustible, and he was a master of just that kind of uncompromising rhetoric that is always welcome in revolutions. Sinn Fein won its first by-election in February 1917, and Mr. de Valera himself secured in July the seat left vacant by the death of Mr. Redmond's brother at the front.

By this time Mr. Lloyd George was Prime Minister, and he had already decided that something must be done. In May he addressed a letter to Mr. Redmond offering either the immediate application of the Home Rule Act outside the six counties or the summoning of a Convention of Irishmen of all parties for the purpose of devising a new scheme of Irish self-government. Mr. Redmond, preferring unknown to known evils, chose the Convention, which forthwith met without the co-operation of the Sinn Feiners, who refused to have anything to do with it. The comments of the *Round Table* on the prospects of this forlorn constituent assembly make strange reading today. 'It must be uncomfortably obvious to the leaders of Sinn Fein', says a writer in the September issue, 'that by establishing this Convention England has taken the wind out of their sails.' And again: 'The ultimate settlement of the Irish question is not difficult to forecast; it will follow the recognition that a united Ireland can only be attained through loyal partnership in a United Kingdom.'

The members of the Convention were animated by the very best intentions, but the only result of their deliberations was to reveal the irreconcilable divisions of Irish opinion — even of Irish opinion excluding Sinn Fein. In April 1918 the product of their labours issued in three conflicting Reports, the Majority

Report being carried by 38 to 34 in an assembly originally com-posed of 100 members. This report recommended a new varia-tion of semi-self-government for all Ireland. Of the minorities one stood for absolute self-government on Dominion lines, and one for the maintenance of the Union. The crucial point of difference proved to be not religion but tariffs. The Dominion party demanded complete control of tariffs, and Ulster could not consent to see imperilled the free intercourse with England on which her industries depended. This was a point on which 'safeguards' for Ulster were plainly incompatible with 'freedom' for a united Ireland.

The Convention reported amidst the thunder of the final German advances which filled the last ten days of March and almost the whole of April. The British Government hurried through a new Man Power Bill which extended conscription to Ireland, accompanied by the promise of a new Home Rule Bill 'at an early date'. This was too much for the old Nationalist party. Mr. Redmond was dead. His career had ended in tragedy as deep as Parnell's, and with this difference that the tragedy was no fault of his own. His final defeat had been marked by his resignation, in the previous summer, of the presidency of the National Volunteers which he could no longer control. They had gone over bodily, 150,000 strong to Sinn Fein. Mr. Dillon, his successor, was a very different man, and at once entered into futile competition with Sinn Fein by withdrawing his party from the House of Commons, and opening a savage campaign against conscription. By his policy of Sinn-Fein-and-water Mr. Dillon deprived his party of any excuse for its continued existence—a fact at once realized in Ireland and, after two years' interval, in England. Thus it was that the final German offensives extin-guished the last hopes of the typically Victorian compromise of Gladstonian Home Rule.

With or without Home Rule, however, conscription in Ireland was an impossible undertaking. The Government dropped both their Irish projects into the same grave, and sent out as their

Freedom in Ireland 1914-24

Viceroy an Irishman and a soldier, Lord French. Lord French launched a campaign of voluntary recruiting, with inducements such as had never been offered in England, in the form of free settlement on the land. The results were negligible. So the last year of the war dragged away, and a week before the Armistice the Chief Secretary, Mr. Duke, declared that Ireland contained all the material for an armed rising. Immediately after it Mr. Lloyd George and Mr. Bonar Law committed their Coalition to the 'exploration of all practical paths' towards the settlement of the Irish question 'on the basis of self-government'. So Unionism was as dead as Gladstonian Home Rule. What remained?

In the General Election of December Sinn Fein secured 73 seats: the old Nationalist party was reduced to 6: the Unionists improved their position, rising from 18 to 26. The Voice of the People? Perhaps; though the election over the greater part of Ireland was of a kind more familiar to South America than Great Britain. Many refrained from voting in fear of death; others, being dead already, voted as having nothing to fear. Those who voted in Sinn Fein constituencies were but a small part of the electorate. But it was enough. If force had won the election, that was as it should be, for force was everywhere enthroned. Redmond was dead and forgotten; the epoch inaugurated by Sir Edward Carson and the German Emperor had reached its climax.

We enter upon the first post-war period, of exactly three years, between the Sinn Fein electoral victory of December 1918 and the signature of the 'Treaty' in December 1921.

The Sinn Fein M.P.'s did not, of course, take their seats at Westminster. They stayed in Dublin and constituted the first Dáil Eirann. Their first objective was to secure for Ireland a place among the new nationalities at the Peace Conference, and in this policy they hoped, not without reason, to enjoy the support of President Wilson. As the inaugurator of a new and better world and also as a sound party politician dependent on the Irish-American vote, President Wilson could not fail to be inter-

Freedom in Ireland 1914-24

ested in Ireland, and Mr. Lloyd George could not afford to quarrel with President Wilson. In the first months of 1919 many strange things were said and done, but promising beginnings yielded poor results. The representatives of the Irish Republic did not reach the Peace Conference; they had to be content with a private interview with the President in June 1919. At this interview they reminded him of his public statement at the Plenary Session of the Conference five months before, 'that every people of the world should choose its own master'. 'You have touched', said the President in reply, 'on the great metaphysical tragedy of today. My words have raised hopes in the hearts of millions of people. . . . When I gave utterance to those words, I said them without the knowledge that nationalities existed, which are coming to us day by day.' And with this interesting, though quite irrelevant, remark the Irish found they had exhausted the possibilities of President Wilson.

Of course they had their revenge. The Irish-American vote swung over to the side of the enemies of the League of Nations, and was perhaps the deciding factor in the defeat of Wilsonism in Congress and the exclusion of America from the League.

There remained force—a war of independence, in which victory would lie not with the bigger battalions but with the stronger convictions: war between the Volunteers now renamed the I.R.A. (Irish Republican Army) and the R.I.C. (Royal Irish Constabulary).

The R.I.C. had been recruited entirely in Ireland, mainly from the peasantry. Not long since it had been one of the most popular of Irish institutions, and for every vacancy there had been scores of applicants. Murders of police had begun in 1919. Now the R.I.C. was officially marked down for destruction, and sums varying from £60 to £100 were paid from Sinn Fein funds, continuously replenished from America, for every policeman shot. Eighteen policemen were murdered in 1919 and 176 in 1920. These events made much less impression on the British public than they would have done in ordinary times, though it

Freedom in Ireland 1914-24

is astonishing to find that the *Round Table* gives no special article to post-war Ireland until June 1921. In June 1920 four pages suffice for the subject. We read that 'the situation is evidently drifting to a crisis', that 'Ireland is terrorized as it has never been in its previous history', that 'it is difficult to say how far the extreme policy of Sinn Fein secures the sympathy of the general population', that 'the policy of the Government seems to be twofold'—the suppression of disorder and the promotion of legislative reform. If the shades of Gladstone and Parnell were permitted to read about this twofold policy, they may have been moved to smile, as they reviewed the eighteen-eighties in their disembodied minds.

By the end of 1919 it had become impossible to recruit for the R.I.C. in Ireland, and a recruiting office was opened in London to accept the services of men who had served as N.C.O.'s in the war. These reinforcements, clad in khaki with black caps, were nicknamed the Black and Tans, a name which was afterwards extended to an auxiliary corps of ex-officers enrolled as a separate unit for Irish service. These auxiliary Black and Tans were the authors of the once notorious and much-discussed 'reprisals', which began to assume prominence in the autumn of 1920. There was, it need hardly be said, every excuse for the authors of the reprisals, though little for a British Government which appeared to believe that in them lay the solution of the Irish problem. In September 1920 Sir Henry Wilson's diary records a conversation with Mr. Lloyd George. 'He reverted to his amazing theory that someone was murdering two Sinn Feiners to every loyalist the Sinn Feiners murdered. I told him of course that this was absolutely not so, but he seemed to be satisfied that a counter-murder association was the best answer to Sinn Fein murders. A crude idea of statesmanship.' Sir Henry Wilson had a fluent pen and a rather satirical turn of mind, but the speeches of Mr. Lloyd George at this time, and of his Irish Secretary, Mr. Hamar Greenwood, are in tune with Sir Henry Wilson's impressions. We 'had murder by the throat' said Mr. Lloyd George.

Freedom in Ireland 1914-24

Mr. Greenwood pursued a vigorous forward policy, though his 'authorized reprisals' were apparently less effective than those spontaneously undertaken by the bold and exasperated men of action on the spot. The military forces in Ireland were greatly strengthened and by the spring of 1921 the Irish campaign was going decidedly in favour of 'the forces of order'.

Meanwhile, in December 1920, a new Home Rule Bill had become law. It purported to create two Home Ruling units, the six counties of Ulster and the rest of Ireland, together with machinery by means of which the two units might combine if they wished. Ulster accepted the Act, and is governed under its provisions today, Sir Edward Carson handing over the leadership of Ulster to Sir James Craig, now Lord Craigavon. Sinn Fein repudiated the Act as entirely inadequate, but took advantage of its provisions to hold what was called a General Election —in which there were no contested seats. None the less, the new Act proved to be the starting point of a new and better policy.

It was one of those occasions when words spoken by the King could carry a weight and bear a significance denied to the words of politicians, especially such politicians as those of 1921. What part King George's personal initiative played, whether it was his own idea to go and open the new Parliament in Belfast, whether the peculiar and decisive turn of the speech in which, looking beyond the frontiers of the six counties, he appealed for peace, forbearance and conciliation throughout all Ireland— whether these things were his own suggestions is a question on which much has been surmised, though the secret has very properly been kept.

The King's speech was delivered in Belfast on June 22nd, 1921. Two days later the Prime Minister invited Mr. de Valera and Sir James Craig to a Conference in London. After an exhibition of his gift for controversy Mr. de Valera accepted. Sir James had accepted as a matter of course, and the Irish truce was proclaimed on July 11th. Few surely can forget the newspaper—it was a Sunday paper—in which one first read of the

275

Irish truce. There had been nothing quite like it since the Armistice. That was undoubtedly the prevailing impression, but it was not the only one. Sir Henry Wilson records a conversation with Sir Laming Worthington-Evans, who was a member of the Cabinet responsible for these proceedings. 'I told him that in my opinion inviting de Valera over was pure cowardice, and that if a man committed a sufficient number of murders he was qualified to be asked to breakfast at 10 Downing Street. "Worthy" was rather shocked and said *it was done to get England on our side.*' The italics are my own, and surely they are not misplaced.

The rest of the summer was filled with the dialectics of the Irish President and the British Prime Minister. Both were masters of the game of finding formulas, but the Welshman was the better Celt of the two by reason of his sense of humour. The metaphysical point at issue was whether Ireland was in fact, at the moment, a Republic. Mr. Lloyd George scored heavily when he found that there was no word for Republic in the Gaelic language, only Saorstat, which means Free State. By October 11th Mr. de Valera found himself unable to refuse to send delegates to a Conference 'with a view to ascertaining how the association of Ireland with the community of nations known as the British Empire might best be reconciled with Irish aspirations'. Wiser than President Wilson, he did not propose to attend the Conference himself.

A Conference of ten, containing on one side leading members of the late 'murder gang' and on the other leading members of what was still called, rather absent-mindedly, the Unionist party, wrestled with each other's obstinacy for several weeks. Their agonies were ended by an ultimatum from Mr. Lloyd George on December 5th—signature of the draft as it then stood or renewal of war. The Irish delegates conferred in private until nearly three on the following morning, and then appended their signatures.

By this treaty it was agreed that the Irish Free State was to have the same constitutional status within the Empire as Canada, the oldest and greatest of the Dominions, but a very curious oath was substituted for the usual oath of allegiance. Members of the Free State Parliament were to swear 'allegiance' only to the constitution of the Irish Free State, adding 'and I will be faithful to H.M. King George V . . . in virtue of the common citizenship of Ireland with Great Britain and her adherence to and membership of the group of nations forming the British Commonwealth of Nations.' There were those who held that the terms of this rigmarole were insulting to His Majesty, and certainly the language with which Irish supporters of the Treaty recommended the oath to their dissenting brethren were open to that objection. Perhaps it would have been better to leave the King's name out of this business: subsequent events certainly make one think so.

Various articles defined Ireland's contribution to the National Debt, the rights of the British navy in Irish waters, and the compensation due to servants of the crown discharged or retiring in consequence of the new régime. Interest centred on the Ulster clauses. For a month after the ratification of the treaty the powers of the Free State Government were not to be exercisable in Ulster, and during that month Ulster was to decide whether she wished to join the Free State or not. If she did not, a Boundary Commission of three, with a neutral chairman, was to define her frontiers. Ulster at once protested that she was no party to the treaty and that she would have nothing to do with the Commission. She had accepted the Act of 1920 which gave her Tyrone and Fermanagh, the two bones of contention whenever the boundary question had cropped up. To accept the Boundary Commission would be to stake Tyrone and Fermanagh, and possibly parts of other counties, on the judgment of some unknown 'neutral'.

The treaty has proved, on the whole, and in spite of recent events, an act of wisdom, but neither of the parties to it can claim credit for that. It was a compromise representing the

Freedom in Ireland 1914-24

failure of both to secure by the arbitrament of war the satisfaction of their aims: on the side of Collins and his gunmen, independence; on the side of Mr. Lloyd George and his colleagues—what? The damning indictment of their Irish policy lies in the impossibility of answering that question.

Of course Mr. de Valera denounced the treaty, offering instead his own solution. Ireland, recognized as a Republic, was to conclude a 'treaty of permanent association' with the British Commonwealth, recognizing the King of Great Britain as head of this Association and contributing to his Civil List. The difference between this and the terms of the treaty is so elusive that so strong a Unionist historian as Professor Allison Phillips has expressed a regret that the British Government, having already conceded so much, did not concede this much more, assuming that it would have secured Mr. de Valera's support for the settlement. But experience in India has taught us that there is always a *gauche de la gauche*. It may be that Mr. de Valera would have moved on ahead of our advances, and that concession could never have overtaken him.

The Dail carried the Treaty against the remnant of Sinn Fein by 64 votes against 57. Mr. de Valera resigned, being succeeded as President of the *soi-disant* and about to be extinguished Republic by Mr. Griffith, the founder of Sinn Fein and one of the signatories of the Treaty. Michael Collins, another signatory and the hero of the gunmen, became head of the Provisional Government, which however was by no means in a position to govern, for the I.R.A. was divided in allegiance between the Provisional Government and its enemies. Then followed several months of manoeuvring for position, Collins trying to conciliate Sinn Fein with assurances that the treaty was merely a temporary halting place on the road to independence. In April Rory O'Connor, one of the champions of Sinn Fein, seized the Four Courts in Dublin, and from these headquarters directed a Sinn Fein offensive against Ulster. This was too much for the wilder elements of the Orange party, who committed a series of bloody

278

outrages upon the Catholics of the North-eastern towns. Sir James Craig invited Sir Henry Wilson, who had just retired from his official position in the War Office, to take command of the Ulster forces. It was perhaps an unwise choice, for Sir Henry Wilson was notoriously an unconverted Unionist, as anxious for the failure of the treaty policy as Mr. de Valera himself. But criticism was silenced when, a few months later, the British Field-Marshal was murdered by agents of Sinn Fein on the doorstep of his own house in London.

There was very little doubt that the majority opinion in Southern Ireland was strongly in favour of the treaty. This was proved by the singular general election of June, 1922. In spite of the attempt of the rival leaders to stifle the voices of their followers by offering an agreed list of candidates which would preserve the exact balance of strength enjoyed by Treatyites and Anti-treatyites in the previous Dail, the electors refused to be muzzled and returned, against the Sinn Fein candidates endorsed by Collins, a large number of independent men pledged to support the Treaty.

Still Collins hesitated to open the inevitable Irish civil war. It may be that in the end his hand was forced by the British Government declaring that if he did not attack the Four Courts, they would. He attacked on June 28th, and thenceforth until the end of the year Ireland gave an exhibition of what the *Round Table* called 'the extreme deformity of long-thwarted nationalism'. Dublin was cleared after ten days' fighting which eclipsed all memories of Easter Week. The Sinn Fein front was rolled back on to the south-west, from Waterford to Limerick. Ulster experienced instant relief, and the anti-Catholic outrages in Belfast stopped with the cessation of anti-Protestant outrages on the Ulster frontier. But the Free State was, in the words of the Roman Catholic hierarchy, 'wrecked from end to end'. To this day charred ruins of hotels and country houses recall that awful time, though the country folk now talk—to strangers, at least—of 'the troubles' with a kindly fatalism, as though of some visitation of nature for which no human agency was to blame.

The victory of the treatyites was due in part to British munitions; in part to finance, for America was no longer interested in Sinn Fein, and the Provisional Government offered its soldiers terms so munificent that most men of sense who wanted to fight had little doubt which side to choose; in part also to the emergence of a new leader. Mr. Griffith died in the course of the summer; Collins was ambushed and killed by the methods he had himself employed against so many servants of the Crown; Mr. Cosgrave took his place, and displayed at once the vigour and the wisdom which were to make him undisputed master of the Free State for the first eight years of its existence. He treated rebels as rebels and shot them. Not till March 23rd, 1923, did Mr. de Valera announce the impossibility of continuing the struggle, and bade his followers lay down their arms. There was no formal submission, and when, some years later, Mr. de Valera took the treaty oath in order to qualify for a renewal of his political career, there were true-green Sinn Feiners left to repudiate him as a traitor to the cause of Irish freedom.

Long before this the British Parliament had completed its share of the formalities. In December 1921 the Articles of Agreement (i.e. the Treaty) were confirmed by the votes of both Houses, and a year later a new Parliament which had rejected Mr. Lloyd George and contained an overwhelming majority of 'Unionists' supporting a Conservative Government, enacted the Free State Constitution Bill. Of the passage of the first of these measures Lord Carson said: 'The stage management is one of the most perfect things I recollect.' There was indeed a great deal of formal congratulation upon a great achievement, and it was even suggested that the settlement of the Irish question would prove to be one of Mr. Lloyd George's strongest claims on the gratitude of posterity. But no one attempted to answer a question asked by Lord Buckmaster. 'If the change in view is really an act of wisdom, an act of healing differences between nations, why was it not introduced in 1918 after the Armistice?'

Freedom in Ireland 1914-24

Lord Buckmaster was one of those Liberals who, with Mr. Asquith, had urged the granting of Dominion Home Rule ever since the beginning of 1919. As he asked his question he may have had in mind words which Gladstone had used in the course of the debate on the first Home Rule Bill nearly forty years before. 'If it be a just and reasonable demand, we cannot too soon hasten to meet it, and we will not wait until the day of difficulty, the day of disaster and, I will add, the day of dishonour to yield, as we have so often yielded to necessity, that which we were unwilling to yield to justice.'

The Ulster Boundary question was allowed to slumber until the time of the first Labour Government (1924). Ulster had, of course, exercised her option of exclusion from the Free State, and by 1924 Mr. Cosgrave could no longer resist the section of his supporters who hungered for Tyrone and Fermanagh. Mr. MacDonald acceded to his request for the statutory Commission of three, and appointed Mr. Justice Feetham, of South Africa, as the neutral chairman. Ulster refused to make her contribution to the Commission, and an Act of Parliament had to be passed to enable the British Government to appoint an Ulster representative. Thus equipped the Commission entered upon its work, with results apparently most unsatisfying to the Free State representative, who, finding himself in a minority, resigned. The report of the Commission was never published. The Free State consented to accept the 1920 boundary of Ulster on condition of being relieved of its contribution to the public debt of the United Kingdom. Thus both Irelands were made happy —at the expense of the British taxpayer. This excellent arrangement was the work of Mr. Baldwin's Government, the short first innings of Labour having concluded some months before.

CHAPTER XXI

FREEDOM IN INDIA 1914-1922

German forecasts of the effect of a world-wide war upon the fabric of the British Empire were mistaken, but not so mistaken as we sometimes suppose. What the Germans expected happened, but it happened too late to be of any use to them. They expected that revolutionary movements would break forth and paralyse our authority in Ireland, in India, and in Egypt as soon as the good news from Germany had reached the oppressed peoples of these unhappily red-painted countries. The revolutionary movements were indeed to come, and their coming was quickened by the war, but their outbreak on any serious scale was deferred till a time when Germany could draw no advantage from them.

At the opening of the Great War India astonished the world by an exuberance of militant loyalty. Not only the princes of the fighting races but the unrestful western-educated classes were caught up on a wave of spontaneous enthusiasm. The Brahman Bal Gangadhar Tilak, most famous of anti-British agitators before the rise of Mr. Gandhi, though just released from a long detention at Mandalay, gave his support to the war. Mr. Gandhi, just returned to India after his long struggle for the rights of Indians in South Africa, a struggle in which he had been powerfully supported by the Viceroy, Lord Hardinge, abounded in the same sense. His war message was: 'The gateway to our freedom is on French soil. . . . The British Empire has certain ideals with which I have fallen in love. . . . My advice to the country would be to fight unconditionally unto death with Britain for victory.' Before 1914 had drawn to a close Indian regiments were serving in France. To the ordinary Englishman who had never pretended to understand India all this was very gratifying and surprising and romantic; it seemed to suggest that the India of Queen Victoria and Lord Beaconsfield was less a thing of the past than recent 'unrest' had led us to suppose. When Mr. Asquith declared that henceforth Indian questions must be approached 'from a new angle of vision' he was felt to have paid India an altogether appropriate compliment. Indeed, throughout the first two years of the war India presented a warlike and patriotic front unbroken by any apparent dissensions. The Imperial Legislative Council, to which a small number of distinguished Indians had been nominated under the Morley-Minto Reforms of 1909, accepted without a murmur the drastic curtailments of personal liberty contained in the Indian Defence of the Realm Act, and spontaneously voted a hundred million pounds to the war expenditure of the Empire.

But Mr. Asquith's 'new angle of vision' was taken as much more than a compliment by the nationally minded politicians whose numbers, though small by modern standards, were already considerable. It was taken as a promise that India would be given, in the very near future, a constitution conferring on her a status of equality with the self-governing Dominions. At first they were content to wait until after the war, for they assumed, like nearly everyone else, that the war would be short. But when the end of the war seemed to be indefinitely postponed, enthusiasm inevitably ebbed, and voices were heard saying that this European civil war—for such it was from an Indian standpoint—proved the hollowness of Western civilization. The politicians were not inclined to wait and see. In 1916 the Indian members of the Imperial Legislative Council published a vague and ambitious scheme of self-government, or *swaraj*, from which any conceivable British scheme was bound to make considerable subtractions. Later in the same year Congress, the annual gathering of Hindu politicians, which only a year before had accepted a resolution expressing unqualified gratitude for the blessings conferred upon India by British rule, fell under the spell of Mrs. Besant, an eloquent and eccentric English lady who in the course of a long life had championed many mutually antagonistic causes, and was now engaged in preaching the spiritual superiority of Eastern over Western civilization. The All-India Moslem League followed the lead given by Congress and declared for complete and absolute Home Rule.

England's 'new angle of vision' did not however become apparent until Mr. Lloyd George appointed Mr. Edwin Montagu to the position of Secretary of State for India. The appointment was in itself sensational for Mr. Montagu had, only a few days before, electrified anti-British opinion in India by a violent attack upon the weaknesses of Indian administration as revealed in the Report of the Royal Commission on the Mesopotamian campaign. On August 20th, 1917, the new Secretary of State made his historic declaration of the new policy. Its purpose was, he declared, not only 'the increasing association of Indians in every branch of the administration, but also the greatest possible development of self-governing institutions, with a view to the progressive realization of responsible government in India as an integral part of the British Empire'. In these words Indians were definitely encouraged to look forward to the ultimate attainment of 'Dominion status'. The British Government, Mr. Montagu added in words less widely quoted, 'must be judges of the time and measure of each advance: they must be guided by the co-operation received from those upon whom the new opportunities of service will thus be conferred. . . . Substantial steps should be taken as soon as possible.' Mr. Montagu then proceeded to India, and after a winter of strenuous labour completed, in collaboration with the Viceroy, the complicated constitutional scheme embodied in the Montagu-Chelmsford Report.

The summer of 1918, when the Report was issued, was not a

favourable moment for the consideration in England of these deep and remote problems. The war had entered upon its final eight months' agony, and after that the foundations of European peace had to be laid. Not till the summer of 1919 was the Bill based on the Report presented to the consideration of Parliament. After a friendly reception in an overwhelmingly Conservative House of Commons it was remitted to a Joint Committee of both Houses which subjected it to an exhaustive examination, assisted by reports and comments from every relevant Indian authority. The measure, which finally became law on Christmas Eve 1919, was in essentials the same as that devised by Mr. Montagu three years before during his rapid tour of India; it was now endorsed by all the available wisdom and experience of British statesmanship. But before Christmas 1919 much had happened in India.

One and the same month, July 1918, saw the publication of two Reports which vitally affected the history of India. One, the Montagu-Chelmsford Report, was concerned with India's future freedom; the other, a less welcome document, was concerned to secure her against present anarchy.

In view of the oncoming end of the war and the consequential lapsing of the special war measures which had empowered the Government to arrest and imprison the promoters of anarchy and assassination, a committee of five had been appointed under the chairmanship of Mr. Justice Rowlatt to investigate and advise the Government on the steps necessary for the protection of society against its enemies. The members of the Committee were men of the highest authority and qualifications, two of them being Indians, and their report, the Rowlatt Report, after an impressive, and indeed appalling, recital of the facts of Indian political crime during the seven years before the war, recommended certain measures, some permanent and others temporary, for the strengthening of the hands of the administration. These measures were embodied in two Acts, popularly known as the Rowlatt Acts, which were made law in spite of the unanimous protest of the Viceroy's Council, in March 1919.

The Rowlatt Acts are rather disconcertingly comparable with the famous Stamp Act of American history. Both measures were, in themselves, moderate and reasonable: both provoked explosions as unexpected as they were disproportionate to the occasion: in both cases the offending Acts were the occasion but hardly the real cause of the explosions. It is easy to defend both Acts, but it would have been better if neither of them had seen the light of day. The stamp duties were never collected, and the powers granted under the Rowlatt Acts were never used; both were repealed, but only after the damage had been done.

For it seems to have been the Rowlatt Acts which finally extinguished the last remnants of Mr. Gandhi's faith in the British *Raj*. Why a faith which had stood so many trials over so long a period of time should have boggled at measures directed solely against the promoters of violent measures which Mr. Gandhi, with his creed of non-violence, continued to deplore, is a problem beyond the solution of Western minds. One must accept the fact without trying to explain it. On the passage of the Bills Mr. Gandhi proclaimed a *hartal* in Delhi, i.e. a demonstration involving a day's complete cessation of business. This *hartal* led to rioting which spread with unexpected violence in the Punjab and the Bombay Presidency. The *hartal* was held on the last day of March, and by the end of April the Viceroy was able to announce that order had been generally restored. But that April was a terrible month for Englishmen, especially for those with wives and children residing in the provinces affected, much the worst month since the Mutiny; and in the middle of the month there occurred the massacre at Amritsar which, as broadcasted by the Indian native press, stirred the peoples of India from the Himalayas to Cape Comorin as no event had ever stirred them before.

Amritsar is the second city of the Punjab, with a population at that date of 160,000. Five Europeans had been murdered there by the Gandhi-ite mob under circumstances of ghastly brutality, and General Dyer, who was responsible for the restoration of order, considered that it was necessary for the safety of the British community to 'strike terror into the whole of the Punjab'. A crowd of many thousands of Indians, violently excited but for the most part unarmed, had assembled, in defiance of his orders, in a large public square in the city. On this crowd he opened fire for ten consecutive minutes. 379 were killed and 1200 wounded.

British opinion is still divided on General Dyer's action. The General himself had no doubts, either before the event or in retrospect. With deliberation and without panic he did what he conceived to be his duty. Very likely he had in mind the well-grounded opinion that the Indian Mutiny of 1857 would never have spread beyond Meerut if the first mutineers had been immediately and drastically punished; in reply to which it may be said that here was no mutiny, or threat of mutiny, among the sepoys of the Indian army. Some held, and still hold, that General Dyer's action 'saved India'. Others hold that it only made our position in the long run ten times more difficult, and also that it was a flagrant breach of the British tradition that in times of civil disturbance no more than the minimum force necessary to restore order may be used; that it was, in fact, a perfect example of the method of organized 'frightfulness' by which the Prussians had set themselves to cow the civil population of Belgium. Certain it is that the 'massacre of Amritsar' furnished the anti-British agitators with a more powerful argument than they had ever possessed before. To this day Indians write of it as if it had been a slaughter of the innocents; the barbarous murders of British subjects which had preceded it are never mentioned. This is entirely characteristic of the native press, which thrives upon the wildest abuse of every action of the Government, regardless of all European standards of truth.

The situation might have been retrieved if the Viceroy had at once disavowed the action of the General who was, in law, his agent. But British statesmen are, rightly, extremely reluctant to save a situation—and themselves—by that method. So nothing was done. Six months after the event a committee of six Englishmen and three Indians (the Hunter Committee) was appointed to investigate the circumstances of the massacre, and the six Englishmen produced a report exonerating General Dyer, with which the three Indians refused to concur. Meanwhile the British mercantile community had hailed the General as the saviour of India. At long last the problem was reviewed before the High Court of Parliament, where Mr. Montagu's condemnation of General Dyer's action was endorsed by a majority in the House of Commons but rejected in the House of Lords.

The disturbances in the Punjab were the proximate cause of an Afghan war which, though brief and almost unnoticed in England amid the clash of shattering events nearer home, involved the use of more troops than either of the Afghan wars which fill so many tragic and exciting pages in Victorian history. A new Amir, Amanullah, had ascended the throne after the murder of his father. He was a restless and conceited young man whose efforts to modernize his country some years later led him to make a widely advertised European tour, after which he was deposed and made his home on the shore of the Mediterranean. At the time of his accession he was the leader or the puppet of the military faction, and he resolved both to solve his domestic problems by 'busying giddy minds with foreign warfare' and to free the peoples of India from the oppression of British rule. But Amanullah had not reckoned on the aeroplane, and after a month's experience of the military potency of this recent invention he was ready for peace and the *status quo ante bellum*.

Within India disturbances continued, marked from time to time by hideous atrocities often directed as in Ireland against the police. The ill-fated Treaty of Sèvres added fuel to the flames. Three years before the opening of the war Indian Moslem agitators had discovered a somewhat artificial grievance in a supposedly world-wide Christian conspiracy for the destruction of the independence of the surviving Mohammedan states.

Freedom in India 1914-22

France was absorbing Morocco: Great Britain and Russia seemed to be arranging the partition of Persia: Italy and subsequently the Balkan States attacked Turkey whose Sultan, it was remembered, was Caliph, or head of the Moslem world. The Ali brothers, the leaders of this so-called *Khilafat* (Caliphate) movement, had been proof against the wave of pro-British sentiment which swept over India in 1914, and had been interned. They were now once again at liberty, and their agitation revived on a much extended scale. Mr. Gandhi discovered the elements of pure religion in the *Khilafat* movement, and conveniently ignoring the fact that *jihad* or Holy War is of the essence of Islam, accepted its alliance with his own movement for non-violent non-co-operation and salvation by suffering. The most conspicuous result of this uneasy alliance was the Moplah rebellion of 1921. The Moplahs are a vigorous and potentially savage Moslem people in the extreme south of India, descended in large part from the Arabs who had settled in Malabar for purposes of trade along the coasts of the Indian Ocean centuries before the British came to India. In 1921, stirred to enthusiasm by the ill-advised propaganda of Mr. Gandhi's new allies, they rose in rebellion and fell upon their Hindu neighbours. This marked the end of the Hindu-Moslem alliance, and in the years that followed the outbreaks of disorder in India were much more often 'communal' than anti-British. They were renewals of the religious civil wars which were endemic in the country before we established our authority, and would probably become endemic again if our authority were to be withdrawn.

At the end of the same year the Prince of Wales, treading in the footsteps marked by his father ten years before, came out for a three months' visit of ceremony. It had been intended that he should come a year earlier in order to inaugurate the new Constitution. That had been deemed inadvisable, but the visit though postponed was not abandoned. It was a bold experiment, to test once again, in circumstances so radically changed, the magic of the royal name. The visit proved that the magic had lost some, though by no means all, of its potency. There were riots and boycotts, but also scenes of splendid enthusiasm. Whether, as a matter of Indian policy, the experiment justified itself is a point on which opinions appear to differ. What was beyond question was the profound respect felt by British people, at home, in India and all over the world, for the courage of the Prince in undertaking this, the most hazardous of all his imperial progresses.

While all these things had been happening the new Constitution had arrived and was actually in operation. The main conclusions of the Montagu-Chelmsford Report had been that (i) during the whole of the 'transition period' prior to the grant of full self-government unalloyed by British control, the central government of India must remain responsible to the British Government at home, and therefore at liberty to override, in emergency, the vote of whatever elective assemblies might be provided for its guidance; and (ii) that experiments in representative government should at once be made in the eight great provinces of which British India (apart from Burma and certain small units) consisted.

For the central government the Report had recommended the immediate creation of an All-Indian Legislature, consisting of a Council of State, part elected and part nominated, and a Legislative Assembly based on the widest workable franchise. The Viceroy was empowered to override the Legislature if it failed to pass measures or to grant supplies which he was prepared to 'certify' as vital to the peace, safety, and interests of India. Thus a very real royal veto was retained. In the provinces experiments were to be made on the lines of what was called dyarchy. The departments of government were to be divided into two classes. One class, including the maintenance of order and control of the police, were 'reserved' in the hands of the British authorities; the other class, including such social services as education, were to be 'transferred' to ministers entirely responsible to representative assemblies, elected on the widest workable franchise.

Freedom in India 1914-22

Such was the Report, and such the constitution which had received royal assent in England in the last month of the year which had been signalized in India by the Amritsar massacre and the emergence of Mr. Gandhi as the enemy of British rule. Mr. Gandhi rendered the constitution a signal service in recommending all his followers to apply his favourite principle of non-co-operation to the elections of 1920 which constituted the new central and provincial assemblies. The result was the election of a great preponderance of moderate men. The sessions opened everywhere in a friendly spirit, and good practical work, wholesomely dull and humdrum Parliamentary work, began to be done.

And there, for the time being, English people were prepared to leave it. It would be too much to say that they looked upon their work, and saw that it was good. English people felt no enthusiasm for the Indian constitutional revolution which had been consummated in their name. Eighty-five years before Macaulay had foreseen this day and had written about it in his famous Minute on Indian Education. 'It may be', wrote Macaulay, 'that the public mind of India may expand under our system till it has outgrown our system; that by good government we may educate our subjects into a capacity for better government; that, having become instructed in European knowledge they may, in some future age, demand European institutions. Whether such a day will ever come I know not. But never will I attempt to retard it or avert it. Whenever it comes it will be the proudest day in English history.'

The day had come. Perhaps Macaulay was right, and we ought to have been proud. But historical forecasts, omitting all sordid detail, are so much more satisfying than historical events. Macaulay forecasted his own reincarnation in Mr. Montagu but he failed to forecast either General Dyer or Mr. Gandhi, and our pride, if we had any, was overlaid with disillusion, diffidence and anxiety about a future towards which, by our own admission, we had taken only the first step.

CHAPTER XXII

FREEDOM IN EGYPT 1914-1924

The English people have long been ashamed, it would seem, of their performance in Ireland and proud of their performance in India. What they have done in Egypt, though in its own way not less momentous, has never greatly interested them. Their establishment in the country was an inextricable chapter of accidents, and no hearts have ever beat faster at the mention of the name of Tel-el-Kebir, though this little battle has a melancholy interest as the last in which the British soldier wore his famous red coat. Lord Cromer, the maker of modern Egypt was one of the greatest of British proconsuls: he was, beyond question, devoted to the task he performed with such patient skill, but even he never pretended any devotion to the Egyptians on whose behalf he laboured. He never even took the trouble to learn their language. Our occupation of Egypt was always reckoned a temporary expedient, and the leaders of both political parties tried, on different occasions in the last twenty years of the nineteenth century, to get quit of the burden. Before the war Egypt had never been technically within the British Empire —on the maps it was painted not red but pink, for it was technically still subject not to ourselves but to the Sultan of Turkey.

When, however, in the first autumn of the war Turkey joined the enemy, this fiction could no longer be endured. The pro-Turkish Khedive Abbas, who had gone to Constantinople, was formally deposed; a member of his family who was loyal to the British connection was declared 'Sultan' in his place, and Egypt was proclaimed to be a British Protectorate. This last item, though it might be an announcement of a sufficiently obvious fact, was none the less a mistake. The Egyptian Nationalist movement, never entirely extinct, had been markedly reviving since the retirement of Lord Cromer in 1907, and the proclamation of a British Protectorate very naturally suggested to Egyptians that we had now thrown off the mask of our hypocrisy and proclaimed our intention to stay in their country for ever.

At first the war seemed to make little difference to Egypt. No attempt was made to enlist the enthusiasm of the people by inviting them to co-operate with us in the prosecution of the war. Instead, we went out of our way to say that Great Britain 'takes upon herself the sole burden of the present war without calling upon the Egyptian people for aid therein'. Having told the Egyptians that we did not want their aid, however, we soon found ourselves reduced to asking for it, and afterwards to taking it by methods as forcible as regularized conscription and much less fair in their incidence. Egyptian Labour corps not only played an important part in the Syrian campaign, but were employed in Mesopotamia and even in France. At the same time the stock in trade of the Egyptian peasant, his beasts and his cart, were requisitioned for military service. True, he was paid for his property; but as in most cases the money did not enable him to replace it, the payment was a mockery.

Another cause of discontent was the presence of great numbers of British and Australian troops in Egypt; they showed little respect for or courtesy towards the inhabitants of the country. In many cases battalions were required to lend one or more of their officers for administrative tasks which placed them in authority over the natives of the country. Needless to say, battalion commanders did not choose to part with their best officers for these purposes, and the results were sometimes deplorable. In fact we have nothing to be proud of in our management of Egypt during the war.

Two days after the Armistice Zaghlul Pasha, the leader of the ultra-nationalist party, presented to the British High Commis-

sioner a demand for complete independence. When it was rejected, he sought his country's fortunes at Versailles, like the
leaders of Sinn Fein at the same date and under the same circumstances. Thereupon the Prime Minister of Egypt, who had
co-operated loyally with the British Government throughout the
war, asked leave to go to England to confer with the British
Government on the future of his country. He was told that they
had no time to attend to him, and immediately resigned. Every
allowance must of course be made for the immense pressure of
work upon the British Government at that time. None the less,
they must be convicted of a serious and avoidable mistake;
Egyptians of all parties felt that their country had been simply
insulted.

It had in fact become necessary for the Egyptians to employ
the one infallible device for attracting the respectful attention of
a European government. Rioting broke out, and spread all over
Egypt, in March 1919, the month of Mr. Gandhi's *hartal* in
Delhi; much property was destroyed, and some British soldiers
were brutally murdered in a train. The riots were quickly suppressed, but were followed by widespread strikes of government
employees. The British Government now made amends by
sending out a Commission under Lord Milner, who had been a
leading member of Mr. Lloyd George's War Cabinet, to examine
and report upon the situation. It was no doubt natural enough
in the circumstances that the Nationalists, having gained so
much more by violence than they had gained by respectable
behaviour, persisted in methods of unreason, and subjected the
Milner Commission, in spite of its well-known friendly intentions,
to an elaborate boycott supplemented by such salutations in the
streets as 'God crash Milner! Long live Egypt! Long die England.'

Undisturbed by these evidences of hostility, the Commission
pursued its labours, and on his return to Europe Lord Milner
had an interview with Zaghlul Pasha, the upshot of which was
an important 'Milner-Zaghlul Agreement' afterwards incorpor-

ated in the Commission's Report. The British statesman and the 'Egyptian Gandhi', as the newspapers had begun to call him, agreed in recommending a Treaty of Alliance between Great Britain and Egypt, in which Great Britain would recognize the independence of Egypt as a constitutional monarchy with representative institutions, and Egypt would confer upon Great Britain the powers necessary to safeguard her special interests, would undertake not to enter into any agreement with any foreign power prejudicial to British interests, and would confer upon Great Britain the right to maintain a military force upon Egyptian soil.

More irritating delays followed, and more riots. At last, in 1922, Egypt was formally proclaimed an independent State by the British Government, certain questions being reserved for future settlement. The reserved questions were (i) the security of the communications of the British Empire (i.e. the Suez Canal); (ii) the military defence of Egypt; (iii) the protection of European communities living within Egypt; and (iv) the claim of Egypt to the Sudan, or alternatively to a share in the government of the Sudan. These questions continue in reserve, for all attempts to settle them have proved abortive. On the first three points the Egyptians have a case which must command the respect of all who sympathize with nations 'rightly struggling to be free', for until the Egyptian Government controls all the military forces within its territory Egyptian independence must continue to be a figure of speech. On the fourth point Egypt has no case at all. The Sudan is not inhabited by Egyptians, and though its conquest in 1898 was the achievement, under Lord Kitchener, of an 'Anglo-Egyptian army' it is entirely to British and not to Egyptian administration that the country owes its modern prosperity. Egypt's claim is, in fact, a claim of prestige, though she also professes alarm that our policy of using Nile water for the irrigation of the Sudan may starve the lower Nile of its water supply.

So the Egyptian problem has never, from the British standpoint, been completely solved and put away. Zaghlul in particular proved as unable as Mr. de Valera to be content with the measure of freedom which his country had, largely through his own efforts, secured. Exiled from his country during the years of trouble he was at last allowed to return and, supported by the Wafd or Nationalist organization, he secured a sweeping victory in the first Parliamentary elections of independent Egypt, and became Prime Minister. In his hour of triumph he seems to have entirely forgotten both the spirit and the letter of his agreement with Lord Milner, which had been the basis of the constitution under which he now governed Egypt. Anti-British agitation, closely associated with the Egyptian Government, culminated in the murder of Sir Lee Stack, the Governor General of the Sudan, who was shot while driving through the streets of Cairo in 1924. The British Government responded with an ultimatum of dramatic severity. Zaghlul Pasha resigned, and shortly afterwards King Fuad found that he could rule Egypt more effectively without a Parliament, a discovery which has been made by the rulers of many other countries in recent years.

CHAPTER XXIII

THE END OF THE COALITION

Coalitions are, by the law of their nature, temporary arrangements. The parties composing them must either fuse and become a single party or they must drift apart. Mr. Lloyd George's Coalition Government had been formed to achieve victory and end the war. It was renewed to make the peace and to carry through an ill-defined assortment of domestic projects lumped together under the general heading of reconstruction. It was assumed that there would be a clear-cut period of post-war emergencies, a period of transition intervening between the war and 'the normal'. But what was the normal? Would it ever come?

There were some who held that war, which had removed so many landmarks, had rendered the old parties, Liberal and Conservative, obsolete, and that the Liberals and Conservatives now in coalition should merge their identity in a new Centre Party. This view had the support of those Conservatives who appreciated the merits of Mr. Lloyd George, whether as a constructive statesman or as an electoral asset, and despised the old-fashioned and supposedly brainless Diehards of their own party. Prominent among these was Lord Birkenhead (formerly Mr. Smith), Lord Chancellor in the Coalition Government, a man much inclined to emphasize the importance of 'first-class brains' and to indicate the lack of them in others. With him was associated Mr. Churchill, who had been a Conservative M.P. before he became a Liberal Cabinet minister, and now once again found himself, though nominally a Liberal, inclining towards

The End of the Coalition

the Conservative associations of his youth. These two brilliant men and those who followed them held that the fundamental issue of post-war politics was Socialism, and that if the forces opposed to Socialism divided they would be courting defeat.

The argument was hard to resist, but other factors, quite outside the sphere of any argument based on general principles, were strong on the other side. Great historic organizations of men, such as were the Liberal and Conservative parties, gather about them sentiments and loyalties which cut deeper than any abstract argument. An argument for the fusion of Eton and Harrow, even if it were in the interests of educational efficiency, would not gain much sympathetic attention from the Old Boys of those schools. The old parties, judged as abstractions, might appear obsolete to a political philosopher. To those who had devoted their best energies to working for them and in them, they were living organisms with proud traditions of national service and achievement. And what, by contrast, were the traditions and achievements of the post-war Coalition? It had blown hot and cold. It had contradicted and stultified itself in relation to every subject it had touched. It had poured out money on social reforms, and subsequently repealed them. It had prosecuted a barbarous war against Sinn Fein, and subsequently capitulated to Sinn Fein. It had imposed an unworkable settlement on Germany, and was now quarrelling with France in an attempt to whittle away the settlement it had imposed. It had promised everything and accomplished nothing. It had proved a false start. What was wanted was a new beginning, a new Government with a clean sheet. Only the Conservative party, with a Conservative Prime Minister, could supply such a Government. Thus argued an increasing number of the back-bench Conservatives on whose votes the continuance of the Coalition Government depended.

In March 1921 occurred a personal incident of the first importance in this connection. Mr. Bonar Law's health broke down and he had to retire at once from all political activity.

The End of the Coalition

The circumstances of Mr. Bonar Law's accession to the leadership of the Conservative party have been described on an early page of this book. Since that date, ten years before, he had won a position of authority over his followers within the House of Commons such as had belonged to no Conservative leader in that House since the day on which Disraeli became Lord Beaconsfield. His name does not figure prominently in histories of the war because it was not in his line either to stimulate the public or to improve upon the plans of the commanders in the field. But his work had been not the less valuable; he had raised more money by tax and by loan than any other Chancellor of the Exchequer. More than that, he had kept the machine of government going. He had not been at ease in Mr. Asquith's Coalition, and perhaps Mr. Bonar Law's friends are right in saying that Mr. Asquith failed to appreciate his merits, but to Mr. Lloyd George his services had been invaluable. 'My job in the war', he once said to a friend, 'is hanging on to the coat-tails of that little man and holding him back.'

As Prime Minister Mr. Lloyd George had practically abandoned the House of Commons. He had revived, for his own relief, the office of Leader of the House, as known in old days when the Prime Minister happened to be a Peer. This arrangement, originally intended as a wartime innovation, had been prolonged into the era of Allied Conferences, an era which had never come to an end. Mr. Lloyd George's position had come to approximate to that of an American President, surrounded by a personal staff of assistants and prepared to intervene as the personal representative of the nation at whatever point he might be required. Mr. Bonar Law had performed, with full authority, nine-tenths of the duties of the Prime Minister within the House of Commons. He was pre-eminently a House of Commons man, perhaps the most effective debater of his generation. He had been from the first the linchpin of the Coalition. Now he was gone.

The Conservatives elected Mr. Austen Chamberlain as their

The End of the Coalition

leader in his place, and Mr. Lloyd George at once appointed him Leader of the House, but his authority in his own party could not be the same as Mr. Bonar Law's. And then, in the autumn, Mr. Bonar Law's health improved sufficiently to allow his return to the House of Commons as a private member without the burdens of office. It was said that he would never again be a strong man; but perhaps that would prove too pessimistic a forecast. Assuming, the wish being father to the thought, that it did so prove, then the Conservatives had their leader ready, outside the doomed Coalition.

During Mr. Bonar Law's absence from politics his late colleagues had made their Irish *volte-face*, to the indignation of many Diehards. When he returned to the House the Treaty negotiations were in progress. Steps were taken to ensure that he received confidential information about their progress; he approved their result, and for the moment the Coalition was steered clear of a formidable rock.

But in 1922 nothing went well for the Government. The numbers of the unemployed refused to fall much from their peak at two million; the German mark descended into the gulf; the Genoa Conference, the most advertised Conference since that of 1919 at Paris, produced nothing but an ominous *rapprochement* between Germany and Russia; the French entered the Ruhr; Mr. Montagu, Indian Secretary, author of the famous 'Reforms', which had come to be regarded, by those who disliked them, as embodying a policy peculiar to their author, committed a flagrant breach of Cabinet etiquette and had to resign, to the unconcealed satisfaction of the Diehards; and, to cap all, a ridiculous and unsavoury scandal in connection with the bestowal of titles undoubtedly shook public confidence in the Prime Minister.

None the less, the end when it came was unexpected. As late as September the *Round Table* was saying: 'It seems likely that the Government's natural term will be reached' (i.e. the autumn of 1923); and 'Everyone is beginning to realize that in some

300

The End of the Coalition

shape or other the next Government is bound to be a Coalition too.' As late as September 29th Sir George Younger, the formidable Conservative Whip, was praising the Prime Minister's handling of the Chanak crisis. Yet ten days before the end of October the Coalition had fallen and Mr. Bonar Law was Prime Minister of a Conservative Government.

The end of the Lloyd George Coalition has many points in common with the fall of Mr. Asquith six years before. In both cases there had been a prolonged and unmistakable decline in popularity pointing to ultimate disaster at an uncertain date. In both cases also the end was reached with a suddenness which took the public by surprise, resulting as it did from the secret manoeuvres of a small number of powerful individuals: but the manoeuvres of 1922 have as yet been much less completely made known to the general public than those of 1916. Some say that it was the Prime Minister himself who forced the crisis. Trusting in the declared loyalty of Mr. Chamberlain, the Conservative leader, and in fact of all his best-known Conservative colleagues, he determined to bring the back-benchers of the party to heel by means of an immediate election, and Mr. Chamberlain summoned the meeting of the party at the Carlton Club on October 19th, to unfold the new situation. Others say that the Carlton Club meeting was summoned to meet and subdue the rebellious elements in the party, the proximate cause of rebellion being the bellicose attitude of Mr. Lloyd George and the ministers most closely associated with him toward the Turkish crisis at Chanak. An appeal which had been issued claiming the support of the Dominions, issued it was said without the concurrence of Lord Curzon, seemed to portend war, and Mr. Bonar Law had written a letter to the *Times* which was equivalent to a motion of censure on the Government. These two versions of the crisis are not at all incompatible with one another, and may be regarded as complementary aspects of one and the same story.

However that might be, the party met at the Carlton Club on

The End of the Coalition

October 19th, and Mr. Baldwin delivered the speech which settled the issue. At that date Mr. Baldwin was President of the Board of Trade. He was not accounted an important member of the Cabinet, and his personality was unknown to the general public, which was surprised to read in the *Times* on the following morning that he was the 'best-liked man in the House of Commons'. His political career had associated him closely with Mr. Bonar Law, for he had been his Parliamentary Private Secretary and subsequently Financial Secretary to the Treasury when Mr. Bonar Law was Chancellor of the Exchequer. Mr. Baldwin, while expressing respect and affection for his titular leader, Mr. Austen Chamberlain, described Mr. Lloyd George as a dynamic force, and 'a dynamic force is a very terrible thing'. It had smashed the Liberal party to pieces, and was in process of disintegrating the Conservative party also. Mr. Baldwin therefore moved a resolution to the effect that, when the election came, the Conservative party would fight it 'as an independent party with its own leader and its own programme'.

It is said that Mr. Baldwin went to the meeting expecting his resolution to be defeated and his own official career terminated thereby. But the resolution was carried by 187 votes to 87, almost all the Cabinet Ministers voting with the minority. Mr. Lloyd George at once resigned, and Mr. Bonar Law, whose course of action had been doubtful, on account of his precarious health, to the very last, consented to form a Conservative Government and at once dissolved Parliament.

Mr. Chamberlain, Lord Balfour, Lord Birkenhead, Sir Robert Horne, and a few other Conservatives of the Coalition Cabinet refused to serve in Mr. Bonar Law's Government, partly no doubt from a personal loyalty to Mr. Lloyd George and partly from a conviction that the break-up of the Coalition was a mistake and that the result of the election would prove the necessity of another. They went into the election as Conservative-Coalitionists, but the great majority of the 87 who had voted for the Coalition at Carlton House now ranged themselves

The End of the Coalition

as supporters of Mr. Bonar Law. The Liberals offered the electorate two rival parties, Independent and National (i.e. Coalitionist), inspired by all the mutual animosities that had been engendered by Mr. Lloyd George's treatment of Mr. Asquith six years before. Superficially the situation was confusing enough, but in fact the issue presented to the electorate was very simple. Did they, or did they not, want Mr. Bonar Law and his programme of one word—Tranquillity?

It was very little that Mr. Bonar Law offered. He had never been a sanguine man, and he was now less sanguine than ever. In the interests of Tranquillity he discarded from his programme the one great plank on which he had risen to leadership ten years before, the one constructive policy he did not regard with scepticism—Tariff Reform. He promised that his Government, if returned to power, would undertake no fundamental changes in fiscal policy. What he offered was a rest from alarums and excursions, a Government which would leave the country alone. 'I do have at the back of my mind', he said, 'this feeling that in a condition so critical as ours the real cure must come from better trade and better industry.' How restful were such platitudes, and also the assumption that trade and industry would revive if only the Government would sit still and not disturb them.

What were the alternatives? The Labour party offered nationalization of mines and railways, a capital levy, revision of the peace treaties, a higher standard of life for the workers, better housing, better education. For those who wanted more excitement here was value for their money. As for Mr. Lloyd George he was a programme in himself. He had been seventeen years in office, and for fourteen of them he had been the active and fermenting principle in British politics. He was not tired; he could go on for ever. But the country was tired of him. Mr. Bonar Law was not much given to metaphors, but he hit upon a good one on this occasion. After speaking of the late Prime Minister's success in heartening and inspiring the country during the war he remarked that, though the drummer boy was an asset in the

The End of the Coalition

hour of battle, he and his drum were only a nuisance afterwards among the casualties in the hospital ward.

Mr. Lloyd George's reference to Mr. Bonar Law was less happy. 'He is', said Mr. Lloyd George, 'honest to the verge of simplicity.' But that was just the sort of man that was wanted. 'If in truth', said Mr. Baldwin, 'Mr. Bonar Law resembles the portrait which his predecessor has drawn of him, then the public will certainly say "Here is the man for us." '

They did say so. They gave the Conservatives a clear majority over all the other parties, 344 out of 615. Labour doubled its numbers and rose to 142. Mr. Asquith's Liberals secured 60 seats and Mr. Lloyd George's Liberals 57.

'What we want', said President Harding, the successor of President Wilson in America, 'is not heroics but healing: not nostrums but normalcy: not revolution but restoration: not surgery but serenity.' Tranquillity was 'normalcy' translated into English.

PART IV
CONVALESCENCE
1922-1929

CHAPTER XXIV

TRANQUILLITY IN OFFICE 1923

The General Election at the end of 1922 had given the Conservative party a blank cheque, and had instructed them to draw it for as small a sum as possible. In all respects the new Government was to be a contrast to its predecessor, and it was good to see that the new Prime Minister was disinclined to magnify his own office. Soon after the election had established his authority sundry communists and advanced persons, constituting themselves a Council of Action, organized 'hunger marches' of the unemployed, which, converging on London from all, or at least several, points of the compass, demanded an interview with the Prime Minister. Mr. Bonar Law refused to see them, simply directing them to the Ministers of Health and Labour, as the heads of the departments responsible for the redress of their grievances. It was a cool reminder to all concerned that government is a matter of business, not of headlines and supermen.

Among domestic questions the Government singled out housing as a subject requiring immediate attention. There were two intimately connected Housing questions, the provision of new houses and the renting of old ones, and over the second of these questions the Government quickly found itself in collision with the views of its supporters in the constituencies. The Rent Restriction Act of 1920, extending the scope of an Act passed during the war, had prevented profiteering by the landlords of the smaller middle-class and working-class houses during the housing shortage by forbidding the raising of rents beyond a fixed percentage of the rent in 1914, and the eviction of tenants. Unfortunately rent control, while it averted some of the most undesirable results which would otherwise have followed from the shortage of houses, tended at the same time to prolong the shortage by discouraging the building of new houses, since these could not profitably be let at rents equivalent to the controlled rents of the old houses. The Government therefore announced that it would introduce a measure progressively decontrolling rents. But even before it had made clear the detail of its proposals the electorate, in the words of the *Round Table*, 'laid its ears back and kicked'. Three members of the Government who had failed to win seats in the general election, one of them the Minister of Health who would be responsible for the proposed measure, were defeated in by-elections in reputedly safe Conservative constituencies.

Mr. Bonar Law responded handsomely by dropping both his policy and his Minister of Health, offering the vacant post to Mr. Neville Chamberlain. Mr. Neville Chamberlain, the half-brother of Mr. Austen Chamberlain, had pursued a career more closely resembling that of his famous father. He had entered Parliament comparatively late in life, having first made his mark as a successful man of business and an enterprising Lord Mayor of Birmingham. He approached the Housing question with a long experience of its municipal aspects, and carried through Parliament in the course of 1923 a Housing Act which proved one of the most successful measures of Conservative statesmanship since the war. Avoiding both the prodigality of Dr. Addison and the parsimony of the Geddes axe, he gave the building schemes of private builders and local authorities a little assistance and not too much, giving it in a manner which both discouraged extravagance and limited the subsidy to the cheaper types of houses.

Meanwhile Mr. Baldwin, as Chancellor of the Exchequer, had been to America and had secured a settlement of the Anglo-American debt. The circumstances of that debt have already been described: also the Congress Resolution that it should be paid in full with four and a half per cent interest within a period of twenty-five years, and the issue by the British Government of the much-debated Balfour Note. The terms which Mr. Baldwin brought back were a great improvement upon what Congress had threatened. The rate of interest was reduced to three per cent for the first ten years and thereafter three and a half per cent and the period of repayment was extended to sixty-two years. Mathematical calculations proved that the concessions granted to Mr. Baldwin amounted to twenty-eight per cent of the original American demand. Mr. Bonar Law, we have since been told, accepted the settlement with reluctance, and only in deference to the views of the rest of his Cabinet. He foresaw that these annual payments of thirty, and afterwards forty million pounds would some day prove a burden too grievous to be borne; but the nation was glad to have the thing settled. The Balfour Note, if conveniently misread, brought assurance that we should extract as much from Europe as we paid America. The annual revenue for 1922-23 was going to show a surplus of over a hundred millions, and Mr. Baldwin was going to make another reduction in the Income Tax. Sir Robert Horne had reduced it from six shillings to five shillings in 1922; in 1923 it came down to four and six.

When Mr. Bonar Law first contemplated the course of action which placed him in the seat of Mr. Lloyd George, he took the precaution of consulting his doctors. They told him that he was 'good for a year at least, perhaps two'. Thus, with the unobtrusive patriotism that had marked every step in his career since the beginning of the war, he took office under sentence of death. Before the end of May ill health compelled him to resign, and before the end of 1923 he was dead. After his funeral in Westminster Abbey, Mr. Asquith, we are told, remarked to Lord Beaverbrook: 'It was fitting to bury the Unknown Premier by the side of the Unknown Warrior.' Mr. Bonar Law had never become a salient personality in public estimation, but he was a very good Parliamentarian, and as a party leader he must be ranked as easily the most successful of his generation. When he succeeded Mr. Balfour, after the passage of the Parliament Act, many assumed that Conservatism was the faith of a dwindling remnant and that the future lay between the Liberals and the Socialists. The fact that his party occupied the largest number of seats in the House of Commons throughout the whole of the post-war period down to the present day, except during the two years of the second Labour ministry 1929-31,[1] was in large part the result of Mr. Bonar Law's leadership, which combined two qualities not always found in association: it was at once honest and astute. Yet it may well be that, by the spring of 1923, his leadership had served its term of usefulness. Tranquillity could, after all, be no more than a temporary reaction. There had always been, his friends tell us, a vein of pessimism in the temperament of Mr. Bonar Law. England in convalescence needed a guide and counsellor more genial, more robust, more obviously human and obviously English. Such a leader, though few realized the fact, stepped quietly into Mr. Bonar Law's place in the person of Mr. Baldwin.

Mr. Baldwin's succession had remained to the last uncertain. Many thought that the occasion of Mr. Bonar Law's retirement would be seized to bring back into the fold the lost leaders who had remained Coalitionists in 1922. If that happened, the succession would pass to Mr. Austen Chamberlain who had so nearly become leader in 1911, and had in fact succeeded to the leadership of the party under Mr. Lloyd George when Mr. Bonar Law's health first gave way in 1921. But the party was as disinclined to take back Mr. Lloyd George's too recent friends as the German states who deserted Napoleon in the spring of 1813 were disinclined to open their arms to the German states who deserted him in the autumn. Apart from these Coalitionists, however, there was one man whose claims incom-

[1] Even in the 1929 election the Conservatives polled more votes than any other party.

parably surpassed all others, if length of distinguished service were the criterion. Viceroy of India, Member of the War Cabinet, Foreign Secretary ever since the signature of the Treaty of Versailles—Lord Curzon himself was by no means the only person who confidently expected that Lord Curzon would be the next Prime Minister. But it would not do. Apart from the inconvenience of having a Prime Minister in the House of Lords, Lord Curzon himself was much too like a Victorian nobleman as envisaged by a Victorian caricaturist to serve as a Prime Minister in post-war England. In any case he was too old; a man who was old enough to be Viceroy of India in 1898 could not possibly be young enough to learn the duties of the Premiership in 1923. With his usual magnanimity he accepted his heartfelt disappointment and consented to remain Foreign Secretary.

As for Mr. Baldwin, at that date few of us knew anything about him except that he had played a leading part in the break-up of the Coalition, and had negotiated the American debt settlement. The *Round Table* could say little more than that he had long been 'an enlightened and successful employer' and that 'the intellectual interests which are naturally suggested by his family connection with Burne-Jones and Kipling are an assurance against the limitations of the pure business view'.

All through this year the French were in the Ruhr, and seemed determined to stay there until—until what? Formally they were determined to stay there until they had exacted from Germany the uttermost farthing of what under the Reparations Agreement of 1921 was due to them, but as a financial investment the occupation of the Ruhr was so plainly unproductive that the onlooker was driven to look for some further purpose—the permanent cession of the Rhineland, or perhaps the break-up of the German Federal Republic. Actually the French were in that state of angry desperation in which people hardly know what they want for themselves; they only want to injure their enemies. Someone said that the clue to the French view of reparations was to be found in the fact that the word itself, so alien and technical in its English dress, is to be found outside every motor garage in France. It is simply the French for 'repairs'. Northern France had been battered to pieces by the German invasion. The French set themselves, in haste and in many cases with extravagance, to rebuild their ruined towns and villages. The money was for the most part subscribed in loans by the thrifty French bourgeoisie and peasantry: interest and principal were to be repaid from Germany. Germany's default meant that the French investor lost his money, and meantime German industry was enjoying the hectic and temporary boom which always accompanies inflation of the currency. It was too much; the result was the occupation of the Ruhr.

English opinion was entirely out of sympathy with France, and was irritated by the apparent impotence of the Conservative Government. It bitterly resented the official hypocrisy of Lord Curzon's statement, in April, that the Anglo-French Entente was 'the one solid and stable factor in a world of flux'. The word *entente* was supposed to mean 'friendly understanding' and that was surely the very last term to describe our present relations with our ex-Ally, who had become the principal obstacle to the resettlement of Europe. However, Lord Curzon's speech, apart from this unpopular sentence, contained what might prove a fruitful proposal. He urged Germany to make a new offer to France, proposing guarantees for the continuance of her payments. Germany at once responded with an offer in terms which, whatever their feasibility, were fantastically generous if judged by standards which became commonplace a few years later. M. Poincaré rejected them within twenty-four hours of their reception. After this the British Government could do, and did, nothing, except throw out the suggestion that Germany's creditors would have to look for their security not to an indefinite occupation of German territory but to an international control of German finance. This suggestion afterwards bore fruit in the Dawes plan. For the moment nothing came of it, and in its December issue the *Round Table* foreboded that 'before these words reach the reader Germany may be once again a mere geographical expression, a collection of weak and independent states, as she was in the time of Napoleon'.

It was in fact the darkest hour which proverbially precedes a dawn. Italy under Mussolini, following the example of France, had seized Corfu and was defying the League of Nations. The Poles had for some time been in occupation of the city that was supposed to be the capital of Lithuania. 'Nationalism', says the writer of another article in the December *Round Table*, 'has been exalted to the dignity of a universal religion, and in its defence the armies of Europe can boast, on a peace footing, of one and a half million men more than in 1913. The spirit of nationalism is insatiable: no sooner has it made political boundaries conterminous with those of race than it is driven by a restless fever to absorb alien peoples. Peaceful co-operation between men of different races within the same state—perhaps the highest achievement of humanity in its political life—is not even sought as an ideal, but rejected as an absurdity.' As for the democracy for which President Wilson had hoped to make the world safe: 'The Parliamentary system is not indigenous to the Continent. . . . Continental democracy since the war has scored only one important success. It has effectively obstructed the application of the principles of sound public finance, and it seems likely to perish from the completeness of its own triumph.' As for the British Government and the British people they were reduced to the role of mere spectators at a tragedy, to all appearance 'as powerless to influence or postpone as it is beyond the power of the spectator to divert the destiny of an Oedipus or an Othello from the path conceived for him in the imagination of the poet'.

But before the end of the year the reign of Tranquillity in Great Britain had come to an abrupt and unexpected end. The Prime Minister was dissatisfied with his position. The figures of unemployment obstinately refused to fall below about 1,300,000.

Tranquillity in Office 1923

Mr. Baldwin had been a protectionist since Joseph Chamberlain's tariff reform campaign twenty years before and he believed that in a policy of protection might be found at least a partial cure for unemployment.

The free trade system which Joseph Chamberlain had challenged in vain was, in 1923, no longer intact. In 1915 Mr. McKenna, Chancellor of the Exchequer in Mr. Asquith's Coalition, had imposed import duties on various manufactured articles of which the most important were motor cars, and in 1921 Mr. Lloyd George's Government had gone further in the same direction with the Safeguarding of Industries Act. This Act legalized the protection by duties of $33\frac{1}{3}$ per cent of (i) certain industries which were defined as 'key industries' since their maintenance was considered indispensable in the event of war; (ii) any industry, other than foodstuffs, which could prove that it was subject to competition that was unfair, either by reason of dumping or because the competing product came from a country with a depreciated currency. But the practical results of the Act had been small, because the Government which passed it had been, for the most part, strongly suspicious of protectionist doctrine in general and reluctant to apply it to any particular industry. Mr. Baldwin now wanted to go much farther along the road to protection, and found his hands tied by the pledge against fundamental change in the fiscal arrangements of the country, given by Mr. Bonar Law in the previous year. Somewhat suddenly, at the end of October, he announced the dissolution of Parliament and went to the country on a policy of protection and imperial preference, without food taxes. It is quite possible that he had in mind, as an ulterior object, the reunion of his party with the small but distinguished body of Coalitionist-Conservatives.

The election which followed was welcomed only by the Liberals, for the defence of free trade recalled their famous victory in 1906 and enabled Mr. Asquith and Mr. Lloyd George to reunite their forces. The Conservatives were vexed at being

led out of the fortress of power to fight in open and confused
country, and Labour was notoriously short of funds.

The results of the election presented an interesting study to
those arithmeticians who deplore the rough and ready methods
by which we measure the modulations of the Voice of the
People. The percentages of votes cast for the three rival parties
varied hardly at all from those of the election of the previous
year. To be exact, the Conservative percentage fell from 38 per
cent to 37.5 per cent; the Labour percentage rose from 29.2 per
cent to 30.7 per cent; the Liberal percentage rose from 29.1
per cent to 29.9 per cent. Yet in the House the Conservative
party fell from 344 to 257, Labour rose from 142 to 192, and the
Liberals from 117 to 157. (In each Parliament the addition of a
few independent members must be made to raise the totals to
615.) Yet, arithmetic apart, the result was decisive enough.
Mr. Baldwin had declared that in his judgment the country
required a policy of protection, and the electorate, by returning
a majority of nearly a hundred free traders, had declared that it
did not wish this experiment to be made.

Ever since the days of Disraeli it had been usual for a Prime
Minister, when defeated at the polls, to resign without waiting
for the formal vote of the House of Commons. The present
occasion, however, was peculiar in that the Conservatives were
still the largest party in the House, and Mr. Asquith was under
no obligation to support a Labour vote of censure. Mr. Baldwin
therefore retained office until Parliament met in the new year,
thus giving ample time for Mr. MacDonald to consider the
problem of the construction of the first Labour Government,
and for the press and public to speculate upon the possibilities
of the situation. Lord Rothermere made his readers' flesh creep
in the *Daily Mail* with horrid prognostications, and exhorted Mr.
Baldwin and Mr. Asquith to save the country from imminent
ruin by combining their forces. It is quite likely that Lord
Rothermere and the professional journalists who took the same
line were not affrighted by their own alarums, for the manufac-

ture of sensations was their daily trade; but their readers took the matter to heart and inflicted on Mr. Asquith a correspondence surpassing in volume and vehemence his postal experience at any period of the war. On the other side, some of the detached intellectuals of Labour, such as the editor of the *New Statesman*, urged Mr. MacDonald to offer and Mr. Asquith to accept high office in a Labour-Liberal Government which would command a clear majority for the 'cause of progress'.

None of the party leaders were impressed by these conflicting adjurations. Forecasting his line of action in a speech at the National Liberal Club in December Mr. Asquith said that, since sooner or later the country must make trial of a Labour Government, it would be well that the trial should be made under such conditions as those of 1924, in a House of Commons that could turn it out of office as soon as it had a mind to do so. When Parliament met in January the course events would follow had been predetermined. Mr. Asquith rose to support the Labour amendment to the Address. After admitting, with a gesture towards his colleague Mr. Lloyd George, that he had known 'administrations which had done more actual mischief' than that which confronted him on the Treasury bench, he declared that he certainly had no mandate to keep it in office. The amendment was carried, and the stage was cleared for an interesting and harmless experiment.

CHAPTER XXV

THE GROWTH OF THE LABOUR PARTY

A student of the photographic group of the Labour Cabinet which took office in January 1924 might perhaps receive the impression that most of the persons there represented fell into one or other of two sharply contrasted types. He would observe on the one hand men of obviously intellectual temperament and high-strung nervous organization, lean and hungry men, bookish and theoretical men, men sicklied o'er with the pale cast of thought, men such as can often be seen abstrusely pacing the courts and quadrangles of Oxford and Cambridge. But alternating with these he would also observe men of a very different order; solid, broad-shouldered men whose book is the book of life only, instinctive and practical men accustomed to manage and lead, men of the type who, in different circumstances, earn knighthoods as successful captains of industry. No doubt the contrast can be pressed too far, and some members of the Labour Cabinet could be adduced to prove our physiognomical analysis too simple, but as far as it goes it will serve our purpose. The Labour Party, like the rest of us, had two parents: it was the offspring of an alliance between Socialism and the Trade Union Congress; between men who believed in a fundamental reorganization of society and desired a new political party as the instrument of their purpose, and men who, not necessarily socialists at all, desired a new political party which would give expression to whatever might from time to time be the practical demands of the organized bodies of trade-unionist wage earners.

317

The Growth of the Labour Party

The peculiar, and to foreigners elusive, character of the British Labour Party is the result of its history. It was at once a party with a creed and the party of a class; but class counted far more than creed. The woolliness of its socialism has always been the despair of its continental friends. 'Labourism' has never got much beyond the all too simple demand that the wage-earning classes shall have their 'fair share' of the national income. Mr. Snowden was supposed to be one of the great brains of the movement, but we find him saying in the House of Commons (4th May 1909): 'My object is to make the rich poorer and the poor richer, *because there is no other way under heaven by which you can make the poor better off except by making somebody else poorer than they are.*' Only in England could a Socialist politician of the front rank talk such nonsense.

The search for the origins of the Party leads us back to the great industrial depression which cuts across the middle of the Victorian Age, from the early 'seventies till near the end of the 'eighties. Looked at as a whole, it is of course true to say that the seventy years from the building of the main line railways down to the Great War was a period of unprecedented expansion, when population grew as it had never grown before and the wealth of all classes grew faster than population. But if one resists the temptation to look at the period as a whole, one finds that it is divided into three parts—the early prosperity, which was the golden age of Matthew Arnold's Philistines; the late prosperity of the Jubilees and the Imperialists; and cutting across like a dark shadow between them, fifteen lean years.

Those fifteen years—we may concentrate on the central core of them in the early 'eighties—brought the Victorian optimism of Samuel Smiles and his school to a halt. It became plain that economic progress was not automatically cumulative; that poverty and all that went with poverty would not retreat inevitably and indefinitely before the blast of the trumpets of steam power and free trade. The problem was not so simple, and those who set themselves to think it out afresh found ready to their hands the revolutionary theories of the continental socialists, more particularly of Karl Marx, whose industrious researches in the library of the British Museum were just then drawing to a close. And in the nick of time there came a book from America, more readable and convincing to British minds than Marx, Henry George's *Progress and Poverty*. It is a long and elaborate economic treatise but, unlike most economic treatises, it is almost exciting. It is lucid, aggressive, and optimistic in tone, and the whole argument is made to lead up to a single and apparently simple remedy for the ills of society, namely a 'single tax' on land. Young Ramsay MacDonald read it while still a boy at Lossiemouth, and it decided the bent of his career as of many others. Long afterwards he wrote of this book: 'It familiarized people with the idea of common use of property, of common creation of values, of common claims to share in aggregate wealth. It led them to discuss the problem of poverty, not as the result of personal shortcoming, but as an aspect of a certain form of social organization.'

Thus arose the little Socialist societies of the early 'eighties, such as the Social Democratic Federation which inclined to believe in revolution, and the Fabian Society which held that the essentials of socialism were so obviously in the logic of the future that no new political party was needed to secure their enactment by the ordinary processes of legislation. This society was the stronghold of the Webbs who, from the 'nineties onwards, exerted over the social politics of both the old political parties an unofficial influence which is made very apparent in the *History* of M. Halévy.[1]

But there was another factor of the same period predisposing the minds of an important class towards socialism, quite apart from the alternations of prosperity and depression. So long as the factory system was in its experimental stage, when factories were small and the normal type of business was the 'one-man show', every able and enterprising workman had a good chance

---

[1] *Histoire du Peuple Anglais au XIX Siècle*. Epilogue. 1895-1914.

The Growth of the Labour Party

of becoming a master. Most of the first generation of mill owners were self-made men. As late as 1859, when *Self Help* was published, and indeed much later, Samuel Smiles could convince his thousands of readers with his picture of the virtuous employee, whose virtues transform him into an employer. But those days were passing. The industrial structure had stiffened; the organization had become infinitely more complicated. The normal type of business was coming to be the limited company, with its hundreds or thousands of employees, owned by shareholders scattered over the country and directed by economic supermen. A capitalist class stood over against a working class, and the gulf between them seemed to have become unbridgable.

The Liberal individualist of the first half of the nineteenth century had been content that there was a natural 'ladder', whereby the enterprising could climb into the upper regions of the social and industrial system. He was prepared to demand that this natural ladder should be broadened by the introduction of free elementary education. But this artificial broadening of the ladder was of somewhat illusory benefit if those who climbed it found all the seats at the top of the ladder already occupied. This was roughly the position of many of those who now became working-class leaders. In the previous generation these men of more than the average intelligence and energy had drifted up out of the wage-earning class. Now they found themselves confined within it, and were very rightly disposed to criticize a system which thus confined them. The men who would otherwise have been 'self-made men' became leaders of the class in which they had been born, and the trade unions gave them their opportunities.

But the trade unions of the 'eighties were a long way from Socialism. They were scarcely even democratic, for the unions were organizations of skilled craftsmen, jealously guarding their crafts against the competition of the vast unorganized hordes of unskilled Labour. The Trade Union Congress had been established in 1868 to agitate for certain clearly defined reforms in the

The Growth of the Labour Party

status of the unions. These reforms had been secured in the course of the next eight years, and thereafter the Congress had relapsed into routine and somnolence. Twice in the early 'eighties it rejected by large majorities motions in favour of manhood suffrage for Parliamentary elections. A few individual trade unionists, such as John Burns, afterwards one of the first Labour members entirely independent of the old parties, were in active protest against the conservatism of Congress, but they had little following.

The democratizing of trade unionism came with surprising suddenness in the 'nineties, after the famous Dock Strike of 1889. The result was a rapid extension of trade unionism among the unskilled, and thereafter the building up of the great industrial unions which, like the Miners Federation and the National Union of Railwaymen, aimed at the inclusion in a single organization of all grades of workers within a single industry. Under such circumstances as these Socialism and Trade Unionism could draw closer together. The trade unions awoke to a livelier interest in politics, and the Socialists could forget Utopian dreams in the practical task of inspiring a new and more ambitious trade-union policy. The time was ripe for the birth of the Labour party, as soon as the Socialists could persuade the trade unions to untie their purse strings.

This was not so easily done, and a Scottish Socialist miner, Keir Hardie, having failed to persuade the Congress to found a Parliamentary Labour Party, founded one himself, and was elected member for West Ham in 1892. In 1895 his organization put up twenty-nine candidates, one of them Mr. MacDonald who contested Southampton; but all except Keir Hardie himself were defeated. These events, however, stirred the trade unions to action, and the year 1900 saw the establishment of the Labour Representation Committee, consisting of delegates from the Trade Union Congress, from Keir Hardie's organization, known as the I.L.P. (Independent Labour Party), the Fabian Society and the Social Democratic Federation. It was the mar-

The Growth of the Labour Party

riage of the parents of the Labour party—Trade Unionism and Socialism—and the secretary to the Committee was none other than the eloquent and handsome young Scotsman who, twenty-four years later, became the first Labour Prime Minister.

The Committee failed to score any successes in the Khaki election of 1900, but the next year conferred upon it the choicest of boons in the shape of a first-class grievance. The Taff Vale judgment, undermining the foundations of the complicated edifice of trade-union privilege, provided a platform topic which came home, in Bacon's phrase, to the business and bosom of every trade unionist, a topic in which neither of the other parties consented to interest itself. As a result twenty-nine candidates of the Committee secured election in 1906. These, with twenty-two other Labour members elected with Liberal support, combined to form what was now for the first time formally christened the Parliamentary Labour Party, with fifty-one members.

The new party was able to score smartly in the course of the first weeks of its Parliamentary career. The Liberal Government introduced a moderate measure dealing with the grievance of trade unions under the Taff Vale judgment. Labour at once tabled a much more radical measure, and the Liberal Government grafted on to their own measure the principal features of the Labour Bill. Whatever may have been the reasons for this display of Liberal weak-mindedness, it counted as an effective advertisement of the new party. None the less, the eight years that followed marked no perceptible advance. It was Lloyd George and not any of the professing Socialists who secured the limelight as the leader of the projected onslaught upon the citadels of the rich. Indeed in the elections fought upon the Budget and the Veto Bill in 1910 the Labour party shrank from fifty to forty, and the 'Labour' that secured headlines in 1911-13 was not the party in the House but the leaders of the big unions.

The outbreak of the war showed up at once the dual character of the party. The intellectuals of the I.L.P., the 'men who had

The Growth of the Labour Party

never done a day's manual labour in their life', Mr. MacDonald and Mr. Snowden, opposed the war from start to finish. With them was Keir Hardie, the real founder and the first leader of the party. He had, it is true, been a miner from his childhood upwards, but he was temperamentally always more of an idealist than a trade-union boss. He deserved the reverent affection with which his followers regarded him, and it must be reckoned a pity that *Punch*, that infallible index of the limitations of the British bourgeoisie, could never discover in him anything but a subject for rather spiteful jesting. The war broke his heart and he died of it. The great majority of the Labour members, however, were as 'sound' on the war issue as the trade unionists who had sent them to Parliament. Mr. MacDonald, who had succeeded Keir Hardie as leader some years before the war, was at once deposed in favour of Mr. Henderson, an iron moulder and trade unionist from the Tyne, who assured the Government that his party would do all in its power to maintain the 'splendid unity' of the nation. When coalitions became the order of the day various Labour members accepted office. Mr. Henderson was a member of Mr. Lloyd George's War Cabinet of five, until his colleagues refused to allow him to attend a Socialist International Conference at Stockholm, when he was succeeded by Mr. Barnes, and Mr. Clynes greatly distinguished himself by his efficiency as Food Controller during the last year of the war.

None the less it cannot be doubted that the war, though at the time it split the party and obscured its independent existence, was in the long run of the very greatest service to its fortunes. The war, as everyone understood, closed a great epoch of history and opened a new one. The terms 'pre-war' and 'post-war' became fundamental categories of thought on every conceivable subject. In these circumstances it was natural, indeed inevitable, that all who were not temperamentally conservative should feel that Labour's lack of experience and historic tradition would be a positive advantage in the post-war age. 'The old men have ruined the world: it is for the young to build it up again.' Facile

The Growth of the Labour Party

generalizations of this kind were all in favour of a party unencumbered, it might be supposed, by political inhibitions which the war had rendered obsolete. As for Labour's successful competitor in the pre-war years, the Lloyd Georgian variety of Liberalism, where was it now? The Lloyd George of the Budget had become the Lloyd George of the War Lords and the profiteers. The so-called Lloyd Georgian Liberals of 1918-22 were crypto-Conservatives, and their subsequent reunion with the Independent Liberals brought with it not peace but a series of squabbles which destroyed whatever chances the party may ever have had of regaining its pre-war position. Many of the keenest Liberal supporters of the pre-war Lloyd George were going to drift over to the Labour party.

In view of the future before it, a Labour Party Conference in February 1918 amended the party constitution and adopted a new programme. The aim of the new constitution was to broaden the basis of the party which hitherto had rested on the membership of its constituent organs, the Trade Unions, the I.L.P. and the two Socialist societies. The new constitution invited the membership of all who 'produce by hand or brain'; in fact, it proclaimed that the party was henceforth to be national, and no longer an instrument of restricted classes and sects. At the same time Socialism was for the first time formally adopted as the programme of the whole party: 'To secure for the producers by hand or by brain the full fruits of their industry, and the most equitable distribution thereof that may be possible, upon a basis of the common ownership of the means of production and the best obtainable system of popular administration and control of each industry and service.'

The profit which Labour was ultimately to draw from the war was hardly to be realized in the 'Coupon' election of December 1918. The party withdrew its representatives from the Coalition Government, and fought as an independent organization. In winning 57 seats it made a slight numerical improvement in its position, but the pacifists, who were also the most skilful Par-

liamentarians, were heavily defeated. The Parliamentary history of the Labour party during the four years of the Aftermath
is uninteresting and insignificant. Mr. Clynes, the new leader on
the strength of his Food prestige, proved no expert in the arts of
opposition.

Meanwhile Mr. MacDonald, deprived of his seat in the House
by an overwhelming hostile vote at Leicester, was diligently going to and fro and up and down the country. By speech and
pamphlet, by personal intercourse with local leaders, he gathered together the broken pieces of Labour idealism, and re-
established his claim to become, when the war fever was over,
the only possible leader of his party. When he stood in 1921 as
candidate at a by-election in the Labour constituency of Woolwich, all the forces of 'patriotic' demagogism were mobilized in
support of the V.C. who was his carefully selected opponent.
Mr. MacDonald failed to win the seat by a few hundred votes,
but there were many convinced anti-Socialists who agreed with
Mr. Garvin of the *Observer* in wishing that he had won.

A student of the output of Mr. MacDonald's prolonged campaign will be more impressed by the courage, the energy, and
the eloquence of the man, than clear as to the nature of his
programme. Mr. MacDonald, like Gladstone before him, is
primarily a man of words, and the more the words the less
certain their final application. The post-war Coalition policy
offered many broad targets for criticism, and that Mr. Mac-
Donald criticized effectively goes without saying. It was when
one came to construction that the purple mists of his beloved
Scotch mountains began to descend. What was this Socialism so
continuously on Mr. MacDonald's lips: was it a programme for
the next Parliament or for Utopia? a creed or a sentiment?

Lenin, who never minced his words, said of this campaign:
'Ramsay MacDonald's speeches and articles are the best example that could be given of that smooth, melodious, banal, and
Socialist-seeming phraseology which serves in all developed
capitalist countries to camouflage the policy of the bourgeoisie

inside the Labour movement. MacDonald remains throughout a bourgeois pacifist and middle-class reformer, recognizing the class struggle only as a figure of speech, just as do all the deceivers, sophists, and pedants of the bourgeoisie.' There was a kind of truth in this. Real socialism of the continental sort had very few adherents in England, however matters might stand on the Clyde and in the Rhondda. In order to secure a majority in the House of Commons MacDonald had to consider the marginal voter in the doubtful constituency. This marginal voter— and there were millions of him—was a deeply discontented man. He was thoroughly disillusioned about the old parties, their promises and performances; he was losing faith in the possibility of 'reforming capitalism'. He was ready to take up the cry of Socialism provided its appeal was merely destructive and Utopian. If he had been told that Socialism meant what it means in the continental textbooks, he would have recognized it as a tyranny worse than conscription or prohibition. What Mr. MacDonald gave him was the kind of Socialism he could swallow, and the reason why Mr. MacDonald gave it so effectively was that it was the kind of Socialism he had for thirty years been swallowing himself.

Reviewing the past history of his party at Cardiff in February 1923 Mr. MacDonald said that though 'born' in 1900, Labour was the heir of all the Liberal opinion that had been hammered out before it, heir of all the experiments and ideals of the nineteenth-century Radicals. Mr. MacDonald, in fact, was shaping for the part of a post-war Gladstone. In this he represented his own generation, growing old and mellow and worldly-wise. It was the sort of thing to draw the marginal men to his standard, but hardly the sort of thing to satisfy the keen young Socialist workers at the core of his party, who stood now where the eager MacDonald had stood, when he shook the dust of Liberalism from his strong young feet and joined Keir Hardie in the 'nineties. These young men would have preferred not a Gladstone but a Parnell.

The Growth of the Labour Party

The election of 1922 more than doubled the party representation. They were now 142 strong and could displace the Liberals as 'His Majesty's Opposition'. The intellectuals, the pacifists, and the younger trade unionists, especially those from Scotland and Wales, combined to depose Mr. Clynes in favour of Mr. MacDonald, but before Mr. Baldwin's first Government was out, some of them had become much less certain of their man. It was noticed that as Leader Mr. MacDonald allied himself with the solid moderate men who had split with him in 1914 and voted against his leadership at the end of 1922, rather than with the stalwarts of Socialism to whom he owed his position. In fact the simple analysis of the party into trade unionists and socialists had been complicated by several cross currents. The pre-war men among the socialists combined with the older trade-union leaders to form a front bench of politicians, supported by whatever was docile and disciplined on the back benches, whereas the younger trade unionists, especially those from the Clyde, found allies among the youthful and intransigent intellectuals, who looked not for office in the near future but for 'Socialism in our time'. Their time might be long. The front bench were quite as old as most front benches, and had lost most of whatever interest they ever had in the fundamental reorganization of society.

The election of 1923 was not wanted by the Labour party, and it brought them no distinct accession of strength at the polls. Accidents in the distribution of the voting, however, gave them an extra fifty seats, and office dependent on the goodwill of the Liberals. What was about to be tested was not Socialism, which was ruled out from the start, but the capacity of the party calling itself Socialist to improve upon the current domestic and foreign policy of a capitalist state in a capitalist world.

CHAPTER XXVI

THE FIRST LABOUR GOVERNMENT 1924

A fortnight before he became Prime Minister Mr. MacDonald delivered a speech at the Albert Hall which, though it was preceded by the 'Marseillaise' and followed by 'The Red Flag', was welcomed by a prominent Liberal politician as 'pure Liberalism', and the personnel of the new Cabinet foreshadowed a policy of conciliation designed to preserve as long as possible the delicate balance of forces which had entrusted office to a party commanding less than a third of the votes of the entire House of Commons. It was an elderly Cabinet. Lord Haldane was Lord Chancellor, an ex-Liberal and a philosopher whose greatest national service had been his reorganization of the army for the war of which Mr. MacDonald had disapproved. The Admiralty was entrusted to Lord Chelmsford who consented to serve in the Cabinet as a non-party man. Two members of the Cabinet, Lord Olivier and Mr. Sidney Webb, had been contributors to the well-known volume of *Fabian Essays* thirty-six years before. Mr. Snowden was at the Exchequer, and most of the principal administrative offices were occupied by experienced trade-union leaders, several of whom had held office in one or other of the War Coalitions. The only advanced man to attain Cabinet rank was Mr. Wheatley, a Clydesider, who became Minister of Health. Mr. MacDonald himself took the Foreign Office in addition to the burden of the Premiership. The objection to this course was obvious, but the public fully shared Mr. MacDonald's own view that he was much the best man for the Foreign Office, and he doubtless hoped to relieve himself of some of his Parliamentary duties by appointing the worthy Mr. Clynes as Deputy Leader of the House. The Prime Minister took an early occasion to announce that his Government, being in a minority, would accept adverse votes on departmental issues, and indeed, during its brief existence, it suffered about a dozen defeats such as, under other conditions, would have involved the resignation of the Government or the dissolution of Parliament.

In its social policy the Government had to select proposals which would secure the support of at least one of the opposing parties. The easiest line of advance was a more generous treatment of the unemployed. Accordingly the benefits received under the Insurance Act were increased by a few shillings a week, and the restrictions on the payment of 'uncovenanted benefit' to those who had exhausted their claims were somewhat relaxed. All this increased the burden which the already bankrupt insurance fund imposed upon the Treasury, but it could be excused on the ground that unemployment had fallen to very near the million mark and might be presumed (the wish being father to the thought) to be going to fall still farther. But in the more important sphere of legislative remedies for unemployment itself the session proved that all assertions that the Labour party had a 'cure for unemployment' had been nothing but the hot air of electioneering. On this subject Mr. Shaw, the unfortunate Minister of Labour, found himself riddled with derisive criticism from front and rear. He could only tell his Conservative critics across the floor of the House to 'wait and see', and retort to his back-benchers at a party meeting that 'remedies for unemployment could not be produced like rabbits out of a hat'. The valid answer to this was that, during the election, he and all his friends had declared that the hat was bulging with rabbits.

The only really successful legislator of the Labour Government was Mr. Wheatley, whose Housing Act, though severely criticized and amended in the course of its passage through the House, proved a solid contribution to the Housing problem. Mr.

The First Labour Government 1924

Chamberlain's Act of the previous year had been designed primarily to stimulate by subsidy the activities of private builders, though it also assisted schemes of local authorities. The Labour party found its results disappointing, and Mr. Wheatley's measure, with a more generous subsidy, was designed to assist schemes of local authorities, subsidized from the rates, and producing houses for renting only, not for sale. In effect these two Acts, politically rivals, proved to be complementary and worked on side by side. Between them, in the course of the next half dozen years, they went a long way towards wiping off the arrears of housing that had been accumulating since before the war. The number of houses built under each Act was nearly half a million. The subsidies given under both Acts were reduced in 1927 owing to the decrease in the cost of building materials. A surprisingly large number of houses were also built without assistance from either Act.

The Budget only proved how sound, how bigoted a Gladstonian was Mr. Snowden. He inherited a surplus of £48,000,000, half of which he devoted to 'the great Radical ideal of the free breakfast table', reducing or abolishing the duties on tea, coffee, cocoa, and sugar. He refused to proceed with the proposals for Imperial Preference which had been drawn up by the Imperial Conference of the previous year, and announced the abolition of the McKenna duties which for the last eight years had been levied on various manufactured imports including motor cars. This prospect gave pleasure to very few outside the old guard of Liberalism, and stirred murmurs of protest from many Labour members sitting for constituencies in which the McKenna industries were carried on. But few men were less responsive to 'murmurs' than Mr. Snowden. His back-benchers toed the line, and with Liberal support the McKenna duties were sacrificed on the altar of free-trade principle.

Apart from this sacrifice to his religion Mr. Snowden's Budget was a popular—critics said a vote-catching—measure. It made no provision for the cost of the new Housing Bill, or for the project of Widows' Pensions which was adumbrated as an event of the near future. The next Budget would presumably be much less agreeable. Perhaps Mr. Snowden had a shrewd idea that he would not be called upon to frame it.

An abundance of strikes, none of them very long or very expensive, proved that Labour in office was no insurance against Labour unrest. There was, of course, no reason to suppose it would be, but the fact was none the less a cause of disappointment and disillusion to the average voter. There was a strike of the Locomotive Engineers and Firemen, reduced to impotence by the fact that large numbers of the workers in this trade were members of the National Union of Railwaymen, which did not call its members out. There was a strike of the dockers, a strike of the London bus and tram conductors, and a strike on the London underground railways. A coal strike was narrowly averted. In fact industry was beginning to recover from the slump which attacked it in 1921, and the strikes were the inevitable result of a Labour offensive to recover some part of what had been lost in wages during the bad years. They were entirely unconnected with the merits or demerits of the Labour Government.

None the less they were a cause of anxious distraction, as was also the almost continuous insubordination in the ranks of the Parliamentary party. Labour, as everyone was saying, 'spoke with two voices'. One voice was that of Mr. Maxton, a young schoolmaster M.P. from the Clyde, whose attractive personality won him many friends among those who were amused by his conflicts with his own leaders. 'Politics', said Mr. Maxton in May, 'is no game, it is a very definite and bitter class war, which could not be fought with kid gloves, because the common people were not to be raised until the wealthy and powerful were pulled down.' That was real socialism, indistinguishable from communism. Mr. MacDonald, on the other hand, wanted the very name of Socialism to be dropped as a party label 'because after all there is a sort of bookish association about Socialism'. Let the party be called Labour, 'and then you will have a heart and spirit that in some sort of mystical way associates yourself with the great simple godlike heart of the common people, with all its failures yet with all its divine potentialities and possibilities.' The Labour party in the House contained, it was said, fifty men who had been preachers in chapels or other religious institutions, but the Prime Minister was far the finest preacher of them all. Like President Wilson and like Mr. Gladstone he made great audiences feel good, and only a few of those who heard him afterwards enquired within themselves what exactly it had all amounted to.

One of the first duties of Parliament in the early months of the year is the presentation of departmental estimates, and the back-benchers at once became critical when they found the army and the navy left intact and the air force positively increased. They were angry when Lord Olivier, as Secretary of State for India, condemned the agitation for *swaraj*, and maintained the policy of the preceding Government. Mr. Maxton attacked the Government for supporting a guaranteed loan to a 'private enterprise' called the Sudan Cotton Plantation Syndicate, and carried forty-two supporters with him into the opposition lobby.

The Labour party, unlike other British parties, elects an Executive Committee to manage its affairs, and while Mr. MacDonald selected a Cabinet of the Right, the party elected an Executive of the Left, of which Mr. Lansbury was the leading spirit. Mr. Lansbury had for many years been editor of the *Daily Herald*; he was a vigorous old Christian Socialist with a warm heart and a muddled head. Old age had not yet cast over his temperament the chill of moderation, and he and his Executive Committee summoned Minister after Minister to appear before them to answer for their shortcomings. Mr. Henderson, for example, was censored for his policy as Home Secretary, because he had taken no steps to reinstate the police strikers who had been expelled from the force after the strike of 1919.

But the chequered and humiliating experiences of the Government at home were balanced by the striking successes of Mr. MacDonald in foreign policy. When he entered office the French were still in the Ruhr, and it was not likely that the acidulated despatches of Lord Curzon would ever get them out. If Mr. MacDonald could solve the Franco-German problem, such a national and international service would much more than compensate for the few months' muddling at Westminster. In fact he succeeded. He was favoured by a combination of auspicious events on the Continent, but that does not detract from his achievement, for the essence of statesmanship is to seize upon auspicious events and extract the good things latent within them. Mr. MacDonald by his art in establishing friendly personal contacts and his skilled management of the Conference of London proved himself a great international statesman.

The circumstances which favoured him were three in number. In France the franc began to slip, and with it the security in office of M. Poincaré, the author of the Ruhr policy. He was defeated in the general election held in May, and succeeded by M. Herriot, the leader of the Coalition of the Left. M. Herriot could approach the Ruhr problem with an uncommitted mind, and the complete failure and indeed discredit of the French attempts to establish German 'separatist' governments in the Palatinate and the Rhineland had weakened the resolve of those who had hoped to detach these districts permanently from the German Republic. Meanwhile Germany had re-established her currency on the basis of the *Rentenmark*, and a German general election in the same month as the French, though indecisive like all German elections between the establishment of the Republic and the victory of the Nazis, had given the country a Reichstag likely to support the Chancellor, Dr. Marx, and his foreign minister, Dr. Stresemann, in the conciliatory policy they were already pursuing in the Ruhr. Finally, there was the Report of the Dawes Committee, issued in April. The occupation of the Ruhr has been the measure of the failure of the Inter-Allied

Reparation Commission, and towards the end of 1923 that body had in fact been superseded by a new committee of experts to investigate Germany's financial position and produce a new scheme for the payment of reparations based on economic facts instead of political passions. On that Committee America consented to be represented and an American, General Dawes, was elected chairman. The essential feature of a necessarily highly technical Report was the establishment in Germany of an international Transfer Committee to which reparations should be paid. This Committee was to fix the amounts that Germany could and should pay at any given time, and to be responsible for the transfer of Germany's payments into the currencies of the creditor states.

These were the cards in Mr. MacDonald's hands, and it may well be that the Opposition parties prolonged the life of the Labour Government in order to give him the chance of playing them. He had already established, in a remarkable manner, relations of personal cordiality with M. Poincaré, but with M. Herriot his chances of converting personal friendliness into political agreement were obviously much brighter. After entertaining M. Herriot at Chequers, he was able to issue invitations to a Conference in London of all the states interested as creditors in German reparations, and the Conference, after wrestling with intractable problems for three weeks, established terms on which the American financial houses would consent to make to Germany the loan of £40,000,000 which was an essential preliminary of the Dawes Plan. The Conference was then in a position to invite the Germans to London, and the Dawes Plan was accepted by all members of the Conference, France undertaking to complete the evacuation of the Ruhr within a year from that date.

It was a great achievement, and very likely it was beyond the range of any statesman in the world at that moment except Mr. MacDonald. He was fully entitled to pride himself on the fact that he, a consistent opponent of the war, had negotiated, exactly ten years after the war began and nearly six years after it ended, the first amicable agreement between the principal belligerent powers. 'Almost for the first time in five years,' said the *Round Table* for September, 'it seems reasonable to expect some alleviation of the plagues that have tormented Europe.' The Dawes Plan was not to be regarded as in itself a final solution of the reparations problem, but 'it gives Europe a breathing space, possibly of several years duration. In that time passions may have abated and the pressure of financial problems may be relaxed. In a changed atmosphere political feuds may become susceptible to mediation, and the nations of Europe ripe for a complete settlement.'

Unfortunately Mr. MacDonald had other international fish in fry. Concurrently with the Reparations Conference there was also sitting in London an Anglo-Russian Conference, which, under the guidance of Mr. MacDonald and his Under Secretary for Foreign Affairs, Mr. Ponsonby, produced a treaty which sealed the fate of the Labour Government.

It is curious to recall that these same two statesmen had already got themselves in trouble over Russia long ago, in the distant past before the war. In 1908 King Edward VII paid a visit to the Tsar at Reval. The abortive Russian Revolution of 1906 had been suppressed with violence only two years before, and Mr. MacDonald contributed an article to the press in which he protested warmly against His Majesty 'hobnobbing with a bloodstained creature . . . a common murderer' and various Liberal and Labour members drew up and signed a memorial protesting against the royal visit. A debate in the House of Commons followed; 'disloyal' speeches were made, and the King omitted Mr. MacDonald and Mr. Ponsonby from the list of persons invited to the royal garden party at Windsor. It is said that Mr. MacDonald was subsequently forgiven, but not Mr. Ponsonby, because 'being born and bred in the purple'—he was, in fact, a son of Queen Victoria's Private Secretary—he ought to have known better.

The First Labour Government 1924

It was now the turn of Mr. MacDonald and Mr. Ponsonby to 'hobnob with bloodstained creatures'.

As soon as he was installed at the Foreign Office Mr. Mac-Donald had reversed Lord Curzon's Russian policy, and had despatched a note recognizing the Union of Socialist Soviet Republics as *de jure* rulers of Russia, and inviting the Soviet Government to send plenipotentiaries to London to discuss the question of the Russian debts and the means of establishing friendly relations and full commercial intercourse between the two countries. The project in itself, as an attempt to break away from the barren anti-Bolshevism of the previous régime, was altogether to be commended, but the public and the Opposition parties awaited the outcome with considerable anxiety. Mr. MacDonald's great merit as an international statesman was that he was always prepared to be magnanimous, to believe the best of the foreign governments with whom he had to deal. People feared that in dealing with the Russians his magnanimity might degenerate into credulity. They feared also that he might be preparing to throw a sop to his mutinous back-benchers. However, they elicited in June a promise from the Prime Minister that on no account would Great Britain guarantee a loan to the Russian Government.

When, two months later, and at the very end of the session, the Conference completed its labours, the Treaty, as described to the House of Commons, was found to contain the offensive loan, though so hedged about with conditions that it was never likely to become operative. At once opposition flared up. A Conservative speaker asked the Prime Minister whether he would refrain from initialling the Treaty until empowered to do so by Parliament. He refused to do so and in fact appended his signature on the following day, an action which placed the position of the Government in a new light. In the sphere of legislation nothing could be done without the assent of a majority of the House of Commons, but in making treaties the Prime Minister acts on behalf of the Crown, and though the House may subsequently

render his position untenable, it cannot control his actions so
long as he occupies his position.

Another awkward question made its appearance in the last
days of the session, a trivial thing in itself, but just the sort of
question on which tottering Governments are brought down.
The Attorney General, acting on instructions from the Home
Office, issued apparently without the knowledge of the Home
Secretary, instituted a prosecution for sedition against one J. R.
Campbell, editor of an obscure Communist paper, on account
of an article urging soldiers to disobey orders rather than shoot
their fellow countrymen when on strike—a dilemma with which
the soldiers of the British army were in no immediate danger of
being confronted. This prosecution irritated Labour members
who only a few years before had conducted a national campaign
against the prosecution of the veteran agitator Tom Mann for a
precisely similar offence. Questions were asked in the House and
ambiguously answered. A few days after the end of the session
the prosecution was dropped on the alleged grounds that Campbell had an excellent war record and (or) that the words of his
article were found to be not seditious within the terms of the
law. Campbell, however, brushed aside these allegations, and
declared that he had been released on account of the pressure
brought upon the Government by their own back-benchers.

Thus the political discussions of the summer holidays, which
might otherwise have been devoted to expressions of satisfaction
over the really great achievement of the London Reparations
Agreement, centred upon the Russian loan and the Campbell
case, and it became more and more certain that the Opposition
parties would combine to destroy the Government on one or
other of these issues. It became common form to say that Mr.
MacDonald had 'surrendered' to his extremists. In actual fact
he had done nothing of the kind. The Russian Treaty was the
Prime Minister's personal and considered policy. He held that
its terms were harmless and that the 'gesture' it involved, with
its offer of a loan which would never be lent, was internationally

The First Labour Government 1924

wholesome. As for the Campbell case, it was one of those muddles which illustrate the fallibility of politicians but involve no principles. One need not be a socialist to hold that the prosecution of an obscure communist writer was a game which, on second thoughts, was not worth the candle. If proof were needed of the Prime Minister's essential 'soundness' on the subject of Maxtonism, it could be found in the new preface which he wrote at this time for a reissue of his book on *Socialism: Critical and Constructive*, a preface which is in fact a vigorous attack on socialism as understood by most of its enemies and as preached by most of its friends. In it he told trade unionists that 'profiteering' was as rampant among trade unionists as among capitalists, and that 'public doles, Poplarism, strikes for increased wages and limitation of output were not only not Socialism but might mislead the spirit and policy of the Socialist movement'.

The Government fell because both the Prime Minister and the Liberals had come to the conclusion, for different reasons, that the experiment had lasted long enough. The Prime Minister had proved in his own person and in those of, at least, several of his colleagues that Labour was 'fit to govern'. He had scored one resounding success in the international sphere, and his colleagues had managed to pass several little social reforms through a hostile Parliament. To go on farther would be almost certainly to fare worse: to exhibit the weakness of his position and the dissatisfaction of his more ardent supporters. It is likely that he also took account of the fact that the numbers of the unemployed, which had flattered his Government by declining in the early months of the year, were again on the increase. The absurd practice of all post-war Governments in claiming credit to themselves for any decline in unemployment rendered them as deservedly liable to blame whenever the figures moved in an adverse direction.

The Liberals, on the other hand, had been in a wretched position from the first; they had been the 'patient oxen' dragging the Socialist car, only to be sacrificed at the end of the journey. The very fact that their conditional support circumscribed the policy of the Government and compelled it to be no more than 'Liberal' increased the weakness of their own hold upon the electorate. As the Prime Minister said after his defeat, 'Our success has been our trouble. If we had made a mess of things we should not have been turned out.' These words excited much amusement in Opposition circles, but they contained a measure of truth. As a Socialist Mr. MacDonald had proved a disappointment, but regarded as a Liberal Prime Minister he was the most inspiring since Gladstone whom in his strength and his weakness he resembled much more closely than Mr. Asquith or Mr. Lloyd George had ever done. Every exhibition of the Prime Minister's Gladstonianism transferred Liberal votes to Labour; every exhibition of Maxtonite mutiny transferred other Liberal votes to the Conservatives. It was imperative to bring this attrition on both flanks to an end.

It so happened that Parliament had to meet at the end of September, a month before the usual time, to carry legislation which would enable the Government to appoint an additional member on the Ulster Boundary Commission, in face of Ulster's refusal to appoint one of her own. The Campbell case came up as soon as the Ulster business was through the House of Commons. The Prime Minister's defence of the conduct of his Government was at once provocative and obscure. He declared that if defeated he would dissolve Parliament, and the two Oppositions took him at his word.

A few days before the end of the electoral campaign the Foreign Office published a communication which it had despatched to M. Rakovsky, the Russian Minister in London, to which was subjoined the celebrated Zinoviev letter. This was a document which, if genuine, had been sent by Zinoviev, the head of the Third International (which was in effect the Propaganda Department of the Russian Government) to the Communist party in Great Britain, urging British comrades to work for the violent overthrow of the British constitution. Whether or not the letter was genuine, and how or why it was published at that moment are matters which remain obscure and are not important. No one disputes that Zinoviev was in the habit of addressing the subjects of foreign Governments in this manner. The letter could be regarded as an additional argument against the Russian Treaty, but it is doubtful if it affected the result of the election as much as Labour apologists like to think. The notion that it was the prime cause of the overwhelming Conservative victory, which followed it, is quite preposterous. It is true that the 'swing-over' of the electorate surpassed expectations, but that has been a feature common to many elections since the war, because the prophets have made their forecasts in accordance with pre-war standards. They forget that, with the enfranchisement of women, the proportion of the electorate which floats with the tide of emotional circumstance, unmoored to party allegiances, is very much higher than it used to be.

The Conservatives gained 161 seats, and came back to Parliament with 413 members, a majority of over two hundred over both 'progressive' parties combined. Labour seats fell from 193 to 151. The Liberals lost over a hundred seats and came back with only 40. The figures of the total votes cast for each party revealed the very remarkable fact that Labour had polled over a million more votes than in 1923. In fact the party scored a much greater increase of votes in the election which drove its leaders out of office than in the election which had put it in. The first Labour Government might lie mouldering in its grave, but the cause was marching on. This paradox is easily explained. In 1923 many Labour candidates owed their seats to the fact that the anti-Labour majority was divided, on the issue of Protection, between Liberal and Conservative candidates. In 1924 Mr. Baldwin dropped Protection from his programme, and the number of three-cornered contests was greatly reduced, Liberals who could not hope to win the seat for themselves retiring in the interests of Conservative candidates.

The decision of the electorate taken as a whole was plainly

inscribed on the result. Most people wanted a strong Government, and gave their votes to the only party which seemed likely to be able to supply one. They were to be rewarded with a five years' exemption from service at the polling booth.

CHAPTER XXVII

MR. BALDWIN'S SECOND GOVERNMENT: LOCARNO

The general election which drove Labour from office was attended by one of those semi-secret intrigues, the complete history of which will only be known, if it is ever known, to a later generation.[1] It was an attempt to revive the Coalition, or Centre party, at the expense of the leadership of Mr. Baldwin. Sir Robert Horne was to be Prime Minister, and the scheme had the support of Lord Birkenhead, Mr. Churchill, and perhaps Mr. Lloyd George; also of certain Lords of the press who, as later events proved, cherished a curiously vindictive animosity towards Mr. Baldwin. Mr. Churchill and Mr. Lloyd George were both of them statesmen of the type that does not easily confine itself within the channels of a single party; it is a type to which some of our greatest statesmen have belonged—Chatham, Palmerston, Joseph Chamberlain. Mr. Lloyd George had received anything but a warm welcome in the ranks of the Liberals after the reunion of that party in 1923. Mr. Churchill had never returned. In the election of 1922 he had encountered one of the strangest mishaps of his adventurous career, being defeated at Dundee by a Socialist-Prohibitionist of the name of Scrymgeour, and since then he had, like the sun in Shakespeare's simile, been 'wandering with the antipodes', seatless and unattached. Early in 1924 he had unsuccessfully contested the St. George's division of Westminster as an Independent anti-Socialist, being defeated

---

[1] My account is based on that given by Mr. Wickham Steed in his book *The Real Stanley Baldwin*. Mr. Steed, who had recently ceased to be editor of the *Times* was no doubt in personal touch with many of the parties concerned.

by the orthodox Conservative candidate. Only on the eve of the election had he rejoined the Conservative party which he had left on the tariff issue twenty years before.

But it would be wrong to suppose that the leaders of the Centre party intrigue of 1924 were influenced only, or even mainly, by personal considerations. There was a real case for a fusion of all Liberal and Conservative elements opposed to the advancing tide of Labour. It would be possible to argue that the case of the Centralists of 1924 was proved good by the formation of the National Government of 1931, though by that time the roles were reversed, and Mr. Baldwin was a principal architect of a fusion from which both Mr. Churchill and Mr. Lloyd George stood aloof.

However that may be, and whatever the precise details of the intrigue of 1924, it was swept off the map by the overwhelming character of the Conservative victory, which made the official party leader unquestioned master of the situation. All the Coalitionist Conservatives who had stood aloof in 1922-23 accepted office under him, except Sir Robert Horne who is said to have refused the thankless post of Minister of Labour. Mr. Churchill became Chancellor of the Exchequer, and Mr. Austen Chamberlain Foreign Secretary. This last appointment was perhaps the best available, but it was not very inspiring. Everybody liked and respected Mr. Austen Chamberlain, but no one had ever supposed him to possess the touch of genius for which his office called. He would probably be an improvement on Lord Curzon, but he seemed commonplace in comparison with Mr. MacDonald. It was easy enough to reverse the engines where Mr. MacDonald had run off the rails, and to inform Mr. Rakovsky that the Russian Treaty would not be ratified. What was much more important and much more difficult was to build the superstructure on the foundations which Mr. MacDonald had so well and truly laid, to carry on the task of Franco-German reconciliation.

Fundamentally it was the problem of Security. France was

determined to be, or to feel, secure. Left to herself she believed she could only attain security by the time-honoured methods of Louis XIV and of Bismarck, by maintaining a position of dominance which was intolerable to her neighbours and inconsistent with international justice. How could Great Britain contrive to give France security of another and better kind without committing herself to continental obligations from which she was determined to keep free? 'It is evident', said the *Round Table* in June 1924, 'that great pressure will be put upon Britain, not only by her Allies, not only by some powerfully organized bodies of opinion in the British nation itself, but also by the logic of European history since the Armistice, to enter into specific obligations, with naval and military liabilities, to maintain the European *status quo*.' To put the matter very bluntly, there would be an attempt to blackmail us into undertaking undesirable and impossible military and naval obligations, with the threat that only so could be restored that economic prosperity in Europe on which our own economic prosperity so largely depended.

There was, of course, the League of Nations. It was primarily an organization through which the nations could, if they were wise, co-operate to secure the peaceful settlement of their mutual differences and discover thereby how much they had to gain by such co-operation. It was a vital element in the Covenant that all nations should agree that any nation which resorted to war without giving time for the League to invoke arbitration, to try to arrange a peaceful settlement, or at least publish to the world an impartial statement of the matter in dispute with proposals for its peaceful solution, should be regarded as a common enemy. The exact nature of the obligations of members of the League in their treatment of a 'common enemy' as thus defined, was uncertain, and there were some who held that the obligations imposed by the wording of some clauses of the Covenant went dangerously too far, and that, when the issue arose, members would be found to be unwilling to live up to them. The Covenant had assumed that America would be a member of the League. As she was not, it was certainly dangerous that Great Britain should be committed in advance to the use of her navy in a manner which might bring her into collision with the United States.

There were in fact two schools of thought among convinced supporters of the League of Nations. The predominating British view, at any rate in Conservative circles, was that the real security for peace was to be found in the wisdom and charity of the policies pursued by the various States of the world, and that the League was primarily an organ of co-operation to advise and encourage them in the pursuit of wise and charitable policies. Where the terms of the Covenant went beyond this, those terms were unwise and would prove inoperative. But on the Continent and in schools of thought represented in England by the League of Nations Union, an opposite view prevailed. According to this view the League did not go far enough. What was wanted was a more cogent Covenant, ensuring that in any outbreak of war all members would actively participate on the side which the League found to be in the right.

A scheme to secure this purpose had been prepared in 1923 by a Committee of the League under the chairmanship of Lord Robert Cecil, known as the 'Draft Treaty of Mutual Assistance'. The object of the treaty was to induce States to limit armaments by offering to those which did so on an agreed scale guarantees against aggression much more complete and far-reaching than anything in the Covenant itself. The argument for this plan might be stated in the following terms: Armaments are a form of insurance against being attacked, but unfortunately these same armaments afford a means of attacking others against which they in turn have to insure. We therefore offer an alternative and innocuous form of insurance to all States willing to accept it, namely the guarantee that if they should be attacked, the armaments of all other members of the League will be at their disposal. It was in fact a new variation on the old French scheme for an armed League, and it was rejected by the British Labour Government in July 1924.

Mr. MacDonald, however, was very rightly not content with a gesture of mere negation, and in September, just before his downfall on an entirely different issue, he attended the Assembly of the League in the company of M. Herriot. The presence of the two Prime Ministers focused the attention of the political world upon Geneva, and their speeches were an interesting study in what oratory can do to conceal the disagreements of men who wish to agree. Mr. MacDonald emphasized disarmament, while agreeing that security was also necessary; M. Herriot emphasized security, while agreeing that disarmament was also necessary. Under the impulse of their initiative two committees got to work, presided over by a Greek and by a Czecho-Slovak, and the result was a document known as the 'Protocol for the Pacific Settlement of International Disputes',[1] and accepted provisionally by the Assembly of the League, including the British delegates, Mr. Henderson and Lord Parmoor.

The Protocol aimed at 'stopping up the gaps' in the Covenant and in this it certainly succeeded. Its object was to abolish aggressive war by creating a system under which every international dispute should be decided by judicial or arbitral means: all members of the League were to be under an obligation to go to war with any States who refused to accept these decisions. 'It gives', said the *Round Table* for December 1924, 'to an unknown group of men, responsible to nobody, the power to legislate for the world and to decide when and for what purpose nations should go to war.' The only redeeming feature of the scheme was that it was not to become operative unless success was achieved at the projected Disarmament Conference of 1925. Since a general measure of disarmament such as would place France and her allies on a level with their late enemies was quite inconceivable as an event of the near future, the Protocol might be regarded as a harmless exercise in hypothetical idealism.

[1] Protocol is simply a technical term for a Draft Treaty.

Mr. Baldwin's Second Government: Locarno

It was, however, much better that Great Britain should indicate clearly that along this road she would in no case proceed. The Protocol represented, in substance, the policy of France and her allies in Eastern Europe, such as Poland. These allies of France had secured, at the expense of Germany, Austria and Hungary, slices of territory which they would almost certainly some day have difficulty in retaining, and were perhaps not entitled, on an impartial award, to retain. The Protocol could quite reasonably be regarded as an attempt to stabilize these and all the other frontiers by the guarantee of the British navy. It was not strange that the scheme was condemned in England, not only by the Conservatives but also by Mr. Lloyd George, who denounced it as a 'booby-trap', and by the *New Statesman*. What is strange is that it found any defenders. Labour politicians no doubt recognized in it their own offspring and defended it as such, but in general the reluctance to slay the Protocol, as evinced for example by the *Observer*, must have been prompted by a reluctance to condemn anything put forward as a contribution, however misguided, to the cause of universal peace. The *Round Table* put the sounder view in a nutshell when it wrote: 'It has never been any part of British policy to sign a blank cheque. . . . There is all the difference in the world between the influence of the Empire being thrown into the scale at Geneva or elsewhere, in accordance with the deliberate views of its own statesmen, and its being used at the discretion of five arbitrators sitting at Geneva.'

France had immediately ratified the Protocol, and so had a number of small States of the kind much in need of protection and not likely to be called on to bear an important part in the task of protecting others. From the French point of view the problem of security had become all the more urgent because January 1925 was the scheduled date, under the Treaty of Versailles, for the evacuation of one of the three areas into which the occupied Rhineland was divided, that of Cologne. January passed without evacuation, on the ground that Germany had not yet fulfilled all the Allied demands in the matter of her disarmament, but evacuation could not be indefinitely delayed without working up a new spasm of Franco-German animosity as bitter as that which was now subsiding by reason of the French withdrawal from the Ruhr. However, the German Foreign Minister, Dr. Stresemann, made proposals in February which were to prove not only the solution of the Cologne problem but also an acceptable alternative to the Protocol. These proposals enabled Mr. Chamberlain, after decisively rejecting the Protocol at Geneva in March, to point forward to what subsequently became the Locarno Treaties.

The German proposal was that France, Germany, Belgium and Great Britain should enter into a Security Pact recognizing the permanence of the present western frontier of Germany. M. Briand, who had become Foreign Minister in France on the fall of M. Herriot's Government, at once raised in his negotiations with Mr. Chamberlain the point that France could not disinterest herself in the security of her Allies on the German eastern frontier, Poland and Czecho-Slovakia. Indeed the suggested guarantee in the west had immediately lowered the political barometer in the east, Poland in particular resenting the implication that her own frontier was less axiomatic than that of France. The implication was, none the less, in accord with the facts as understood in Great Britain. The claim of France to Alsace-Lorraine stood on a very different footing from the hazardous and questionable experiment of the Polish corridor. We were prepared to guarantee the former, but not the latter.

The Conference which met at Locarno in October 1925, in the autumn, had therefore to deal with the two frontiers in separate treaties. France, Germany, Belgium, Poland and Czecho-Slovakia, the States with the frontiers affected, undertook in no case to go to war with one another, but to invoke arbitration in its place and to abide by its results. Great Britain and Italy guaranteed that this procedure should be observed in

Western Europe; France guaranteed that it should be observed in Eastern Europe.

The Locarno Conference was made the occasion of a variety of symbolic festivities expressive of the inauguration of a new era of peace, and its proceedings were followed in England and elsewhere with almost rapturous enthusiasm. It marked, in the words of the *Round Table*, 'the definite termination of the war era'. None the less it was no more than a beginning of better things. It did not entail the evacuation of the Rhineland, outside the Cologne area, and it did not touch the thorny question of disarmament. Moreover, scrutinized closely, it involved Great Britain in extremely hazardous commitments. True, we refused to guarantee the Eastern settlement, but could East and West be kept apart? The war of 1914 had not originated in a Western quarrel, but it had none the less begun with the violation of the western frontier. Suppose war arose between Germany and Poland on an issue on which British sympathies were predominantly with Germany, and French sympathies with Poland, and suppose that Germany, to secure herself against French attack violated the French frontier—where would our duty lie under the Locarno Treaties? Perhaps, as Horatio said to Hamlet, 'it were to consider too curiously to consider so.' None the less, we had committed ourselves to Europe more deeply than we ever consented to commit ourselves before the war. Before the war our commitment was limited to Belgium. If Palmerston in 1839 had made not a Belgian but a 'Locarno' Treaty we should have been under an obligation to take part in the Franco-German War of 1870, and it is by no means obvious which of the parties to that war would have had the better claim to our alliance. The defenders of Locarno may, of course, reply that if Palmerston had made a 'Locarno', the war of 1870 would never have been fought. It may be so. In 1925 the price of Locarno was worth paying, but it may none the less be found some day to have been a heavy one.

As an implied condition of the Locarno Treaties Germany

Mr. Baldwin's Second Government: Locarno

was to be admitted in the following March to the League of Nations and simultaneously elected, as one of the Great Powers, to a permanent seat on the Council of the League. Unhappily the 'Locarno spirit', of which so much had been heard, had now evaporated, and the March meeting of the Council of the League produced nothing but scandal and farce. The fault seems to have lain with M. Briand, but also with Mr. Chamberlain, now Sir Austen K.G., for complying too readily with his French friends. M. Briand wanted the election of Germany to be balanced by the election of Poland. Then other claimants stepped forward. Spain wanted to have her temporary seat made permanent; so did Brazil. In the end, after a succession of fantastic wrangles, Brazil vetoed the admission of Germany, and the business was adjourned until the Council could be remodelled and more seats provided. Germany's admission in the autumn was a huddled anticlimax.

CHAPTER XXVIII

THE COAL CRISIS AND THE
GENERAL STRIKE

If Labour had its Reds, Conservatism also had its True Blue Diehards. Being haunted by fears rather than exalted by hopes they were the more amenable group of the two, but occasionally they insisted on having their fling, and one of these occasions arose early in the first Parliamentary session of Mr. Baldwin's ministry when Mr. MacQuisten, who like Mr. Maxton came from Scotland, insisted on introducing a Bill to amend the law relating to the trade unions' 'political levy'.

The history of this controversial levy stretched back to the very beginnings of the Labour party. It had been from the first the custom of the trade unions to finance out of their funds the expenses of Labour members, until in 1908 a Mr. Osborne, who was a Liberal trade unionist, secured a judgment of the courts which declared this illegal. One result of this judgment was to hasten the introduction of State salaries for M.P.'s. Another was the enactment in 1913 of a measure which enabled trade unions to levy subscriptions to a special political fund, trade unionists who did not wish to subscribe being allowed to 'contract out' by signing an application to that effect. Conservatives had always disliked this arrangement. They objected to its implied assumption that trade unionists were normally and naturally Socialists, and they held that, human nature being what it is, the Bill enabled trade unions to secure many subscriptions to which they were not morally entitled, because of the trouble involved, and possibly odium also, in signing the contracting-out form. Conservatives held that the arrangement ought to be the other way round, and those who wanted to subscribe ought to be put to the trouble of 'contracting in'.

The MacQuisten debate was significant not so much on account of the Bill, as for the speech in which Mr. Baldwin secured its rejection. This speech, quaintly described in the *Annual Register* as 'earnest and almost sentimental', made a deep impression upon the House and the country. It may be taken as marking the establishment of Mr. Baldwin as a salient personality. Under his guidance and inspiration the term 'Unionist', which had originally meant nothing more than opposition to Irish Home Rule, began to take on a deeper and more permanent meaning. It stood for the union of all classes for the common good of all, as opposed to the doctrine of class war into which Socialism so easily degenerates; and for the maintenance of the unity of the Empire against those who seemed to assume that, in every controversy between native peoples and their British rulers, the British rulers were in the wrong. About this time Mr. Baldwin began to give a variety of addresses on subjects not connected with politics. He spoke on the Classics, on English literature, but most of all upon the old English countryside, the wholesome and happy ways of a merrier England. These addresses were marked by an intense sincerity of feeling and a curious felicity of phrase. They were in their own way as distinctive as anything written by Rudyard Kipling who was, one remembered, Mr. Baldwin's first cousin. Mr. Baldwin's Worcestershire began to have as honourable a place upon the map of ideal England as Thomas Hardy's Wessex.

We have compared Mr. MacDonald with Gladstone. The parallel between Mr. Baldwin and Disraeli might seem to present greater difficulties. The mere fact that Disraeli kept peacocks whereas Mr. Baldwin kept pigs presents at the start an almost insuperable obstacle. Mr. Baldwin was English of the English. Disraeli was hardly that, but at least he was not Scottish or Welsh, and when he dug his roots into our soil it was in a county as unspoilt by London in 1850 as Mr. Baldwin's

The Coal Crisis and the General Strike

Worcestershire. Certainly Mr. Baldwin looked back for the inspiration of his party past his own immediate predecessors to the great Jew, whose novels he constantly recommended to his audiences, especially to *Sybil*, whose sub-title was *The Two Nations*, and whose theme the need for making them one. Unfortunately the task of making the two nations one during 1925 and 1926 was going to prove altogether too difficult for Mr. Baldwin. He failed, and it is difficult to see how in the circumstances of the time anyone else could have succeeded. What is certain is that the failure might, with leadership less firm, less cautious and patient than his, have been much more disastrous.

The factors making for the crisis which involved the General Strike were the bankruptcy of the coalmining industry; the general drift of Labour towards the industrial Left after the failure (as it was considered) of Mr. MacDonald on the political Right of the movement; and the link between these two furnished by the personality of Mr. Cook, the Secretary of the Miners' Federation.

The fundamental irony of the situation lay in the interaction of good and evil at home and abroad. In 1923 and 1924 the British mining industry enjoyed a period of hectic prosperity—because the French were in the Ruhr. The export of coal in 1923 surpassed that of 1913, the best of pre-war years. In the spring of 1924, the miners secured, with the aid of the Labour Government, a new wage agreement which marked a big advance on the wages paid under the agreement of 1921. Then came the Dawes Agreement, the evacuation of the Ruhr, the recovery of Germany and the pacification of Europe, and the British coalmining industry, once again exposed to the full blast of continental competition, and handicapped by the Seven Hour Day which had been imposed on the industry in 1919, plunged once again into the depths of depression. In the spring of 1925 a committee of owners and miners set to work to investigate the position. The committee agreed on the facts, but could not even begin to agree on the remedies and, on the last day of

The Coal Crisis and the General Strike

June, the owners gave a month's notice to terminate the existing agreements, offering in their stead terms which would have reduced coalmining in the worse-paid districts to the level of a sweated industry. These terms were immediately rejected.

In rejecting these terms the miners were relying not so much on the sympathy of the general public, which though widespread and freely expressed in the press was not likely to be of much use to them, as on a sympathetic strike on the lines so nearly secured by the Triple Alliance in 1921. The Triple Alliance was dead, but another and more effective organization had taken its place. The Trades Union Congress, having long regarded itself as 'the Parliament of Labour', had recently equipped itself with a kind of Cabinet or General Council, commonly described as the Trades Union Council, and some of the members of this Council were firm believers in the weapon of the General Strike. They regarded it as a means, more effective than the ballot box, of compelling the Government of the day to obey the will of 'the democracy'. It is a well-known fact that the elected representatives of trade unions are nearly always men of more venturesome opinions than the majority of those they represent, simply because the moderate men are often too lazy or too much occupied with their wives and families to play an assiduous part in attendance at the innumerable meetings on which trade-union activity is based. Moreover in the trade-union world as a whole there had been a decided drift towards a forward policy. While the political Labour party was busying itself in expelling its Communists, under pressure from Mr. MacDonald and Mr. Snowden, these same Communists and many more who, without calling themselves Communists, agreed with them, were improving their position in many trade unions. The Trade Union Congress of 1924 received Mr. MacDonald with marked coldness, but listened with appreciation to Mr. Tomsky, the fraternal delegate from Russia, and presented him with a gold watch.

Foremost among trade unionists of this way of thinking was

The Coal Crisis and the General Strike

Mr. A. J. Cook. In early youth he had been a lay preacher for the sect of the Baptists, but in the South Wales coalfield he had found a more congenial religion and he had been, in 1912, one of the authors of the notorious pamphlet called *The Miners' Next Step*, which advocated the intensive use of the strike weapon as a means of bringing down capitalist society in ruins. During and after the war he had been in the van of a number of extremist movements and had served several sentences in prison. In 1924 he became Secretary of the Miners' Federation and a member of the Trades Union Council.

Mr. Cook was a man of febrile energy and transparent sincerity: it was noticed as characteristic of him that when he made a speech he took his coat off and spoke in his shirt sleeves, instead of holding the lapels of his coat after the manner approved among men of moderate views. He described himself as 'a humble follower of Lenin', and his methods bore no more resemblance to peaceful persuasion than those of the author of the Bolshevik Revolution. Had he, any time in 1925, or the spring of 1926, approached his colleagues on the Trade Union Council with a reasoned motion pledging them to order a General Strike, they would have turned him down. He knew that he was, like Lenin, in a minority and he acted accordingly. He went up and down the country assuring his audiences that if the miners were driven to strike, the T.U.C. would support them. The T.U.C. did not feel equal to contradicting him, so that, when the time came, they found themselves morally involved by his pledges. He had bluffed them into it, and they came to believe that they could bluff the Government into coercing the mineowners. Whatever credit or discredit attaches to the General Strike and the eight months' stoppage in the mines must go almost entirely to Mr. Cook.

After the strike Mr. Cook went to Russia, and on his return moved rapidly in the direction of Right. More than once, during the mines controversies of the Second Labour Government he pleaded the cause of compromise and moderation. When he died in 1931 he had, in fact, completed his education: it had been a prolonged education, and very expensive to the community which paid for it.

The month of July slipped all too quickly away while the Government exerted itself in vain to bring the parties together, appointing at the same time a Court of Enquiry under Mr. Hugh (afterwards Lord) Macmillan, who had held office as a non-party law officer in the Labour Government. Though the owners gave evidence before this Court of Enquiry and the miners refused to do so, the Court upheld on the whole the miners' contention that the bankrupt condition of the industry was in part due to bad management on the part of the owners. Meanwhile the Trade Union Congress, which happened to meet in July for another purpose, fully supported the resolution of its Council to call out the transport and railway unions in support of the miners.

Both sides were conspiring to drive the Government into granting a subsidy to the industry. Most unfortunately Mr. Baldwin, when replying to a vote of censure on his Government for neglecting the general problem of unemployment, had let fall that fatal word. 'I think it would be useful', he had said, at the end of June, 'if the House itself would examine and consider, as the Government are proposing to do, whether any form of subsidy may be possible to give . . . that stimulus and lift in the region of those industries which seem at the moment beaten down into a position of helplessness.' It was, it seems, an unpremeditated rumination of a rambling mind, the sort of 'thinking aloud' which should be indulged in only by persons whose thoughts do not matter. Asked at once whether his speculation applied to the mining industry Mr. Baldwin begged to be excused. But the mischief was done. With a subsidy in the air both owners and miners were tempted to indulge their native unreasonableness to the utmost.

Throughout twenty-nine days of July and the greater part of the thirtieth Mr. Baldwin refused a subsidy. On the evening of

The Coal Crisis and the General Strike

the thirtieth he gave way. The Government would appoint a Royal Commission to make a detailed examination of every aspect of the industry. For nine months, the greater part of which the Commission would require for its task, the owners would pay the new wages and the miners would receive the old ones, the difference being made up from the Exchequer. At the cost, as it turned out, of twenty-four million pounds, the nation secured an expert Report, and the postponement of the crisis till the end of April 1926.

The Commission was a very different body from that which, under the chairmanship of Mr. Justice Sankey, had investigated the same industry seven years before. This time the parties to the dispute were allowed no members on the board. The chairman was Sir Herbert Samuel, once a Liberal minister under Mr. Asquith and recently returned from several years as High Commissioner of Palestine, and his colleagues were each selected in virtue of the fact that, though unconnected with coalmining, they possessed experience which would give them an expert's understanding of one or other of its problems.

The Samuel Report, which was published on March 11th, was an elaborate and carefully reasoned document. It found that, under present conditions, three-quarters of the coal raised was being produced at a loss, and it recommended a thorough reorganization of the industry which would require active participation both by the State and by the owners. It proposed that the State should buy out the royalty owners (i.e. the landowners on whose property the collieries stood, and to whom the mineowners—popularly miscalled coal-owners—had to pay a royalty on every ton of coal raised). The purpose of the State purchase of landowner's rights was to facilitate the reorganization of the industry itself, an important feature of which was the amalgamation of the multitudinous colliery companies in a much smaller number of large concerns. These amalgamations should if possible be negotiated by the mineowners themselves, but the State should not hesitate to bring pressure upon them if they

357

proved recalcitrant. For the rest, the Commission recommended substantial improvements upon existing methods of scientific research, improved methods of transport and selling, and a greater degree of combination between the coal-producing and the coal-using industries.

These reforms would take time, and a still longer time would elapse before their results were reflected in a renewal of the prosperity of the industry. In the meantime there must be a reduction of wages, though less drastic than that demanded by the mineowners. The Commissioners emphatically rejected the idea that the subsidy should be prolonged in any form whatever, and rather less emphatically deprecated a repeal of the legislation of 1919 which had limited the working day below ground to seven hours.

The Report was unanimous and was universally regarded as highly creditable to the Commissioners. While all other parties to the dispute incurred some share of blame for the disasters which followed, no one has ever ventured to depreciate the work of Sir Herbert Samuel and his colleagues.

As soon as the Report was published Mr. Baldwin appealed for a fortnight's 'moratorium' during which all concerned might master the implications of the Report, undisturbed by controversy. The truce was well kept, and at its conclusion the Prime Minister announced the Government's policy. There were some things in the Report which he and his colleagues did not like. None the less, since the Report had to be taken as a whole, the Government would accept it, and would do all that the Report demanded of it if the owners and the miners would do the same.

From this point onwards the miners' leaders maintained continuous contact with the body popularly known as the T.U.C. but more exactly as the Industrial Committee of the General Council of the Trades Union Congress. The chairman of this Committee was Mr. Pugh who neither at this time nor before nor afterwards made any great impression upon the public mind. The 'T.U.C.' appeared as a group of secondary person-

The Coal Crisis and the General Strike

alities, entirely dominated by Mr. Cook, until they ran away from him.

The miners' argument against the Report was a strong one, though it may not, in the circumstances, have been a wise one. The Report, they held, proved up to the hilt their main contention: that the industry as conducted by their masters was hopelessly inefficient. They were prepared to support the whole of the Commissioners' scheme for the reorganization of the industry, even though it was not their own scheme and excluded nationalization. But they held that, on these premises, it was unjust that they should be expected to bear the cost, in reduced wages, of what was in fact not their fault but the fault of the owners, and also the fault of successive Governments for refusing to compel the owners to set their house in order long before. Even now the owners, while accepting the Report, had done so with such ill grace and in such ambiguous terms as to strengthen the miners' attitude, which crystallized into Mr. Cook's slogan: 'Not a cent off the pay, not a minute on the day'. The miners in fact believed that out of a General Strike they could extract a permanent subsidy for the industry. It was an error which cost everyone dear, and themselves most of all.

April passed away in abortive negotiations, the T.U.C. being disowned by the miners whenever they showed signs of weakening towards a compromise with the Government. With the end of the month came the end of the subsidy and work ceased throughout the mining industry, the miners refusing to accept the unsubsidized wages which had been the owners' terms ever since the previous July. The purists in technical terms insisted that it was not a strike but a lock-out, and they may have been right. They also insisted that what followed was not a General Strike but a combination of sympathetic strikes. The terms used do not very much matter if the facts are fairly stated.

On the afternoon of May 1st the T.U.C. decided to declare a strike in certain vital industries, including all transport services and the printing trades, to begin at midnight on May 3rd, and

The Coal Crisis and the General Strike

on the same day (May 1st) the Government, by Royal Proclamation, declared a state of emergency, thus bringing into operation the elaborate and, as it proved, exceedingly efficient arrangements for safeguarding the essential services of the country, which had been worked out in the preceding autumn. The intervening day, May 2nd, was spent in a final effort on the part of the T.U.C. to secure a fortnight's extension of the subsidy, as they 'felt confident' that a settlement would be reached within that time 'on the lines of the Report'. The miners' leaders took no part in these negotiations, and it was difficult to believe that the T.U.C. were in a position to speak for them. While these negotiations were still in progress news came that the printers of the *Daily Mail* had, under the direction of their union, refused to set up an article on the situation for the next day's issue of that paper. On this pretext the Prime Minister broke off negotiations. The experiment in Direct Action was left to take its course.

The Government was severely criticized for this step. Those who like to think that they know what happens in the secret conclaves of Cabinet Ministers say that at this point the 'militarists' of the Cabinet, Mr. Churchill and Lord Birkenhead, took the bit between their teeth and the control into their hands, flouting the authority of poor Mr. Baldwin who was, to the last, ingeminating 'Peace! Peace!' in chorus with Mr. Pugh. It is wiser to assume an agnostic attitude on such subtle points as these. Suffice it to say what is obvious: that some members of the Cabinet would naturally be more disposed for a 'fight to the finish' than others, and that the absurd insubordination of the printers would be likely to bring over waverers to their side. The point is not important. By the evening of May 2nd the General Strike was inevitable, and the action of the printers merely gave a quietus to a futile negotiation with the T.U.C. who were, in the circumstances, men of straw. Mr. Cook was not at that council table; he was already where a general ought to be, in the field.

The Coal Crisis and the General Strike

The General Strike was a nine days' wonder, from May 4th to May 12th inclusive. The first and most fundamental impression of the ordinary citizen living outside the industrial areas was that it felt curiously like the first weeks of the war. He had forgotten what those weeks had felt like: now he remembered, because he was feeling the same again. There was the same sense of vague insecurity, a feeling that the underpinnings of society had been loosened, that all was adrift and anything might happen, that one certainly ought to do something but did not quite know what. In one respect it was like those first weeks 'only more so', for there were no newspapers on the breakfast table. Nothing did more to turn the public against the General Strikers than the attempted suppression of the press. The idea in the mind of the T.U.C. was that the press, being a capitalist organization, would be biased against their cause. The ordinary man, even when admitting the truth of this, was extremely vexed by the further assumption that he would be the slave and the dupe of his newspaper. Newspapers, after all, contain facts as well as dope, and the ordinary man had a right to his daily facts, let the dope be what it might.

But the scheme for the suppression of news proved as ineffective as all the other schemes of the T.U.C. The ordinary newspapers gradually struggled back to life, publishing, at first, half-sheets of what looked like typescript, and afterwards issues which were, like Milton's rebel angels, 'in their own dimensions like themselves', though the pages were much fewer. There was also an official organ of the Government, the *British Gazette*, under the supervision of Mr. Churchill, running from May 5th to 13th and an organ of the T.U.C. called the *British Worker* which lasted a few days longer. The first issue of the *British Gazette* did its best to restore a sense of calm and normalcy by means of 'Notes from the Zoo', in which we read of the arrival of a white elephant. The cross heading 'Brooding Lovebirds' was in itself a sermon by implication, and the announcement under 'Latest Wills' that a member of a well-known mine-owning family had left £271,769 net personality was a reminder to those who needed it that the mineowners were not quite so near to becoming a Mendicant Order as the more vehement critics of the miners sometimes seemed to suggest. The first issue of the *British Worker* had nothing to say about the Zoo, and offered no comic relief of any kind.

Even more important was the wireless. Broadcasting, which had begun in America with President Harding's election in 1920, had already become a fairly common feature in English life. Most people had not yet got sets of their own, but had friends who had a set in the next street. The General Strike gave the B.B.C. its best advertisement, and at the appointed hours we all queued up at the house of the friend in the next street to hear Mr. Baldwin, or some other accredited leader, report the day's progress. The Government refused its enemies and its critics access to this means of publicity, and neither Mr. Cook nor the Archbishop of Canterbury, who appealed for compromise, was allowed access to the microphone. The Archbishop's appeal was also, very foolishly, excluded from the *British Gazette*, though it appeared in all other papers.

As an attempt to bring the national life to a standstill the General Strike was a failure from the first. Before its first day was over a vast number of volunteers were engaged all over the country in transporting food supplies by motor, running trains and buses. There was no food shortage anywhere, nor, it is said, any general rise in prices except an additional twopence on the quart of milk in the London area. Day by day the army of volunteers increased in numbers and efficiency. At first they were mainly drawn from what Socialists call the bourgeoisie but, as the tide flowed ever more strongly in favour of the Government, the unemployed sought employment, and the strikers themselves drifted back to work in large numbers. The British public, freed from anxiety about primary essentials, began to be amused, and stories of the expected sort began to circulate, such as that of the young sportsman who was entrusted with the

The Coal Crisis and the General Strike

driving of a train due at Waterloo at 6.30, and arrived at 6.10 with the gates of two level crossings impaled on his buffers.

There was another story which ought to be true even if it is not. A detachment of the Guards, it is said, was sent down to the London Docks where a disturbance was expected. As the Guards marched down the Whitechapel Road the officer commanding observed signs of hostility in the crowd and some stones were thrown. He halted and held a consultation. 'Why don't you play your bloody band?' came a voice from the crowd. 'Oh! is that all?' said the O.C. and instructed the bandmaster to strike up his lightest and brightest dance tune. In a few moments all Jewry was dancing in the highway.

On the whole the General Strike was a masterpiece of orderliness and good feeling, for which the moderate counsels of the T.U.C. and their reiterated professions that they were not striking against the established order but only in sympathy with the miners, deserve a share of the credit. Foreigners were astonished, and the pound rose above its gold parity. There was indeed some exaggeration of the orderliness of the country as a whole, and it was rather a shock to learn, next month, that there had been during May, in England and Wales, 1760 prosecutions for incitement to sedition and 1389 for actual violence.

Mr. Baldwin took the line that the General Strike was, whatever the professions of its leaders, an unconstitutional attempt to coerce the Government, duly installed in power by an enormous majority less than two years before, into doing what it believed to be wrong; a conspiracy against the constitution which was the only true embodiment of the national democracy. He refused all parley until the General Strike was called off, and in this policy he was supported by all the leading Liberals except Mr. Lloyd George. The Labour leaders were placed in a humiliating position. Everyone knew that Mr. MacDonald detested the strike, as also of course did Mr. Thomas, who had 'betrayed' the Triple Alliance in 1921, but as party politicians they felt compelled to give it an indirect official blessing by denouncing what they conceived to be the provocative action of the Government.

After the strike had been going on a week, all that was needed to end it was some formula which would enable its leaders to call it off without excessive humiliation. This was furnished by Sir Herbert Samuel, who, acting as he pointed out on his own initiative and without the authority of the Government, drew up a Memorandum of terms 'suitable for adoption and likely to promote a settlement in the coal industry'. These terms involved nothing inconsistent with his Commission's Report except the granting of a final subsidy of £3,000,000 to assist the restarting of the industry. Mr. Baldwin at the same time promised in a broadcast message that the Government would do all they could to see that the strikers were fully and without victimization reinstated in their jobs. This message was the more welcome as Sir John Simon had, in an impressive speech, depicted in the blackest colours the illegalities in which the unions, whose men had struck without proper notice, had involved themselves. The T.U.C. took the Samuel Memorandum to the miners' leaders, who at once rejected it because it involved reduction of wages. Thereupon they went to Mr. Baldwin and informed him that they would at once call off the strike in order that negotiations about the future of the coal industry might be renewed.

The end when it came was a ragged and bewildering affair. Many of the strikers, never quite clear for what they had struck, were now no more clear why they had struck in vain, and suspected that they had been 'let down' by their leaders. For five days after the General Strike had ended, sectional strikes of its major component parts continued. But in the end the employers fully responded to Mr. Baldwin's plea for magnanimity, and work was resumed except in the coalfields.

At the end of the General Strike Mr. Baldwin's prestige stood higher than that of any British statesman since Mr. Lloyd George had lost in peace the reputation he won in war. There was a general feeling that even if, by some measure which his

The Coal Crisis and the General Strike

critics never succeeded in defining, he could have averted the General Strike, he had more than atoned for his fault, if it was one, by the consistent magnanimity of his attitude throughout those eventful days. 'With malice toward none: with charity for all: with firmness in the right, as God gives us to see the right, let us strive to finish the work we are in: to bind up the nation's wounds. . . .' The words of the greatest and most completely Christian of modern democratic statesmen, spoken when the civil war which he, too, was accused of having provoked, was drawing to its end—Abraham Lincoln's last message to an America distracted by four years' civil war would not have been inappropriate in the mouth of Stanley Baldwin in the middle of May 1926. It only remained to settle the coal industry. That seemed at the moment, and by comparison with the General Strike, a small matter.

But the miners still held by their slogan 'Not a cent off the pay, not a minute on the day', and, exhibiting a quality for which Englishmen have often praised themselves, they did not know when they were beaten. It would be wearisome to chronicle the various 'peace offensives' of the Government, which proved as ineffective as President Wilson's proposals of neutral intervention between the belligerents in the Great War. In June the Government carried through Parliament, against bitter Labour opposition, a Bill enabling the miners to work eight hours instead of seven for the next five years, and another Bill designed to carry out some of the recommendations of the Royal Commission for the improved organization of the industry. As soon as the Eight Hours Bill was law the owners posted revised terms of wages. In districts employing three-quarters of the mining population they offered the same or better terms than were paid before the stoppage, and in nearly all the remaining districts the reductions demanded were not greater than ten per cent. But 'not a minute on the day' still held the field.

In July a committee of religious leaders, formed under the auspices of the Industrial Christian Fellowship, established con-

365

The Coal Crisis and the General Strike

tact with the miners' leaders, and secured their acceptance of certain proposals, which were rather contemptuously rejected by Mr. Baldwin on the ground that they involved a subsidy to the industry. Mr. Cook, however, accepted the terms provisionally, though they involved an almost certain reduction of wages, and summoned a conference of the delegates from the mining districts, the first meeting of the 'Miners' Parliament' since before the General Strike. The delegates met in no complaisant mood, and Mr. Cook found that he could not now damp down the fires he had previously heaped up; in spite of Mr. Cook, they rejected the churchmen's proposals.

Meanwhile the Government were importing foreign coal in large quantities, and the National Union of Railwaymen expressed their disapproval of the miners' obstinacy by refusing to place an embargo on its transport. Before the end of July, in time for the summer holidays, the railways were able to re-establish their normal time-tables, though the dirt and the smell of much of the foreign coal was such as to suggest to experienced travellers the illusion of a holiday abroad. But though the railways might run, the mills stood idle from lack of coal, and the figures of unemployment which, just before the strike, had dipped to the one million mark for the first time since 1921, rose into the neighbourhood of two million, a figure which did not, of course, include the million miners on strike. Those who visited the moorlands around Bradford that summer heard everyone saying that never before had one really seen the colours in the view. The same remark was made, no doubt, in every industrial area. The air was clean of coal dust as it had not been since Watt and Arkwright conferred their dubious blessings on the human race.

At the end of August Mr. Churchill, acting for the Prime Minister who was taking a holiday, made a fresh approach to the miners and drew from their leaders the welcome announcement that they were willing to enter into a new national agreement 'with a view to a reduction of labour costs'. The phrase 'reduction of wages' was avoided much as the American Constitution avoided the mention of the word 'slaves', but it was understood. It was now the turn of the owners to display their quality. The Mining Association announced that it had, a fortnight previously, surrendered its powers to the associations of the various districts; that, in fact, as an organ for negotiating a national settlement it had ceased to exist. Henceforth the owners would only negotiate district by district. Mr. Churchill expressed his opinion of this manoeuvre in no measured terms, but he could do no more with Mr. Evan Williams, the President of the Association, than Mr. Baldwin had been able to do with Mr. Cook. Meanwhile the drift back to work was beginning. It was strongest in the Midland coalfield, where the local leaders had for some time been at open variance with Mr. Cook. The miners' national executive was left, as it were, in the air by the abdication of its opposite number on the owners' side. The Government could do no more. Terms were settled, district by district, on the basis of the eight hours' day and the wage terms offered by the owners in the previous July. The worst industrial dispute in our history was practically over on Armistice Day, 1926.

It was not strictly true to say that the miners had been 'starved' into surrender. Though there was obviously much privation in other directions there is no evidence to suggest that miners or their families suffered at any stage from want of necessary food. Some hundreds of them found a lucrative occupation in digging and selling outcrop coal. Many millions of pounds were granted in outdoor relief to miners' dependants from local rates. Large sums were subscribed by the general public, irrespective of party, to funds opened by the Labour party and other bodies. A million pounds came, in instalments, from Bolshevik Russia, where the terms which the miners refused would have been accounted luxurious, but the attempt of the miners' delegates to secure charitable assistance from the bulging pockets of the working classes of America proved a dismal failure.

The Coal Crisis and the General Strike

Locarno in 1925 and the crisis of the coalmines in 1926 had this much in common. Each in its respective sphere was the end of a long story, and the beginning of a new epoch much quieter than what had gone before. Never had the strike weapon been so utterly discredited as at the end of 1926. It might be hoped that Mr. Baldwin's mission of conciliation might thereafter be received with more respectful attention. No doubt interested parties would continue to say that Mr. Baldwin had favoured the owners, had put himself in the pocket of the Mining Association, and so on. A candid review of the facts could not fail to show that this was not so. Mr. Baldwin had done his best to preserve peace. He had treated the industry with a generosity—at the expense of the taxpayer—never accorded to any other British industry. At the cost of a nine months' subsidy he had secured an expert Report of unimpeachable impartiality, and had offered, in spite of the fact that his party did not entirely like the Report, to carry out all the recommendations in it which called for legislative action. All had been done in vain. Both belligerents had insisted on fighting it out, with the inevitable result that the stronger side had won. The Government had been able to make only one positive contribution: they had enabled the miners to choose between the day and the pay, and they had preferred to retain all, or nearly all, their wages in exchange for an extra hour's work.

As for the cost of all this industrial warfare, it was beyond accurate calculation. Among measurable items, imports for the year were less by £77,000,000 than those of 1925, exports less by £150,000,000. Instead of exporting fifty million tons of coal we exported twenty millions—and imported another twenty millions. The consumption of beer and spirits was drastically reduced, that of tea hardly at all; and the consumption of sugar and tobacco was greater than ever!

CHAPTER XXIX

MR. BALDWIN'S ADMINISTRATION 1924-1926

The rest of the acts of Mr. Baldwin's Administration and all that it did, after Locarno and the coal crisis have been removed from the list, present materials for a very miscellaneous chronicle—a chronicle of events which by comparison with what has filled most of the previous pages of this book, might be called almost humdrum. We begin to be reminded of the old saw which runs, 'Happy is the country whose annals are dull.' But it is to be remembered that we have only secured this illusion by isolating for previous treatment the two major events of the time.

The circumstances of the defeat of Mr. Baldwin's first Government, in the autumn of 1923, had persuaded him to face the new Parliament and therefore to compose a King's Speech which was not so much a last will and testament as a series of promises contingent upon resurrection. It was a Speech of unusual amplitude, forecasting no less than seventeen Bills dealing with various social problems. Mr. MacDonald drily remarked that it was a very good King's Speech, and that he thought his own party was more likely to live up to its good intentions than Mr. Baldwin's. It was, at any rate, an indication that the Conservatives had abandoned Tranquillity in favour of Progress; and Progress was their keynote on their return to power. Unfortunately there was another keynote, Economy, which when sounded in conjunction with Progress produced the harshest of discords. The best one could hope for was as much Progress as was consistent with Economy, and as much Economy as was consistent with Progress.

Mr. Baldwin's Administration 1924-26

The Conservatives had promised at the election that there should be no general tariff, but the McKenna duties were restored at the first opportunity and a new Safeguarding of Industries Bill introduced, a Bill designed, as someone said, to safeguard Safeguarding against the charge that election pledges were being broken. Under this Bill each suppliant industry had not only to satisfy a Special Committee of Enquiry that it was of substantial importance, conducted with efficiency, and subject to abnormal foreign competition; it had also thereafter to run the gauntlet of criticism in the House, since no protective duty could be imposed except through the Annual Finance Bill. Under this system duties were imposed in the course of 1925 on imports of lace, cutlery, gas mantles, fabric gloves, and packing paper. The purists of free trade began to raise their voices, but were reassured when the privilege of safeguarding was refused to the iron and steel industry on the ground that import duties protecting a basic industry of such dimensions would amount to an instalment of 'protection' beyond the pledges of the Government.

Housing was at last making really good progress. Mr. Chamberlain, who had returned to the Ministry of Health, was able to reduce the State subsidies to local authorities and private builders, as, with the fall of the price of building material, the gap between the economic rent and the fair rent diminished. There had been much controversy over the steel houses designed by Lord Weir as a cheap and temporary substitute for the product of the building trade. The builders' trade union, always more interested in their own wages than in the provision of houses, had fairly successfully suppressed the Weir experiment by insisting that the unskilled labour employed upon it should be paid at builder's rates. However, with the marked increase in normal building, the Weir experiment lost urgency and soon faded out of public discussion.

Mr. Churchill was expected to be as interesting at the Treasury as at all the other many departments over which he had presided. He was the only Home Secretary who had ever besieged Sydney Street, and since then the limelight had followed him up and down both sides of Whitehall. His first *coup* was to restore the pre-war gold standard of the pound. No ordinary person could understand what this would involve, but there was a general feeling that, as a symbol of returning normalcy, it was 'a good thing'. It was gratifying to know that 'the pound could now look the dollar in the face'. For some time past it had been creeping up to its pre-war parity; what Mr. Churchill did was to clamp it there, and Mr. Snowden's speech on the subject seemed to indicate that he would very probably have done the same had he still been in office. Mr. Lloyd George opposed the measure, as did Sir Alfred Mond, whose word carried weight as one of the leaders of industry. Six months later, our export trade was found to have declined, and Mr. Churchill's *coup* began to look more questionable. One gathered that financiers were for it and industrialists against it; and as the ordinary man can understand industry and cannot understand finance, he was prepared to back the judgment of the industrialists. He was supported by Mr. Keynes in a pamphlet called *The Economic Consequences of Mr. Churchill*.

The gold standard was only one item in Mr. Churchill's first Budget, which also reimposed the McKenna duties, and levied taxes on silk, natural and artificial, whether imported or manufactured at home. At the same time he introduced a substantial instalment of Imperial preference, reducing the existing duties on tobacco, wines, and sugar when imported from Empire countries. Assisted by a preference which knocked a shilling off the quarter-pound across a tobacconist's counter, and by the discovery that their tobaccos were more palatable when blended with American varieties, the Imperial grower and the home consumer of tobacco began from this date to establish a contact which was of advantage to both. But the most substantial boon conferred upon a predominantly Conservative class was the improvement introduced into the scales of allowances and abatements of the income tax on small earned incomes. How great these boons were the recipients of them were forcibly reminded when the National Government of 1931 took them all away.

So much for Mr. Churchill's first Budget. But the longest passage in his Budget speech was quite another matter. It was a forecast of a Bill which he was not going to introduce and for which his department would not have to begin to pay until the following year. In the course of the year the Government was going to introduce and carry through a scheme, which the *Round Table* called 'gigantic', including pensions for the widows and children of all men at present within the Health Insurance scheme, and old age pensions for all persons over 65 instead of only for those over 70, in all an insurable population of fifteen million persons. The scheme was to be financed, like the existing State compulsory insurances, by contributions from the beneficiaries, the employers, and the State. On the last it would impose progressively increasing liabilities, with the increasing longevity of the population, liabilities which Mr. Churchill set against progressive decline in the cost of war pensions. Here was what Mr. Lloyd George in his old days called 'rare and refreshing fruit'. Mr. Snowden had vaguely promised something of the kind. The Conservatives fulfilled the promise. The Bill on its introduction was opposed by Mr. Wheatley on the ground that it exacted contributions from the workers, and by Sir Alfred Mond on the ground that it imposed an intolerable burden upon industry, but in the main it enjoyed a smooth passage.

The Budget of 1926 was introduced on the eve of the General Strike, and its most interesting, because most controversial, item was a tax on betting, or rather on legal betting as carried out on a racecourse or through a credit bookmaker. It seemed absurd that an industry which battened upon one of the vices, or at least one of the weaknesses of human nature, an industry which showed no signs of suffering from the prevailing depression, should not contribute to the nation's needs. The tax was attacked by the racing fraternity on the ground that it would discourage the breeding of racehorses, an industry still assumed to be of national importance in spite of the mechanization of the army; it was also attacked by many organizations of the virtuous on the ground that taxation of a vice signified its official condonation. The argument was hard to follow, for teetotallers have never objected to the taxes on alcoholic drinks, and would certainly protest vigorously if they were abolished. The Labour party, speaking with the voice of Mr. Snowden, its financier and its leading Puritan, denounced this traffic in unclean things, though it was asserted that few papers contained better racing tips than the *Daily Herald*.

The tax became law, but difficulties of administration proved insuperable, and a few years later it was abandoned by its author. Its only legacy has been the introduction of the continental betting machine called the totalizator, which was legalized on racecourses for the purposes of the tax.

In 1926 we began to extract perceptible contributions from our foreign debtors. Reparation receipts yielded £10,000,000 and the French and Italian war debts had been funded, the latter on terms which remitted 86 per cent of the sum involved. The French debt settlement involved much more controversy because the French demanded that their payments should be wholly or partly contingent on the receipt by France of reparations from Germany. Against this we were firm and France gave way. We surrendered only 62 per cent of what we were technically entitled to. France agreed to pay four million pounds in 1926 and then six, eight and ten millions in successive years: twelve and a half millions yearly from 1930 to 1956, and fourteen millions yearly from 1956 to 1987. One wonders whether Mr. Churchill and M. Caillaux, like Roman augurs, forbore to smile as they fixed up the later stages of this agreement.

The domestic legislation of 1926 was uninspiring, its principal items being an Economy Bill which did very little economizing, and an Electricity Bill which would, at some future date, produce cheap electricity. What it really produced was pylons, and an interesting discussion as to whether these add to or subtract from the amenities of English landscape.

In no direction did the Government raise more hopes and subsequently disappoint them more bitterly than in that of agriculture. On taking office Mr. Baldwin had declared that the continual shrinkage of the arable area was a danger to the whole community. Unemployment and agriculture were, he declared, the principal problems facing the Government. The plan of calling a conference of owners, farmers and labourers to consult with the Minister of Agriculture and the officials of his department had been foiled by the refusal of the labourers' trade union to participate, but the Minister had declared that this would not prevent him from consulting all interested parties and formulating a far-reaching policy. Eighteen months passed, and in June 1926 the Minister announced that the Government had given up all idea of assisting the industry; he refused to see that there was anything seriously wrong with it, and he felt confident that the farmer would pull through with his own resources.

It was easy to blame the Government. The only answer the Government could have given was that it had its own remedy for the agricultural depression, namely taxes on imported foods, but it knew that the urban electorate would not allow the remedy to be tried. The Labour party stood for the nationalization of the land, and Mr. Lloyd George, taking up again what had always been one of the causes nearest his heart, declared that he agreed with them in a voluminous report, entitled 'Land and the Nation', which embodied the conclusion of a committee of enquiry he had himself appointed. The other Liberal leaders emphatically did not agree with Mr. Lloyd George. They also wanted to know why he would not place at the disposal of the party organization the mysterious political fund which he had retained on the break-up of the Coalition. After the General

Strike, over which Mr. Lloyd George dissociated himself from the other leading Liberals, the feud between the two sections of the party broke out with renewed violence, and the forty Liberals in the House of Commons lost all pretence of cohesion. They became a fortuitous concourse of political atoms, distributing their votes between the Government and opposition lobbies in accordance with their individual judgments. Several of them left the party altogether, some joining the Conservatives and some the Labour party.

The Labour party was much more successful in preserving an appearance of unity. Though Mr. MacDonald's leadership had been bitterly denounced, and not only by extremists, after his defeat in 1924, he remained the only possible leader, and the attempt of Messrs. Lansbury, Wheatley, Maxton and Colonel Wedgwood to form a kind of 'Fourth Party' which would treat him as Lord Randolph Churchill's famous group had treated Sir Stafford Northcote in the early 'eighties, ended in complete fiasco. After the General Strike Labour began to gain markedly in by-elections, but it is a common experience for a Government with an enormous majority to lose its by-elections after it has exhausted its initial impetus.

Thus Parliamentary politics lost interest, but the affairs of the nation were as urgent as ever. How was Great Britain to maintain, or rather revive, in the post-war world the industrial prosperity and the export trade on which the very life of her crowded population depended? In the first years of the post-war slump we had attributed a large part of our unemployment to the economic ruin of our customers in Central Europe. It now looked as if their economic revival would hit us equally hard. In March 1925 the public heard that a well-known British firm had placed a contract with a Hamburg firm of shipbuilders for five 10,000 ton motor ships at a price lower by £60,000 than the most favourable British tender. At first it was assumed that the German Government had subsidized their nationals, but this was soon found to be not the case. German organization was more efficient and consequently more economical.

About this time it became very much the fashion to study and to praise the industrial methods of the United States, which was enjoying the unexampled prosperity associated with the Presidency of Mr. Coolidge. Mass production, mass distribution, scientific management, expert salesmanship, high wages and low prices seemed to be the clues to prosperity. Only one kind of brick, we read, was now made in the United States instead of forty different varieties, only four kinds of bed instead of seventy-eight. 'Such horrid uniformity', says a writer in the *Round Table* of September 1925, 'may revolt the artistically minded, but the ordinary householder is probably indisposed to grumble if he can purchase the best kind of blanket or kitchen range cheaper than he could previously obtain inferior varieties. . . . Is there no room for a "department of Simplified Practice" in the Board of Trade, working in close harmony with the trade organizations?' What was needed was a 'rationalization' of industry, a grouping of industries in scientifically planned aggregations, horizontal and vertical. Horizontal aggregation was the combine as usually understood, the co-operation of competitors in the same field. Vertical organization was, to the general public, a less familiar notion: it meant the co-operation of units representing different stages in the manufacture of the same product. The closer co-operation between coal-getting, coal-transforming, and coal-using industries, as recommended in the Samuel Report, was an application of the vertical idea.

Rationalization would deliver the goods. Whether there would be a public to buy them was another question. Rationalizers had to admit that their remedies would probably increase unemployment before they diminished it.

At the end of 1926 the public, weary of the coal stoppage, was invited to look elsewhere and applaud a triumph of academic definition. The hero of the occasion was Lord Balfour. His

career, apparently closed in stormy controversy as long ago as
1911, had after all enjoyed a prolonged and golden sunset. He
had become a national institution, and his name was associated
with a curious miscellany of Declarations. In 1917 he had declared that Palestine should become a National Home for the
Jews; in 1921 he had negotiated the Washington Agreement
which had established a ratio for the strength in battleships and
battle cruisers of the five great navies of the world; in 1922 he
had declared British policy on the subject of inter-Allied debts;
and now in 1926 he defined the British Empire.

The self-governing Dominions had achieved nationhood and
equality of status with Great Britain. They had become the
sisters of their Mother country. They had been separately represented at the Versailles Conference, and as nations they were
members of the League. Were they not then, independent? and
if independent, where was the British Empire? The problem of
finding a formula to reconcile this independence and this inter-
dependence, this unity of the Many and plurality of the One,
might seem as insoluble as the problem confronting the author
of the Athanasian Creed. Nor was the problem entirely academic; dissatisfaction with the present uncertainty was not confined to Ireland and South Africa, Dominions in which a strong
party was traditionally suspicious of whatever remained of the
Imperial tie. At the time of the Chanak crisis of 1922, when the
British Government was on the edge of war with Turkey, an
unwise telegram to the Canadian Government, calling on
Canada for armed support of British policy, had caused deep
resentment. The Dominions, though co-signatories of the Treaty
of Sèvres, had refused to have anything to do with the making
or the signing of the Treaty of Lausanne, which replaced it, and
they had insisted on the insertion in the Locarno Treaty of a
proviso expressly excluding them from responsibility for active
measures in guarantee of the Franco-German frontier.

Into these difficulties it was best not to probe too deeply. But
something could be done, and the Imperial Conference of 1926

appointed a Committee under the chairmanship of Lord Balfour, which, while expressly leaving out of account the colonial dependencies, produced the following definition of 'the group of self-governing communities composed of Great Britain and the Dominions'.

'They are', runs the definition, 'equal in status, in no way subordinate one to another in any respect of their domestic or external affairs, though united by a common allegiance to the Crown, and freely associated as members of the British Commonwealth of Nations.'

There was, in fact, much truth in the view often expressed by General Smuts, himself one of the principal authors of the Covenant of the League, that the British Commonwealth of Nations is itself a League of Nations. In the British Commonwealth a number of once insignificant and subordinate colonies had grown to free and equal partnership with their Mother country. In the League a far larger group of entirely independent states, with long records of rivalry and warfare behind them, sought a better future by means of free and equal partnership. Starting from opposite ends, the members of the League and the members of the British Commonwealth had worked towards the same result. When war between any two members of the League has become as improbable as war between Australia and New Zealand, the League will have achieved its ultimate ideal.

CHAPTER XXX

MR. BALDWIN'S ADMINISTRATION 1927-1929

The years 1927 and 1928 were beyond question the quietest in the whole of the reign of George V. Mr. Baldwin's Government remained in office, and there was never any great likelihood that the Parliament which gave it so comfortable a majority would fail to live out its five years' term. It was in fact the first Parliament to die a natural death at the proper time since quinquennial Parliaments had been established by the Parliament Act in 1911. The first Parliament under that Act had had its life prolonged for eight years owing to the emergencies of the war, and its three successors had perished in their prime. As for the Government, it would be untrue to say that, like Gilbert's House of Lords, it 'did nothing in particular', but nothing that it did in these its later years stirred more than a ripple of interest outside professionally political circles. It curtailed the privileges of trade unions, enfranchised women under thirty, and carried through a drastic and complicated reform of local government and local taxation; it despatched troops to Shanghai; it broke off relations with Russia; it wrestled, most unsuccessfully, with the problem of naval disarmament. But none of these things ever created the impression that they were vitally important. Perhaps the best measure of the quietness of these years is the fact that their principal sensation was the New Prayer Book—the point at issue being whether certain clergymen should be legally empowered to conduct certain services in a manner in which they were already conducting them, and would continue to conduct them whether legally empowered or not.

379

Curtailment of the powers of the trade unions had long been the desire of a considerable section of the Conservative party, and one of Mr. Baldwin's most striking Parliamentary performances had been his speech in deprecation of this policy a year before the General Strike. After the General Strike he either modified his own opinions or allowed his judgment to be overruled by the will of his majority, and all and more than all that Mr. MacQuisten and his friends had hoped for was included in the Trade Disputes and Trade Unions Bill which was the principal Government measure of 1927. The Bill was declared by Sir Douglas Hogg, the Attorney General, who moved its Second Reading, to be founded upon four propositions: that a general strike is illegal, and no man shall be penalized for refusing to take part in it; that intimidation is illegal, and no man shall be compelled by threats to abstain from work against his will; that no man shall be compelled to subscribe to the funds of any political party unless he so desires; that any person entering the established civil service must give his undivided allegiance to the State, i.e. that the civil servants' trade unions must disconnect themselves from the Trade Union Congress and all other association with the Labour party.

Everyone knew that the first and the second of these propositions involved notorious difficulties of definition. For what, in the first proposition, is a General Strike? Labour maintained that there had been no General Strike in 1926, but only a combination of sympathetic strikes. The ground here was at once difficult and, by law, untrodden. As for the second proposition —intimidation—its legal pitfalls had been familiar ever since the trade union controversies of the Gladstone-Disraeli epoch, and the bad old days when seven Welsh women were sent to prison for saying 'Boo!' to one 'blackleg'. The original proposals of the Government on these two subjects went much too far, and Mr. Baldwin was constrained to admit that the Bill 'could be vastly improved' in the Committee stage. Improved it was; but the Labour party was at first too angry to co-operate with the

Government in this task. Its leaders had declared, even before
they saw the text of the Bill, that it was an attack upon the rights
of the workers. They planned to fight it with passion across the
floor of the House, and to organize a whirlwind campaign to stir
the passions of their followers throughout the country.

They failed, with a completeness of failure that surprised
themselves and everyone else. The ordinary trade unionist was
sick of strikes, whether general or particular. He inclined to
agree with Mr. Williams, of the Transport Workers Union, when
he said 'the era of effective strikes has passed'; and Mr. Williams
had been a vigorous Direct Actionist only a few years before.
The ordinary trade unionist was not interested in what the Bill
might say about General Strikes and Intimidation; at least, not
sufficiently interested to dance to the piping of his Parliamentary
leaders. Perhaps he thought that, in so far as it mattered at all, his
own party would have plenty of time to put the law to rights
again before he required its services. As for contracting-in instead of contracting-out, it was after all no more than a scrap of
paper. The results, after the new system came in action, proved
that contracting-in was no great hardship; the numbers that
exerted themselves to perform this feat of penmanship fell very
little short of the number of those who, under the old system, had
refrained from contracting-out. The Trade Union Congress
turned down, almost with derision, the proposal that there
should be another General Strike in protest against the Act
forbidding General Strikes. Mr. Citrine, the Secretary of the
Trade Union Council, took occasion to reprove those trade
unionists, mostly irresponsible young persons, who talked as if
their unions were simply fighting machines, and Mr. Hicks, the
Chairman of the Congress, suggested that the Council might
with advantage enter into negotiations with the employers'
organizations to consider with them the promotion of peace in
industry.

This invitation, though ignored by the official organization
of employers, was taken up by Sir Alfred Mond and some of his

friends among the supermen of industry. The result was the 'Mond-Turner conversations' which continued, with much goodwill though without any constructive results, throughout several months of the year following.

Outside the world of Labour some regarded the Trade Union Act as a necessary corollary to the General Strike, others regarded it as a welcome, or unwelcome, sign that the Baldwin Government was 'swinging to the Right'. These others found support for their view in the melodramatic raid upon 'Arcos', the Headquarters of the Russian Trade Agency in London. The hero of this raid, in which safes were blasted open with dynamite in the best Edgar Wallace manner, was the Home Secretary, Sir William Joynson-Hicks, who had already endeared himself to the public as the comic member of Mr. Baldwin's Government. He preferred, it was said, to be known as Jix, a monosyllable worthy of a great comedian, the equal of Mutt or of Jeff; but Jix though he might like to seem, the Sir William and the Joynson were also always very much in evidence. He took himself intensely seriously and he was right to do so, for he personified the average; he was the Platonic idea of the suburban Conservative voter.

The pretext for the raiding of Arcos was that nefarious Bolsheviks had got hold of an important secret document relating to His Majesty's Forces; it was a pity that in none of their blasted safes could this document be found. The real justification for the raid was that the Russian Government had never been true to the undertaking to refrain from hostile propaganda which had been given to Mr. MacDonald's Government when the Trade Agreement of 1924 was signed. Possibly the machinations of the Bolsheviks did us no particular harm; perhaps they would continue them as easily without Arcos as with it; perhaps on the other hand the Trade Agreement with Russia had proved sterile of benefit and might as well be terminated. It did not seem to matter very much, either way. The most interesting and important fact connected with the Arcos raid was that Labour, apart from a few Labour politicians, was quite unmoved. A very few years back Labour had insisted on looking at the Soviets through rose-coloured spectacles and presenting a gold watch to Mr. Tomsky. Now, when Mr. Tomsky chose to be exceedingly rude about all things British, the Trade Union Congress decided to take a leaf out of the Book of Jix, and to wind up its fraternal relations with the trade unions of Russia. Several leading trade unionists who had for years been sustaining fraternal relations with the Russian unions, gave a variety of very good reasons for their change of opinion—one of them was that their Russian brethren appeared to believe that the end justified the means.

It was one thing for the Government to abuse the trade unions and break with Russia; quite another thing to rehabilitate the House of Lords. 'Reform of the House of Lords', which implied and included a restoration of some of the powers it had lost by the Parliament Act, had long figured on the Conservative programme, and a sound debating point could be scored whenever one called attention to the famous Preamble to the Liberal-Labour Parliament Act, which declared that measure to be merely preliminary to a reconstitution of the membership of the Second Chamber. But wiser heads were inclined to leave the subject alone.

In June 1927, however, when the Arcos raid was still a novelty and the Trade Union Bill was in mid passage, the Lord Chancellor intervened in a debate introduced by a peer outside the Government, to describe an official scheme for the Reform of the House of Lords, and Lord Birkenhead declared that the Government intended to pass a Bill based upon this scheme before the dissolution of Parliament. The new House of Lords was to consist of peers elected by the peerage and of members nominated for ten years by the Crown on the advice of the Government, and the Parliament Act was no longer to apply to any measure affecting the constitution and powers of the Second Chamber. There were other provisions, but this was the important one. In effect it would render the new House of Lords and its powers immune from alteration except with its own consent.

One would like to know more than is known at present about the incubation of these proposals. In what light were they regarded, for example, by Mr. Baldwin, who certainly showed himself on other occasions as shrewd a judge of democratic sentiment as most of the statesmen of his day? Did he foresee what in fact inevitably happened, and allow his reactionary colleagues to learn from experience what he knew by instinct in advance? Certain it is that the proposals had what is called 'a bad press'. Mr. Garvin dealt with them in his most trenchant style, in an article entitled 'Doomed!' and concluding with a comparison between the Conservative party and the Gadarene swine. The younger Conservatives in the House of Commons took early occasion to make their opinions known, and before time could be found for the expected Vote of Censure to be debated, Lord Cave's scheme had already become 'the late proposals'. Mr. Baldwin's official defence of them was at once detached and elegiac, like a funeral oration in praise of a very distant relative, and he indicated that he would make no further attempt to solve the problem which, as Mr. Asquith had said, 'brooked no long delay'.

Abandoning their attempt to make the British Constitution less democratic, the Government addressed themselves to the simpler task of making it more democratic by giving the vote to women between the ages of twenty-one and thirty. This was, sooner or later, an inevitable measure for, if women were to have the vote at all, there was no evidence to suggest that they took longer to emerge from 'infancy' than their brothers and their boy friends—rather the opposite, some would say. The reason for postponing their enfranchisement until a later age had been the reluctance of a male House of Commons to create an electorate in which their own sex was outnumbered; but a few years' trial had dispelled whatever fears there may have been that the ballot box would prove a vehicle for sex expression. This, the

Fifth, and presumably the last, Reform Bill was accepted without any particular enthusiasm. The young women who had tied themselves to lamp-posts and starved themselves in prison before the war were now a long way past thirty, and the younger generation were much less interested in the vote, either because they were less earnest in their outlook on life or else because their earnestness ran into other channels.

Only in the *Daily Mail* and other papers controlled by Lord Rothermere was there any appearance of excitement. Lord Rothermere's henchmen industriously denounced the measure and insulted its intended beneficiaries. The 'Flappers' Vote', it seemed, would be the ruin of England, and when the next election gave the Labour party a precarious majority Lord Rothermere was quick to call attention to his own merits as a prophet of woe. But when, two years later, the same electorate gave an overwhelming verdict in favour of the National Government, the *Daily Mail* omitted to comment on the Flapper contribution to this result. In any case, why 'Flappers'? for a Flapper is a Victorian maiden in her teens, with long hair in pigtails flapping against her shoulders.

Mr. Churchill's Budgets continued to be, as it were, among the best sellers of each spring season. In 1927, for example, we all expected to suffer just, though vicarious, punishment for what Mr. Churchill called 'the shocking breakdown of our island's civilization' in the previous year. Revenue fell short of estimates by thirty-six millions, not so much on account of the General Strike, which was an inexpensive experiment, as on account of the prolonged paralysis of the coal industry, and it seemed that unless the Sinking Fund were raided the taxpayer would have to pay. The Chancellor, however, confounded his critics and accomplished the feat Mr. Tom Shaw had deemed impossible; he produced the rabbits from his hat. By antedating the payment of various tax instalments and by sundry technical rearrangements he swept into the revenue of 1927-28 all, and indeed rather more than all, the money required to cover his deficit, the only additional taxes being a trifle on wines and tobacco and two new safeguarding duties.

Mr. Churchill's 1927 financed the past follies of Labour; his 1928 financed the boons which the wisdom of his own party was about to confer. The Government had in prospect a Derating Scheme, which would relieve agricultural land of all and industrial plant of three-quarters of the burdens at present imposed on them by local rates. It was necessary, therefore, to ensure to the Treasury a revenue from which the local authorities would receive compensation for the rate revenue they were about to lose. The money for this purpose was to be raised by a tax on petrol, one of the few commodities which was much cheaper than before the war, and for which the demand was continually increasing. Motorists had long been pointing out how much fairer it would be to tax them through their petrol consumption than by measuring, by very questionable standards, the horse-power of their cars. Mr. Churchill took them at their word—but retained the horse-power tax. The petrol tax would also help to redress the balance of power in the competition between road and rail, which had recently become acute. Indeed, the longer one looked at it, the more admirable this tax appeared. Besides financing the Derating scheme the 1928 Budget gave further assistance to domestic establishments by affording increased allowances for the children of income-tax payers. Finally the Chancellor outlined a far-reaching policy of debt redemption which would, if his successors lived up to it, extinguish the whole of the National Debt in fifty years. It was, in the opinion of the *Round Table*, the most remarkable and thought-provoking Budget since the 'People's Budget' of 1909.

In the financial year 1927-28 for the first time, and also very nearly for the last, our receipts from our European debtors practically covered our payments to America.

Not much could be expected of the Budget of 1929, since it was introduced within a few weeks of the dissolution of Parliament, and had therefore to be composed of ingredients easily

Mr. Baldwin's Administration 1927-29

and rapidly digestible. But even here Mr. Churchill had his little *coup*. He abolished the remainder of the tea duty, thus putting an end, for the time being, to a tax which in one form or another went back to the reign of Queen Elizabeth.

The Derating policy involved, apart from the Budget which financed it, three measures of legislation: a Bill authorizing a revaluation of ratable property and two Bills reorganizing the system of local government, one for England and one for Scotland. The English Local Government Bill was one of the most elaborate measures ever presented to the House of Commons, and it was introduced by Mr. Chamberlain in a speech recognized by all who heard it, without distinction of party, as a masterpiece of lucid exposition. The Bill was, in fact, designed to serve many purposes besides Derating: it was a comprehensive attempt to reform, in face of changed conditions, the system of local government as established by Acts passed in the days of Mr. Gladstone and Lord Salisbury. Mr. Chamberlain summed up the deficiencies of the existing system under five heads. First there was the overlapping of the spheres of the elected guardians of the poor with the spheres of other authorities; secondly, the unfair burden of road maintenance imposed on rural district councils; thirdly the lack of elasticity in the boundaries of local districts; fourthly the inequitable system of rates, payable by agriculture and industry irrespective of profit or loss; and fifthly the chaotic relations between national and local expenditure.

For each of these evils the Act had remedies to offer. It was, as one of Mr. Chamberlain's admirers remarked, an excellent example of disinterested statesmanship. It was an attempt to tackle a whole complex of problems at once difficult, important, and dull. Undertaken and carried relentlessly through in the last year before a general election, it conferred real boons which could not be experienced until the election was over, and in all probability it did not catch a single vote.

In 1917, as everyone knows, President Wilson declared war

upon Germany and thereafter began to create the greatest army in the world. There were some who wished that he had begun to create that army earlier.

A fact less widely remembered is that, in 1916, President Wilson, feeling himself, as he confessed to Colonel House, urged almost irresistibly along the path that led to war with Great Britain, gave orders for the beginnings of what was to be the world's greatest navy, ten first-class battleships, six battle cruisers and a number of smaller craft being the first instalment. This programme was interrupted by the declaration of war on Germany, and American shipyards were switched over to the construction of mercantile vessels to replace the victims of the U-boats. After the war the American navy was resumed. The purpose of this great navy, except as an expression of American pride, was not altogether obvious even to Americans themselves, and when President Harding summoned his naval disarmament conference at Washington in 1921 he and his advisers hoped to kill three birds with one stone. They would impose limits upon the navies of their rivals, offer the naughty world an example of how disarmament could be done, and save themselves a great deal of probably useless expenditure.

The Washington Conference succeeded because it limited itself to the easiest part of its task. It fixed, for the five nations concerned, America, Great Britain, Japan, France and Italy, maximum tonnages for battleships and battle cruisers, leaving aside ordinary cruisers, destroyers and submarines. It established Anglo-American 'parity' in battle fleets. The other Powers accepted lower maximum figures on an agreed scale.

In the years that followed Great Britain proceeded, without reference to America, to build what cruisers she required, and America did not build cruisers to the same extent because she did not consider that she required them. There was no breach of the Washington Treaty, but Americans began to think that they had been fooled, and in the beginning of 1927 President Coolidge invited Great Britain and the other naval powers to confer once again, with the object of extending the policy of limitation to all types of vessels of war. France and Italy refused the invitation, which was accepted by Great Britain and Japan, whose representatives met those of America at Geneva.

It soon became apparent that Great Britain and America did not see eye to eye on the subject of cruisers. America wanted a cruiser parity which would allow both powers to build a comparatively small number of large and powerfully armed cruisers. Great Britain wanted a very much larger number of small cruisers such as, she declared, were necessary for the protection of the worldwide system of oceanic communications on which her very existence depended. Like France when faced with any suggestion of disarmament on land, she insisted upon her special need for 'security'. Deadlock supervened; the Conference failed, and President Coolidge invited Congress to authorize by far the largest naval programme that any nation had proposed since the Armistice. In England Lord Robert Cecil, the principal British exponent in Conservative circles of the cause of the League of Nations, resigned his Under-Secretaryship of Foreign Affairs, and delivered himself of a stinging criticism of the whole of British policy in relation to disarmament and world peace. As though to prove how unrepentant he was, Mr. Baldwin appointed, as Lord Cecil's successor, an elderly Diehard named Lord Cushendun, of whom little was publicly known except that he had once in anger thrown a book at Mr. Churchill across the floor of the House of Commons; for he was an Ulsterman and Mr. Asquith's Home Rule Bill was the subject of debate on that lamentable occasion.

Viewed in retrospect it was easy to see why the Conference had failed, and how easily failure could have been avoided. Both the British and the American Governments had entrusted the conduct of the Conference to their naval ministers and naval experts, oblivious of the sound maxim that the expert should, in all Conferences, be 'on tap' but not 'on top'. If a British statesman, other than a very worthy First Lord of the Admiralty, had led the British delegation at Geneva, he would not have insisted upon equality with America in the larger type of cruiser. He would have said 'We are not afraid of your cruisers, for we cannot believe you will ever use them against us.' If that line had been taken, America might well have allowed us as many little cruisers as we wanted.

The next American peace offensive was a World Dove with a World Olivebranch in its beak. On April 14th, 1928, newspaper readers all over the world were, as the *Round Table* has it, 'somewhat dazed' by the publication of despatches addressed by Mr. Kellogg, American Secretary of State, to the Governments of France, Great Britain, Germany, Italy, and Japan, proposing that a multilateral treaty should be concluded renouncing war altogether as an instrument of policy and undertaking that international disputes of whatever kind should be settled by peaceful means.

This proposal had behind it a rather curious correspondence. M. Briand, most internationally minded of French statesmen, had for some time been troubled by the fact that his country no longer occupied the privileged position in American sentiment that it had so long retained. The land of Lafayette had become, in American eyes, the land of Clemenceau and Poincaré. To rectify this unfortunate state of things M. Briand proposed a Franco-American treaty by which both countries would 'renounce war as an instrument of their national policy towards one another'. The 'outlawry of war' had become a popular watchword across the Atlantic, and a treaty on these lines would please the Americans without doing any harm to the French. M. Briand made his proposal first in speech and then formally in writing in the spring and summer of 1927. It received no answer until the end of the year, when Mr. Kellogg replied that his country would welcome an opportunity of signing a multilateral treaty by which all nations, each to each, would pledge themselves in the terms M. Briand proposed.

This was embarrassing. It would mean that France would no

longer be entitled to go to war with Germany, if Germany repudiated the Treaties of Versailles and Locarno. M. Briand's reply suggested that the multilateral treaty should be limited to a
renunciation of 'wars of aggression'. He pointed out that France
was bound, both by the Covenant of the League and by one of
the Locarno Treaties to enter upon war—a righteous war—if
circumstances definitely specified in those engagements were to
arise: that the defence of society against the crime of war depended upon the 'institution of international sanctions calculated to prevent and repress it'. But Mr. Kellogg swept all this
triumphantly aside. He refused to see that an engagement universally undertaken to refrain from the crime of war could
possibly do anything but facilitate any reasonable arrangements
for the suppression of that crime. To this M. Briand's reply was,
as the newspapers said, 'distinctly frigid'. He reiterated and
underlined his ifs and buts. But Mr. Kellogg, who had scored
in every stage of this correspondence, proceeded to score again
by simply sending his draft Treaty of three clauses to all the
Great Powers.

To most English people 'the outlawry of war' was no more
than a grandiloquent metaphor, a substitution of an easy phrase
for all the carefully calculated provisions of the Covenant which
America had renounced. This view was not entirely just, for the
phrase contained an idea, even though it had been coined by
Mr. S. O. Levinson, a company lawyer of Chicago. The idea
was an implied criticism of the League, along lines with which
the British public, outside the school of thought which had supported the Protocol, was very ready to sympathize. The League
stood for the prevention of war by methods which, in the last
resort, approved the use of war against those who defied it. It
assumed, and in fact approved, the retention of armaments, only
distinguishing between lawful and unlawful wars. The Covenant
declared that any member could go to war after nine months
unless its opponent had accepted a unanimous verdict of the
Council of the League. Similarly the Locarno Treaties obliged

the guaranteeing parties to go to war if the Treaties in which the
boundary states renounced war should be broken by any one of
them. The 'outlawry' school held that this was all wrong; they
held that the threat of war would never cease to trouble the
nations until they disarmed, and that they would never disarm
until they had renounced war under any and every circumstance.

In the end the Kellogg Pact was signed, in Paris, not only by
the Great Powers but by almost every independent State in the
world. It was, however, made subject to certain reservations
and interpretative declarations. Nothing in the Pact was to be
held inconsistent with the obligations imposed by the Covenant
of the League and the Treaties of Locarno, and nothing in the
Pact 'restricted or impaired in any way the right of self-defence'.
That right was declared by Mr. Kellogg himself to be 'inherent
in every sovereign State. Every nation is free at all times, and
regardless of treaty provisions, to defend its territories from
attack or invasion, and it alone is competent to decide whether
circumstances require recourse to war in self-defence.' Whether
the Kellogg Pact, as thus interpreted, was a contribution of any
substance to the cause of peace was a question on which various
opinions were held. At least it gave the Americans an adequate
pretext for abandoning the greater part of their new cruiser
programme.

But before the ink on the Pact was dry, indeed before the ink
of ratification had been deposited upon it, Sir Austen Chamberlain, inspired as always with the best intentions and anxious to
promote European disarmament, had manoeuvred himself and
his country into a most unfortunate position. For some years
past there had been in existence an organ of the League called
the Preparatory Disarmament Conference, and it had made
almost no progress. One of its troubles was that we could not
accept the French demand that reservists should be excluded
from the computation of the military forces allowed to the
several nations. It seemed quite impossible to get France to

recede from this demand; so Sir Austen Chamberlain gave way, bartering our reluctant assent in exchange for French concessions to British views on naval disarmament. France had hitherto demanded that all naval tonnage below the rank of battle cruisers should be treated as it were *en masse*, and each Power allowed to use its allotted quota in any way it pleased, e.g. for cruisers or for submarines. The French now accepted the British policy of limitation for the larger types of cruiser and of submarine, coupled with free building in the smaller types of each category. Such was the Anglo-French Convention, announced in July 1928, and Sir Austen at any rate was happy to think that as a result of his diplomacy Britain and France could at length present an amicable and united front on disarmament. The result was not answerable to his expectations.

Sir Austen had only a little time before declared, on one of his visits to Paris, that he 'loved France as one loves a woman, for her defects as well as for her qualities'. The compliment was not received quite in the spirit in which it was offered, for France is the kind of woman that does not like her lovers to know that she has defects; but as a self-portrait of the British Foreign Secretary it was all too true to life. Sir Austen could not be trusted alone with a Frenchman, especially if the Frenchman was as seductive a charmer as M. Briand. In this precious Convention he had assented to a series of propositions which were, no doubt, extremely popular in Paris but gave dire offence in Germany, Italy and America. Americans saw in the Convention a document which proposed to limit the type of cruiser favoured by America while allowing unlimited programmes in types America did not want; Italy envisaged an Anglo-French naval alliance to dominate the Mediterranean; Germany saw in it a reversal of the Locarno Treaties in which France and Germany had met as equals and Britain had presented herself as the good friend and guarantor of both alike. There was some ground for these peevish protests. In Paris the Convention was in fact acclaimed as an Anglo-French entente—almost an alliance. For years the

Mr. Baldwin's Administration 1927-29

French had been trying to 'hook' Great Britain, and land her in the basket which already contained Poland and Roumania and other trusty allies, and now they seemed to have succeeded. Of course Sir Austen intended nothing of the kind, and the Convention was dead as soon as it was published. It was only a storm in a teacup—a world storm in a world teacup; but it was a pity, for it is so much easier to depress than to raise the world-barometer. Ten months later Mr. Baldwin, on the eve of the election, promised that if he was returned to power he would retain Sir Austen's services at the Foreign Office. The announcement must have cost him several seats.

While Europe and America prattled of disarmament as the only alternative to warfare so scientific that it would involve the suicide of civilization, China suffered endemic warfare of a much more old-fashioned description. No one understood what it was all about; indeed for the most part it was about nothing, being simply the result of the general breakdown of discipline which had followed the fall of the Manchu dynasty in 1911. In the spring of 1926 the Chinese chaos began to define itself and revealed a formidable confederacy of forces in Southern China named Kuomintang. Its policy was announced to be democratic government, a higher standard of living, and the expulsion of the foreigner, and its leaders acted in close collaboration with Borodin and other agents of Soviet Russia. In the first days of 1927 the forces of Kuomintang sacked the British concession at Hankow, the great city five hundred miles up the Yangtze river, and threatened Shanghai, whereupon the British Government, while renewing its offer to negotiate a revision of the Treaties on which the extra-territorial privileges of the British settlements were based, sent a cruiser squadron and a force of 12,000 men to China. The Labour party protested, but the action of the Government was justified in the eyes of all but fanatics by the events that followed. Kuomintang occupied the native city outside the International concession at Shanghai and, while driving its Chinese rivals out of Nanking, began a massacre of Europeans in that city which was in all probability only checked by the presence and prompt action of British cruisers. By the end of the year the situation had grown easier, and most of the British troops were withdrawn. However, no permanent solution of Anglo-Chinese relations could be envisaged until China was once again blessed with a settled government capable of enforcing its authority. The anti-European movement had weakened for the moment only because the rival Chinese warlords were more actively engaged in fighting against each other.

In India there was a record of steady progress so far as acceptance of the Montagu-Chelmsford constitution was concerned. The first elections under that constitution had been boycotted by all the extremist parties. When the second elections were due these same extremists offered themselves at the polls in order to pursue a policy of 'wrecking the Reforms from within'. This project had failed to materialize, and in the third elections, of 1925, the dominant note was 'responsive co-operation'. The *swaraj* party had disintegrated, and most of its leaders were now in various ways and with various aims pursuing the Parliamentary careers which the great experiment offered them.

In these circumstances the British Government decided to advance by two years the date of the Royal Commission which, under the terms of the India Act of 1919, was to report on the working of the new constitution and recommend what further steps could safely be taken along the road to complete Indian self-government. The members of the Royal Commission were selected from both Houses of Parliament—two Conservatives, two Labour men, two Peers, and Sir John Simon, an eminent Liberal lawyer, as chairman. In India furious protests arose because no Indian statesmen were included among the Commissioners. It was, no doubt, a pity that misunderstandings on this point had not been foreseen and eliminated. The Commission was in fact a delegacy from the British Parliament to secure information in India from all representatives of Indian opinion. The task of Indian statesmen was not to write the Report but to supply the evidence on which the Report would be based.

And so Mr. Baldwin's five years drew towards their close. We have given to the period the general title of 'Convalescence', but anyone with personal experience of convalescence after a long and serious illness knows that this 'getting better', which is all that the word means, is a slow and wearisome business. Progress is often imperceptible, there are many disappointments, many relapses into weakness, and the patient is more acutely aware of the fact that he is not yet strong than that he was still weaker a while back. The *Round Table* summarized 1928 as 'the eighth lean year'. It was worse than 1927, and unemployment, which had fallen again to a million after the coal strike, was over a million and a half in the winter of 1928-9 though it mysteriously fell again a few hundred thousand by the summer of the latter year. What had become increasingly plain was the localization of unemployment in the coalfields and the industrial North, in fact in all the iron and steel and the textile industries on which Victorian prosperity had been based. In the London area, on the other hand, the insured population had increased ten per cent in five years and the numbers unemployed had been halved. But in the coalfields the distress was worse than ever. The Lord Mayor opened a fund to relieve distress in the mining districts and the Government, after some hesitation, consented to double whatever sum was raised through this agency. It also established an Industrial Transference Board to organize the migration of surplus labour and its employment elsewhere. The Board did useful work, but what it succeeded in doing was but a small fraction of what it would have liked to do.

What made the situation more depressing was that wherever one looked abroad industry seemed to be booming. In America 'Coolidge Prosperity' was the envy and admiration of the world. In Germany unemployment had fallen from two millions to less than half a million since France had evacuated the Ruhr. In France there was practically no unemployment at all, and steel production, to take but a single industry, had increased almost a hundred per cent since the last pre-war year. How did they do it, one would like to know. The *Round Table* had no doubt of the answer: 'By ruthlessly scrapping all methods, machinery, and management which do not come up to the most modern standards.' Our trouble was, partly, that we had so much more to scrap, having been so much more completely industrialized on lines now obsolete, so long before. A visitor to a Yorkshire industrial town, confronted by grimy and almost venerable structures, in Victorian semi-Gothic, bearing Gladstonian and even Palmerstonian dates over their porticoes, could not but wonder whether these places were fit to compete with the post-war structures of Germany, America and northern France. But that was not all our trouble. Our employers and workers alike were too firmly and complacently set in old-world ways. Many businesses were hereditary. Too many employers owed their position to the merits of their fathers, and were content to carry on in the ways their fathers had taught them. As for the men, nothing is more desperately conservative than a trade union when confronted with new ideas for 'speeding up' the industry on which its members are engaged. It was remarked that the new British industries, such as motors and artificial silk, and the old ones which had revolutionized their practice on modern lines, such as chemicals and tin plate, easily held their own in the international market.

It was not enough to make the best article; one had got to sell it. Early in 1929, speaking at the British Industries Fair, the Prince of Wales called attention to the importance of cultivating the art of salesmanship, and practising it in all the competitive markets of the world. So often British goods were not sold only because they were not in the right place at the right time, because they were not designed to satisfy the requirements and even the fads and fancies of remote markets, because the agent in charge of them was not properly acquainted with either the language or the national characteristics of his intended customers.

These were vital matters, but they were hardly politics; they offered no ready-made ammunition for the three parties now girding up their loins for the general election which was to take place at midsummer 1929. Of these three parties the Liberals had, since 1927, enjoyed a quite perceptible revival. Mr. Lloyd George had become, for a brief interval as it proved, undisputed leader of his party, after handing over to it 'without conditions' a large slice of his famous fund. Sir Herbert Samuel had returned to active party politics, and, unlike the other Big Brains of Liberalism, he was ready to co-operate unreservedly with Mr. Lloyd George. A series of bulky Reports were produced, under Liberal auspices, on the principal social problems of the day, and before the election the Liberal leader declared roundly and without qualification that, if returned to power, he could, and would, 'conquer unemployment', attacking it 'in the same spirit as we attacked the emergencies of the war'. The sixpenny pamphlet in which this promise was expanded and expounded was mostly about roads, bridges, houses and telephones—and a loan of £200,000,000.

The Labour party continued to suffer from its internal stresses. Briefly, those behind cried 'Forward!' and those in front cried 'Back!' For example there was, in 1927, much talk among the more sanguine Socialists of a programme according to which the next Labour Government was to establish a minimum wage of £4 a week. Mr. Snowden, Labour's official financier, expressed himself somewhat sharply on this project in the columns of the *Daily Herald*. It would cost, he said, £500,000,000 a year more than the total national income. 'It was all very well,' he continued, 'when the Socialist movement was in the propagandist stage, to be content with phrases about "exploitation" . . . but now that we are likely to have the responsibility of attempting to put our propaganda into practice, we have got to get down to the hard facts, and hard facts do not square with the licence of propaganda patter. My own experience must be the common experience of all Socialist speakers. Unless we use the word "Socialism" at least twice in every sentence, and unless we interlard our remarks with all the stock phrases of propaganda patter, we are sure to be charged with having sold ourselves to the capitalist.' The Mr. Snowden who could write thus in 1927 was already ripe for the National Government of 1931. He already despised his own party more than he hated Mr. Churchill.

The Labour Party Conference of 1928 had before it for consideration a voluminous official programme recently issued under the title of 'Labour and the Nation'. It was a programme full of saving clauses designed to reassure the marginal voter, and entirely merited the caustic criticism it received from real Socialists like Mr. Maxton and Mr. Cook, but even so it was much more than Mr. MacDonald could swallow in a single mouthful. With Gladstonian adroitness he removed the greater number of its items from the region of practical politics, declaring that it was a manifesto not merely for 1929 but for many elections to come, and that it was 'pregnant with programme after programme'. In his political campaign Mr. MacDonald preferred to devote himself to the errors of the Conservative Government, especially in the sphere of foreign policy. Most of his lieutenants, however, followed the lead of Mr. Lloyd George and promised, if returned to power, to abolish unemployment.

As for Mr. Baldwin he proceeded with his usual honesty. He and his friends had been doing their best for five years. If the public gave them a further lease of office they would continue to do their best along the same lines, neither more nor less. The principal Conservative poster for election purposes was a big picture of good old Father Baldwin smoking his good old briar pipe, over the legend 'Safety First'. If the Conservative Government had disfranchised everyone under forty instead of enfranchising several million women under thirty, this might have proved a very shrewd appeal. As it was, a large number of the electorate had sized up Mr. Baldwin's team as a lot of old and tired men, without courage and without vision. The Prime Minister had resisted the frequently repeated appeals of his candid friends, the editorial staff of the *Times*, to get rid of the less brilliant of his old cronies, and promote the best men of the post-Victorian generation. He had refused; these old men were his loyal colleagues; no doubt the time of some of them was nearly up, but he would not eject them at the bidding of journalists and in the interests of political window-dressing.

The 'Safety First' election was a dull affair, though in one respect it was the biggest election ever fought. Not only was the electorate larger by five millions, the candidates were more numerous by three hundred than in 1924. Each party put forward over 500 candidates, and few indeed were the constituencies with a straight fight between Government and Opposition. The *Round Table* had some interesting remarks on the similarity of the rival programmes. 'The Socialist party has been moving towards the Right, as the Conservative party has been moving to the Left. The wild and subversive ideas of a few years ago have faded into the background. The Socialist programme no longer requires for its adornment the old flag of revolution; rather it appears top-hatted and frock-coated, bespatted and adorned with the Albert watch-chain of respectability. Liberalism is more socialist than the Labour party. Conservatism is more advanced than Victorian Liberalism. Labour is approximating to nineteenth-century radicalism. These changes, however disconcerting they may be to the partisan, are eminently satisfactory to the patriot. Parliamentary government is only possible when all parties accept the general structure of society. . . . It may perhaps be said without exaggeration that Socialism is dead in all except the rank and file of the Socialist party. Its leaders have ceased to believe in it.' The writer conjectured that this change would be found, by the ver-

Mr. Baldwin's Administration 1927-29

dict of history, to be in large measure due to the conciliatory policy uniformly pursued by the Conservative leader. Not that, in the conditions of the moment, he was likely to profit by the situation. 'This steadying process may prove to be at once Mr. Baldwin's political grave and his political monument.'

Both Conservatives and Labour party polled rather over eight million votes, and the Liberals five million. The allocation of seats was, however, dramatically different. The Labour party increased its holding from 160 to 290, becoming for the first time the largest party in the House. The Conservatives fell from 396 to 260, and the Liberals rose from a miserable 46 to a scarcely less miserable 60. Labour failed, as in 1924, to secure an independent majority, but Mr. Baldwin resigned at once, and the King sent for Mr. MacDonald.

Undramatic as the 1929 election may have been, it will be, or should be, always memorable as the first in which the whole adult population, male and female, was enabled to take part. It was also a very fair and easy test of democratic intelligence, for there was no issue involved over which there was any excuse for getting irrationally excited. The slight but definite drift of votes away from the Conservative party was probably due to a natural desire, not based on any careful analysis of rival programmes, to give Labour an innings. The Conservative party did not lose heavily, for they had a good and varied record to defend, and their abstention from extravagant promises very likely gained them as many votes as it lost; for in spite of his apparent taste in newspapers the average Englishman respects good sense and moderation of statement. The Liberal party had promised most, and it was easily at the bottom of the poll; but the electorate had evidently decided that, if it wanted bold social experiment, it would entrust itself not to Mr. Lloyd George but to the party which called itself Socialist.

Pure Socialism of the continental variety was certainly not wanted in 1929. Of the twenty-five Communist candidates twenty-one forfeited their deposits by failing to poll one-eighth

Mr. Baldwin's Administration 1927-29

of the votes cast in their constituencies. None was elected, not even Mr. Saklatvala, the ingenious and eloquent Parsee who had upheld Communism in the two previous Parliaments as the representative of the electors of Lambeth.

CHAPTER XXXI

THE PRAYER BOOK

I t is impossible to assess the comparative importance of events
which belong to different categories. Which, for example, is
to be held the more important of two events of the period
1927-28, the successful introduction of greyhound racing or the
unsuccessful introduction of the Alternative Prayer Book? The
question, like all foolish questions, admits of no answer, and the
chronicler of historical events would do well to admit that his
selection of topics is, in the last analysis, quite arbitrary; he
writes about what happens to interest him, and he hopes that
his readers' taste in these matters is not altogether different from
his own. Those who take pleasure in historical studies, while in
no way denying the significance of 'the Dogs', may be excused
for preferring the Prayer Book. It has, for those trained to hear
them, the richer overtones. In an age all too exclusively post-
war, all too obsessed with economic intricacies such as our
fathers never knew or needed to know, it is exhilarating to open
up a controversy in which the rival champions take their stand
upon arguments which were the very stuff of history when men
wore wigs, when men wore armour, when the Pope was the
centre of Europe and there were no Presidents in America.

The questions at issue were apparently remote and mysterious;
it might be said that they were incomprehensible, but, when
brought to the popular test, they were certainly not found uninteresting. 'Not for a long time', says the *Round Table*, 'has a
decision of the House of Commons moved the people of England
in the way that its rejection of the Prayer Book measure on

The Prayer Book

December 15th (1927) moved them. The venerable Archbishop of Canterbury, widely regarded as the very prototype of Christian statesmanship and charity, who thus saw the principal work of his long archiepiscopate rejected; the dramatic manner in which the labour of the twenty-one years expended on it was overthrown on the last test to which, by law, it had to be submitted; the fact that this occurred on one of those rare occasions when a first-class issue is decided on the debate preceding the division, the result uncertain to the last; the innate instinct in most people for theological controversy; the ever-surviving force of the cry of "no Popery", and the determination of the Protestants to oppose any compromise of what they regarded as essential to the Reformation settlement; the zeal of the Anglo-Catholics; all combined to make the occasion in every way memorable.'

The issue had been raised by the pouring of new wine into old bottles. The old bottles were the Prayer Book of 1662; the new wine was the Anglo-Catholic movement, itself the offspring of the early-Victorian Oxford Movement whose leaders had been Keble and Newman. Newman went over to Rome in 1845, and when, writing a Preface to a novel in 1870, Disraeli said that the Church of England 'still reeled' under that blow, most of his readers must have thought that he was amusing himself over a subject he did not understand. In essentials Disraeli was right. The secession of Newman and his friends indelibly tarred the Anglo-Catholic movement with the Roman brush; it contributed, from its remote and scarce consciously remembered past, to the rejection of the Alternative Prayer Book.

The leaders of the Oxford movement were dons, and their activities were centred upon theology and doctrine. They ransacked the Fathers and disintegrated the Articles, but they hardly concerned themselves with those outward and visible signs whereby differences of religion make themselves apparent to the ordinary churchgoer. By 1870 there were, however, already a few clergymen performing services which bore but little resemblance to those ordained in the Prayer Book of 1662, and in 1874 Disraeli, with the wholehearted approval of Queen Victoria, carried through Parliament a Public Worship Regulation Act, to suppress what he called 'mass in masquerade'. Beyond inflicting upon a few clerical extremists the honours and the advertisement of a mild martyrdom the Act proved an entire failure. Irregularities multiplied, and in 1906 a Royal Commission was appointed to enquire into the subject of ecclesiastical discipline. Though including members well known for their strongly Protestant views, the commission unanimously reported that discipline could not, and ought not, to be enforced until the disciplinary norm, the Prayer Book, had itself been revised. 'The law of public worship', they wrote, 'is too narrow for the religious life of the present generation.'

That was in 1906. It was, in fact, an invitation to the Church, from the highest competent authority within the State, to undertake the revision of the Prayer Book. The Church accepted the invitation and from that date onwards pursued, without haste but also without rest, the delicate and difficult duty that had been laid upon it.

Before that task was completed, another movement within the Church, the so-called Life and Liberty Movement, secured the passage of an Act of Parliament which gave to the Church a new system of representative assemblies, and a new relationship to the legislature of the State. It had become improbable that, under modern conditions, a House of Commons would ever spare the time to put through all the stages required by Parliamentary procedure any complicated and important ecclesiastical Bill. Gone were the days when members of parliament debated Tonnage, Poundage, and Predestination at equal length and with equal enthusiasm. Tonnage and Poundage had crowded Predestination out of the legislative arena. Under the Enabling Act of 1919 all the spade work of ecclesiastical legislation was to be done in a new National Assembly of the Church and in the Houses of Convocation. The finished product of these ecclesiastical assemblies then passed to an Ecclesiastical Committee of both Houses of Parliament. If the Ecclesiastical Committee certified the measure as constitutionally within the competence of the assemblies of the Church it was then laid before Parliament, and became law after an interval of three months unless its rejection was moved and carried in either House of Parliament. Under this procedure several small measures, creating new bishoprics and the like, had already become law, and one such measure had been rejected.

At last, by 1927, the New Prayer Book was completed. It was not proposed as a substitute for the Prayer Book of 1662, but as an Alternative, as a repertory of authorized variations upon the historic text. By far the greater part of the New Prayer Book was acceptable to all parties and outside controversy. On controversial subjects the arts of compromise had been so effectively exercised that the Book was adopted in the House of Bishops by a majority of 38 to 4; in the House of Clergy by 253 to 37; in the House of the Laity by 330 to 92. It was certified by the Joint Ecclesiastical Committee and accepted by the House of Lords. The 'no Popery' societies of what the Bishop of Durham, himself a Protestant, stigmatized as 'the Protestant underworld' were conducting a vigorous agitation, and threatening members of the House of Commons with consequences at the next election, but it was assumed that the exceptional prestige enjoyed by the principal sponsor of the Book, the Archbishop of Canterbury, would suffice to conciliate the waverers.

Those who reasoned thus had not taken sufficient account of the Home Secretary, Sir William Joynson-Hicks. That sturdy British patriot had found in the defence of our traditional Protestantism a theme exactly suited to his quality. He was the average man made eloquent by genuine resentment and apprehension; and there was, when one considered it from his point of view, much cause both for resentment and alarm. The New Prayer Book legalized the reservation of the sacrament, and the leaving of the consecrated elements upon the altar after the conclusion of the Communion Service. There were, it was admitted, excellent practical reasons for reservation; it made possible the administration of Communion to the sick on a scale never contemplated in an easy-going past. None the less, the practice of reservation made possible the worship of the sacred elements, the worship of 'God in a box' as ultra-Protestant champions called it and, however much the Church might officially frown upon such superstitious practices, once reservation was admitted these practices could not be prevented. Again, the original purpose of the revision of the Prayer Book was to make possible the prohibition of all practices that went beyond it. Did the extremer Anglo-Catholics intend henceforth to confine themselves within the limits set by the New Prayer Book? Did the bishops, all the bishops, undertake henceforth to enforce the rigour of the law against all those who did not so confine themselves? The supporters of the Book could not answer either of these questions in the affirmative. The measure was defeated in the House of Commons by 238 votes to 205.

After the measure had been rejected the bishops at once met and introduced a number of alterations designed not so much to modify the careful compromise on which the Book was based as to meet certain objections which could be met without sacrificing any point of principle. The debates on these amendments in the assemblies of the Church were not auspicious. They brought into clearer light the disunity of religious opinion within the Church itself. It became clearer than before that the Book, while straining the allegiance of such Protestants as the Dean of St. Paul's, fell far short of the requirements of the Bishop of Truro. When the Book came a second time before the House of Commons in June 1928, the result was hardly in doubt. After one of the most brilliant of Parliamentary debates, the measure was rejected by a larger majority than on the previous occasion. It was remarked that both in June and in the previous December the measure had a small English majority. It owed its defeat to an English minority supported by the representatives of Scotland, Wales, and Ulster, homes of a sturdy Protestantism

The Prayer Book

where the writ of Canterbury did not run. In no Scottish, Welsh, or Ulster church would any practice have been legalized or il-legalized by Parliamentary acceptance of the New Prayer Book.

What then was the result of the rejection of the measure? It was, that things remained as they had been before the measure was introduced. Reservation of the sacrament remained in the same category as driving a motor car at more than twenty miles an hour. It continued to be illegal, and it continued to be allowed.

PART V

RELAPSE—AND RECOVERY

1929-1934

CHAPTER XXXII

THE LITTLE VICTIMS

It is possible that a completely articulated socialistic system would provide a sure haven of refuge in any economic storm, but the policy of the British Labour Party was made in, and for, times of fair weather. It was, as its elder statesmen never tired of professing, a policy of gradualness, less concerned to construct socialism than to sap capitalism, bleeding its profits for the benefit of the social services. It assumed that the capitalist was, and in spite of indefinite bleeding would continue to be, conveniently 'bloated'. But if the capitalist slowly and suddenly pined away, the major premise of Labour policy was gone, and Labour leaders would find themselves in the position of the egg-vendor whose goose has lost the capacity to lay her golden eggs. That was what was happening throughout the two years' lifetime of the second Labour Government. Almost immediately after the Labour Government took office the Great Slump announced its oncoming with the collapse of the American stock market, and from that moment onwards the economic barometer began to fall all over the world. The Labour politicians shut their eyes to what they did not want to see, and went ahead with their fair-weather policies. In August 1931, the Prime Minister and a few of his colleagues opened their eyes, and entered the National Government; others opened their eyes and, not liking what they saw, shut them again; and others again did not open their eyes at all or had no eyes to open. These latter groups crossed over into opposition.

The Little Victims

But that crisis was still two years ahead. We have first to survey the domestic futilities of 1929-31.

> 'Alas! regardless of their doom
>   The little victims play:
> No sense have they of ills to come
>   No care beyond today:
> Yet see how all around them wait
> The ministers of human fate,
>   And black Misfortune's baleful train!
> Ah, show them where in ambush stand,
> To seize their prey, the murderous band!
>   Ah, tell them they are men.

Warning voices in plenty were to be heard before the two years were over, and facts which spoke louder than any voice. But, in the summer of 1929, it was not only Labour men who seemed very well satisfied with the result of the election. 'The electorate', says the *Round Table*, 'rejected the slogan of Safety First but achieved the result. With the uncanny good sense (or perhaps good fortune) of the British people the electors have, in however blind and groping a fashion, produced a Parliamentary situation almost exactly suited to the present needs of the country.' A cryptic and, in retrospect, a fatuous judgment; the writer means to imply that the electors had done well in restoring Mr. MacDonald to the control of foreign relations, but had at the same time, by making his Government dependent on Liberal goodwill, prevented the hotheads of his back benches from driving him into Socialistic experiments. The list of the new Cabinet confirmed a forecast along such lines as these. Mr. Wheatley, the only aggressively Socialist minister in the Government of 1924, was excluded from that of 1929. Mr. Snowden returned to the Treasury; Mr. Henderson took the Foreign Office, and Mr. Thomas, as Lord Privy Seal, was entrusted with the campaign against unemployment. It was said that Mr. Thomas knew no economics but had many influential friends

The Little Victims

in the City, and the advantages of such ignorance and such friends were widely canvassed. Some said that Mr. Thomas had been entrusted with this task by his enemies, in the hope that his failure would discredit him. But this was not true, and events were to prove that it would take much more than a World Slump to discredit Mr. Thomas.

For the past five years and more, throughout the period of economic recovery in Europe and hectic prosperity in America, British unemployment had stuck obstinately at a figure which oscillated slightly above the million mark. Labour had climbed into office on a promise to abolish this unemployment which Conservatives had failed to cure, so Mr. Thomas's responsibility was no light one. We will follow his fortunes—and the fortunes of the unemployed—throughout the two years' period before passing to other topics. He was given three political assistants: Mr. Lansbury, Mr. Johnston, and Sir Oswald Mosley, a brilliant and aggressive young man, said to be extremely rich, who had already served in, and quarrelled with, the Conservative and Liberal parties, and was soon to found a New Party of his own invention. There was also an entirely new department with a staff of distinguished civil servants to work out the details of Mr. Thomas's far-reaching schemes.

For several months nothing happened except that Mr. Thomas went to Canada. What he would or could do there was a mystery, but he returned 'satisfied in my mission, and certain that work for the unemployed will result'. These comfortable words had been cabled from Canada. On landing he declared, 'I have a lot of things up my sleeve'; and further, 'I have a complete cure.' Needless to say, Mr. Thomas's speech in exposition of his cure was awaited with unusual interest. When it came, in October, it was found to amount to just nothing; it was one of the notable Parliamentary fiascos of modern times. But Mr. Thomas was not outwardly discouraged. He seems to have remembered the system of Professor Coué, who a few years earlier had taught us to eliminate our evils by simply telling ourselves

413

that we were getting better and better in every way, every day. Mr. Thomas did not repeat his formula; he found a new metaphor for it in every speech. We were pulling through; we had reached the bottom; we were not down and out; the worst was past; the cloud had a silver lining; the day was dawning; the tide had turned. After eleven months of this sort of thing unemployment figures had risen from 1,100,000 to 1,700,000 and Mr. Thomas was transferred to the Dominions Office to prepare for the Imperial Conference.

Meanwhile Sir Oswald Mosley had taken a line of his own and had produced a memorandum on somewhat Lloyd Georgian lines—a big scheme of public works financed by a big loan. For some months the Cabinet concealed this memorandum in their pigeon-holes until Sir Oswald lost patience, resigned from the Government, and published the memorandum on his own responsibility. He was now the hero of the rank and file and was looked upon by many as the future leader of the party. At the annual Conference of the Labour party in the autumn of 1930 a resolution in favour of his policy was very nearly carried against the party leaders. But by this time Sir Oswald had nearly done with the Labour party. He left it and formed his New Party in the spring of the following year. In his new role he was angrily rejected by Labour audiences, but sympathetically considered by the editor of the *Observer*. He put up two dozen candidates in the general election of 1931 offering independent support to the National Government. They were all defeated, and Sir Oswald was soon afterwards found to be the leader of the British Fascists.

As for the figures of the unemployed, they rose even more rapidly after Mr. Thomas's encouragements had been withdrawn, and reached two and a half million in the last week of 1930, half a million worse than the worst of the 1921-22 slump. They were to remain somewhere between that and three millions until 1933. The Government had failed to cure unemployment, but it had other pledges which it could more easily fulfil. It had promised to make the lot of the unemployed more com-

The Little Victims

fortable, and with this object in view an Insurance Bill was introduced before the end of 1929.

It is impossible in an outline sketch of general history to give any adequate idea of the immense and exasperatingly technical confusion in which the whole system of unemployment insurance had become involved. When the system was first instituted in 1912, and extended in 1920, its object was to assist wage earners to insure against a measurable risk. It was never intended to succour the chronically unemployed, and confusion began as soon as the needs of these were allowed to encroach upon the Fund. Those who had exhausted their actuarial claim to benefit were given 'extended' or 'uncovenanted' benefit, and the Insurance Fund was driven to borrow from the Government. The Insurance Bill of 1929 took one step towards clearing up the confusion by relieving the Fund of responsibility towards those whose insurance claims were exhausted. These were henceforth to receive what was frankly a 'dole', not from the Fund, but from the Exchequer. Relieved of this cost, estimated (and underestimated) at £8,500,000 a year, it was hoped that the Insurance Fund would maintain its solvency.

These arrangements however, were of no interest to the unemployed and of little to the supporters of the Government. The part of the Bill designed for popularity was an increase—a despicably small increase—in the allowances given to dependants and young persons, and the abolition of the clause restricting benefit to those 'genuinely seeking work'. Few remembered that this unpopular formula had been devised by the previous Labour Government. Its intentions were obviously good but, in places where employment was notoriously non-existent, it was certainly an aggravation to expect the unemployed to make a weekly peregrination in search of work. These, the compassionate clauses of the Bill, were expected to add about £12,000,000 to the annual charge on the fund.

But of course all the financial estimates of 1929 were rendered valueless by the doubling, and more than doubling of the

The Little Victims

figures of unemployed. The cost of the 'uncovenanted' benefit henceforth falling directly upon the Treasury rose towards thirty millions a year. The borrowings of the still insolvent Fund, renewed in dismal debate every few months, first for £10,000,000 at a time, and afterwards for £20,000,000, totalled £115,000,000 before the crash.

In the autumn of 1930 the Government appointed a Royal Commission to look into these grave matters and its Report, published in the following June, was one of the first of the really sensational warnings that national bankruptcy was not far away. In addition to its deadly arithmetic the Report contained a vivid and authoritative account of the 'scandals' which too easy conditions of relief made possible; married women drawing dole for months after they had gone off the labour market, professional footballers drawing dole for the half of the week in which their weekly match did not fall, and so on. The Government could not let this continue and introduced an Anomalies Bill, dealing with some, though not all, of the abuses recorded in the Report, and saving, it was estimated, a trifle of £3,000,000 a year. It was almost their last legislative achievement.

In the days when Labour Government was still a matter of speculation, most people had thought that it would be efficient at home and incompetent abroad. 1924 had corrected both these estimates, and 1929 confirmed the correction. The autumn of 1929 was filled with international events, most of which afforded general gratification. The first minister to take the limelight and the applause was Mr. Snowden.

Ever since 1925 Germany had in effect been paying her stipulated reparations with money borrowed from America, who got some of her money back again from the receivers of reparations under the name of inter-Allied debts. This was all done under the arrangement known as the Dawes Plan, and, as it was thought unlikely that the Plan would work much longer, another international committee with an American chairman had

been appointed in 1929, and produced a new scheme for reparation payments known as the Young Plan, which had for
no very good or obvious reason increased the share of the loot
allotted to France at the expense of Great Britain. The plan
would not, of course, become operative until it was accepted by
the Governments concerned, whose Finance Ministers assembled
at the Hague for its consideration. Here Mr. Snowden was in his
element. He said 'No' with shocking emphasis. The assembled
Finance Ministers, who had never seen a real Yorkshireman
before, were painfully impressed, and retreated in disorder.
England was delighted; it was Lord Palmerston back again.
The welcome accorded Mr. Snowden on his return to England
had something very old-fashioned about it. It suggested that the
old unregenerate British lion, apparently so out of date, was still
alive and could roar with all his old menacing geniality.

But it is necessary to take a wider and less cheerful view.
During the previous five years Western Europe, Locarno-
Europe, had been held together by a trio of allied foreign ministers, Chamberlain, Briand and Stresemann. None of them had
at any period secured unqualified approval in his own country;
each was frequently accused of undue subservience to one or
both of the other members of the trio. Each of them had made
mistakes, no doubt, but on the whole all of them had markedly
advanced the cause of peace. Now reaction from their policies
was setting in. Stresemann was dead, and the name of Hitler
was beginning to be heard. Briand was soon to fail in his candi-
dature for the French Presidency. Snowden marked the reaction
from Chamberlain. Chamberlain had no doubt been too partial
to France to be quite fair to Germany. But Snowden had not
improved our relations with Germany; he had merely been rude
to France, and for what? For nothing; inasmuch as the Young
Plan, with all the figures and calculations attached to it, was
soon to be proved waste paper.

While Mr. Snowden was at the Hague, Mr. MacDonald was
preparing the ground for his visit to President Hoover, which

was of course a huge success. His arrival in New York coincided with the first crash of the American stock market, and as he drove to the City Hall his friends explained to him that Wall Street was so busy that it had no time to throw from office windows the usual quantity of 'ticker tape', which is the essential feature of every triumphal progress in the New York streets.

But Mr. MacDonald was not concerned with investments; his business was to arrange with the President the programme of the London Naval Disarmament Conference to which they would jointly invite the representatives of Japan, France, and Italy. The Conference met early in 1930 and it settled as between Great Britain, America and Japan the thorny cruiser question which had wrecked the Conference of 1927. But France and Italy were left at loggerheads. Italy demanded naval equality with France but France replied that naval equality would leave Italy preponderant in the Mediterranean where both had equal interests, since France had also to consider her position in the Atlantic and the Channel. Ultimately, however, after a year of patient diplomatic effort, the British Foreign Office brought Italy and France to agreement, and the way was held to be well prepared for the more formidable Land Disarmament Conference which was to meet in 1932.

With Mr. Snowden impersonating the British bulldog at the Hague and Mr. MacDonald pouring oil on international waters at Washington, the titular Foreign Secretary, Mr. Henderson, was reduced to playing third fiddle in his own department. He achieved however what looked like a great step forward, in securing the complete evacuation of the Rhineland by the Allied forces, five years before the date accepted in the Treaty of Versailles. Unhappily what should have been an occasion of goodwill was made by the Germans a pretext for defiantly nationalistic demonstrations. The gesture had come too late.

In other quarters of the world Mr. Henderson found his task ungrateful. The sudden dismissal of Lord Lloyd, the too im-

The Little Victims

perialistic British Agent in Egypt, preluded a fresh attempt to settle the four reserved points (see page 295) with that country. But it failed like other attempts before it. Also as in duty bound Mr. Henderson undertook and carried through a treaty with Russia to restore the officially friendly relations with that country which had been broken off at the time of the Arcos raid (1927), but incidents connected with these negotiations suggested that Mr. Henderson's spoon was hardly long enough for a supper with the Bolshevik devil. Unfriendly incidents continued after the treaty as before it, and Mr. Henderson was kept busy writing protests which evoked evasive replies from Moscow, and offering equally evasive replies to Parliamentary questions at Westminster.

Meanwhile the attitude of the general public towards Russia was entering on a new phase, which first became articulate with the appearance of Russian grain upon the British markets in 1930. There had been a time, very shortly after the war, when Russian grain had seemed a most desirable thing, and Mr. Lloyd George, having failed to secure the overthrow of the Communist régime through the instrumentality of the Russian royalist armies, had pointed to the 'bulging cornbins' of Russia as the reward of reconciliation. But shortly after that Russian corn had failed to feed its own people and by 1930 one had almost forgotten that pre-war Russia had been an important contributor to our supplies. Agricultural science had developed so rapidly that even without Russia there was too much corn for the market. The Russian grain of 1930 was not wanted and was therefore described as 'dumped'. But it invited respectful attention to the Russian Five Year Plan, which had been inaugurated two years before. Little books on this subject began to pour from the printing presses, and the *Times Literary Supplement* could devote a leading article to reviewing at least half a dozen of them at once. The American boom had crashed, and it almost looked as if Stalin would take the place of Coolidge as the world's best advertised architect of prosperity.

The Little Victims

But what was the Five Year Plan? A difficult question, admittedly. The *Round Table* declared it to be 'such a mixture of elemental forces and planned efforts that it defies concrete and simple definition'. It was 'the offspring of Revolution and of Big Business', and it was, like all else Russian, a tyranny. Foreign trade was no longer to go its own way seeking immediate profits, but was to be regulated by the Government in the ultimate interests of the community. Imports and exports were henceforth to be 'not a manifestation of the actual demands of the population but an integral and calculated element in the reconstruction of the country'. The Planners, in short, applied to foreign trade Cromwell's well-known maxim of Government—'Not what the people want, but what's good for them'. Ignorant persons supposed that Russia was dumping goods abroad in order to injure capitalist societies. Actually the Plan was much more interested in imports, and the purpose of the exports was to pay for these. The principal imports thus fostered were machines which would ultimately enable Russia to dispense with the foreigners' manufactured goods.

Was the Plan succeeding? There again it was hard to arrive at the truth. Secrecy and lies were the staple of Russian news, and even when, by accident, the facts reported were the truth it was easy to misinterpret them. But whatever the plan might accomplish in Russia it made much flesh creep elsewhere. Just as in 1925 we had been urged to imitate Henry Ford so now in 1930 people began to ask whether England did not need a Five Year Plan of its own.

Early in 1931 a new grievance against Russia was found in the large-scale importation of Russian timber produced, it was said, under conditions of slavery by gangs of political prisoners. The cheapness of this timber ruined the prospects of Canadian exporters to the British market, and, not for the first time in our history, arguments based on humanity and arguments based on Imperial interest were harnessed in support of the same policy. But nothing was done in this matter until the National Govern-

The Little Victims

ment brought this and much other foreign trade under the
control of its tariffs.

The domestic policy of the Government was determined
throughout by a desire to conciliate the Liberals, the Maxtonites,
and the Miners' Federation. Of these claims the first was the
most urgent, for the Liberals could at any moment of a Parliamentary session turn the Government out of office. They were
only sixty strong, but they were more than enough for this
purpose, and many thought that Mr. Lloyd George, after
seven years of eclipse, was about to reassert himself as an
effective statesman. To conciliate the Liberals the Government
appointed a Parliamentary Committee under Lord Ullswater to
enquire into the possibilities of reforming electoral law by the
introduction of some system for the representation of minorities.
Under the existing system the Liberals, as the weakest of the
three parties, obtained a representation in the House far short
of their voting strength. They had polled nearly a quarter of the
votes cast in the late election, and should, on proportional principles have held one hundred and fifty instead of only sixty seats.
The Liberals on their side were very ready to be conciliated, for
they felt little confidence in the upshot of another election under
the present system.

It was less necessary to conciliate the Maxtonites, and also less
possible. These were a group of Labour extremists fluctuating in
numbers with the circumstances of the moment, with their
headquarters in the I.L.P., the Socialist society which Keir
Hardie had founded in the far-off 'nineties, when the few so-
called Labour members in the House still accepted the Liberal
whip. It had been the training school of Mr. MacDonald and
Mr. Snowden, in fact of nearly all the Labour politicians who
had not come in through the trade unions or seceded from the
Liberals, but it had now become the organ of a younger generation. The strength of the Maxtonites, in so far as they had
strength, lay in the fact that most Labour back-benchers agreed

with them, even though they did not dare to vote with them. These men believed in carrying at once to their logical conclusion the processes by which, in the opinion of most economists, the economic welfare of British society was already being undermined. They held that the State, through taxation, should appropriate the national income and redistribute it in social services and guaranteed minimum wages. They believed that they could cure unemployment by increasing the purchasing power of the masses. They seemed to ignore the existence of the export trades, and indeed all the ulterior consequences of the policy they proposed. It was difficult for the Prime Minister to argue with these people, and unnecessary. He contented himself with resigning his membership of the I.L.P. and administering a stern rebuke to its members. They had, he said, lost their grip of Socialism, and their sense of the meaning of the word 'comrade'; their salt had lost its savour and was henceforth good for nothing. In 1931, just before the National Government election, the Labour party formally expelled the Maxtonites from their fellowship.

The Miners' Federation was a menace, because the Government had pledged itself to repeal the Eight Hours Day enacted by the Conservatives after the General Strike, and it was notorious that the industry could not stand a return to the Seven Hours Day without a drastic reduction of wages. No doubt the official programme in 'Labour and the Nation', had given many other pledges as difficult to fulfil as this pledge to the miners. But, as the *Round Table* remarked, 'election pledges can often be evaded when they affect the electorate as a whole. But when, as in this case, they have been given to a powerful and well-organized interest, commanding over forty seats in the House of Commons, the matter is not so easy.' This seems to be the converse of Lincoln's well-known dictum about fooling some of the people all the time, but it is none the less true.

In these circumstances the Government introduced a Coal Mines Bill reducing hours from eight to seven and a half, with a series of provisions establishing a National Board and dividing the coalfields into statutory areas, each with its own marketing scheme and output quota. On its introduction the Bill was described by Mr. Lloyd George, who held its fate in his hands, as 'incredibly bad', and the *Round Table* took an exceedingly cynical view of the character of the measure and the motives of its authors. It was, in the view of the *Round Table*, a Bill in the interests of coalowners and miners at the expense of every coal-using industry in the country. Mr. Lloyd George, however, decided to support the Bill on the acceptance of certain Liberal amendments, and though it encountered stiff opposition on all its major provisions it has on the whole justified itself. Indeed it may be regarded as an application of the same quota system as the National Government subsequently applied to a variety of agricultural products. The argument in favour of such a system is that, where supply exceeds effective demand, the price of the article in question may fall to a figure at which no producer can continue profitably to produce. All such quota schemes are difficult to work, and may easily at any time run, as it were, off their rails and do more harm than good. But they are probably a necessity of the present economic chaos, and their object, which is to keep prices at a figure which ensures a reasonable return to the producer, is in the interests not only of the producer but, in the long run, of the users and the whole community. The minister in charge of the measure was Mr. Graham, President of the Board of Trade, an able man whose early death, shortly after the next general election, was a great loss to his party.

Having passed the Commons the Coal Mines Bill became a bone of contention between the two Houses, the Lords demanding the amendment of the hours clauses so as to allow what was called the 'spreadover', a system of calculating hours by the fortnight instead of the week, which would improve output without perceptibly lengthening the duration of work. The Government insisted, and the Lords gave way. But the last laugh was with the Lords, for the miners in several districts, faced with the alternative of reduced wages, agreed with their employers to adopt the 'spreadover' which the Government had been at such pains to render illegal.

The Bill was accepted as satisfying the pledge, and it had occupied so much Parliamentary time that the Government could excuse itself from fulfilling other pledges until the next session.

Throughout the session of 1930-31, beginning in the autumn of the former year and extending to the eve of the crisis, three pledges struggled desperately for fulfilment by means of an Electoral Reform Bill, a Trade Unions Bill and an Education Bill. None of them reached the Statute Book, but their fortunes illustrate the political futility of their day and afford abundant illustration of the drawbacks of the three-party system.

On the first of these problems the Government received no help from the Ullswater Committee it had appointed, which threw in its brief in the summer of 1930 having done no more than elucidate the fact, already well known, that the Liberals wanted the Alternative Vote and that both the other parties were opposed to it. The Alternative Vote is an electoral device used in the States of Australia, providing that when there are more than two candidates the electors shall indicate not only the candidate they prefer but also the one they like next best, and that, in calculating the result of the election, if no candidate has an absolute majority over all the others combined, the returning officers shall add the 'second preferences' indicated on the voting papers, beginning with those of the lowest candidate, and continuing until either some candidate secures an absolute majority or all the second preferences have been exhausted. It sounds complicated, but it is simple enough in practice, though whether it is likely to secure a more accurate representation of the real mind of the electorate is a question that can be endlessly debated. The Liberal affection for it is easily explained. They thought that, being the middle party, they would secure most of the second preferences on Conservative and Labour voting papers, and the Government decided that the Alternative Vote was a price worth paying to ensure their continued support. The Bill contained provision for this system, and a few additional clauses designed to please the Labour party, such as the abolition of University representation, and a really ridiculous clause forbidding the use of motor cars at elections except those which were placed at the disposal of returning officers for equal distribution among the three parties. Both these clauses were removed from the Bill by the combined action of Liberals and Conservatives in the House of Commons, and when what was left, namely the Alternative Vote, reached the House of Lords, it was sent back to the House of Commons with an amendment restricting its application to London and the larger boroughs. And thus things stood with it at the end of the session.

Its twin brother, the Trade Unions Bill, was designed to satisfy and placate the stalwarts of trade unionism and to repeal the Conservative measure enacted after the General Strike. Once more 'contracting-out' was substituted for 'contracting-in' (see page 351); once more Civil Servants were to be entitled to join unions affiliated to the Trade Union Congress; once more 'peaceful picketing' was to be a lawful occupation. The crux of the Bill was the clause about general strikes. A sympathetic strike, that is a strike of one body of workers in support of the claims of another body of workers, was declared legal. Such a sympathetic strike might extend to all workers and become 'general', yet remain legal, so long as its objects were industrial and not political. The nature of the objects of any particular general strike could only be ascertained by an appeal to the courts. The opposition at once asked whether the Bill would legalize a repetition of the strike of 1926, and received evasive and contradictory replies. It was left to the Liberals to kill the Bill by carrying, with Conservative support, an amendment defining illegal strikes in a manner regarded as intolerable by the Trade Union Council.

The Little Victims

The Education Bill was intended as a contribution to a reform of the elementary-school system which had been in progress for some years with the cordial approval of all parties. In the bad old days the Elementary Schools were conceived as restricted to a function which hardly deserved the name of education—the three R's, it was called, reading, writing, and arithmetic. As the conception of elementary education advanced teachers found it more and more difficult to do justice to the more gifted of the elder children in schools containing all ages from seven to fourteen. A new educational philosophy arose, holding that primary education, for the normal child, ended at eleven, and that at that age there should be for all children a change of school, the most gifted securing free places in Secondary Schools, and the rest passing to what were called Central or Senior Schools, which in big urban areas could themselves offer varieties of education, some catering for backward, and some for more gifted pupils, some concentrating on commercial, others on industrial subjects, and so on. As soon as the movement of reform reached this stage there arose a demand to extend the Senior School Course from three years to four, in other words to make education compulsory up to the age of fifteen. This was the purpose of the Government's Education Bill. It added a year to the age of compulsory education and also, to gratify working-class parents, conferred a five shillings weekly allowance on the parents of all children attending school for the additional year, to compensate for the loss of wages they might otherwise have earned. This, too, might seem to be an excellent arrangement, if the country could afford it; though many people felt that the subsidizing of schoolchildren was a dangerous innovation, which might be extended backward from the fifteenth year to the cradle.

Finance was to be the doom of this Bill—finance and the old sectarian complications. First the Liberals insisted that the coming into force of the measure should be postponed until the autumn of 1932, a very reasonable provision on any grounds, for the education authorities would need a full two years to organize additional staffing and accommodation. Then the strong Roman Catholic section of the Labour party carried an amendment against the Government to the effect that the Bill should not come into operation until provision had been made for a grant to assist 'non-provided' schools to equip their school buildings for the change. The House of Lords did what little remained to be done. Mr. Snowden had recently admitted, in reply to an economy debate, that the financial situation was grave and that schemes involving heavy expenditure, however desirable, would have to wait until prosperity returned. The Lords, unlike his own party, took him at his word and rejected the Bill as untimely. After all, the birth rate was falling, and in a few years' time the pupils of an extra year could very likely be accommodated without any such formidable additions to staff or equipment.

The fate of the Education Bill brings us back to the high road of finance, from which we turned aside after watching the unemployed approach the three million line, the broad road of finance which was leading to the destruction of the Government. Mr. Snowden's first Budget, and the speech with which he introduced it, were in deliberately designed contrast with the brilliant displays with which Mr. Churchill had kept himself conspicuous throughout the previous five years. The House of Commons and the Departments had decided to spend so much; existing taxes would yield so much less; it remained to find the difference, and the most economical way was to add to the weight of taxes already in operation. What could be simpler, or duller? Mr. Snowden had to find an additional thirty millions, and he found it by adding sixpence to the income tax, and increasing the supertax and the death duties. He also illustrated his passion for free trade by abolishing the safeguarding duties imposed by Mr. Baldwin's Government, and promised in the following year to introduce a scheme of land taxes. This was the

The Little Victims

best form of flattery to Mr. Lloyd George, whose land taxes, long since repealed by himself in his Coalition days, had been a leading feature of the 'People's Budget' of 1909. But land taxes were a scheme after Mr. Snowden's own heart also, for he belonged to that old generation of Victorian Socialists which had been greatly exercised about the land; indeed it was the only sort of Socialism that still remained in his political composition.

A by-election at Nottingham showed that the repeal of the duty safeguarding the British lace industry was anything but popular with the working men who had profited by it. But such trifles did not bother Mr. Snowden, and the Government soon afterwards announced that the Dyestuffs Act, behind the protection of which a prosperous industry had been built up in the previous ten years, and which was about to expire, would not be renewed. Then again, as on so many occasions in the lifetime of the Second Labour Government, the House of Lords, that supposedly powerless assembly, asserted itself with effect. It reinserted the Dyestuffs Act in the Expiring Laws Continuance Bill, and thus sent it back to the House of Commons. The Government moved to disagree with the Lords, but many Labour back-benchers disagreed with the Government, whose majority, even with Liberal support, fell to six. The Lords reinserted the Dyestuffs Act, and the Government did not venture to cut it out a second time.

In his speech on his first Budget Mr. Snowden forecasted that, if the situation got no worse, he would not have to impose any further burdens upon industry by way of taxation in 1931. But the premise was not fulfilled. Revenue shrank, and the indebtedness of the unemployment fund mounted up towards £100,000,000. In February 1931 Mr. Snowden uttered the famous warning to which reference has already been made. It delighted the Conservatives and the majority of the Liberals as much as it disgusted the majority of his own party. Sir Herbert Samuel followed it up by proposing the appointment of an Economy Committee, after the model of the Geddes 'Axe' Committee of nine years before, and Mr. Snowden accepted the proposal with characteristic contemptuousness, saying that he could write its Report himself. Mr. Lloyd George, however, went off at a tangent with a trenchant attack on the City of London and its 'money barons', to whose sinister miscalculations most of the major mistakes of the last ten years were said to be due. This was much more to the taste of the Labour back-benchers, and indeed gave them the line they were to take in the crisis that followed six months later.

Of the financial position at the end of the Budget year 1930-31 all that could be said was that it was better than that of France and Germany, both of which had heavily defaulted. Our own default on the year's balance sheet was eight millions short of the amount of the annual contribution to the sinking fund. As Chancellor of the Exchequer in a Labour Government Mr. Snowden was obviously in a false position. He was an ambassador of economy in Socialistic chains. His 1931 Budget was a makeshift and a gamble, only balanced by bringing back into the year then opening a large amount of income tax which would normally be paid in the year following.[1] He sought an anodyne in his Land Taxes, which were generally held to be more likely to raise money than those of 1909, but also to be even more obviously unfair. They were severely cut about in their passage through the House of Commons, but they reached the Statute Book, where they reposed in innocuous suspense till repealed by the Budget of 1934. With these the Labour Government made its last contribution to the economic welfare of a tottering world.

When the National Government won its unparalleled majority in the autumn, there were some who held that this was in fact a mandate for Protection, and others who held that it was nothing

---

[1] For many years past income-tax payers had paid half their dues in January, and half in July. Mr. Snowden made three-quarters payable in January. The National Government returned to the fifty-fifty system in 1934.

The Little Victims

of the kind. In anticipation of that controversy it may be well to
consider here some of the evidence suggesting that there was in
the eighteen months before the General Election of 1931 a
general movement of the national mind towards Protection, irrespective of party allegiance. The unpopularity of the repeal of
the lace duty, and the rebellion of Labour members against the
expiry of the Dyestuffs Act, have already been noticed. There is
indeed no obvious affinity between Socialism and Free Trade
except the rather vague aspiration towards a closer human
brotherhood which Labour is sometimes inclined to regard as
a virtue peculiarly its own. Free Trade is an offshoot of *laisser-
faire*, which Socialism abhors, and those whose main object is
to raise the standard of the working classes could always make
out a case for protection against the products of foreign industries with a markedly lower level of wages. Many imports were
in fact disliked and as such were described as 'dumped', a term
which in popular parlance had lost its strict significance, and
was applied to any product one wished to exclude without
abandoning the general principle of Free Trade.[1] The proposals
for which Sir Oswald Mosley very nearly secured the support of
a majority vote at the Annual Labour Party Conference included a scheme for regulating imports by Import Boards and
'insulating' so far as possible the trade of the British Empire.
Apart from Mr. Snowden and a few others on the front bench
there was little devotion to the pure theory of Free Trade in the
Labour party; only a general feeling that tariffs involved a
closer liaison between Government and the big employers'
organizations.

The Liberal party was the Headquarters of Free Trade, and

[1] When the word 'dumping' was first introduced, in the tariff controversy
of 1903, it applied only to foreign goods placed on the British market at a
price below their cost of production, in order to destroy a British industry
and supplant it on ultimately profitable terms. The device had been made
familiar by the methods of American trusts who thus reduced their small
competitors to bankruptcy before buying up their stock and taking over
their business.

430

The Little Victims

Mr. Lloyd George, in spite of the protectionist character of many measures for which he had been responsible when in office, even as far back as his Edwardian period at the Board of Trade, had become a fanatically devoted free trader. But even in the Liberal party there were defections. Sir John Simon, who had separated himself from his leader and refused to conspire with him any longer to keep the Labour Government in office, had suggested that a general tariff might be necessary for revenue purposes, and another man of the same name, Mr. E. D. Simon, the chief Liberal authority on slum clearance, had fluttered the dovecotes of the Liberal Summer School with his protectionist heresies.

The Conservative party had been pledged to Protection ever since Joseph Chamberlain's campaign, but earlier pages of this book have shown what embarrassments and disasters the 'whole-hog' protectionist policy had entailed for the party. It was difficult—most people thought, before the slump, that it would be for ever impossible—to persuade a predominantly urban electorate to allow the taxation of its sea-borne food in the interests of British agriculture. One of the few facts of modern history which the ordinary man had got into his head was that the Victorian prosperity opened immediately after the repeal of the Corn Laws. It was useless to try to persuade him that *post hoc* is not *propter hoc* and that the Victorian prosperity may have been mainly due to railways, steamships, or even the opening of goldmines in California and Australia. Mr. Baldwin had failed with a full protectionist programme in 1923 and succeeded with a drastically emasculated programme in 1924. His private opinions probably remained unchanged, but as a politician he had become very cautious on the subject.

The gingering up of Mr. Baldwin and his party was undertaken by Lord Beaverbrook of the *Daily Express* assisted by Lord Rothermere of the *Daily Mail*, and the Protectionist issue was thereby unhappily involved with other issues. Lord Beaverbrook had once, as Mr. Aitken, been a member of the House of Com-

mons. As a close personal friend of Mr. Bonar Law he had
played an important part in the manoeuvres which overthrew
Mr. Asquith in 1916, and, as he tells us with charming frankness
in his own account of that crisis, he was disappointed that his
services were not rewarded with office in the Lloyd George
Coalition. Instead, he took a peerage and went out of Parliamentary life, but no doubt he continued to occupy a powerful
and entirely irresponsible position in the conclaves of the mighty
until the retirement and death of Mr. Bonar Law. Mr. Baldwin
succeeded Mr. Law, and was another kind of man. He was not
a fellow Canadian, and between him and the great press mag-
nate there seems to have developed the same kind of mutual
antipathy and contempt as had previously marked the relations
of Mr. Asquith and Lord Northcliffe. Lord Beaverbrook was a
perfectly sincere adherent of the full doctrine of the Chamberlain School, and no doubt in his private mind his policy assumed
a perfectly sensible and feasible shape: but in his public manifestation as a seller of sensational news he found that it paid
him to advocate what was neither sensible nor feasible. Moreover he wanted also, and in any case, to destroy Mr. Baldwin,
and drive him from the leadership of the party. With all this
Lord Rothermere was in essential agreement, though he naturally
preferred to run his own movement in the *Daily Mail* on
slightly different lines. But Lord Beaverbrook's campaign was
the more effective, and was conducted with greater ability.

The slogans of the movement avoided the term Protection:
they were Empire Crusade, Empire Free Trade, and United
Empire Party, appeals to that pride in Empire and in splendid
isolation supposed by some to be obsolescent survivals of the
Victorian age. The Empire was to enjoy Free Trade with all its
component parts and to impose an Empire tariff on all that
came from outside. This was what the message seemed to be,
and it was of course nonsense in view of the declared protection-
ism of the Dominions, but the movement had more weight than
its message, and early in 1930 Mr. Baldwin promised that if he

won the next election he would submit Food Taxes to a Referendum. Thus did history repeat itself, for Mr. Balfour had made the same offer in 1910. But the Referendum did not content Lord Beaverbrook for long, and it was allowed to fade into oblivion.

Meanwhile the Imperial Conference approached, and a really formidable consensus of opinion in favour of tariffs began to manifest itself. The Manchester Chamber of Commerce, the historic centre of the Free Trade Movement, declared for Safeguarding and Imperial Preference. A representative gathering of bankers followed suit, and the Economic Committee appointed by the Trade Union Congress declared that Britain must enter an 'economic group' with other nations 'free trade being maintained within the group but, if necessary, protection against outsiders'. At the same time the Federation of British Industries issued to its members a questionnaire, the answers to which revealed an overwhelming preponderance in favour of some protective system, and the Federation thereupon combined with the trade unions to address a joint memorandum to the Prime Minister, urging that the Imperial Conference should be made the occasion of establishing an inter-Imperial organization to frame proposals for Imperial Preference, with the consequential abandonment by Great Britain of her free-trade system.

It may be presumed that Mr. Thomas, the Minister specially in charge of the Government's policy at the Conference, would have been willing to advance in this direction, but his hands were tied by his colleagues. Nor was he helped by the principal Dominion premiers whose offers of tariff concessions in the highly protected Dominion markets were far from generous. So the Imperial Conference did nothing of note but debate the elaboration of the constitution of the Commonwealth on lines laid down in Lord Balfour's famous definition of 1926. The results of these debates were subsequently embodied in the so-called Statute of Westminster, and enacted shortly after the General Election.

The Little Victims

Mr. Baldwin on the other hand gave the Dominions offer a warmer welcome than intrinsically it deserved, and seized the occasion to issue a sketch of a complete Conservative programme for the next election. It included economy in public expenditure; the reform of unemployment insurance; safeguarding of industries; an emergency tariff on all imported manufactured goods; Imperial Preference; and the quota system for the encouragement of British agriculture. An interesting programme, for it is in effect that on which the National Government subsequently worked; but it was not good enough for Lord Beaverbrook.

The last act of the Baldwin-Beaverbrook comedy was played out early in 1931, at a moment when Mr. Baldwin's leadership was also threatened from another quarter by reason of his support of the conciliatory policy pursued by the Government and by Lord Irwin in Indian affairs. It was the time when the 'naked fakir' of Mr. Churchill's rhetoric was allowed to visit and negotiate with the Viceroy at his official Residence in Delhi. There was a by-election at St. George's, Westminster, a safe Conservative seat, and the Conservative candidate declared himself an opponent of Mr. Baldwin's leadership, with the full support, of course, of the Lords of the popular press. For some time Conservative headquarters could find no candidate to oppose him, but ultimately Mr. Duff Cooper entered the field and won the election by a handsome margin. Mr. Baldwin took occasion to break through the established custom that party leaders do not speak in by-elections, and addressed a meeting in the Queen's Hall.

Mr. Baldwin has a well-earned reputation as the least acrimonious of politicians. Accusations of dishonesty and other vices, so common on the lips of many politicians that they are inevitably accepted in a Pickwickian sense, had scarcely ever fallen from his lips. On this occasion his previous economy of abuse served him well, for when he now accused Lords Beaverbrook and Rothermere of falsehood, misrepresentation, suppres-

434

The Little Victims

sion of facts, and unscrupulous insinuation, and declared that
they sought, 'power without responsibility, the privilege of the
harlot throughout the ages', the ordinary man knew that Mr.
Baldwin really meant it and that it was probably true. Four
days earlier he had won a decisive victory over the malcontents
in the House of Commons on the subject of India. He was, after
all, the only possible leader, and though his Toryism might not
be of a sufficiently crusted vintage for the electorates of south-
country health resorts, he was the only man who could win back
a hundred lost seats in the manufacturing towns of the Midlands
and the North. Lord Beaverbrook, with characteristic good
humour, entered into negotiations with Conservative headquarters, and accepted, for the time being, the party programme
and its leader.

The case for tariffs could be argued this way and that. The
case for economy could only be met by running away from it.
As prices declined from their post-war peak the burden of the
service of the National Debt grew heavier and heavier; yet while
the purchasing power of money increased the amount spent
upon the social services, instead of decreasing in proportion,
grew more and more. Meanwhile conditions quite outside the
control of British politics were bringing on the World Slump,
and vitally impairing the economic prospects of the nation
which depends more than any other on foreign trade. 'It seems',
says the *Round Table* of September 1930, 'as though the whole
system of international exchange of goods was slowly wither-
ing'; and in March 1931, 'there are signs that economy may
become the issue which will decide the colour of political labels.'
But was economy possible? Ninety years before, Disraeli had
written of 'the Two Nations', yet scarcely even in the hungry
'forties were the interests of rich and poor in such apparent antagonism as now, when money paid by the rich in exorbitant
taxes was distributed among the poor in barely adequate 'doles'.
Could an electorate in which the majority were, in one form or

435

another, recipients of public bounty, be persuaded to forgo claims which were strangling the community? But where, except in the social services, could economies be made?

There was no sign in the early summer of 1931 that the working classes would respond to any call for economy. In May the Trades Union Council, giving evidence before the Committee on Unemployment Insurance, put forward a scheme to abolish the principle of insurance altogether, and to substitute a general scheme of relief for all unemployed at rates higher than the existing rates, and at a cost to the Exchequer of an additional £150,000,000, which would mean another two shillings on the income tax.

At the end of July, at the end also of the Parliamentary session which had wasted so much time on other subjects, the Economy Committee, appointed so contemptuously by Mr. Snowden four months before, produced its Report. It estimated, and as subsequent events show underestimated, the deficit on the existing basis of receipts and expenditure at £50,000,000 for the current year, and £120,000,000 for the year following, and it recommended drastic cuts in many directions, the most conspicuous being the salaries of teachers in State schools and the benefits of the unemployed. The Government appointed a Cabinet committee to study the scheme during the vacation.

CHAPTER XXXIII

THEIR DOOM—AND THE NATIONAL
GOVERNMENT ELECTION

To explain all the causes of the Great Slump or World
Depression, which began in 1929 and reached its crisis, so
far as Great Britain was concerned, in 1931, is a task before
which the boldest must quail, and the present writer, who is no
economist, can only offer a few simple observations on the more
easily comprehended aspects of the matter. For the trouble had
many and diverse roots—mechanization, speculation, tariffs,
war debts, gold; each played a part in sinister interaction with
all the others.

Probably the most popular, because the most easily comprehended, explanation was mechanization. As a result in part of
the war stimulus, in part of the natural acceleration of things,
labour-saving devices were multiplied in the post-war decade as
never before. To take but a single example from the motor
trade: it was asserted that within five years one workman was
enabled to turn out ten times as many tyres, which lasted six
times as long. But examples are really unnecessary; everyone
knew that fewer and fewer men were needed to produce more
and more goods, and as a result fewer and fewer men had, except by means of doles, the money to buy the goods produced.
It was easy to envisage with the mind's eye a logical conclusion
to this process, in which one man, manipulating the world's
super-engine, produced all the goods the world required, the
only worker in a world of unemployed, the only salesman in a
world of paupers. But this hypothesis, taken alone, was too
simple. It did not cover the facts. Mechanization had progressed

continuously, but the facts showed a slump in 1921-22, a recovery which in many countries brought abounding prosperity from 1923 to 1929, and then another slump. Something besides mechanization was obviously at work here.

The fact is that, in the long run, and sometimes in the very short run, mechanization creates new wealth for producers and consumers alike because it creates new wants. The world, for example, has been immeasurably enriched by the application of labour-saving devices to the production of the motor car. Demand expands in response to supply. But there are articles the demand for which can expand little or not at all. Those sombre philosophers, the classical economists, used to mention coffins in this connection; we all want one and none of us want two. But bread, the staff of life, is an example more to our purpose. During the post-war decade mechanization and biological research had between them enormously increased the potential output of the staple foods; there was no equivalent increase in human population or human appetite, and the horse, who had been the farmer's customer as well as his servant, had been succeeded by the internal-combustion engine which lived on oil. The world agricultural depression is a simpler and more inevitable phenomenon than any other part of the World Slump, and it is one of the contributing causes to the whole of which it is a part. In pre-war days some economists traced the cyclical depressions of industry to the periodic incidence of bad harvests and the consequent high price of food supplies. In the great depression which began in 1929, a contributory cause was the fact that farmers starved in the midst of the plenty they were capable of producing.

Those who were not satisfied with the mechanization theory of the World Slump turned to the War. The war, no doubt, was long past, but it could be shown that after the Napoleonic Wars there was a first slump, followed by comparative prosperity in the 1820's—was there not an English Chancellor of the Exchequer in that decade nicknamed 'Prosperity Robinson' on account of the agreeableness of his Budgets? Yet this was followed by a greater and longer slump in the 'thirties and the 'hungry 'forties'. This may well be true, but it does not get us very far. Much long and painful argument is needed before the Great War can be connected in a cause-and-effect relationship with the slump which began eleven years after its conclusion.

Sir Arthur Salter in the brilliantly lucid pages of his book *Recovery* shows how the nineteenth-century world had developed without conscious effort or premeditation a perfectly workable and continuously expanding system of production and exchange of goods. 'The distinctive feature of the system was its self-regulating and automatic quality. Over the whole range of human effort and human need, demand and supply found their adjustments without anyone estimating the one or planning the other. . . . The signal merit of the system was that under it the multitudinous economic desires and activities of the world were, so to speak, democratized. They governed themselves with the liberty, elasticity and variety of freedom. . . . By a process almost as automatic, the balance of payments and the balance of trade between different parts of the world were adjusted by the working of the monetary system. . . . The economic and financial structure was indeed more like one of the marvellously intricate structures built by the instincts of beavers or ants than the deliberately designed works of man.'[1]

This delicately adjusted system had been completely dislocated by the war, and reason seemed powerless to reconstruct it. Was it possible to ascertain and remove the causes of dislocation, or was it necessary to look forward and strive towards some entirely new system of world-planned economy? There is a story of a rebuke administered by Mr. Keynes to someone who thought, like Mr. Thomas, that the darkest hour must, by all reasonable calculations and precedents, be passing. 'No,' he said, 'none of us have ever seen a Great Slump before. The last one lasted nine hundred years, and is generally called the Dark,

[1] Salter, *Recovery*, pp. 10-13.

or Middle, Ages.' And in fact modern economic research into the causes of the downfall of the Roman Empire has revealed many factors which can be roughly paralleled with what we see around us in the world today.

In a world which had lost its automatic system and had hardly begun to realize the necessity of a world-planned economy it was inevitable that each nation should struggle desperately for its own immediate interests. It could hardly be otherwise, for even if the statesmen had believed what philosophers and economists with an international outlook had to tell them, their peoples would not have allowed them to sacrifice immediate profits at the expense of their neighbours for a less comprehensible prospect of a greater but more distant good. 'It is very unfortunate', says a contemporary philosopher, 'that the experiment of democracy is being given its first extended trial at the very moment when the problems confronting governments have become insoluble to all but first-class mathematicians.'

The most conspicuous examples of this short-sighted nationalism were the claims to reparations and inter-Allied debt payments, but it is unnecessary to recapitulate here what has been said earlier in this book about these international millstones. France was the principal profiteer of reparations and America of inter-Allied debts. Such debts and reparations could in the long run only be paid in goods, but both France and America set high tariffs in the way of goods, with the result that the gold supplies of the world, which should have been oiling the machinery of international exchange, piled themselves up in useless heaps in the vaults of Paris and Washington. The consequent shortage of gold in the rest of the world further contributed to the fall of prices which was paralysing industry in all countries.

Nowhere was the conflict between national ambitions and international ideals illustrated so plainly as in tariff policy. One approaches the entanglements of the Free Trade—Protection controversy as reluctantly as one would approach an argument on Free Will and Predestination, but one may hazard the axiom that the world as a whole would ultimately be richer under a Free Trade system than under any other. It is also fairly obvious that under such a system some regions of the world, now happily and healthily occupied by an agreeably diversified society reasonably attached to the homes of their fathers, would either be specialized into a single industry or entirely depopulated. If *everything* Ruritania produces can be produced cheaper elsewhere, what, under free trade, becomes of Ruritania? So, unless we think it reasonable that the Ruritanians should leave their country a desert and go to Chicago in the interests of the maximum world wealth, it is obvious that the tariff question cannot be settled by purely economic considerations.

None the less one need not be an unconditional free trader to accept the considered opinion of the World Economic Conference of 1927 that the excessive and frantic tariffs of the post-war world were the chief impediment to the growth of the world's prosperity. This was not a Conference of Governments but of some two hundred unofficial persons selected by their respective Governments as experts in finance, commerce, industry etc. Their recommendation on the subject of tariffs was unanimous: and its result almost nothing. Creditor countries insisted on protecting their home producers against the goods with which their debtors wished to pay them, and debtor countries, unable to expand their exports, set themselves to secure by tariffs and a restriction of imports the favourable balance of trade which would enable them to pay their debts.

But tariffs and reparations are no more helpful than mechanization in accounting for the curious feature of the *two* slumps, and the six or seven years' interval of prosperity between them. It must be remarked that neither the first slump nor the prosperity that followed was an absolutely world-wide phenomenon; America escaped the first slump, and England shared very inadequately in the six years' prosperity. One may take Germany as an example of a country that experienced both the first slump and the subsequent recovery in a marked degree, and of economic Germany one could say what used to be said of revolutionary France—'When Germany sneezes, her neighbours catch colds.' What then raised Germany out of the depths in the early 'twenties? And what plunged her back again at the end of the decade?

The answer to the first of these questions is not obscure. The first breakdown of reparation payments, the occupation of the Ruhr, the collapse of the mark were followed by a series of recuperative measures: the stabilization of the mark, the Dawes Plan, the Treaty of Locarno. After the establishment of the Dawes Plan American loans poured into Germany. America was at this date (1924) almost incredibly prosperous, and the wealthiest nation of the world began to discover, during the Prohibition epoch, that the stock market was a very colourable substitute for the saloon. The salesmen of the great issuing houses of New York and Chicago worked their enormous market with the efficiency one would expect of them, and the surplus incomes of ten thousand Main Streets poured across the Atlantic in loans not only to Germany but to many other countries in clamant need of reconstruction. These loans were for the most part made to Governments, and they were short-term loans used for long-term purposes. Visitors to Germany round about the end of the decade often wondered where the money had come from which had built such magnificent new buildings of every kind, factories, offices, museums of art and science, and palaces of officialdom, as are to be found in all the greater German cities. The answer was, borrowed money, mostly from America. Reparations were paid in punctual accordance with the Dawes Plan, and no wonder, for the sum borrowed from America alone amounted to half as much again as the total sum paid out in reparations. The foreign lending of America was, however, quite unrelated to American trade policy, and was bound unless continued indefinitely to lead to a crash; for America was not prepared to take, from the countries to which she lent, payment of interest in the form of goods and services. It was a hectic prosperity, as inevitably ephemeral as the industrial prosperity that accompanied the Great War. And all the while the value of money was rising (i.e. prices were falling) and the real burden of the interest on all loans and other debts was increasing.

In 1928 American loaning to Europe slackened off, and money began to be recalled for the more exciting purpose of gambling in the American share markets. That insane gamble, the climax and abrupt conclusion of 'Coolidge prosperity', the South Sea Bubble of modern times, reached its peak and crashed in the autumn of 1929. All over the American industrial world production fell until it was at about half its Coolidge rate, and America learnt the meaning of unemployment, though not of unemployment insurance. Henceforth America refused to lend abroad the money without which the interest on her previous loans could no longer be paid, and other lending countries followed, at a distance, her example. The economic situation grew darker all over the world. A financial breakdown, threatening the solvency of governments, was only a matter of time.

It began, like the Great War, in Austria, with a declaration of insolvency by the Credit-Anstalt, the principal bank of that country, in June 1931. This caused 'a run on Germany', in other words a demand by Germany's creditors for the repayment of floating debt and short-term loans. President Hoover tried to save the situation by proposing a year's moratorium of reparation and war-debt payments, to which Great Britain assented at once and France after what may have been a fatal fortnight's delay. The principal international bankers met and made a 'standstill' agreement by which they agreed to renew their advances to Germany until the end of the following February. This in turn reacted upon the position of the Bank of England, whose extensive credits in Germany were henceforth 'frozen' while its liabilities remained assailable. Gold began to be withdrawn, especially by France, before the end of July.

The weakness of Great Britain's industrial and commercial position, her millions of unemployed, her bankrupt unemployment insurance system, her unbalanced Budget, had long been advertised to her own citizens and to the world at large with a wealth of unimpeachable statistics. On top of these came the May Report (i.e. the Report of the Economy Committee) with its stark and simple arithmetic, and its apparently impossible schedule of economies. The May Report pointed the way to the solution of the crisis by bringing facts home to our own electorate; it also precipitated the crisis by bringing home the same facts to the foreigner. We pursued in the financial crisis a policy of publicity the exact opposite of that pursued by all Governments in the war. We gave the world the uncensored facts of our situation, and the advantages outweighed the undoubted disadvantages of the policy. But the 'flight from the pound', a possibility which the *Round Table* had discussed as early as September 1929, had become an apparent fact. It began before, and was accelerated after, the publication of the May Report.

It is now possible to return to the narrative of the fortunes of the Labour Government, which we broke off at the end of the Parliamentary session and the month of July.

The Cabinet Committee of five members with Mr. Snowden at their head, appointed to examine the May Committee Report, itself reported on August 13th that the Budget must be balanced, and that it must be balanced on the principle of 'equality of sacrifice', half the money being found by reductions in expenditure and half by additions to taxation. Their plan was considered by the full Cabinet on August 19th. The Cabinet flinched before the ten-per-cent cut in unemployment benefit, which its own committee had accepted from the May Report, but it did not, as was afterwards pretended, reject the proposal *in toto*: it accepted certain lesser reductions which would have amounted to a cut of about three per cent. It also considered and rejected the possibilities of a tariff, designed for revenue rather than protection. These proposals were immediately laid before the Executive of the Parliamentary Labour Party, the

Trades Union Council, and also before the leading members of both the Opposition parties. With these last the Prime Minister had already been in consultation. When the run upon the Bank was renewed after the publication of the May Report, Mr. MacDonald had, while his Cabinet Committee was still sitting, invited the Opposition leaders to share with him the responsibility of framing proposals. They had refused, but had promised to give him full support if the plans evolved by his Government appeared to be adequate to the situation. From these negotiations Mr. Lloyd George was inevitably excluded as he was still in the early stages of recovery from a serious operation.

The Government's proposals, then, were laid before three outside bodies. They were accepted by the Party Executive, but rejected by the Opposition leaders, on the ground that the 'cuts' were inadequate. The Opposition leaders held that seventy-five per cent of the money should be found from 'cuts' and only twenty-five per cent by taxation. The trade-union leaders rejected the proposals for the opposite reason. They refused to allow any cuts in unemployment benefit, and expressed the view that the whole crisis was exaggerated; that it had been invented by 'the bankers' and that it was no concern of the Government to bolster up the Bank of England. This was very much as though, during the retreat from Mons, one had suggested that the retreat had been invented by the War Office, and that it was no concern of the British Government to bolster up the British Expeditionary Force.

The Government was now in a cleft stick, for the Trades Union Council could count on the support of a large part of the Labour back benches, whatever the Party Executive which the back-benchers had themselves elected might say. The Cabinet began to fall into two groups. Of the four most conspicuous members three were on one side, the Prime Minister, Mr. Snowden, and Mr. Thomas; and with them was the Lord Chancellor, Lord Sankey. On the other side was Mr. Henderson and the rest of the Cabinet.

There had long been talk, in quarters where gossip on such subjects circulates, of antipathy between the Prime Minister and Mr. Henderson. Both had been leaders in the Labour party since its earliest days, and their contributions to its welfare had been, in the judgment of many, not unequal. Mr. Henderson had many qualities which Mr. MacDonald lacked. He was shrewd and genial, a good manager of men, a good mixer; he had long been known affectionately to all the younger generation as 'Uncle Arthur'. He had made foreign affairs his special subject, and the post of Foreign Secretary may well have had its galling aspects under a Prime Minister who was himself an expert on the same subject. Mr. Henderson was no theorist and not very much of a statesman; he was before all else a party man and a party organizer, and for him the Labour party was primarily the organ of trade unionism. Thus, though he was well aware, one presumes, that the talk about the crisis as a 'banker's ramp' was arrant nonsense, he took the side of the T.U.C. and consented to give the support of his great prestige to the party of ignorance.

At first the Prime Minister's section seemed to yield ground and accepted a plan which made some concessions to the trade-unionist demands. This was submitted to the Opposition leaders, and at once rejected by them on August 21st. Throughout the next day the Prime Minister wrestled with his colleagues, and in the evening the King took train from Balmoral to London.

It is always difficult, until the secret archives have been published, to decipher the part played by the Sovereign in political crises, and the natural tendency of caution, based upon the maxim that the King reigns but does not govern, is to minimize that part. Only since the publication of the nine volumes of Queen Victoria's Letters we have realized how active a part Victoria played in the political events of her reign. It is believed, though it cannot be positively asserted, that the King came to London on his own initiative on the night of August 23rd, and that he played a decisive part in the events of the following day,

Their Doom—the National Government Election

when Mr. MacDonald resigned office as Prime Minister of the Labour Government, and reaccepted office with a commission to form a National Government. The suddenness of the event took the country completely by surprise. An article in the *Round Table*, written certainly not earlier than August 11th, and not published until a week after the new Government had taken office, declared that 'our financial and economic dangers may produce a new alignment of parties, but at the moment there has been no substantial change. . . . All talk of the formation of a National Government is premature.'

The new Government offered itself to the country as an emergency institution. The Cabinet consisted of only ten members, four Labour, four Conservative, and two Liberal. It was not, said the Prime Minister, a Coalition, but a Government of co-operation for the single purpose of balancing the Budget and dealing with the 'national emergency'. When this purpose was accomplished the Government would resign and the political parties would resume their respective positions.

This declaration may have been expedient: it may have helped, in those first days, to reconcile the strong party men in Conservative and Liberal camps to the service of their leaders under a 'Socialist' Prime Minister. But in every other aspect it had little relation to realities. Balancing the Budget was one thing: dealing with the emergency another. Mr. MacDonald might perhaps have taken a leaf out of Lord Kitchener's book, and claimed support for three years or the duration of the slump.

When Parliament met for its emergency session on September 8th almost the whole of the Labour party ranged itself in opposition under the leadership of Mr. Henderson. On the side of the Government were the Conservative and Liberal parties, and about a dozen Labour men, giving the Government a majority of fifty. The work of the session was a supplementary Budget and an Economy Bill, which between them would cover deficits of £75,000,000 in the current year and £170,000,000 in the year

447

following. The Budget was a drastic measure, even though it was designed to go rather less than halfway to bridge the gap between revenue and expenditure. Two-thirds of its new money was raised by income tax and supertax. The rate of the former was raised by sixpence to five shillings and, what hit the small taxpayer much more severely, the amount of income exempt from taxation and the allowances for wives and children were drastically cut down. For the family man with a salary or earnings of between £500 and £1000 it meant that direct taxation was increased by something like fifty per cent.

Labour was little interested in the Budget and reserved its artillery for the Economies; cuts in all official salaries from the Prime Minister downwards; judges, insurance doctors, members of parliament, soldiers and sailors, police, teachers; in most cases the cuts were ten per cent, and those for the teachers, though first fixed at fifteen per cent, were reduced to the lower figure. There was also, of course, the ten-per-cent cut in unemployment benefit. With the cuts and the new taxes it was estimated that the Budget would be balanced.

The formation of the Government had been followed by remarkable demonstrations of financial patriotism. The King and the Prince of Wales took the lead in surrendering substantial fractions of their incomes, and the Treasury post bag was filled with cancelled war bonds and saving certificates. But there was also a very natural ferment among certain sections of the victims of the cuts. What excited special attention, magnified as it inevitably was in the popular press, was the 'mutiny' of certain sailors in the Atlantic Fleet at Invergordon. The incident, like the curiously parallel incident of the Curragh during the Ulster crisis of 1914, was an accidental product of tactlessness and misunderstanding. When it was explained, it was explained away. But it acted on the apprehensive foreigner as the May Report had done. Was this the English Revolution, beginning, as the German Revolution had done, in the navy? Certainly if the eloquence of the Labour opposition meant anything, it meant that England was not going to take her economic medicine with docility. Once again, and more formidably, the drain upon gold began, and on September 21st the Gold Standard was abandoned. In other words the clause of the Gold Standard Act, which compels the Bank to sell gold on demand at a fixed price, was suspended until further notice. The pound was no longer anchored to gold, and thereby to the currencies of other gold using countries. Many people, remembering the fate of the mark and perhaps forgetting that England had been off the gold standard from the beginning of the war down to 1925, began to prepare themselves for the worst.

The National Government had been formed in view of the run upon the gold reserves. Yet the country had, after all, gone off gold, and it soon began to find that it was none the worse. Internal prices remained stable, and the rapid fall of the pound to about two-thirds of its former value in relation to gold currencies provided at once a welcome encouragement to the export trade. It served another equally valuable purpose in giving the leaders of the Government a pretext for revising their plans for the future. Whatever the meaning, in 1931, of the terms Liberal and Conservative, it was obvious that on the fundamental issues of the future they were in one camp, with the Prime Minister and his ex-Labour colleagues. To resolve the National Government bloc into its component parties in the autumn of 1931 would be simply to hand over the tiller to the T.U.C. That could not be done. Then arose a further question: should the Government continue to work through the old House of Commons elected on quite other issues in 1929, or should it boldly appeal to the country? This question gravely embarrassed the Liberal party because they feared that such an election, even though not explicitly fought on the tariff issue, would give a decisive majority for a tariff policy. In the present House, the Liberals were in the position so gratifying to themselves (but to no one else) of being able to prevent whatever party was in power from carrying out the policy it professed. As previously they had prevented Socialistic legislation, so now they could impose their veto on protection. The Conservatives, on the other hand, were eager for the fray and confident of victory.

But apart from Liberal fears and Conservative hopes the argument for an immediate election was overwhelming; for, until an election was held, the question of the date of the next election would hang like an obsession over the Government. To restore confidence at home and abroad it was vitally necessary to prove that the vociferant Labour Opposition, though they occupied nearly half the existing House, had not got half the country behind them. What was wanted was a decisive national vote, a handsome majority, and the prospect of a clear run thereafter for any length of time up to five years. Early in October the Prime Minister announced that he would go to the country immediately; he would offer no detailed programme; he would ask for a 'free hand', a 'doctor's mandate' to employ whatever measures, including tariffs, seemed to be called for by a rapidly changing situation and an unpredictable future. The result of his appeal surpassed all expectations.

The election placed the Liberals in an embarrassing position. Sir Herbert Samuel, who had become leader in the absence of Mr. Lloyd George, gave a qualified and reluctant consent to possible experiments with tariffs as temporary measures. He was opposed in his own constituency by a Conservative, and probably owed the retention of his seat to a strong appeal from Mr. Baldwin that he should be supported as a member of the National Government. A considerable group calling themselves National Liberals, under the leadership of Sir John Simon and Mr. Runciman, who had been associated with a strong appeal for economy some months before, separated themselves from the main body of the party, and took a line indistinguishable from that followed by the Prime Minister and Mr. Baldwin. Mr. Lloyd George, from his sick bed, gave his blessing to the Labour Opposition. Thus there were three Liberal parties.

The candidates were fewer by three hundred than in the

election of 1929. On that occasion each of the three parties put roughly five hundred candidates in the field, and three-cornered contests were the general rule. In 1931 the Conservative and Labour parties again produced a little over five hundred candidates, but the Liberals only one hundred and sixty, of whom one quarter were National Liberals. There were twenty-one National Labour supporters of the Government, and the usual sprinkling of Communists and the like, nearly all of whom forfeited the £150 which candidates have to deposit, and only recover if they secure one-eighth of the votes polled in their constituencies. Thus in most places there was a straight fight between Government and Opposition.

Though Mr. Snowden was not himself seeking re-election, his manifestoes were one of the leading features of the campaign. He had long been known as the owner of the most biting tongue in British politics, but invective tires when its objects remain unchanged. Now he was free to shift his ground and pour forth the long-accumulating reservoirs of his contempt upon his late associates. These fell with their most devastating force upon Mr. Graham, a former Labour Minister, who ventured to affirm that the cut in unemployment benefit had been made at the dictation of the New York bankers as a condition of a loan which they had made to the Bank of England early in August. This silly falsehood had already been issued in the *Daily Herald*, and denied by the Prime Minister. Mr. Snowden reaffirmed the denial, and proceeded to convict Mr. Graham of a variety of other untrue statements about the events preceding the fall of the Labour Government. Mr. Graham made no reply, and it was safe to assume that no reply was possible. The Government's case was indeed, on all points, as nearly unanswerable as any case in party politics can be. To those who were uneasy about dictation by bankers the most effective, even though not the most complete, answer was a reminder that the Labour ministers who 'ran away' had themselves acted on the dictation of an outside authority, the Trades Union Council. The National

Government represented the cause of Parliamentary democracy as surely as did Mr. Baldwin in the General Strike.

The result was overwhelming. 558 Government candidates were elected, against 56 for the Labour Opposition. Of the Government candidates 471 were Conservative, 35 National Liberal, 33 Liberal, and 13 National Labour. Two candidates won seats as 'National' with no prefix or suffix. It did not escape notice that of the Liberal candidates who had given the Government wholehearted support, seven-eighths were elected, whereas in Sir Herbert Samuel's party only one candidate in every four secured a seat. There were also elected five Lloyd-Georgians, a figure which included Mr. Lloyd George himself, his son, and his daughter. The Prime Minister and Mr. Thomas retained their seats in constituencies which had long been regarded as safe for Labour, but of the ex-Ministers who had broken with Mr. MacDonald in the Cabinet meetings of August all but one were defeated. The exception was Mr. Lansbury who, at the Office of Works, had certainly deserved well of London, where his constituency lay, by establishing 'Lansbury's Lido' for mixed bathing in Hyde Park.

Of course the turnover in votes was not proportionate to these results, but when one remembers how often a general election effects a decisive change in the strength of parties by means of an almost imperceptible change in voting strength, the figures are striking enough. The Labour poll fell from eight millions to six and a half. The Conservative vote rose from eight millions to over eleven millions, the total vote recorded for Government candidates being fourteen and a half millions.

Before meeting Parliament the Prime Minister reconstructed his Cabinet, enlarging it to the normal dimensions. Mr. Baldwin retained the office of Lord President, holding a position of second-in-command similar to that of Mr. Bonar Law under Mr. Lloyd George. It was understood that the heavy work of leadership in Parliamentary business would rest for the most part on his broad shoulders. The offices of Chancellor of the

Exchequer and President of the Board of Trade, pivotal offices
in view of tariffs, went to Mr. Neville Chamberlain and Mr.
Runciman. Sir John Simon took over the Foreign Office. Mr.
(henceforth Lord) Snowden retired, but free trade was entrenched at the Home Office in the person of Sir Herbert
Samuel. The great majority of the posts both within and without the Cabinet were held by Conservatives, but some conspicuous Conservatives remained outside the Government altogether:
Sir Austen Chamberlain who stood aside at his own suggestion
to make way for younger men; Mr. Churchill, who was in active
rebellion against the Indian policy on which the leaders of all
three parties had agreed; and Mr. Amery, who had long been
recognized as the leader of the extremer Protectionists.

Before the end of the year the Government had enacted its
first protective measures: an Abnormal Importations Bill em-
powering the Board of Trade to impose duties up to one hundred
per cent on the value of the article, on manufactured goods
which were being imported in abnormal quantities in anticipation of the Government's considered tariff policy, which was
reserved for the following year; and a Horticultural Imports
Bill imposing a prohibitive tariff on next year's early vegetables,
fruit and flowers. This could hardly be regarded as a tax on the
food of the working classes, and the more difficult problems of
wheat and meat were postponed for further consideration. It
was already apparent that the Samuelite Liberals were going to
be uncomfortable supporters of the Government and that a
large section of the Conservatives would ask for more Protection
than the 'doctor's mandate' was likely to give them. Unemployment was a trifle down, but bleak vistas stretched indefinitely
ahead, and the National, as distinct from the Conservative, outlook was to trust less in tariffs than in the various International
Conferences which would meet in the ensuing year.

But there was one thing the ordinary voter could do, and he
did it with a will. His income tax due on January 1st, three-
quarters of the tax imposed upon him by the revised Budget,

Their Doom—the National Government Election

was the heaviest on record, and he was urged to pay it with unprecedented punctuality. Accordingly New Year's Day 1932 witnessed the entirely novel spectacle of queues outside the offices of the tax collectors. Many were reminded of the queues outside recruiting offices in August 1914, and indeed some rather absurd remarks were made about the 'heroism' of the punctual taxpayer. There were, after all, very large sections of the middle classes who were no worse off at the end of 1931 than they had been in the so-called prosperous years of 1924-29, and there was a rather ridiculous exhilaration about living through a 'crisis' which one experienced only in the daily newspaper. Still, the income taxpayer's demonstration was sound enough, and it was well advertised abroad. It makes a cheerful ending to a chapter of history which opens with an S.O.S. from the Bank of England.

CHAPTER XXXIV

INDIA

A n earlier page of this book (p. 395) recorded the appointment of the Simon Commission 'for the purpose of inquiring into the working of the system of government, the growth of education, and the development of representative institutions, in British India', and of reporting 'as to whether and to what extent it is desirable to establish the principle of responsible government'. The Commission was appointed at the end of 1927. Towards the close of 1929, after the Labour Government had come into office, Sir John Simon addressed to the Prime Minister a letter of epoch-making importance. He suggested that he and his colleagues should be authorized to extend the scope of their Report, and to include in it recommendations regarding the future relations of British India with the Indian States. He further suggested that, if this proposal were adopted, it would be necessary to summon 'some sort of conference' at which the British Government could meet representatives of both British India and the Indian States 'for the purpose of seeking the greatest possible measure of agreement for the final proposals which it would later be the duty of His Majesty's Government to submit to Parliament'. After securing the assent of the leaders of both Opposition parties, Mr. MacDonald cordially accepted both these suggestions.

A few weeks later the Viceroy, Lord Irwin, declared in a message to the peoples of India that 'the natural issue of India's constitutional progress' as defined in the Montagu Declaration of 1917, was 'the attainment of Dominion Status'.

India

These words, well calculated to pour oil on troubled Indian waters, roused an unexpected storm at home. What was Dominion Status? Did it mean a status in all respects the same as that of Canada or Australia, with no safeguards for European and other minorities, with no British regiments, or British officers in Indian regiments, responsible for guarding the frontier and also, in the last resort, for the maintenance of internal order? If Lord Irwin had had to consider no public but the British he would doubtless have avoided the grandiloquent and misleading phrase. But India thinks in catchwords, and 'Dominion Status' had become the Mesopotamia of the great majority of politically minded Indians who cherished the ideal of 'freedom' within the Empire. They did not read into the phrase all the details that it implied for Englishmen familiar with the constitutional development of the White Dominions. For India Lord Irwin said the right thing, but his words, taken in conjunction with Sir John Simon's recent proposals, marked the beginning of the conscious cleavage in the Conservative party. Lord Irwin was himself a Conservative, but there had long been a suspicion in some Conservative circles that he was too much of an idealist to be quite a statesman. Indian politicians were most of them half saint and half crook. Might not the element of saintliness so unmistakable in Lord Irwin's own character respond too readily to the saint and allow itself to be beguiled by the crook? And did he realize that in all revolutionary movements there is, as the French say, 'une gauche de la gauche'? An agitator's trade is agitation. Grant him the point for which he agitates and, by the law of his being, he moves on to the next point and agitates for that. Such was the line of thought developing at the Diehard end of the Conservative party; though it made less stir at the time than the Empire Crusading antics of Lord Beaverbrook, it was in the long run the most important element in the anti-Baldwinian movement.

The Simon Report was published in the following June in two stout volumes, the first, an historical and analytical account

India

of the problems involved, preceding by a fortnight the second volume containing the proposals. It enjoyed a wider publicity than any previous Blue Book, forty thousand copies being sold in the first few days. Its main proposals can be very roughly summarized under four heads.

(i) In the Provinces 'Dyarchy' was to be abolished, and ministers responsible to the elected legislatures were to be entrusted with the charge of all departments of government, including that of police. The authors of the Report recognized the obvious risks involved in entrusting the control of the police to ministers who would be at the mercy of the vagaries of Indian elected assemblies, but they held that the risk must be taken. It was indeed fundamental to the conception of responsible government. They reserved, however, to the Governor of each Province, and thus ultimately to the British Government, the right of intervention, and of overriding his ministers in certain extreme emergencies.

(ii) The ultimate destiny of India was envisaged as a federation of self-governing states or provinces, like Canada or Australia. That being so, the Legislative Assembly of British India established by the Montagu-Chelmsford Act should give place to a Federal Assembly, elected by the members of the Provincial Legislatures. But the supreme executive authority was to remain, as before, with the Governor General in Council. In other words, while the Provinces were to enjoy the benefits and risks of a complete Parliamentary system, the central Government, controlling the army, was to retain for the present full freedom of action, and be capable of giving support to the Provincial governments in case of need.

(iii) The Indian Federation of the future must include not only British India but also the Indian States. Therefore the framework of the Federation had to be designed in such a way that Indian States could enter it as full members, if and when they pleased.

(iv) The new Indian constitution should be a flexible constitution, capable of self-development without further intervention of the British Government through the British Parliament.

The response of Indian politicians to the Report was an outburst of shrill indignation, in which both those who claimed to have read it and those who boasted that they would not dream of doing so, spoke with one voice. For that reason, if no other, the Report was accorded a rather surprisingly uncritical welcome by the anti-Baldwinian Conservatives at home. Interest, however, rapidly shifted from the Report to the prospective Round Table Conference which was to meet in the autumn. The British delegates were to be representative of all political parties, the members of the Simon Commission alone being excluded. The exclusion of Sir John Simon and his colleagues seemed ungracious, and from a practical Western point of view it was obviously absurd to exclude the men who had spent the last three years making themselves experts on every aspect of the subject; but it was above all things necessary to convince India that the Round Table Conference was not merely a conference for the discussion of the hated Report, but a conference which, if it thought good, could make a fresh start, open up new ground, and reach entirely independent conclusions.

The first session of the Round Table Conference, which sat in London from the middle of November 1930 to the middle of January 1931, did in fact satisfy the largest hopes of those who wanted to advance towards a scheme less cautious and tentative than that of the Simon Commission. The Indian delegates, about eighty in number, represented most of the leading Indian Princes, and all the principal organizations, communities, and parties of British India, with the exception of Mr. Gandhi's Congress party. The Princes made it plain from the first that they were ready and anxious to enter into a federal union with British India, but that they could only do so if the Federation enjoyed real self-government 'at the centre'. The British delegates on their part were unanimous in their readiness to abandon those parts of the Simon scheme which set the Governor

India

General in Council completely outside the control of the Federal Legislature. The new All-Indian Government was to be a fully responsible government—with 'safeguards'; for during a transition period, to which no end could be descried, there must be safeguards, to enable the executive to deal with emergencies, to protect the rights of minorities, and to preserve in experienced hands the control of foreign policy and of the army. The first Round Table Conference could not go beyond general principles, but it was to have a successor in the following winter, for the work of which preparations would go forward at once.

The debate on the work on the Conference in the House of Commons was marked by an outspoken attack from Mr. Churchill on all that had been done by the party leaders since the issue of the Simon Report, but though his words expressed misgivings widely felt in 'European' circles they received no open support in the House. In India the outcome of the Conference effected an almost magical transformation. The year 1930 had been marked by much the worst disorders since the year of Amritsar, eleven years before. Most of the Congress leaders, including Mr. Gandhi, had been incarcerated and, though the forces of order might re-establish the rule of force, there seemed, in the words of the *Round Table*, 'every reason to suppose that the Civil Disobedience movement must continue until it gradually petered out in a fog of bitterness and misunderstanding luridly illuminated by outbreaks of terrorism'. With the coming of the new year the situation began to change with startling rapidity. The first news to strike the Indian mind was a speech of Lord Reading, a Liberal delegate to the Round Table Conference who spoke with the unique authority of an ex-Viceroy, accepting in all its fullness the conception of a self-governing Indian Federation. This was followed a fortnight later by the Prime Minister's official summary of the conclusions at which the Conference had unanimously arrived. Then came news of the release of Mr. Gandhi and other Congress leaders. Mr. Gandhi declared that he had come out of prison with an

India

absolutely open mind, prepared to study without bias what was admittedly an entirely new situation. There followed his private conferences with Lord Irwin at the Viceregal Lodge, resulting in the Irwin-Gandhi Agreement. In return for concessions none of which affected vital matters or could be considered in any way damaging to the prestige of the Government, Mr. Gandhi consented to call off the Civil Disobedience movement.

The Mahatma was at this time at the very height of his unprecedented prestige and was an object of worship rather than of admiration to the vast crowds which thronged around him wherever he allowed his presence to be known. Even so Europeans judged it uncertain whether he could persuade Congress to follow him in his new departure. This too proved to be within the compass of his powers, and in March, at Karachi, Congress accepted the terms of the Irwin-Gandhi agreement without a single dissentient voice. In the autumn it sent Mr. Gandhi to the second Round Table Conference as its sole representative.

These encouraging events were followed by a series of reactions which disappointed though perhaps they hardly surprised those who were aware of the complexities of the Indian problem. Almost as soon as the ideal of an All-India Federation had been brought within the sphere of practical politics its implications began to disconcert the very people who had demanded it. Indians are very ready to claim to be 'all one' as a tactic of opposition to British rule. As soon as the claim is granted the unity dissolves. In particular the Moslem minority of some seventy millions prepared themselves to hold up all advance until their claims to security against Hindu domination were granted. Their claims included a demand for a clear majority of the seats on the Councils of the Punjab and Bengal, the creation of a new Province in Sind, separated from Bombay, and the establishment of complete self-government in the North-West Frontier Province, claims which, if granted, would make the Moslems masters of North-Western India. At the same time the Princes became more nervous about their own position

460

India

within the Federation the more they examined its implications, and, on the other side, Congress, the organ of militant Hinduism in British India, regarded with alarm their own prospects in an All-India in which it was likely that the Conservative forces of the Princes and the Moslems would, on many issues, be combined against them.

And so the Second Round Table Conference, meeting in London at the time of the National Government election, proved a complete failure, all business of importance being held up by the deadlock on the Minorities sub-committee, whose duty was to distribute the seats in the new Councils between the rival communities. The Moslem claims were inadmissible, and Mr. Gandhi, who was chairman of the sub-committee, was equally unwilling to grant separate representation to the Depressed Classes, claiming that they were an integral part of the Hindu community. At the end of the Conference Mr. MacDonald could do little more than announce that the British Government was determined, in spite of difficulties and obstructions, to proceed along the path that the First Conference had marked out.

Some time before these events Lord Willingdon had succeeded Lord Irwin as Viceroy. Never had the selection of a Viceroy been a matter of such importance and such general interest. Lord Irwin was a difficult man to follow. His character had secured for him, in the estimation of the best leaders of Indian nationalism, a peculiar and very personal prestige. Everything that he did excited unusual interest and contributed, without any intention on his part, to the atmosphere of unwholesome excitement in which all India was involved. To find a personality of equal or greater distinction seemed at once desirable and impossible unless, as was quaintly suggested, the Prime Minister himself should make way for Mr. Baldwin in Downing Street and transfer the centre of his activities to the Viceregal Lodge. The choice of Lord Willingdon was a move in the opposite direction, and it proved to be admirably calculated. Lord Willingdon had been an excellent Provincial Governor in

India

Madras and Bombay. His knowledge was unsurpassed, his sympathetic outlook well known, and his tact immaculate. It was a completely unsensational and entirely adequate appointment. It suggested what President Harding would have called 'normalcy', and implied that, whatever the future might have in store, for the present the King-Emperor's government would be carried on. The Congress leaders intended to make 1932 a year of unprecedented disorder. Before many months had advanced both they and Mr. Gandhi, their delegate, returned from the Conference, found themselves in jail. This policy of the firm hand proved very effective. Civil disobedience dwindled away in most of the Provinces, and by the end of 1933 the Government was in a position to release without undue anxiety more than two-thirds of the political agitators who had been in prison in the spring of 1932.

It is not necessary to record the events of 1932 in any detail. The British Government produced its own award on the issue of communal representation, an award which perhaps proved its fairness by giving equal offence to all sections of Indian opinion. There was a third session, on a reduced scale, of the Round Table Conference towards the end of the year. In March 1933 a further milestone on the advance towards the unknown was reached when the British Government issued its White Paper, containing a complete scheme of an All-Indian Federal Government, combining the principles of 'responsibility' and 'safeguards' as accepted in the first Round Table Conference. The White Paper was then submitted to exhaustive examination by a Select Committee of both Houses of Parliament.

The Committee under the Chairmanship of Lord Linlithgow contained representatives of all parties including many with official experience of India, headed by three ex-Viceroys. It produced in November 1934 a closely reasoned, detailed and impressive Report. The main principles of the proposals in the

India

White Paper were approved. There were, however, certain alterations and additions of importance and the Report emphasized, as had the Simon Commission, weighty practical reasons for establishing an all-India Federal Government.

The Report did not obtain the approval either of the Conservative Diehards or of the Labour Party. The former said that it went too far and the latter said that it did not go far enough. A meeting of the Central Council of the Conservative Party and a full-dress debate in the House of Commons showed, however, that the Committee's proposals were accepted by a very large majority of the Conservatives, including many who had been critical of the White Paper, and by the Liberals.

In India there has been criticism and some hostility. This did not come as a surprise. Until the matter is definitely settled it was hardly to be expected that Indians anxious for increased responsibilities should not ask for more and cavil at the safeguards. There are, however, undoubtedly very many Indians who realize and welcome the great opportunities for self-government afforded in the Proposals and there seems little, if any, disposition to boycott or to refuse to work the new Constitution once it is set up.

These lines are written before the introduction of the Government bill which is to be based on the Committee's Report. It seems reasonably certain that this bill will be on the Statute Book before the end of 1935. Some seven years of concentrated work by Englishmen and Indians lie behind the present proposals. When the Act is passed a new chapter will open in Indian history, in which both races will have their own contributions to make in the great advance of India towards her declared goal of responsible self-government.

CHAPTER XXXV

THE VERY RECENT YEARS—THE
WORLD IN GENERAL

A narrative of events continuing up to the moment at which the narrator writes must be content to leave off ineffectively upon a comma. The General Election of 1931 was the last full stop in our history, and the events of the three years 1932-34 can only be provisionally estimated. If one takes a very general view of England and the world during those three years, the first impression is the contrast between the quietude at home and the catastrophic noises proceeding from many other quarters. The English should beware of self-satisfaction, for it is one of their least popular qualities, but it is hard to refrain from quoting, in connection with these last years, the old saw which says that 'Happy is the nation whose annals are dull'. Germany has destroyed her Weimar constitution and proceeded through revolution to a singularly flamboyant and intolerant dictatorship. France, as though to justify her neighbours' anti-parliamentarism, has washed with her usual frank publicity some unusually dirty political linen, and, by changing her government ten times in three years, has exhibited the levity of a democratic assembly uncontrolled by ministerial discipline. There was even a moment when Tennyson's lines about 'the red fool-fury of the Seine' became once more appropriate. America, without a formal change in her constitution, has entrusted her President with powers not far short of those wielded by a Hitler or a Stalin. Japan has fought China, and established a client state under a Manchu Emperor in Manchukuo. Within the Empire the Irish Free State, under de Valera, has found that Dominion Status is not enough, and, across the Atlantic, Newfoundland has found it altogether too much and has surrendered her liberty in return for the Mother Country's financial protection.

At home we have nothing to show dramatically comparable with these things. Tragedians of the distant future may find themes for their art in Hitler, Roosevelt, or De Valera; they will not, we hope, find material in Mr. Walter Elliot and his agricultural marketing schemes. It may, however, be found that, in their unexciting way, he and his colleagues have achieved as much of permanent significance in 1932-34 as any of our neighbours. It may be that historians of the future will point to these years as the time when the groundwork of post-war economic reconstruction was at last, after a dozen years' delay, well and truly laid down. It may be so; but it would be very presumptuous to feel certain of it.

This at least can be said, that we have stopped the rot and turned the corner without dislocating a single cog-wheel in our ancient and well-tried constitutional machinery. There is as much liberty and democracy in England today as at any time before the slump. The Mother of Parliaments survives most of her daughters, and her health is as good as ever it was.

Looked at in another way there is, however, a parallel rather than a contrast between what has happened in England and what has happened elsewhere.

On an earlier page it was suggested that the economic diseases of the post-war world had international causes and could, in the long run, find none but international cures; but that, very naturally, each nation turned to its own medicine cupboard, as being the only cupboard of which it possessed the key, and dosed itself with drugs which often accentuated its diseases. When the World Slump, beginning in 1929, spread its ever-deepening darkness over the nations, the Governments, while not forswearing the use of their own national remedies, turned with a hopefulness bred of desperation towards the instruments of international co-operation. 'Never', says the *Times* Annual Summary of 1932, 'was there such a year of international conferences and consultations.' A year passed, and when the *Times* again issued its recapitulatory supplement it declared that 'the most remarkable developments of the year have been the rise of an aggressive and self-conscious nationalism in Germany and the great economic experiment begun by President Roosevelt in the United States'. It was no accident that, of the two principal world conferences, the Disarmament Conference was disabled by the former, and the World Economic Conference broken by the latter of these great exponents of resurgent nationalism. The international cure might be the safest, but it was also the slowest. The patients were not prepared to die while the prescriptions were being written out. With gestures of impatience they turned back to their own cupboards and took longer and stronger pulls at their own mixtures.

In our own undramatic way our own policy followed the same course. As the nation more dependent upon the ebb and flow of world conditions and consequently more internationally minded than any other, we had set our hope upon the World Conferences. The millions who voted National in 1931 had provided a strong and genuinely representative team to play for England in these great fixtures. On these our weal or woe was believed to depend. But in fact the Conferences failed and the patient, being still alive, dismissed them to the limbo of forgotten things. He fell back upon his second line of remedies, which he had already been preparing, his tariffs, his quotas, his internal reorganizations, and he began to think that he was doing fairly well.

The change of outlook along these lines has been so gradual that it is necessary to furnish evidence that it has really occurred. Once again the quarterly pronouncements of the *Round Table* may be called to witness. In June 1932, when the Disarmament Conference was four months old at Geneva, when the Reparations Conference was about to meet at Lausanne and the Imperial Economic Conference at Ottawa, the *Round Table* declared that 'within a few months, conclusions must be reached in the financial and economic field the effect of which will probably be decisive for or against the happiness of at least one generation of human beings all over the world'.

Three months later the Lausanne Conference had produced an agreement abolishing reparations which would, however, be ratified only when America agreed to an acceptable revision of her claims in respect of inter-Allied debts. The eggs of Ottawa were not yet hatched, and the Disarmament Conference had 'adjourned in very unsatisfactory conditions'. The *Round Table* of September had to revise its forecast of June. 'The last three months were by general consent destined to be a decisive epoch in the history of the crisis. . . . But as usually happens in human affairs, nothing quite turned out as pure reason might have anticipated. On none of the vital points have events given the definite verdict which either the optimists hoped or the pessimists feared. We are not yet basking in the sunshine of renewed confidence, nor, however, are we plunged into the cold shades of despair. We are still forging ahead under a grey sky.' In spite of which the writer of the same article forecasts: 'It may be that the World Economic Conference will meet towards the end of the year under far more promising conditions than seemed likely when it was planned in July. In any case, however, it will be faced by formidable problems, which must be solved if the world is to regain anything like its old prosperity.'

Move on six months, and we find the Disarmament Conference still prolonging its sickly days, but the World Economic Conference postponed till the summer of 1933, and the Lausanne project of giving dead reparations a decent burial frustrated by the refusal of the United States to discuss inter-Allied debts. The *Round Table* for March 1933 writes:

'The world is, in fact, at this moment moving steadily towards national socialism, a form of socialism which is, however, put into effect by Nationalist Right-wing parties, and not by the socialist or revolutionary Left wing.' These words have in their

context no special reference to England, but in the article on
current politics in Great Britain we read: 'There are people who
argue with some show of reason that this Government has been
more socialist in outlook and legislation than either of the two
previous Labour Governments.' And again, with reference to
the American debt negotiations: 'It may be that if these negotiations break down, the forces of economic nationalism in this
country will become too strong to be controlled, and the World
Conference on which so many hopes are fixed, which has already
been so often postponed and, according to the Prime Minister,
cannot even now be held for at least three months, will end in
failure.'

And finally, in September 1933. 'The great international
conferences have come to little. The pulse of the Disarmament
Conference is beating feebly. . . . The World Economic Conference has failed to reduce the obstructions to international trade
or even to make a tentative approach to agreement upon a
solution of the world's monetary problems. . . . The Assembly of
the League of Nations will probably attract less attention this
September than in any year since its inception, for at the moment public opinion is tired and sceptical of the efficacy of
international gatherings.' And elsewhere in the same issue: 'The
break-up of the Economic Conference has had fewer immediate
psychological effects than might have been expected. The shock
—if it could be called a shock—was the less disturbing because
already in most countries for the last six months there have been
symptoms of internal recovery. The manner of the Conference's
dying made it a subject for ironic jest. . . .' One could hardly feel
funereal when unemployment figures had fallen 600,000 in six
months.

The Conference of representatives of the German Govern-
ment and of Germany's reparations creditors which met at
Lausanne in June 1932 had no very difficult task before it.
Whatever French *rentiers* might think, every politician, includ-

ing French politicians, knew that reparations had got to go. The only problem, as a Frenchman put it, was how to conceal the fundamental accord with which the delegates met behind the veil of superficial discord which their public opinions demanded. The one-year moratorium of all reparation and inter-Allied debt payments initiated by President Hoover in the previous summer expired at the end of the month, and a return to the old system was quite unthinkable. By the Lausanne Convention Germany undertook to make one final payment of £150,000,000 in the form of bonds carrying interest at five per cent. The various ingenious arrangements made in connection with these bonds need not, for obvious reasons, be detailed. This convention was accompanied by a so-called gentlemen's agreement of the creditor countries to the effect that they would not ratify the Convention unless and until they secured a satisfactory settlement of their own debts to the United States. There, and not in Europe, lay the crux of the problem.

It would be possible to distinguish four schools of thought in America on the subject of the Allied war debts. First, there were those who held a view identical with that almost unanimously accepted in European countries—that whatever one might think of the morals and economics involved in the past history of these transactions, the debts had now become unpayable, mainly because America could not afford to accept payment in the only feasible form, namely foreign goods and services, and that any attempt to renew them would do nothing but harm to all parties concerned; that America should therefore meet her debtors in conference, and treat them very much as the Lausanne Convention proposed to treat Germany in the matter of reparations. Unfortunately this view obtained almost no support outside the expert circles of professional economists and international financiers, and by the American public such circles are regarded as the reverse of authoritative. The very name of Wall Street has a sinister connotation, and 'bankers' have long, and rightly, been regarded in America as anything but persons to be trusted.

A second school of thought would include those who accepted the views of the first school on the subject of the debts, but not on the corollary of the Conference. They preferred that the debtors should default in order, presumably, that America might be able to make rude remarks about them.

The third school of thought was of greater influence and included many leaders in the press and in big business. These held that the debts were dead and could not be brought back to life, but that America's right to the money survived and should be 'traded' for concessions by the debtor countries in other fields. A picturesque proposal was that England and France should hand over their West Indian colonies. More serious was the suggestion that we should re-stabilize the pound in terms of gold, or grant American imports preferences in our newly protected home markets. To this school of thought President Hoover seems to have belonged.

But all these schools were, on any system of counting heads, completely obliterated by the school of the Great Uneducated who held the simple view that a debt's a debt for a' that, and that the debtor must be made to pay. These simple folk did not grasp the fact that, as creditors, they were simultaneously demanding payment and refusing to accept the goods in which alone it could be paid. The position of a creditor claiming his debt yet refusing to be paid is a difficult one for the ordinary man to grasp because it cannot arise in ordinary domestic life. The average American said in effect: 'We don't want your goods, your services, or your gold: we want your *money*.' And what is money?

Meantime the unwieldy engine of the American Constitution interposed seasonable, or unseasonable, delays. From the end of the Lausanne Conference until November 10th, the United States were in the throes of a Presidential election, traditionally a close season for unpopular topics. On November 10th Mr.

The Very Recent Years—the World in General

Roosevelt was elected by an unprecedented majority, but as he did not assume office until March 4th there was a further close season of four months with two Presidents, one dead, the other powerless to be born.[1] During this interregnum half-yearly instalments of the debt fell due. President Hoover was unable and Congress unwilling to extend the moratorium, and, after setting forth its arguments against the renewal of debt payments in a despatch of overwhelming cogency, the British Government shipped £33,000,000 of gold, equalling in weight, as some playful statistician computed, seventeen double-decker motor omnibuses. The French Chamber refused to allow M. Herriot to pay the French instalment. Italy paid, and of the minor European debtors some followed the example of Italy, some that of France. At the same time Great Britain, while paying her instalment to America, waived all claim to the instalments due to her from her European debtors.

When Mr. Roosevelt took office in March the bubble of American prosperity, first pricked in the autumn of 1929, had reached its ultimate point of deflation. In the first phase securities—ironic term!—crashed, and realized but a fraction of the prices that had been paid for them; in the last, people demanded their money from the banks and found that it was not there. Dozens of the far too numerous banks of the Union had to close their doors. The President at once took heroic measures which were, in their initial stages at least, completely successful. But with the national income halved, or worse, and something like twelve million unemployed without any State system of insur-

[1] This curious provision of the American Constitution dates from its foundation in 1788, when its authors assumed that an Electoral College would meet and choose a President after careful and possibly prolonged debate, with further delays occasioned by the travel conditions of the pre-railway epoch. The four months interregnum has often proved a nuisance, notably on the occasion of Lincoln's election in 1860, when but for the interregnum there might have been no Civil War. By an amendment carried after Roosevelt's election, the waiting period has now been reduced, and Presidents will henceforth take office on January 23rd.

ance the President and his fellow citizens had neither leisure
nor inclination to study the problem of inter-Allied debts. The
Prime Minister crossed to America in April, and before he
arrived the United States had abandoned the gold standard.
The instalment due in June was larger than that paid in the
previous December, but the American Government consented
to accept a 'token payment' of about £2,000,000's worth of
silver, and a similar payment of about £1,500,000 was made in
December.

Between the dates of these two token payments the World
Monetary and Economic Conference had come and gone. It was
opened by the King in the Geological Museum at South Ken-
sington on June 12th, and was attended by representatives of
sixty-six governments. It adjourned on July 27th for an indefinite
period with no concrete achievement to its credit except an
agreement between the principal silver-producing and silver-
using countries to restrict the sales of that metal, and an international agreement to control wheat production and export
with a view to maintain prices.

The idea of some such conference as that which thus met and
failed was implicit in the very nature of the monetary chaos and
economic collapse to which the world had succumbed. It was
the ideal remedy, the remedy which would have yielded ideal
results in an ideal world—though perhaps an ideal world would
not first have suffered such chaos and such collapse. As to the
facts of the collapse, one was weary of their recapitulation.
Never had there been such wealth of statistics; wherever defect
might be, it was not in the hospital charts of the World Patient.
When one passed to remedies it was, again, not very difficult to
offer an outline of what was needed. In the first place it was
necessary that the nations should transcend their national limitations, and think and act in terms of the common good. Industry
and finance could only fulfil their possibilities if free to function
as worldwide organizations. In other words, it was necessary to
liberate productive enterprise from hampering national con-

trols. In the second place, it was equally necessary to liberate industry from the dead weight of debt. War debts were but a small fraction of this dead weight. All the world had borrowed from its neighbour in the post-war period; the slump in prices had doubled the weight of every debt, and the halving of world production had redoubled the ratio of debt to income. The problem was to secure what the revolutionists of ancient Rome called *novae tabulae*, new account books, without either general inflation of currency or general bankruptcy. Such was the need; easy to state, impossible to accomplish.

When the Conference met President Roosevelt was in the midst of his labours for the restoration of economic health in his own country, and he was not prepared to allow the activities of his delegates in London to hamper his own freedom of movement. A month before the Conference he declared that the exchange stabilization of currencies was one of the great objectives of the Conference. Yet when the Conference met he declared that it was 'an old fetish of so-called international bankers'. In fact he was embarrassed by the existence of the Conference, and he killed it; but there is evidence to suggest that, even if he had given it his blessing, it would not have thriven.

First to meet and last to part was the Disarmament Conference, which met at Geneva early in 1932, under the chairmanship of Mr. Henderson, who had been elected to that position when he was Foreign Secretary in the Labour Government. This Conference had been in a very real sense on the world's agenda paper ever since the Treaty of Versailles. That Treaty imposed a drastic reduction of armaments on Germany 'in order' as it stated 'to render possible the initiation of a general reduction of the armaments of all nations'. Since that date many things had happened, including the Locarno Treaties and the admission of Germany to the Council of the League of Nations. The naval powers had dealt with various aspects of naval disarmament in a succession of conferences, but the much more difficult problems of disarmament on land remained not merely unsolved but untouched. The political stability of Europe, if stability be the right word, still reposed upon the artificial and inevitably temporary predominance of the victorious states; in other words, on the military superiority of France and her allies, Poland and the States of the Little Entente. No one outside France and few within it supposed that this state of affairs could last for ever. Either the armed powers would proceed to reduce, or the unarmed to augment their forces, and these augmentations, if augmentations there were to be, would either proceed by amicable agreement or in mutual defiance. Either the signatories of the Treaty of Versailles would fulfil the programme contained in their treaty, or Germany would tear the treaty to pieces. The difficulties here were not of our making. Throughout the post-war period, while Continental armies tended to increase, our own army and air force had been steadily reduced. In 1932 we stood only fifth, it was said, among the Air Powers of the world. We had set an example and it had not been followed.

The Conference met, and France advanced her classic and impracticable programme for creating an international force under the control of the League of Nations. The debate proceeded and the world lost interest.

Meanwhile Germany had already entered upon the course of development which led in 1933 to the establishment of the Nazi autocracy. Previous pages of this book have already described the false dawn in the Germany of the middle 'twenties, the immense reorganization of German industry financed by American money borrowed on short-term credits, the stubborn effort of Stresemann to secure for Germany what she considered her international rights, and the growing conviction of Germans that those rights could never be secured by his conciliatory methods. With the failure of Stresemann and the calling in of American money a violent reaction was inevitable—either Communism or Fascism.

474

The Very Recent Years—the World in General

Fascism makes in all countries a twofold appeal. It offers a satisfyingly drastic scheme to those who believe that democracies are too stupid and parliaments too slow to cope with the problems of the post-war world, and to those who dread communism it offers a bourgeois alternative which is prepared to fight communists with their own weapons of violence and tyranny. The Germans both feared communism and distrusted their Parliament. As for communism they had lived nearer to Russia, both geographically and spiritually, than any other great nation. As for their Parliament, the pedantries of the Weimar constitution-builders had created a system fruitful only in deadlocks, a system carefully calculated, one might think, to blur clear-cut issues, confuse the straight fight, and prevent the development of Gladstones and Disraelis who might become the heroes of a Parliamentary Germany. For the German must have heroes; it is no accident that the term hero-worship was popularized in England by the most Teutonic of our Victorian prophets.

In such a Germany as that of 1929-33 the Nazi (National Socialist) movement made a strong appeal. It attracted the impoverished bourgeoisie because it was anti-capitalist without being proletarian. It preached the supremacy not of the class-conscious proletarian but of the race-conscious Nordic man. It offered as victims to revolutionary lust not bourgeois but Jews. It was robustly national, and frankly denounced not only the Treaty of Versailles but all German politicians who had accepted the Treaty with meekness for the previous ten years. Finally it appealed to the German love of uniforms and quasi-military pageantry. The Nazi movement was the German equivalent of the *revanche* of which the French had so often talked after 1871. Of the French *revanche* sentiment it was often and truly remarked that it did not necessarily imply an intention to go to war for the recovery of Alsace and Lorraine. Similarly the Nazi movement was mistakenly interpreted by those who read into Hitler's speeches an intention of ultimately re-fighting the Great War. Hitler talked in military metaphors because they are the fav-

475

ourite metaphors in Germany, but his actions were much more pacific and conciliatory, at any rate in the sphere of foreign policy. It may even be maintained that his movement has served the cause of international peace by sublimating the militaristic complexes of his people. He supplied brown shirts instead of battles, and diverted the violent impulses of his fellow countrymen from the Polish frontier on to the Jews and Marxians in their midst.

It is no part of our task to follow the complicated course of events which began with the suppression of Parliamentary control by means of emergency orders which were within the provisions of the Weimar constitution. First Brüning, a professed parliamentarian, ruled with emergency powers; then Papen succeeded Brüning, and Schleicher succeeded Papen. Hitler was offered and refused various subordinate posts. There were several general elections, and only in the last of them, in the summer of 1933, did the Nazis secure a bare majority over all other parties, with the aid of the Reichstag fire. But a bare majority sufficed to give Hitler a power as Chancellor comparable with that exercised by Stalin and Mussolini. Freedom of every kind was suppressed, and the world was presented with a picture of what was called a united Germany, the fact being that one half of Germany had the other half under psychological lock and key. Never, it is said, had any political movement owed its triumph so largely to unscrupulous propaganda, and Hitler declares that he learnt the power of propaganda from the British use of it during the last years of the Great War.

These developments were not favourable to the prospects of the Disarmament Conference. In vain the various armed powers put forward their own, and criticized each other's plans. Early in 1932 Germany announced that she would accept no plan which did not admit the principle of equality of status between herself and her late enemies, and not till the end of the year was a formula found which brought Germany back without driving out France. In the spring of 1933 the Conference was stimulated by a visit from the Prime Minister with a British Draft Convention which embodied all that was most promising in earlier proposals and included elaborate schedules of figures for every kind of land armament. The Convention was given a 'first reading' in June, but with an amendment proposing a preliminary period of four years before the process of disarmament should begin. This gave fresh offence to Germany, who announced her withdrawal both from the Conference and from the League of Nations in October; after which the Conference was suspended and further discussion of disarmament relegated to the channels of diplomacy.

Germany was not the only Great Power to leave the League in 1933. Her action had been anticipated by Japan.

Early in 1932 Japan fought China, without any formal declaration of war, drove her armies out of Manchuria, and established in that province, henceforth Manchukuo, an 'empire' dependent on her armed support, the Emperor being the young man who, as a small boy, had been deposed from the throne of China in 1911. The Sino-Japanese war aroused a general alarm for world security which seems, in retrospect, to have been somewhat excessive. It proved, what most people must have already suspected, that the League could not prevent a war at the far end of the world between two nations, the stronger of which was determined to fight and the weaker practically unable to resist. An attempt of the British Government to curtail hostilities, by placing an embargo on the sale of arms to either belligerent, failed and was abandoned because no other nation would co-operate. Indeed the futility of such an embargo, unaccompanied by more positive 'sanctions', was self-evident; it would give the victory to the belligerent which had made the completer preparations for war, and was therefore presumably the aggressor.

The merits of the dispute were far from clear, and British opinion was divided. Liberal and Labour schools of thought condemned the Japanese as the militarist and imperialist power, and appeared at times to be anxious to preserve the peace of the world by declaring war on Japan. In Tory circles there was much sympathy on the other side. True, the population of Manchuria was overwhelmingly Chinese, but Japan had legitimate commercial interests in the province, in which the Chinese government was notoriously unable to keep order. It was Japan who had conquered Manchuria from Russia in 1904-5, and returned the province to China. Now she was only pursuing very much the same course of policy as, a hundred and fifty years earlier, had laid the foundations of our own dominion in India. The League of Nations appointed a Committee of Enquiry under Lord Lytton, which issued a Report showing that both the Liberal and the Tory views outlined above were very much too simple, and that there was a very great deal to be said on both sides. The Lytton Report was an admirable document, but it exercised no influence whatever on the course of events.

In Russia the famous 'Plan' reached its Five Year's limit at the end of 1932 and left the toiling millions more short of food than they had been at any time since the famine ten years before. That does not mean that the Plan had failed, for its object was not to secure comfort for the Russians of today, but industrial supremacy for the Russians of the day after tomorrow, to 'catch up with and pass the capitalist countries'. On the industrial side the statistics of increased production were astonishing. In many departments the programmes of the Plan were surpassed. Indeed Communist orators went mad with statistics, like the Americans in the days of Coolidge prosperity, and columns of figures replaced quotations from Marx as the staple diet of propaganda. But in many directions quality was sacrificed to quantity, more haste meant less speed, and communist overseers spoiled the complicated machines supplied by the contractors of capitalist countries. It became necessary for the rulers of Russia to prove to their countrymen that the foreign capitalists were the villains of the piece. Just as the German tyranny sought to prove, in the Reichstag trial, that foreign communists had burnt the Reichstag, so the Russian tyranny sought to shift the blame for the breakdown of an important power station on to the shoulders of certain British engineers employed in Russia by the Metropolitan Vickers Company. Mr. Monkhouse and his colleagues were arrested in March 1933.

The trial ran a course similar to that of the Reichstag trial later in the same year, except that there was no equivalent of Van der Lubbe, the apparently insane Dutch communist who insisted throughout the German trial on asserting his own guilt. The innocence of the prisoners was as unmistakable as the iniquity of the trial. Some of the Englishmen accused were acquitted, others were sentenced to terms of imprisonment but subsequently released.

The British Government had, some months before the Moscow arrests, given notice to terminate Mr. Henderson's commercial treaty with Russia as a necessary consequence of the Ottawa agreements, and negotiations for a new treaty had already begun. These were suspended, and an embargo placed on imports from Russia so long as the British engineers were in duress. After their release negotiations were resumed and a new treaty accepted early in 1934, designed to secure that, in a few years time, Russian purchases from Great Britain should be a fair equivalent for British imports from Russia.

In a dubious borderland between domestic and foreign affairs lies the renewal of disharmony between Great Britain and the Irish Free State. It may fairly be called a borderland case, for one party to the dispute claims to be a stranger whereas the other party claims that both are members of the same family.

Under the wise rule of Mr. Cosgrave the Irish Free State enjoyed rest for nearly ten years, but with a Parliamentary system the best of Governments must some day change places with its Opposition. The Parliamentary system requires, if it is to produce good results, that the policies of Government and Opposition should differ sufficiently but not too much. Where there is too little difference, changes of Government become a mere alternation of Tweedledums and Tweedledees; it would be easy to point to periods in English history, and in the history of other countries, when party politics has amounted to little more than the competition of otherwise undistinguishable groups for the fruits of office. The result is a degradation of public life.

But when the difference between the parties is too great the danger is of a less insidious but more alarming order. If there is no agreement between the two sides of the House upon the fundamentals of the national being, each change of Government threatens a revolution. If, for example, the alternative to the present National Government should prove to be not a Labour Government such as Mr. MacDonald and his previous colleagues gave us under that name, but a Socialist Government after the pattern of Sir Stafford Cripps, Parliamentary institutions in England will be faced by a danger such as we have described. A similar danger besets a country where, as in Ireland, one party accepts and the other repudiates the charter to which the State owes its legal existence. In the spring of 1932 Mr. de Valera secured a following which, with the support of the Labour party, gave him a majority over all other parties in the Dail. It was a bare majority, but it is fair to add that Ireland enjoys a system of proportional representation, and, if the election had been conducted in accordance with the English method, his majority would have been substantial. This is still more true of the second election, which Mr. de Valera forced upon his opponents a year later. The election of 1933, if conducted on English lines, would have given him a majority as big, relative to the numbers of the Dail, as any majority ever enjoyed by Peel, Gladstone or Disraeli.

Mr. de Valera has been the cause of more irritation in post-war England than any other political personage except Mr. Gandhi. The *Times* has called each of them, on different occasions, 'a casuistical fanatic'. Indeed the two men are in many ways alike. 'He considers that the Irish people, by reason of their belief in intellectual and spiritual rather than in material values, are specially fitted for the vital task of helping to save civilization. Ireland, in his view, must recall men to forgotten truths and place before them the ideals of justice, of order, of freedom rightly used, and of brotherhood. Ireland today, has, he claims, no dearer hope than humbly to serve the truth, and to help by truth to serve the world. The result of the election does not, as he sees it, indicate hostility to Great Britain, but simply a desire for independence. His economic aims, if vague in detail, are clear in outline. He wants to ruralize and decentralize industry. He has no use for mass production. He envisages a frugal Christian Ireland where no man is rich and no man is hungry. He belongs to that category of mankind with whom one cannot argue but must only agree. He is not in the least like an ordinary politician who proceeds by negotiation to compromise.' Nine readers out of ten, if they came across this passage with the name of Ireland and one or two topical allusions omitted, would assume that it was a description of Mr. Gandhi. It occurs in a *Round Table* article on Ireland.

There is a good deal in Mr. de Valera's programme with which one can sympathize. In his preference for the country against the town, for the field against the factory, he is in tune with Mr. Baldwin and, oddly enough, Herr Hitler. Englishmen who maintained throughout a whole pre-war generation that Ireland must accept or refuse Home Rule as a single unit, can hardly be surprised that he desires to obliterate the irritation of the frontier between Dublin and Belfast. When he asserts that the Treaty of 1921 was forced upon Ireland at the point of the sword and is therefore not morally binding, he is only saying what Germany said about the Treaty of Versailles, and Germany's plea seems to have received a fairly general acceptance. When he declares that the land annuities are a price paid by Ireland for the recovery of goods stolen from her by England three hundred years before, he is telling the truth even though not the whole truth. When he claims that the cancellation by the rich creditor of the debts of the poor debtor would be really in the interest of both parties, he is addressing to England an argument not far removed from that which England had addressed to America. When England replied that a bond was a bond, she gave Ireland the answer which the average American has been giving to his European debtors ever since the debt negotiations began.

But whatever the merits of Mr. de Valera's case, his manner of presenting it was the reverse of conciliatory, and the rejoinders of the British Government, speaking with the voice of Mr. Thomas, Secretary of State for the Dominions, seem to have won general approval in Great Britain. To the Irish measure abolishing the oath we could reply only by protest, but to the policy of withholding the payment of annuities under the Irish Land Purchase Acts, and certain other payments, in all about £5,000,000 per annum, we could and did reply with special tariffs on imports of Irish agricultural goods. Mr. de Valera responded with tariffs on imports from Great Britain, and with bounties on Irish exports designed to counteract the effect of the British duties. The annexation of Northern Ireland was not practical politics even in Mr. de Valera's vision, but in so far as a reply was necessary it was given by the completion of the new Parliament House outside Belfast, which was opened by the Prince of Wales in 1932. The finely truculent statue of Lord Carson, already set up in Belfast, could confidently bid defiance to Parnell on his pedestal in Dublin.

CHAPTER XXXVI

THE VERY RECENT YEARS—OURSELVES

When the National Government, already four months old, entered the year 1932 the first and certainly the most indispensable of its services was already behind it. Indeed its achievement in this respect was so complete that it is in danger of passing into irrecoverable oblivion. It is almost impossible to remember today that in the early autumn of 1931 citizens in every walk of life were preparing themselves for a winter of such distressful emergencies as had not been experienced in living memory. Many expected that the pound would go the way of the mark and the rouble, that the comfortable would lose their savings and the uncomfortable would starve. In the following spring Mr. Chamberlain, a man not given to romantic phrases, described the steadiness of domestic price levels as 'almost miraculous'. No doubt our fears had been based to some extent on false analogies. No doubt other factors besides the wisdom of the Government contributed to make the winter of 1931-32 not so very much worse than many other winters; but who can doubt that it would have been catastrophic if the Labour Government had been left to continue in the courses which were brought to a sudden stop in the previous August?

With this grand negative achievement behind them, the Government in 1932 could settle down to the multifarious problems involved in the positive part of their programme. Their task was to overhaul and reconstruct the whole economic policy of the country.

In this task they were going to receive singularly little help or

483

hindrance from their political opponents. Never had Parliamentary politics so lacked the dramatic touch, for never had there been so ineffective an Opposition. The Labour remnant was not only small in numbers but poor in quality, and the best Opposition speeches were generally made by Mr. Maxton or Mr. Buchanan, who had been driven out of the party at its leftward extremity. In the House and in the present the Labour party could do almost nothing, and it concentrated its attention on its own future. A movement arose, led by Sir Stafford Cripps, a distinguished barrister, to have done with gradualness, to stand or fall in future by a programme of pure socialism. Sir Stafford Cripps outlined a policy according to which the Labour party, as soon as it secured a clear majority in a General Election, would introduce measures to muzzle the House of Lords and secure for the Labour Government almost dictatorial powers. In fact Sir Stafford Cripps, like Sir Oswald Mosley, the leader of the British Fascists, seemed ready to dispense with Parliamentary government. The bulk of the party were not prepared to follow him in this direction, and an unwisely contemptuous allusion to 'Buckingham Palace' was very ill received. Labour has certainly not surrendered to the Crippsian programme, but it does not seem to have found any satisfying alternative.

Of the three Liberal parties, the National Liberals, with Sir John Simon and Mr. Runciman, have become as integral a part of the National combination as their Conservative and Labour colleagues. Mr. Lloyd George has never asserted himself, and his little group has in consequence remained insignificant. The two dozen 'Samuelites', or Liberal free traders, detached themselves from the Government by easy stages. At first Sir Herbert Samuel and the three ministers who acted with him consented to retain their posts under an 'agreement to differ' with their colleagues on tariff questions. After the Ottawa Conventions they resigned, but continued to occupy seats on the Government side of the House. A year later they went into formal Opposition.

The Very Recent Years—Ourselves

This carefully graduated development of hostility amused political connoisseurs but did not interest the electorate, and recent
by-elections suggest that whatever dangers may threaten the
Government when the time comes for it to abide by the verdict
of the electorate, the danger of condemnation by millions of
outraged free traders is hardly one that need be taken into
account.

Before the end of 1931 the Government had hurried through
Parliament certain emergency tariff measures which were described in a previous chapter. These were due to expire after six
months, and early in 1932 permanent foundations were laid in
the Import Duties Act which passed through all its stages in a
very few days. Thus was quietly consummated the fiscal revolution which the disciples of Joseph Chamberlain had been preaching for thirty years, and it was characteristic of the way things
go in politics that the minister in charge of the measure, Mr.
Runciman, President of the Board of Trade, had always been a
free trader, and claimed to be one still. The Bill imposed a
general ten-per-cent duty on all imported goods, other than
certain goods on a free list, and imports from the Dominions
which were to be the subject of negotiation at the Ottawa Conference. Further, a Tariff Advisory Committee was set up to
make recommendations for increases or reductions on the general
ten-per-cent rate. Thus responsibility for the details of tariff
adjustment was, for more than one good reason, removed
from the shoulders of the House of Commons and taken out of
the political arena. The Tariff Advisory Committee, under the
chairmanship of Sir George May, got very quickly to work and
raised the duties on a large number of articles to twenty or
thirty-three per cent, in the latter class being a large number of
steel products, the British manufacturers of which had constantly
claimed, but failed to obtain, protection under the Safeguarding
Acts of the previous decade.

Statistically, the new duties fell upon rather more than half of the foreign imports of 1930, the last full year of the old free-trade system. Rather more than a quarter of foreign imports were on the free list. The remaining fraction, about one-sixth of the whole, consisted of articles, such as wines and tobaccos, on which duties were already levied for revenue purposes.

The tariff was to serve many different purposes; to correct the balance of trade by diminishing the excess of imports over exports, a balance which had gone so far against us in the course of the last year or two, that not all our 'invisible exports' could rectify it; to raise revenue, and thus assist the cuts and extra taxes of the previous autumn to balance the budget; to afford protection to home industries; to make possible a completer system of Imperial preferences; and to put the Government in a position to negotiate mutual reductions of tariffs with foreign countries. Of these five purposes the last three had been in Joseph Chamberlain's campaign of 1903; it was the novel and urgent circumstances of an adverse balance of trade and an unbalanced budget that converted the average voter from free trade to protection.

On the free list of 1932 were all the major food imports. Food taxes had always been the most unpopular items in the protection programme, yet no industry stood in greater need of protection than agriculture, or more entirely deserved it. The greatness of the need could be measured by the fact that 100,000 wage earners had left the land within the previous six years.

How to protect the producer of home-grown food without raising the price of the consumers' necessities—that problem which had baffled economists and embarrassed Conservative politicians for so many years, was now tackled with a very large measure of success by the Board of Agriculture under Mr. Walter Elliot. It would be true to say that the direness of the need facilitated the remedy. As the world slump developed and ramified, the bottom fell out of agricultural prices. It became possible to protect the home grower by imposing duties on all foreign agricultural produce except wool and meat, without the consumer suffering any rise of price whatever. So far as he was concerned all that happened was that prices fell less than they would otherwise have done. The operation proved painless, and probably a large part of the urban electorate, which used to be deeply moved by Free Trade posters depicting the Big and the Little Loaf, is unaware of the fact that it has been performed.

But tariffs were not the only, nor the most interesting, of the instruments of the new agricultural policy. Under the quota system foreign imports were rationed, on lines rendered familiar by the expedients of war time, and the home producer thus assured an adequate market; and he has been assisted to make the best use of it by the Government marketing schemes, which now cover almost the whole range of the agricultural industry.

These marketing schemes have undoubtedly been the most ambitious and the most interesting essays in the national reconstruction of the last few years. Things have not always gone in accordance with plan and grumbles have been heard, though surprisingly few considering the novelty of the venture and the complexity of the circumstances. Such schemes, involving close co-operation between Government and industry, schemes in which Government action stimulates private industry to organize itself, are a manifestation of the new 'socialism of the right'. It is likely enough that 'Walter-Elliotism', as it has been called, will be applied in the future to other industries besides the production of food.

As the summer of 1932 opened up, one set of ministers went to Lausanne to bury German reparations and European inter-Allied debts, and another to Ottawa to clear the channels of better trade between the constituent parts of the British Empire.

Of the results of the Ottawa Conference its enemies speak more distinctly than its friends. Lord Beaverbrook condemned it for accomplishing so little; the Samuelites left the Government because it accomplished anything at all. The friends of the Conference were, in retrospect, more impressed by the difficulties that had been surmounted than by the prizes secured. 'The Con-

ference', says the *Round Table*, 'was a liberal education for many
people who thought that it would be a simple matter to reach
agreements', that the Governments concerned would quickly see
eye to eye, that the Dominions could or would easily grant to
Great Britain the concessions that she desired. Still, mutual concessions there were, and the ratio of inter-Imperial to foreign
trade rose perceptibly in the following year. The *Annual Register*
for the year expressed the view that 'more important to British
manufacturers than any of the actual preferences given was the
undertaking by Canada and Australia that their Tariff Boards,
before which British manufacturers were free to appear, would
review the position so as to ensure that, within a reasonable
period, their protective duties should be reduced to a level
which should give to United Kingdom producers full opportunity of reasonable competition in the Dominion markets'. It is
certainly a valuable concession that British manufacturers should
be enabled to state their own case before the Dominion Tariff
Boards, but the twice-repeated epithet 'reasonable' is one to
which the parties may 'reasonably' attach different interpreta-
tions.

Perhaps the most encouraging verdict on Ottawa was that of a
great American industrialist, Mr. Charles M. Schwab, quoted
by Mr. Chamberlain in the House of Commons. 'The Ottawa
agreements', said Mr. Schwab, 'are going to hit America. They
are going to hit my own concerns, especially in the Canadian
markets.'

After Ottawa the British Government negotiated commercial
treaties with a variety of foreign States: Argentina, Germany,
the Scandinavian States, and others. These treaties had their
critics. Sir Austen Chamberlain, for example, attacked the German Treaty because, in return for concessions to British coal in
the German market, it relaxed the protection of Birmingham
industries against German clocks, watches, and the like. It
would increase employment in the coalfields by increasing unemployment in the workshops. The answer was that one could

not secure concessions without sacrifices; the Government claimed that what was lost on the roundabouts of Birmingham was rather more than regained on the swings elsewhere.

Another group of industries as much in need of protection as any of those occupied with production were the great transport industries, railways and shipping. The railways needed protection against the alarmingly rapid transfer of goods traffic from rail to road. Something was done to redress the balance by the Road and Rail Traffic Act, dealing with the licensing and regulation of goods motor vehicles. The protection of shipping was an even more difficult problem. Owing both to the shipbuilding and shipping subsidies lavished on their national industries by other States, and to the shrinkage of overseas trade in every part of the world since the beginning of the slump, the tonnage at the disposal of the world was vastly in excess of its requirements, and Great Britain, as the greatest carrying-trader of the world, suffered more than any of her neighbours, even though some others had a still larger proportion of their shipping unemployed. The obvious remedy seemed, to those outside the industry, to be to follow the bad example of our neighbours and subsidize our shipping. But the shipping industry was itself divided and uncertain on the subject, and the cost of a subsidy anything like adequate to balance the subsidies given by the United States, a richer community, to their own smaller industry, would be prohibitive. Another policy would be to return to the methods of the old Navigation Acts and exclude foreign shipping from certain routes between British Imperial ports. America excluded our merchantmen from carrying goods and passengers between many of her own ports, yet was at the same time competing with us in the trade between Australia and New Zealand. On this path, too, the British industry was somewhat reluctant to enter. More than any other industry it was traditionally devoted to freedom of trade, and it feared that a Navigation Act policy would provoke reprisals and leave the last state worse than the first. In 1934 an experimental subsidy of three millions was granted for the assistance, under conditions, of tramp steamer companies.

The fall of prices which enabled the Government to tax food imports without raising the price for the consumer enabled them, in another department, to bring to an end the granting of housing subsidies. Of course the annual payments of subsidies already granted, on houses built when the cost of building was high, continues under the terms of the Acts of 1923 and 1924 until the middle of the century or later, but no further grants under these Acts were to be made. The object of the subsidy had been to enable working-class houses to be let at 7/9 a week, and by 1933 the economic rent, based on the cost of building, had practically fallen to that figure. Already by that year more than two million houses (exclusive of houses with a rateable value of over £78) had been built since the war, rather more than half of them with State assistance. Of course the abolition of the subsidy was severely criticized, but the critics were answered by the statistics of the year following its abolition, in which over a quarter of a million houses were built, considerably more than in any single year since the war—or, for that matter, before it. With the termination of the housing-subsidy policy the Government was able to throw its energy and its available financial resources into a campaign of unprecedented dimensions for the elimination of slums.

The Slum Clearance Campaign is the greatest constructive contribution of the Government to the policy which Disraeli described as 'the improvement of the condition of the people'. It is worth remembering that that great man was responsible for the first direct action of government in this direction, through the Artisans' Dwellings Act of 1875; worth remembering, also, that in one of his earliest election speeches he exhorted his hearers to drop their factious labels of Whig and Tory, 'two names with one meaning and used only to deceive you', and to unite in the formation of 'a National party'.

In April 1933 Sir Hilton Young, the Minister of Health, issued a circular to the 1716 housing authorities of England and Wales, calling upon them to submit programmes calculated to secure the demolition of all slum properties and the rehousing of their populations within a period of five years. The programmes submitted in accordance with this circular involve the demolition of about 300,000 houses and the rehousing of nearly a million and a half people, about one twenty-fifth of the total population. The capital cost of the whole scheme is estimated at £115,000,000, expended in subsidies over a period of forty years, one-quarter of which will be borne by the local authorities and three-quarters by the national revenue. The campaign will provide employment, directly and indirectly, for over 100,000 workers throughout the five years within which it should be completed.

Another equally necessary task, undertaken by the Government in 1934, has been clearing up of the unemployment insurance muddle, and the establishment of a solvent and self-regulating system. There have, it seems, been no less than thirty empirical Unemployment Insurance Acts in the last fourteen years. The Act of 1934 should do for unemployment insurance what the Code Napoléon did for the legislation of the French Revolutionary Assemblies. Under the terms of the Act wage earners between the ages of fourteen and sixteen are brought within the insurance system, and the gap between the age of education and that of unemployment is thus closed. The Insurance Fund is relieved of responsibility for those whose actuarial claims to insurance are exhausted, and its solvency is secured. The future development and extension of the system is entrusted, under Parliamentary control, to a Statutory Committee, analogous to the Tariff Advisory Committee which deals with the details of tariff proposals. One of the most important of the constructive tasks of the Statutory Committee will be to deal with demands for the extension of the insurance system to bodies of workers at present outside the scope of the scheme, particularly the 'black-coated' workers with incomes over the £250 limit.

The Very Recent Years—Ourselves

Outside what is properly called insurance, the Act establishes an Assistance Board to deal with the claims to relief of those insured persons whose claims to benefit are exhausted, claims which will be subject to the Means Test which has been the target of much abuse. There is no question that when the means test was first imposed, by the National Government, it dealt unduly harshly with the owners of small savings and the holders of small pensions. An Act passed in 1932 made reasonably generous allowance for cases of this kind, but it did not meet the really difficult cases that arise when two or more persons, employed and unemployed, comprise single household. If, for example, a son in employment got a rise of ten shillings a week, the same amount was knocked off the allowance made, under the means test, to the unemployed father. Yet the objection to taking no account of household earnings in assessing the needs of the unemployed person who has exhausted his claim to insurance, are too obvious to call for exposition. The new Act contains some provisions for elasticity in the treatment of these cases, but it is at present too early to say how they are going to work.

On the whole, however, criticism of the means test today comes from those who hold that there should be no means test at all. On this subject the Labour opposition speaks with an uncertain voice. The ending of the means test 'root and branch, without equivocation or qualification' is a tempting slogan for an irresponsible Opposition. It is answered by the leader of the Opposition himself, Mr. Lansbury, who declared in the early days of the National Government that 'if a person has gone out of ordinary benefit, and has means of his own to maintain himself, I am not prepared to pay him State money'.

Such were some of the principal legislative activities of the National Government. Mr. Chamberlain, with his usual tendency to understatement, described it as a policy of 'pegging away'. It was a good deal more than that; but friends of the Government began to fear that ministers were so intent upon their work that they had forgotten the electorate. In an age of sensational and mendacious advertisement, an age in which good salesmanship sells more goods than good workmanship, the best of Governments can only survive by means of unremitting propaganda. The whole range of the so-called popular press was on the other side. The *Daily Herald* supported Labour, the *News Chronicle* supported the Samuelites, and the organs of Lords Rothermere and Beaverbrook belittled or opposed the Government without supporting anything in particular. In every constituency where the Conservative seat was supposed to be safe, and in many where it was not, there were groups of Conservatives who chafed against the Government because it was not a monopoly of their own party. By-elections suggested that the balance of power between Conservatism and Labour was rapidly moving back towards the point it had stood at in 1929, when the parties polled almost equal and the Liberals held the balance. What results, measurable in such terms as can be converted into electoral ammunition, had the Government to show for its first three years in office?

The first convincing evidence that the Government had done something more than avert the evils threatened in the summer of 1931 was the successful issue of the three and a half per cent Conversion Loan in the summer of 1932. It was the biggest operation of its kind ever carried out by any Government. Practically the whole of the £2,000,000,000 of the five per cent war loan was converted to the new figure with a net saving to the Exchequer of £23,000,000 a year. Further conversion operations on a smaller scale followed and as a result over one-third of the nation's internal debt has been converted from rates averaging nearly five per cent to one of less than three and a half per cent, with the result that the interest payable annually on the National Debt has been reduced by £52,000,000, a decrease of almost exactly one-fifth. This did not only mean a reduced burden for the taxpayer; it meant a lowering all round of the standard rate of interest. It meant cheap money, which is the stimulus of business enterprise.

The Very Recent Years—Ourselves

Unemployment figures did not respond so readily to the turn of the tide, largely because though the tide had turned in England it had not yet reached its ebb in most other countries. Throughout 1932 the volume of production and of exports fell rapidly in France, Germany and the United States, as compared with that of 1931; that of Great Britain did not rise, but neither did it fall. The total figures for the two years were almost exactly the same, in itself a signal achievement. Putting the same facts another way, Great Britain advanced from the third to the first place in the list of exporters, and she was the first to profit by the general recovery which began in 1933. In these circumstances it is not surprising that the monthly returns of unemployment were for a long time disappointing, and furnished easy figures to superficial critics. In January 1933, sixteen months after the Government took office, they were higher by a few thousand than they had ever been before, though they fell far short of the unemployment totals of America and Germany. That month, however, was the worst. Throughout 1933 the figures fell continuously, and after a rise in January 1934 they resumed their steady descent, though they were, until 1935, still above the two million mark. One has to remember, however, that the unemployment figures represent a fraction of a steadily, though slowly, expanding population, and, if one takes the correlative figures of employment in insurable occupations, one finds that, by the spring of 1934, there were more persons employed in Great Britain than at any time since 1929, when the world depression began its first advance.

Even so there was no ground for more than a very restrained optimism, and certainly Mr. Chamberlain's earlier Budget statements did not encourage more. His was perhaps the most typical, though not the most conspicuous, figure in a Government which played very little to the gallery and never spelt its plans with a capital P. Those cuts in salaries and unemployment benefit, those emergency additions to the income tax—when should we see the last of them? As early as in the spring of 1932

494

'most prophets', says the *Round Table*, 'expected some *small* relief.' Mr. Chamberlain's response was to leave burdens as they were and to reimpose the tax on tea which Mr. Churchill had remitted. 'The denial of a penny a pint off beer, which had been generally expected, added particularly to the universal gloom.'

In 1933 the same wistful hopes, and much the same response. The Chancellor had to choose between a grim Budget and a gambling Budget, and advocates of gambling budgets are commoner in Fleet Street than in Whitehall. The beer drinker was given his penny, and the income taxpayer was allowed to keep till July one quarter of his tax, previously payable in January. That was all and, seeing that the previous year had ended with a deficit of over thirty millions, it was as much as he could expect.

A year later not only had wistful hopes changed to 'Great Expectations'—the Chancellor allowed himself a Dickensian joke in his Budget statement—but some at least of the more reasonable expectations could be gratified. The previous year had yielded a surplus of thirty-one millions, all of which was devoted to redemption of debt, though some would have liked Mr. Chamberlain to depart from orthodoxy and devote it to extinguishing one-third of the hundred-million debt of the Unemployment Insurance Fund. The surplus for 1934-35 was estimated at £29,000,000, and the Chancellor used it to abolish the whole of the 1931 cuts in unemployment benefit, and half the cuts in State salaries, and to take the National Government sixpence off the income tax. Some thought that Mr. Chamberlain had intentionally underestimated his prospective surplus in order to have still better gifts in store for a time nearer the next General Election. It may be so, though such political window-dressing does not accord with the accepted estimate of Mr. Chamberlain's character. The reader will be in a better position than the writer is at present to express an opinion on this point.

CHAPTER XXXVII

THE KING

If all is well King George will on 6th May 1935 celebrate the twenty-fifth anniversary of his accession. Judged by the Victorian standard the period of time is not a long one, though it is curious to reflect that only two of his male predecessors in the last four hundred years, George II and George III, have reigned longer. It may in any case safely be said that no quarter-century in past history has been so packed with great events and unimagined developments.

The King's name has not often occurred in the course of this chronicle of his reign, and the fact is a tribute to his uniform success in the discharge of his difficult duties. He has been the first of his line to achieve with completeness the ideal towards which our constitutional monarchy has through two centuries been approaching, the ideal of a King who, in the accepted phrase, 'reigns but does not govern'. To govern is to act, to take decisions and, human nature being what it is, to make mistakes. To reign is simply to be—to be always there, the one representative of the nation who, not being elected, represents not a majority but all. To be universally recognized throughout twenty-five years, through extremes of good and evil fortune, as the adequate representative of a great nation is a singular triumph of personal character. No King ever reigned in a more restless and critical age, an age which has lost more of its faiths in things human and divine, and yet King George's manner of wearing his crown has never been unacceptable to any section of his subjects. We take this so much for granted that we

496

The King

forget that it is unique. We are hardly conscious of the incalculable consequences that might have followed if the King had not been a very wise and good man. We take him for granted, and that is the essence of his achievement.

On some early pages of this book an attempt was made to analyse the impression made by the King upon his subjects in the first years of his reign. To go much further than the slight sketch attempted in those pages is not an easy matter. At first sight the public life of the King might seem to consist entirely of ceremonies and loyal platitudes. If that were so the nation's, and the empire's, loyalty would be no more than a useful convention, an acceptance for constitutional convenience of the maxim that the King can do no wrong. The public person of the King would be a symbol unrelated to his human character. But it is not so. The purely conventional aspect of royalty has its value, not to be underrated, but it does not explain the peculiar personal esteem in which the King is held by his subjects. In the course of every year of his reign the King has made personal and friendly contact with a very considerable number of people in all ranks of life. Each of these carries away his impression and imparts it to his acquaintance. As a symbol in a pageant others would have served the same purpose; it is as a man among men that the King has found his way to the hearts of his people. What manner of man, then, is the King who is thus known to his subjects?

All that we know of the King suggests that at the foundation of his character are the qualities which the simplest can appreciate and enjoy. As a young naval cadet—and he was the youngest cadet ever placed on the books of the training ship *Britannia*—he appears to have been what old wives call 'a regular pickle'; he delighted in the practical jokes approved by his fellow cadets, and not always by their officers. At the same time no cadet worked harder, and was more invariably punctual in the discharge of every duty. During his naval career, which occupied all his ambitions until, when he was twenty-seven, the death of his elder brother placed him in the direct line of succession to the throne, he did well in every position he occupied, and there is no doubt that, had his position in life been different, he would have become a distinguished admiral. That was not to be; but the qualities he revealed on the *Britannia* have remained with him. The age of practical jokes is long past, but no one more enjoys hearing or telling a good story; no one works with more assiduous conscientiousness; and the King's punctuality, which he achieves himself and insists on in others, is said to be the despair of those who are less gifted with this useful virtue.

No King ever received a better training for the position he was to occupy. Ruler of a worldwide empire he has seen more of the world he rules than any but a very few of his subjects. The ocean cruises of the *Bacchante* in 1879-82, when Prince George as a boy of fourteen had just been released from the *Britannia*, and of the *Ophir* twenty years later, have been more fully described in print than any other parts of King George's life. The *Bacchante* visited Gibraltar, the West Indies, Buenos Ayres, South Africa, and most of the Australian colonies; Japan, Shanghai, Hong Kong, Singapore, Ceylon, and returned by way of the Red Sea. The Prince saw Cape Colony immediately after Majuba, and Egypt just before the bombardment of Alexandria. The *Bacchante* was a sailing ship with steam engines used only in emergencies and both on water and on land the Prince had as many rough and adventurous experiences as any spirited boy could desire. The cruise of the *Ophir* was a more sedate and ceremonious undertaking. Its main objective was Australia where the Prince of Wales, now a man of thirty-six and heir to the throne, was to inaugurate the first session of the Parliament of the Australian Commonwealth. This duty accomplished, the *Ophir* visited New Zealand, South Africa, where the second Boer War was drawing towards its close, and Canada, where the royal party crossed the Dominion to Vancouver and back.

These were only the most extensive of the many tours the Prince undertook to many parts of the Empire. Twice he visited India, once during his father's reign, and again after his acces-

The King

sion for the purpose of the Coronation Durbar. It is hardly necessary to say that these tours served a double purpose. During their progress they powerfully stimulated the sentiment of unity upon which in the last resort the very existence of the Empire depends. But they also equipped the King with vast stores of knowledge and reminiscence which enable him to give a congenial welcome in England to visitors from every part of the Empire which he has himself visited.

But the most important event in the King's life was his marriage, in 1894, with his cousin Princess Mary.

Writing shortly after the marriage of King George's parents, when our present King was one year old, Walter Bagehot says in his shrewd and rather quizzical way: 'A *family* on the throne is an interesting idea. It brings down the pride of sovereignty to the level of petty life. A princely marriage is the brilliant edition of a universal fact, and as such it rivets mankind. A royal family sweetens politics by the seasonable addition of nice and pretty events. It introduces irrelevant facts into the business of government, but they are facts which speak to men's bosoms, and employ their thoughts.'

When Bagehot wrote the Crown, though it had more than half relinquished its ambition to play an active part in politics, had not yet, in spite of the strenuous efforts of the Prince Consort, discovered the many lines of activity along which members of the Royal Family now contribute to the national welfare. Bagehot's gesture of patronizing homage is to an ornamental royal family enshrined in a glass case. He writes as a Whig, and the Whigs were always half republican. They valued royalty as the Roman philosopher valued religion; it provided a suitable object for the worship of those who knew no better.

No one could write thus of King George and Queen Mary, and their children who have followed in their footsteps. It would be quite outside the scope of this short epilogue to attempt any sort of enumeration of the activities of the Royal Family, and of the good causes that have benefited by their support. If a single instance may be offered, to stand here as a representative for all the rest, no better or more characteristic example of royal statesmanship could be found than is furnished by the history of the British Industries Fair. This annual institution, which in 1934 covered an area of thirty acres, with a thirty-two mile frontage of stands, exhibiting almost the entire range of British manufactures, began as a temporary expedient to meet the special needs of war time when merchants and retailers, cut off from foreign sources of supply on which they had depended, were eager to get into touch with British manufacturers who could meet their requirements. Having served its wartime purpose the Fair survived to play an ever-increasing part in the stimulation and modernization of post-war industry. In a leading article on the Fair of 1934 the *Times* says: 'It is no disparagement of the splendid work of the officials of the Department of Overseas Trade and of the organizers at Birmingham to pay a tribute—in which they would be the first to join—to the support which the Fair has had from its Royal patrons. It is an open secret that there have been moments of difficulty when the continuity, indeed even the continuance, of the Fair was in doubt, but through good report and ill the Queen has given her unswerving support to the enterprise, and the King has never failed to visit it whenever it has been possible. How much of the success of the Fair is due to the patronage of the Royal House it would be impossible to estimate, and one at least of the improvements at Birmingham this year is the direct result of a suggestion made last year by the Duke of York.'

Indeed the profound esteem in which the King and Queen are held is based upon the conviction of millions of simple people that they, and their whole family, really do care intensely about the welfare of their subjects and pursue it, year in and year out, by every means within their power. So diverse are the good causes they have supported that it might be hard to say where their own particular and special interests lay, but it is no secret that the King is keenly interested in politics, and the Queen in all that concerns health, housing and the domestic welfare of the people. And, in spite of the triumphs of political feminism, this is exactly the division of interests which the ordinary man and woman approves. Only those who have held high office could say how much the King's interest in political detail, enriched by a continuity of experience no party politician can rival, has added to the pleasures and diminished the pains of political eminence, but one outstanding example of the royal touch was, eleven years ago, apparent to every observer. In 1924 the first Labour Government acceded to power. Many of its members had grown up in a tradition which, if not positively republican, had depreciated all the values of which royalty is the supreme symbol; most of them were men unfamiliar with, and perhaps resentful of, the manners and customs of the aristocratic tradition within which previous Governments had moved. It was one of the King's greatest opportunities and he proved triumphantly equal to it. The new ministers found in the King and Queen that touch of nature which makes all men kin. Strangers to office, they were never allowed to feel themselves strangers at Windsor or Buckingham Palace.

Some men live in history as the authors of a single outstanding achievement; others build perhaps a safer and a steadier reputation upon a thousand unostentatious actions. It is high up in the second of these classes that King George will find his place. There have perhaps been only three occasions in the reign when the King made a direct intervention in the course of great events, the summoning of the Irish Conference in July 1914, the speech at Belfast opening the Parliament of Northern Ireland in 1921, and the invitation to Mr. MacDonald to form a National Government in August 1931. On the first occasion the King's project was defeated by the obstinacy of the politicians; on the second occasion his intervention led directly to the pacification of Ireland. The third intervention led to the formation of the National Government, though the historian has not yet under his hand the evidence which will some day enable him to assess the importance of the King's personal contribution to that result. It may be that events would have followed much the same course without the King's intervention; on the other hand, it may be that the King's action was decisive in averting a catastrophe. We cannot say. What we can say with certainty is that the King saw that here was one of the rare occasions on which his intervention in the course of party politics might prove useful, and returned at once from Balmoral to London.

If the judgment of history should assign to the King a decisive part in the national crisis of 1931, an interesting fact will have been added to our constitutional history, but the King's good name stands in no need of such addition. His subjects had made up their minds about him many years before 1931. On the night of August 4th they came in their thousands and stood in front of Buckingham Palace. The vague apprehensions of the previous ten years, the bewildering alarms of the past ten days, had crystallized into a certainty. The Empire was at war. The people wanted to be with their King.

'The excitement', says the *Times* report, 'reached its height outside Buckingham Palace, where a vast crowd had gathered early in the evening, growing denser as time wore on. The Victoria Memorial was black with people. For more than four hours the singing and cheering was maintained without a break. At seven o'clock the King responded to the demonstration. With the Queen, the Prince of Wales and Princess Mary he appeared on the accustomed balcony, and was greeted with tumultuous cheering and singing of the National Anthem. The scene was repeated at half past nine and again shortly after eleven.'

The years that followed revealed as no ordinary years could have done the Royal Family's devotion to the service of their country. Both the King and the Queen visited our own and our Allies' armies in France, the Grand Fleet at Scapa, and innumerable military units, munition works, and hospitals in every part of the country. Wherever they went, then or at any other time, they left the same impression behind them, an impression

The King

of dignity which never obscured the active and discerning friendliness behind it. One royal action of the war years is particularly remembered. At the time of the munitions crisis of 1915 there arose an outcry against 'drink' and there was for a moment a real danger that the Government might be stampeded along the course subsequently followed, with disastrous results, by America. It was the King who gave a wiser lead by ordering that until the close of the war no intoxicants were to be served in the royal palaces.

Four years of war passed, and three months, and once again the crowds assembled outside Buckingham Palace. Now it was not midnight but midday; not summer but winter, the first Armistice Day. The crowd consisted of overworked and underfed people, many of whom were either sickening for or just recovering from influenza. They were in a state of wild excitement. The occasion lacked the tragic dignity of August 4th, but it was one of the great days of history, and once again the people felt that they must see the King.

Ten years passed, and once again night after night through the first ten days of December 1928 the crowds assembled outside Buckingham Palace, to read the bulletins of the progress of the King's very serious illness. In the sombre light of that illness, his people looked back over eighteen years, and many for the first time made a conscious estimate of the King whom they feared they might be about to lose. 'The Reign of George V' took shape in one's mind as a distinct period of history—the pre-war, the war, the after-war, and then during those last years before the King's illness, the period of recovery when, though with a painful slowness, international goodwill and economic order seemed to be gaining ground, and laying the foundations of a great advance. In each of these phases of his reign the King had played the man, and just as circumstances were becoming easier we were to lose him.

The forecast was not fulfilled. King George happily recovered and his reign entered upon yet another phase. The world recovery of the nineteen-twenties proved a false dawn, and now once again, in the middle of the 'thirties we are setting about recovery once again, much more fully aware than we were in 1928 of the difficulties ahead and of the length of the road still to be travelled before the twentieth century achieves a prosperity and a security in any way worthy of its resources. Along that road it is the prayer of every one of his subjects that King George may lead us for many years yet.

INDEX

Index

Index

Index

Index

Index

Index

Index

Index

Index

Index

Index

Index

Index

Index

Index

Index

Index

Index

Index

Index

Index

Index

Index

Index

Index

Index

Index